LIBRARY OF NEW TESTAMENT STUDIES

670

Formerly Journal for the Study of the New Testament Supplement Series

Editor
Chris Keith

Editorial Board
Dale C. Allison, Lynn H. Cohick, R. Alan Culpepper, Craig A. Evans,
Jennifer Eyl, Robert Fowler, Simon J. Gathercole, Juan Hernández Jr., John S.
Kloppenborg, Michael Labahn, Matthew V. Novenson, Love L. Sechrest, Robert
Wall, Catrin H. Williams, Brittany E. Wilson

WRITING WITH SCRIPTURE

Scripturalized Narrative in the Gospel of Mark

Nathanael Vette

t&tclark

LONDON • NEW YORK • OXFORD • NEW DELHI • SYDNEY

T&T CLARK
Bloomsbury Publishing Plc
50 Bedford Square, London, WC1B 3DP, UK
1385 Broadway, New York, NY 10018, USA
29 Earlsfort Terrace, Dublin 2, Ireland

BLOOMSBURY, T&T CLARK and the T&T Clark logo
are trademarks of Bloomsbury Publishing Plc

First published in Great Britain 2022
Paperback edition published 2023

Copyright © Nathanael Vette, 2022

Nathanael Vette has asserted his right under the Copyright, Designs and Patents Act, 1988,
to be identified as Author of this work.

For legal purposes the Acknowledgements on p. vii constitute an extension of this copyright page.

All rights reserved. No part of this publication may be reproduced or transmitted in any form or by
any means, electronic or mechanical, including photocopying, recording, or any information storage or
retrieval system, without prior permission in writing from the publishers.

Bloomsbury Publishing Plc does not have any control over, or responsibility for, any third-party websites
referred to or in this book. All internet addresses given in this book were correct at the time of going to
press. The author and publisher regret any inconvenience caused if addresses have changed or sites have
ceased to exist, but can accept no responsibility for any such changes.

A catalogue record for this book is available from the British Library.
Library of Congress Cataloging-in-Publication Data
Names: Vette, Nathanel, author.
Title: Writing with scripture : scripturalized narrative in the Gospel of Mark / Nathanel Vette.
Description: London ; New York : T&T Clark, 2022. | Series: The library of New Testament studies, 2513-
8790 ; 670 | Includes bibliographical references and index. | Summary: "Nathanael Vette proposes that the
Gospel of Mark, like other narrative works in the Second Temple period, uses the Jewish scriptures as a
model to compose distinctive episodes of Christ's life and tell a new story"-- Provided by publisher.
Identifiers: LCCN 2021037293 (print) | LCCN 2021037294 (ebook) | ISBN
9780567704641 (hb) | ISBN 9780567704658 (epdf) | ISBN 9780567704672 (epub)
Subjects: LCSH: Bible. Mark--Criticism, interpretation, etc.
| Bible. Mark--Relation to the Old Testament. | Bible. Old Testament--Criticism, interpretation, etc.
Classification: LCC BS2585.52 .V48 2022 (print) | LCC BS2585.52 (ebook) | DDC 226.3/06--dc23
LC record available at https://lccn.loc.gov/2021037293
LC ebook record available at https://lccn.loc.gov/2021037294

ISBN:	HB:	978-0-5677-0464-1
	PB:	978-0-5677-0468-9
	ePDF:	978-0-5677-0465-8
	ePUB:	978-0-5677-0467-2

Series: Library of New Testament Studies, volume 670
ISSN 2513-8790

Typeset by: Trans.form.ed SAS

To find out more about our authors and books visit www.bloomsbury.com
and sign up for our newsletters.

Contents

Acknowledgements	vii
Abbreviations	ix

Chapter 1
INTRODUCTION | 1
Mark's use of the Jewish scriptures: expositional or compositional? | 4
Studies on the use of the Jewish scriptures in the Gospel of Mark | 5
The compositional use of the Jewish scriptures in the Gospel of Mark | 22

Chapter 2
SCRIPTURALIZED NARRATIVE IN SECOND TEMPLE LITERATURE | 32
The *Liber Antiquitatum Biblicarum* | 32
Jair and the fiery furnace: *LAB* 38 and Daniel 3 | 48
The *Genesis Apocryphon* | 64
1 Maccabees | 74
Judith | 85
The *Testament of Abraham* | 99
Summary | 107

Chapter 3
SCRIPTURALIZED NARRATIVE IN THE GOSPEL OF MARK | 110
Jesus and Elijah in Mark 1:2-20 | 110
Jesus and Elisha: Mark 6:35-44, 8:1-9 and 2 Kings 4:42-44 | 138
Antipas and Ahasuerus: Mark 6:21-28 and Esther | 148
The Jewish scriptures in the Passion Narrative | 157
The use of the Jewish scriptures in Mark 14:1–15:20 | 162
Summary | 197

Chapter 4
CONCLUSION | 199

Bibliography	207
Index of References	231
Index of Authors	255

ACKNOWLEDGEMENTS

A great many people contributed to the completion of this book. Some contributed with scholarly advice, others with friendship. I am grateful for both.

My sincere thanks goes to Helen Bond for supervising the research that led to this book. Her counsel and helpful criticism have been indispensable throughout my time in Edinburgh. Without her encouragement this project would not have been possible. Thanks is also due to Paul Foster for his thoughtful and constructive criticism. To my doctoral examiners, Mark Goodacre and Timothy Lim, I owe a debt of thanks for their kind and helpful comments. I would also like to thank the faculty and administrative staff at the School of Divinity for their tireless support, especially my post-doctoral supervisor Mona Siddiqui. Special thanks is also due to the Issachar Fund for their generous sponsorship.

To those scholars who were kind enough to offer feedback along the way and send unpublished or hard-to-find articles and chapters, I am grateful for their help: Heike Omerzu, James McGrath, Charles Häberl, Susan Docherty and Crispin Fletcher-Louis. My deep thanks also goes to May Howie who so generously donated to me the theological library of the late Gordon Howie. Thanks also goes to Roy Pinkerton and Calum McIver for their help in this.

I am grateful to Chris Keith and the editorial board of the Library of New Testament Studies for publishing my work in this excellent series. I am also grateful to Sarah Blake for her help, as well as Dominic Mattos and the rest of the Bloomsbury Publishing house.

To my family and friends there is a debt of gratitude that cannot be fully expressed in words. Nevertheless, my thanks goes to Tom Muller, Ally Howell and Brooke Burns for their friendship and encouragement from afar. My thanks also goes to Scott Bickle for his help in all things Hebrew, as well as the rest of the Wednesday-afternoon pub set. Thanks is due to my grandfather, Ken Newman – in whose footsteps I followed spending summer retreats at the Burn in Glenesk. I am also deeply grateful for the support of my grandparents-in-law, Kal LeMaster and Dona Vette, who passed away December 2017 – her kindness and good humour are sorely missed.

The following friends and family deserve special thanks. To my grandmother Margaret Newman I am especially grateful for her generous support and loving correspondence, and for helping make the move from London to Edinburgh a reality. My parents-in-law Laurie Vette and Scott Andrews have been unwavering in their support and encouragement and for them I am so very grateful. My deep thanks and appreciation goes to Will Robinson for his friendship and peerless scholarly input. Will has read every single word and commented on every paragraph of this book and it is all the better for it. I am grateful beyond measure for my parents Rob and Claire Smith, who inspired my love of scholarship in the first place, and who have been ceaseless in their love and support from the other side of the world. This book is the fruit of many years of encouragement and conversations.

Finally, my wife Rachel has been my constant friend and loving partner throughout all of this. Her kindness, generosity and selflessness have made this book possible. To her I owe a life-time of thanks, of which this meagre note is just the start.

Nathanael Robert Newman Smith Vette
June, 2021

Abbreviations

Abbreviations follow *The SBL Handbook of Style*, 2nd ed. (Atlanta, GA: SBL Press, 2014). Journals and series not listed there are abbreviated as follows.

BIBALDS	Berkeley Institute of Biblical Archaeology and Literature Dissertation Series
BibAn	*Biblical Antiquities*
BthSt	Biblisch-Theologische Studien
BU	Biblische Untersuchung
BWANT	Beiträge zur Wissenschaft vom Alten und Neuen Testament
CamSac	Campania sacra
CCME	Culture and Civilization in the Middle East
CS	Cistercian Studies
EC	*Early Christianity*
FZB	Forschung zum Bibel
HTKNT	Herder theologischer Kommentar zum Neuen Testament
IHC	Islamic History and Civilization
JAJSupp	Journal of Ancient Judaism Supplements
LB	Légendes Byzantines
LMW	The Library of Medieval Women
MHS	Monumenta Hispaniae Sacra
PGC	Pelican Gospel Commentaries
SACS	Septuagint and Cognate Studies
SAIS	Studies in the Aramaic Interpretation of Scripture
SBEC	Studies in the Bible and Early Christianity
SBL	Studies in Biblical Literature
SBLEJL	Society of Biblical Literature Early Judaism and Its Literature
SHG	Subsidia Hagiographica
SL	Serie Litúrgica
SPB	Studia Post-Biblica
SPNT	Studies on Personalities of the New Testament
STAC	Studien und Texte zu Antike und Christentum
StANT	Studien zum Alten und Neuen Testament
STML	Studies on Themes and Motifs in Literature
SVTGAASGE	Septuaginta Vetus Testamentum graecum auctoritate academiae scientarum Gottingensis editum

TCAAS	*Transactions of the Connecticut Academy of Arts and Sciences*
TED	Translations of Early Documents
TGST	Tesi Gregoriana Serie Teologia
TM	Tekst en Maatschappij
TTH	Translated Texts for Historiansa

1

Introduction

William Blake once wrote, 'The Old and New Testaments are the Great Code of Art'.[1] For the literary critic Northrop Frye, the slogan means that the 'framework of the Bible, stretching from Creation to Last Judgment and surveying the whole of human history, [is the] framework of the whole of literary experience, [and] the ultimate context for all works of literature whatever'.[2] The Bible is thus the 'Great Code' that provides the mythological structure for all Western literature.[3] One need only look at its most enduring types: each underdog is a David, every favourite a Goliath; rival siblings are Cains and Abels; a mass emigration is an Exodus, its leader a Moses; a paradise an Eden; a tempter a Serpent; a seductress a Jezebel; a betrayer a Judas; a saviour a Messiah; a doubter a Thomas – and so on. The author Marilynne Robinson has written that 'the Bible is the model for and subject of more art and thought than those of us who live within its influence, consciously or unconsciously, will ever know'.[4]

Although Robinson speaks of Western literature, she may as well have been speaking about the literature of the Second Temple period. At the

1. William Blake, 'Laocoön' (*c.* 1826–27). Blake intended this as a critique of the classicists of his day who favoured 'pagan' forms over the biblical. Thus he subverts the classical exemplar 'Laocoön and his Two Sons' (cf. Virgil, *Aeneid* 2.199) as 'יה & his two Sons Satan & Adam as they were copied from the Cherubim of Solomon's Temple by three Rhodians & applied to Natural Fact or the History of Ilium'.

2. Northrop Frye, *The Stubborn Structure: Essays on Criticism and Society* (Ithaca, NY: Cornell University Press, 1970), 170–1.

3. See Frye's oeuvre from *Fearful Symmetry: A Study of William Blake* (Princeton, NJ: Princeton University Press, 1947) to *The Great Code: The Bible and Literature* (New York, NY: Harcourt Brace Jovanovich, 1982).

4. Marilynne Robinson, 'The Book of Books: What Literature Owes the Bible', *The New York Times* (22 December 2011), 22.

heart of these works is a devotion to – and utilization of – the language, symbols, characters, narratives and themes found in the Jewish scriptures.[5] One must be careful to avoid anachronism, as the canon of the Hebrew Bible did not emerge until at least the end of the first century CE.[6] And yet despite the fluidity of textual forms and varying notions of scriptural authority, a collection of writings roughly equivalent to this canon appears to have been at the centre of the ever-expanding literary universe of Jewish antiquity.

But this does not mean that the other literature of the period is merely, as one author puts it, 'paratext, auxiliary material whose purpose is to contextualize and illuminate the biblical'.[7] For the most part, scholars simply do not know how these texts viewed themselves in relation to their literary/scriptural antecedents. Whereas some works appear, at least formally, to supplement a specific writing (i.e. *Pesher Habakkuk*), others explicitly claim authoritative status for themselves (i.e. *Jubilees*).[8] This is reflected in the way that scriptural material was used during the period. Devorah Dimant notes that the Jewish scriptures were not just the objects of exegesis, they were also the means of composing new and independent literature. She distinguishes between the *expositional* use of scriptural material and its *compositional* use:

> In compositional use biblical elements are interwoven into the work without external formal markers; in expositional use they are presented explicitly as such, with a clear external marker. These two distinctive functions have different aims. In the exposition the divine word is introduced in order to interpret it as such, while the composition is employed when the biblical element is subservient to the independent aim and structure of its new context.[9]

5. The term 'Jewish scriptures' refers to those works that eventually comprised the canon of the Hebrew Bible.

6. On this process during the Second Temple period, see Timothy H. Lim, *The Formation of the Jewish Canon* (New Haven, CT: Yale University Press, 2013), 178–85. For a recent alternative account, see Judith H. Newman, *Before the Bible: The Liturgical Body and the Formation of Scriptures in Early Judaism* (Oxford: Oxford University Press, 2018), esp. 14–19, which considers the liturgical process through which texts became sacralized in communities.

7. A view critiqued in Eva Mroczek, *The Literary Imagination in Jewish Antiquity* (Oxford: Oxford University Press, 2016), 7.

8. An exegetical work on a scriptural text may have also been considered authoritative in its own right, so Lim, *The Formation of the Jewish Canon*, 135–9.

9. Devorah Dimant, 'Use and Interpretation of Mikra in the Apocrypha and Pseudepigrapha', in *Mikra: Text, Translation, Reading and Interpretation of the*

1. *Introduction*

The expositional form is found in explicitly exegetical works like the *Pesher Habakkuk*. Here the scriptural lemma is followed by interpretation: '"Why do you stare, traitors, and remain silent when a wicked person consumes someone more upright than himself?" Its interpretation concerns the House of Absalom and the members of their council, who kept silent when the Teacher of Righteousness was rebuked' (1QpHab 5:8-10; interpreting Hab. 1:13). The expositional form is also used to invoke the authority of its scriptural source: 'No-one should offer anything upon the altar on the sabbath, except the sacrifice of the sabbath, for thus is it written, "except your offerings of the sabbath"' (CD A 11:17-18; citing Lev. 23:38). It also appears when one scriptural passage is used to interpret another: 'Accordingly, it is written in the book of the Law of Moses that anyone who is unwilling to raise up posterity for his brother, his shoe should be removed and one should spit in his face. Joseph's brothers did not want their brother to live, and the Lord removed Joseph's shoe from them' (*T. Zeb.* 3:4-5; interpreting Gen. 37:18-28 with Deut. 25:5-10). In the expositional use, the scriptural material appears as something external to the work, so that it can be cited as an authority or so its meaning can be interpreted.

The compositional use of scriptural material features most prominently in works often referred to – somewhat misleadingly – as 'Rewritten Bible'.[10] The book of *Jubilees*, for example, takes the narrative outline of Genesis and Exodus as its compositional model. The Genesis–Exodus material does not appear as something external, but is re-constituted in the new work. The Genesis–Exodus narrative is presented according to the sectarian calendar, whilst the patriarchs are shown performing the Law of Moses, which demonstrates its pre-existence.[11] To this end, the author of *Jubilees* inserts legal material into the patriarchal narrative, composing episodes which are, according to scriptural chronology, anachronistic: Noah celebrates Shavuot (*Jub.* 6:17; cf. Exod. 34:22), Abraham celebrates

---

Hebrew Bible in Ancient Judaism and Early Christianity, ed. Martin J. Mulder (Philadelphia, PA: Fortress, 1988), 382. Note also Michael Fishbane's similar classification of scriptural material as a 'Model for Language' and a 'Model for Composition' in the Dead Sea Scrolls; see his 'Use, Authority and Interpretation of Mikra at Qumran', in Mulder, ed., *Mikra*, 356–9.

10. On problems posed by the term see Moshe J. Bernstein, '"Rewritten Bible": A Generic Category Which Has Outlived Its Usefulness?', *Textus* 22 (2005): 169–96.

11. For example, when Joseph is confronted by Potiphar's wife, he remembers the Levitical prohibition against adultery (*Jub.* 39:6-7; cf. Lev. 20:10) which was written by Abraham (*Jub.* 20:3-4) and read to him by Jacob.

4   *Writing with Scripture*

Sukkot (*Jub.* 16:20-31; cf. Lev. 23:34, 40-42) and Levi, as High Priest, performs Sukkot and the tithe (*Jub.* 32:3-10; cf. Lev. 23:34-44; Num. 29:12-40; Deut. 14:22-23). Into this narrative, the author also inserts scriptural language from outside the Torah. Again, this scriptural language is unmarked and embedded in its new context. When the text reads 'There (will be) no old men and none who is full of days, because all of them will be infants and children' (*Jub.* 23:28), these are the words of the LORD to Moses, not Isaiah (Isa. 65:20). When it reads 'I am old and I do not know the day of my death' (*Jub.* 21:1), the words are those of Abraham, not Isaac (Gen. 27:2). And when God is entreated to 'Create a pure heart and a holy spirit for them' (*Jub.* 1:21), it is Moses who speaks, not the Psalmist (Ps. 51:10). In the compositional use, scriptural elements are woven into the fabric of a new work, providing language and narrative details or serving as a model for a new composition.[12]

Mark's use of the Jewish scriptures: expositional or compositional?

These two approaches to using the Jewish scriptures can be seen in another work of the Second Temple period: the Gospel of Mark. The Gospel begins with an *expositional* citation, partly misattributed to Isaiah, 'As it is written in the prophet Isaiah, "See, I am sending my messenger ahead of you, who will prepare you way; the voice of one crying out in the wilderness: 'Prepare the way of the Lord, make his paths straight'"' (Mk 1:2-3). The passage – which conflates LXX Exod. 23:20, LXX Isa. 40:3 and possibly Mal. 3:1 – is the only editorial citation in the Gospel. Elsewhere, citations or allusions appear in the direct speech of characters. These come in the form of marked citations (Mk 7:6-7, 10; 10:6-8, 19; 11:17; 12:10-11, 26, 29-33, 36; 14:27), unmarked scriptural language resembling a citation (1:11; 4:12; 9:7, 48; 11:9; 13:24-25; 14:62; 15:34) and allusions with a clear scriptural referent (1:44; 2:25-26; 10:4; 13:14). Here the scriptural material appears as something external to the Markan narrative and is invoked to support an argument or interpret an event.

At the same time, the Gospel features unmarked scriptural language woven seamlessly into the narrative. Again, this may appear in direct speech, such as Antipas' offer to the young girl of 'even half of my kingdom' (Mk 6:23) which borrows the language of Esther (Est. 5:3, 6; 7:2). Scriptural language also appears in narrative details, such as the description of John the Baptist wearing 'a leather belt around his waist' (Mk 1:6;

---

12. So Dimant, 'Mikra in the Apocrypha and Pseudepigrapha', 383.

1. *Introduction*

cf. LXX 2 Kgs 1:8) or the image of Jesus' tormentors dividing his clothes and casting lots for them (Mk 15:24; cf. LXX Ps. 21:19). The Jewish scriptures were not just invoked to interpret the Markan narrative, but also to compose details and episodes in the narrative itself.[13]

Studies on the use of the Jewish scriptures in the Gospel of Mark have focused primarily on the expositional use of scriptural material – how Mark's interpretation of the scriptures contributes to the meaning of the Gospel. On this question, scholars can be divided into two camps. One camp, following C. H. Dodd, believes Mark interpreted the Jewish scriptures through an overarching thematic framework or schema of prophetic fulfilment.[14] These scholars identify broad scriptural themes in the Gospel and tend to view the original literary context of a citation or allusion as the key to its interpretation. The other camp, following Alfred Suhl, finds little evidence of an overarching schema.[15] Instead, Mark's use of the Jewish scriptures was ad hoc and atomistic – that is, without concern for its original context.[16] Only a few studies have sought to examine the use of scriptural material in the Gospel as a means of composition, and these with limited success. This chapter offers a history of approaches to the use of the Jewish scriptures in the Gospel, showing the need for a thorough-going compositional approach to the question.

Studies on the use of the Jewish scriptures in the Gospel of Mark

Major studies before Dodd: Strauss to Farrer

Research into the role of the Jewish scriptures in the Gospels began in earnest over a century before Dodd – as with so much in biblical

---

13. The unknown author(s) of the Gospel is referred to as Mark for convenience. As the author's gender is unknown, gender inclusive pronouns are preferred. Where applicable, the possibility of sources or redactional traces will be noted. The author clearly knows of the destruction of the Temple in Jerusalem (Mk 13:2), which establishes the *terminus post quem* as 70 CE. That the Gospel of Mark served as the primary source for the Gospel of Matthew, which was written in the same generation following the Temple's destruction, sets the *terminus ante quem* at *c.* 85 CE.

14. C. H. Dodd, *According to the Scriptures: The Sub-Structure of New Testament Theology* (London: Nisbet & Co., 1952).

15. Alfred Suhl, *Die Funktion der alttestamentlichen Zitate und Anspielungen im Markusevangelium* (Gütersloh: Mohn, 1965).

16. For the classic definition of atomization, see George F. Moore, *Judaism in the First Centuries of the Christian Era: The Age of the Tannaim*, vol. 1 (Cambridge, MA: Harvard University Press, 1927), 249–50.

scholarship – in the work of David Friedrich Strauss.[17] Strauss was among the first to argue that the Jewish scriptures wielded a creative influence over the depiction of Jesus in the Gospels: 'Den reichsten Stoff zu dieser mythischen Verzierung lieferte (dabei) das alte Testament, in welchem die erste, vornehmlich aus dem Judentum gesammelte Christengemeinde lebte und webte'.[18] Following what Strauss saw as the Jewish exegesis of their day, the early Christians manipulated the scriptures to fit the details of Jesus' life whilst also inventing stories about him out of scriptural material.[19] Jesus is shown performing the same deeds as Moses and Elijah whilst his life is narrated using the language of the Psalms and Isaiah. The figure encountered in the Gospels, according to Strauss, is the Jesus of myth, fashioned in large part out of the words of the Jewish scriptures. Strauss had little patience for Mark, however, whom he regarded as a second-rate epitomizer, and even less for the literary world of the Second Temple period.[20] Rather, the guiding force over early Christian exegesis was fanaticism: 'So saben sie, durch ihre Begeisterung für den neuen Messias geblendet, in dem einzigen Buche, das sie lasen dem A. T., ihn überall'.[21]

Over the following century, Strauss' controversial views struggled to gain acceptance outside of German scholarship.[22] Karl Weidel echoed Strauss' sentiments in an article serially published between 1910 and 1912, arguing that the early Christians constructed the life of Jesus out of a *Weissagungsbeweis* drawn from the Jewish scriptures.[23] Put plainly, 'Auf diesem Wege musste allmählich eine Art von alttestamentlichen Leben Jesu entstehen'.[24] Weidel, like Strauss, saw this process going one of two ways: to fulfil the Jewish scriptures, the early Christians invented

17. Beginning with the first edition of *Das Leben Jesu: kritisch bearbeitet*, 2 vols. (Tübingen: Osiander, 1835).

18. Strauss, *Das Leben Jesu*, 1:73.

19. So Strauss: 'Mit dem Messias muß sich nach dem Alten Testament das und das begeben; Jesus war der Messias; folglich wird sich eben jenes mit ihm begeben haben' (*Das Leben Jesu*, 1:109).

20. Strauss characterized contemporary Jewish exegesis as 'bodenlosen Willkühr' (*Das Leben Jesu*, 2:340).

21. Strauss, *Das Leben Jesu*, 2:340–1.

22. See Johannes Weiss, *Die Drei Älteren Evangelien*, Die Schriften des NT 1, 2nd ed. (Göttingen, 1907), esp. 46; Friedrich K. Feigels, *Der Einfluß des Weissagungsbeweises und anderer Motive auf die Leidensgeschichte* (Tübingen: Mohr, 1910).

23. Karl Weidel, 'Studien über den Einfluss des Weissagungsbeweises auf die evangelische Geschichte', *TSK* 83 (1910): 83–109, 163–95; *TSK* 85 (1912): 167–286.

24. Weidel, 'Studien über den Einfluss', 1:169.

1. *Introduction* 7

unhistorical episodes in the life of Jesus, whilst also manipulating scriptural passages to conform to the details of his life.[25] This is nowhere more evident than in the Markan Passion Narrative (Mk 14–15): 'In der Tat der Weissagungsbeweis für weite Strecken der Leidensgeschichte die Quelle gebildet hat, das ser also in diesem Teil der evangelischen Überlieferung in höchstem Masse geschichtsbilden gewirkt hat'.[26] For Weidel, the merging of historical details with wholesale invention on the basis of the Jewish scriptures makes the recovery of the historical Jesus nearly impossible. As the earliest kerygma developed, 'Der Gedanke, dass es sich hier doch um wirkliche Geschichte und lebendige Personlichkeiten handele, verflüchtigte sich allmählich ganz'.[27]

Weidel's views reached a wider audience in the better-known work of Martin Dibelius. According to Dibelius, the early Christians interpreted the life of Jesus through a *Schriftbeweis* drawn from the Jewish scriptures. This began with the simple postulate of the post-Easter faith: 'Daß auch das Leiden Jesu nach Gottes Willen geschehen sei'.[28] This led to the hermeneutical presupposition of early Christian exegesis: 'Gottes Willen mußte in der Schrift zu finden sein'.[29] The early Christians thus began to tell the life of Jesus using the language of the Jewish scriptures. Following Weidel, Dibelius saw no better example of this than the creative use of the Psalms in the Markan Passion Narrative. Indeed, one can hear echoes of Weidel in Dibelius' conclusion: 'Man las die Leidenskapitel des Alten Testaments als massgebende Quelle für die Leidengeschichte'.[30]

---

25. Weidel, 'Studien über den Einfluss', 1:194.

26. Weidel, 'Studien über den Einfluss', 2:289.

27. Weidel, 'Studien über den Einfluss', 1:194.

28. Martin Dibelius, *Die Formgeschichte des Evangeliums*, 6th ed. (Tübingen: Mohr Siebeck, 1966 [1919]), 185.

29. Dibelius, *Die Formgeschichte*, 185.

30. Dibelius, *Die Formgeschichte*, 188; cf. Weidel, 'Studien über den Einfluss', 2:289. This is taken further by Christian Maurer, who distinguishes between a *Schriftbeweis* 'de verbo' and 'de facto', the former characterizing the fulfilment formulae of Matthew, whist the latter is best seen in the embedded scriptural details in the Markan Passion Narrative. Thus, where historical details were lacking, Mark or their source used the Jewish scriptures to compose details in the Passion of Jesus: 'So haben wir sehr damit zu rechnen, dass ganze Perikopen der Passionsgeschichte durch den Schriftbeweis nicht nur geformt, sondern auch geschaffen sind, sofern nicht historische Tatsachen dahinterestehen mögen'; Christian Maurer, 'Knecht Gottes und Sohn Gottes im Passionsberichte des Markusevangeliums', *ZTK* 50 (1953): 1–38 (10). Suhl, however, roundly criticized Maurer for his insistence on the formative role of Deutero-Isaiah in the Passion Narrative, see *Die Funktion der alttestamentlichen Zitate*, 58, 114–20.

8 *Writing with Scripture*

These studies, however, offer little more than provisional comments on the compositional use of the Jewish scriptures in the Gospel of Mark. The purpose of scriptural details in the Gospel narrative is always expositional: it is to demonstrate prophetic-fulfilment (a *Weissagungs-* or *Schriftbeweis*). There is virtually no attempt to place the Markan use of scriptural material in a Second Temple context. Strauss, for example, simply states that early Christian exegesis was indistinguishable from contemporary Jewish exegesis, with the sole exception of Jesus, 'weil der Verstand in jenen Männern durch die Denkart ihres Volks beschränkt war'.[31] Nevertheless, these studies offer a glimpse of what would become the major expositional and compositional approaches to the use of the Jewish scriptures in the Gospel.

During the same period, British scholarship was pre-occupied with the *testimony hypothesis* of J. Rendel Harris.[32] The argument, briefly put, was that there existed a written collection of proof-texts drawn from the Jewish scriptures which was used by the early Christians. Proof of this was seen in the recurrence of peculiar readings, sequences of testimonies and misattributions in early Christian literature.[33] The goal of scholarship was thus concerned with re-constructing these lost testimonia. Perhaps as a result, only one English-language study on the use of the Jewish scriptures in the Gospel of Mark emerged from the period before Dodd. In his *A Study in Mark*, Austin Farrer notes that whilst 'St Mark does not quote the Old Testament much', he was nonetheless 'nourished by the substance of it, and so perfectly assimilates it that he can write it into the matter of his own sentence'.[34] In composing his portrait of Jesus, Mark was guided by the belief that 'All that men had been or done had prefigured Christ, and all they had prefigured, Christ did and was'.[35] Thus, Jesus was typologically modelled after figures from the Jewish scriptures. These

31. Strauss, *Das Leben Jesu*, 4th ed. (Tübingen: Osiander, 1840), 1:180.

32. J. Rendel Harris, *Testimonies*, 2 vols. (Cambridge: Cambridge University Press, 1916–20). For its influence on British scholarship, see R. Hodgson Jr., 'The Testimony Hypothesis', *JBL* 98 (1979): 361–78.

33. Harris, *Testimonies*, 1:8. The testimony hypothesis was effectively put to rest by the criticisms of Dodd and Stendahl; Dodd, *According to the Scriptures*, esp. 126; Krister Stendahl, *The School of St. Matthew and Its Use of the Old Testament* (Philadelphia, PA: Fortress, 1968), 216–17. The discovery of 4QTest and 4QFlor, however, has led some to re-evaluate the claim, see J. A. Fitzmyer, '"4Q Testimonia" and the New Testament', in *Essays on the Semitic Background of the New Testament*, SBS 5 (Missoula, MT: Scholars Press, 1974), 59–89.

34. Austin Farrer, *A Study in Mark* (London: A. & C. Black, 1951), 321.

35. Farrer, *A Study in Mark*, 185.

1. *Introduction* 9

types include Moses, David, Saul and – significantly for Farrer – Elisha. Farrer was perhaps the first to note the extensive parallels between the Elijah–Elisha cycle (1 Kgs 17–2 Kgs 13) and the Gospel of Mark.[36] But Farrer offers little by way of argument for his proposed typologies, his study occasionally veering into 'Typologicalmania'.[37] At the same time, Farrer was uninterested in the use scriptural typology in other works of the Second Temple period. Although Farrer's study has been eclipsed by Dodd's more influential study, its significance is two-fold: it foreshadows the excesses of later compositional studies whilst anticipating the focus on Mark's use of the Elijah–Elisha cycle.

The 'Dodd camp': the 1950s to the 1980s

The publication of C. H. Dodd's *According to the Scriptures* in 1952 ushered in a new era of research into the role of the scriptures in the Gospels. Against Harris' testimony hypothesis, Dodd maintains that the shared features of early Christian exegesis owe their form to the kerygma of the earliest period: a 'common tradition' of testimonia, governed by the concept of prophetic fulfilment, and preserved through oral tradition.[38] In Dodd's words, the early Christians were 'committed [to a] formidable task of biblical research, primarily for the purpose of clarifying its own understanding of the momentous events out of which it had emerged'.[39] By examining passages cited by 'two or more writers of the New Testament in *prima facie* independence of one another', Dodd identifies three major scriptural themes common to all early Christian literature which were seen to have their fulfilment in the person of Jesus:[40] 'Apocalyptic-eschatological Scriptures', 'Scriptures of the New Israel' and 'Scriptures of the Servant of the Lord and the Righteous Sufferer'.[41] The fulfilment of these themes in the person of Jesus can be found in 'all main portions of the New Testament' and, as such, should be regarded as the 'substructure of all Christian theology'.[42] Unlike Strauss and Weidel, Dodd concludes

---

36. Farrer sees the use of 1 Kgs 17:17-24 and 2 Kgs 4:18-37 in Mk 5:21-43; 7:25-29; 9:17-29; 2 Kgs 5 in Mk 1:40-45; 2 Kgs 13:21 in Mk 2:1-12. See *A Study in Mark*, 15–18, 47–52, 91–2.

37. Dale C. Allison Jr., *The New Moses: A Matthean Typology* (Minneapolis, MN: Fortress, 1993), 18.

38. Dodd, *According to the Scriptures*, 29.

39. Dodd, *According to the Scriptures*, 14.

40. Dodd, *According to the Scriptures*, 28–9.

41. Along with the miscellaneous 'Unclassified Scriptures', *According to the Scriptures*, 62–108.

42. Dodd, *According to the Scriptures*, 127.

10   *Writing with Scripture*

that the early Christians paid careful attention to the original literary context of a given citation, remaining 'true to the main intention of their writers'.[43] Whilst he allows for a 'fringe of questionable, arbitrary or even fanciful exegesis', Dodd believes the early Christian use of the Jewish scriptures was 'consistent and intelligent in itself' and 'founded upon a genuinely historical understanding of the process of the religious – I should prefer to say the prophetic – history of Israel as a whole'.[44]

Dodd's approach of examining the expositional significance of broad scriptural themes was continued the following decade in Barnabas Lindars' *New Testament Apologetic*. Lindars traces 'shifts in application' in the early Christian use of the Jewish scriptures. He thus proposes several stages in which the early Christians developed their thematic approach to the scriptures in response to apologetic concerns, beginning with the defence of Jesus' resurrection and culminating in the prophetic-fulfilment schema of messianic exegesis.[45] Lindars compares this to what he calls the 'midrash pesher' of the recently discovered Dead Sea Scrolls, on which basis he concludes that the apparent arbitrariness of Christian exegesis was 'nothing morally reprehensible'.[46] Indeed, Lindars follows Dodd in insisting the early Christians were generally faithful to the original context from which a citation was drawn.[47] At the same time, the early Christians did not compose details to reflect scriptural material, *pace* Weidel and Dibelius. Rather, it was the 'astonishingly accurate' similarities between the scriptures and the 'facts' of Jesus' life that led the early Christians to view events like the Passion of Jesus through a scriptural lens.[48] Often it was Jesus himself who was responsible for the application of scriptural passages to his person. For example, it was Jesus' own use of the 'suffering servant' theme in Isaiah 53 that set in motion a 'doctrine of the Atonement'.[49]

The expositional approach of identifying broad scriptural themes developed by Dodd and Lindars influenced a few important studies in the following two generations of scholarship. These include Ulrich Mauser's study, which argues that Mark developed a pre-existing 'wilderness'

---

43. Dodd, *According to the Scriptures*, 130.

44. Dodd, *According to the Scriptures*, 133.

45. Barnabas Lindars, *New Testament Apologetic: The Doctrinal Significance of Old Testament Quotations* (London: SCM, 1961), 186.

46. Lindars, *New Testament Apologetic*, 27–8.

47. Lindars, *New Testament Apologetic*, 14.

48. Lindars, *New Testament Apologetic*, 33–4, 91 (quoted at 34).

49. Lindars, *New Testament Apologetic*, 79, see discussion in 78–9, 89.

(ἔρημος) theme in the Jewish scriptures, making it the thematic framework for their Gospel.[50] The study of Hans-Jörg Steichele identifies a scriptural theme of suffering in Mark's depiction of John the Baptist (Mk 1:1-8; 9:9-13), Jesus' Baptism and Transfiguration (1:9-11; 9:2-8) and Crucifixion (15:20b-41), through which Jesus is presented as 'der alles erfüllende Sohn Gottes'.[51] Though not limited to Mark, Douglas Moo's study of the use of the Jewish scriptures in the Passion Narratives finds evidence of the thematic application of the Isaianic 'Servant Songs' and the 'Psalms of Lament' to the suffering of Jesus.[52] One can hear echoes of Dodd and Lindars in Moo's insistence that the early Christians were not involved in the 'fabrication of incidents on the basis of Scriptures'.[53] Rather, the influence proceeded from 'history to the text rather than vice versa', so the scriptural content of the Passion Narrative was for the most part generated by the 'correspondence of prophecy with the facts'.[54] At the same time, the original literary context of a citation or allusion is deemed to be of greatest concern for the Gospel writers: '[it] can unhesitatingly be asserted that Jesus and the evangelists have shown a remarkable faithfulness to the original context in their appropriation of OT verses to interpret the passion'.[55] And like Lindars, Moo is – one could say conveniently – able to find shades of reformed dogmatics in Jesus' interpretation of his own death using Isaiah 53, implying the 'efficacy [of his] vicarious, redemptive suffering',[56] which was 'voluntary, sacrificial, [and] substitutionary'.[57]

---

50. Ulrich W. Mauser, *Christ in the Wilderness: The Wilderness Theme in the Second Gospel and its Basis in the Biblical Tradition*, SBT 39 (Eugene, OR: Wipf & Stock, 1963). This wilderness theme was the 'string on which the beads of tradition [were] assembled' (101–102).

51. Hans-Jörg Steichele, *Der leidende Sohn Gottes: Eine Untersuchung einiger alttestamentlicher Motive in der Christologie des Markusevangeliums*, BU 14 (Regensburg: Pustet, 1980), 273.

52. Douglas J. Moo, *The Old Testament in the Gospel Passion Narratives* (Sheffield: Almond, 1983), 360.

53. Moo, *The Old Testament in the Gospel Passion Narratives*, 380.

54. Moo, *The Old Testament in the Gospel Passion Narratives*, 380–1; quoting C. H. Dodd, *The Apostolic Preaching and Its Development* (London: Hodder & Stoughton, 1936), 53.

55. Moo, *The Old Testament in the Gospel Passion Narratives*, 376–7.

56. Moo, *The Old Testament in the Gospel Passion Narratives*, 170.

57. Moo, *The Old Testament in the Gospel Passion Narratives*, 397.

12 *Writing with Scripture*

The 'Suhl camp': the 1960s to the 1980s

As the influence of Dodd and Lindars grew in English-speaking scholarship, the first continental monograph devoted exclusively to the use of the Jewish scriptures in the Gospel of Mark offered a markedly different approach. Reflecting the new interests of the *redaktionsgeschichte Schule*, the 1965 study of Alfred Suhl was the first attempt to examine every citation of, and allusion to, scriptural material in the Gospel, beginning with the Passion Narrative and then the Markan dialogues. Suhl contends that, unlike Matthew and Luke, Mark did not subsume his scriptural material into a 'Schema von Weissagung und Erfüllung'.[58] This belonged to a later stage of exegesis.[59] Instead, Mark simply told their story in the 'colours' of the Jewish scriptures to demonstrate the life of Jesus happened in accordance with the will of God – as the earliest kerygma puts it, κατὰ τὰς γραφάς (1 Cor. 15:3-4).[60] Thus, 'Indem nam das Neue in den »Farben« des Alten erzählte, machte man deutlich, daß es auch im Neuen um dasselbe wie im Alten, nämlich um Gottes Heilshandeln ging'.[61]

For Suhl, this process was ad hoc and showed little concern for the original context from which a citation or allusion was drawn. Rather, it was the Markan context that governed everything: 'der notfalls auch gegen den ursprünglichen Sinn der Schrift diese für sich in Anspruch nimmt'.[62] Suhl criticizes earlier studies for making too much of a 'bloßer Gleichklang einzelner Begriffe' – a mere consonance of concepts or words.[63] For Suhl, an allusion to the Jewish scriptures should not be posited unless 'eine ganze Folge Wörten die Anspielung evident macht oder die syntaktisch auffallende oder gar störende Stellung einzelner Wörter ihren besonderen Charakter schon anzeigt'.[64] This minimalist approach offers a fresh alternative to the broad, often impressionistic

---

58. Suhl, *Die Funktion der alttestamentlichen Zitate*, 44–5.

59. Following his teacher Willi Marxsen, Suhl holds that the Markan community was primarily concerned with the immanence of the parousia. As such, they had little interest in *Heilsgeschichte* – only with the delay of the parousia did the early Christians begin to situate Jesus' place within salvation history. See Suhl, *Die Funktion der alttestamentlichen Zitate*, 169–86; Willi Marxsen, *Der Evangelist Markus: Studien zur Redaktionsgeschichte des Evangeliums*, FRLANT 49 (Göttingen: Vandenhoeck & Ruprecht, 1959), esp. 89.

60. Suhl, *Die Funktion der alttestamentlichen Zitate*, 45, 65, 157–8. Suhl appears to be building on Dibelius, *Die Formgeschichte*, 185.

61. Suhl, *Die Funktion der alttestamentlichen Zitate*, 47.

62. Suhl, *Die Funktion der alttestamentlichen Zitate*, 47.

63. Suhl, *Die Funktion der alttestamentlichen Zitate*, 127.

64. Suhl, *Die Funktion der alttestamentlichen Zitate*, 127.

1. *Introduction*   13

categories proposed by Dodd and his successors.[65] Nevertheless, the rigidity of Suhl's rejection of a Markan prophetic-fulfilment schema has won few adherents. Suhl is often dismissed with little more than a cursory reference to the critical review of Erich Grässer.[66] As Grässer notes, it is difficult to see the formulae in Mk 1:2, 7:6, 14:21 and 14:49 as anything other than some sort of prophetic-fulfilment.[67] The effectiveness of this critique, however, has led to the unjust neglect of this important work. Suhl's most interesting contribution to scholarship – the idea that Mark composed in the 'colours' of the Jewish scriptures – is scarcely discussed outside of the work of South African scholar Willem Vorster.

In two brief articles, Vorster makes the case that Mark tells their Gospel in the 'language of the Old Testament', not as an external source, but as part of the narrative itself.[68] Again, this process was atomistic: citations and allusions were drawn without 'direct reference to their Old Testament context(s)'. In this, Mark was simply 'a child of his time'.[69] Building on Suhl's suggestion, Vorster begins to sketch out a compositional approach to the question: 'One of the inferences one should make from the use of the Old Testament in the Gospel of Mark is that the author created a new

65. Howard Clark Kee criticizes Suhl's approach for failing to take into account more allusive uses of scriptural material. See his influential article 'The Function of Scriptural Quotations and Allusions in Mark 11–16', in *Festschrift für Werner Georg Kümmel*, ed. Erich Grässer and E. Earle Ellis (Göttingen: Vandenhoeck & Ruprecht, 1975), 165–88; as well as the comments in *Community of the New Age: Studies in Mark's Gospel* (London: SCM Press, 1977), 45–9.

66. See Joel Marcus, *The Way of the Lord: Christological Exegesis of the Old Testament in the Gospel of Mark* (Edinburgh: T. & T. Clark, 1992), 2–3; Rikki E. Watts, *Isaiah's New Exodus*, WUNT 2/88 (Tübingen: Mohr Siebeck, 1997), 17; cf. the longer discussions in Thomas R. Hatina, *In Search of a Context: The Function of Scripture in Mark's Narrative*, JSNTSup 232 (Sheffield: Sheffield Academic, 2002), 27–8; Steichele, *Der leidende Sohn Gottes*, 33, who notes that Grässer's review is not entirely negative. Whilst Suhl is often seen to exemplify the excesses of the *redaktionsgeschichte Schule*, this is much better seen in the brief study of Siegfried Schulz, 'Markus und das Alte Testament', *ZTK* 58 (1961): 184–97, itself a continuation of the work of Wilhelm Brandt, *Die Evangelische Geschichte und der Ursprung des Christentums auf Grund einer Kritik der Berichte über das Leiden und die Auferstehung Jesu* (Leipzig: Reisland, 1893).

67. Erich Grässer, 'Review of A. Suhl, *Die Funktion der alttestamentlichen Zitate und Anspielungen im Markusevangelium*', *TLZ* 91 (1966): 667–9.

68. Willem S. Vorster, 'The Function of the Use of the Old Testament in Mark', *Neotestamentica* 14 (1980): 62–72 (66); also Vorster, 'The Production of the Gospel of Mark: Essay on Intertextuality', *HTS* 49 (1993): 385–96.

69. Vorster, 'The Function of the Use of the Old Testament', 67.

14   *Writing with Scripture*

story with the aid of intertextual codes that helped him to communicate his own point of view'.[70] The author creatively weaved together the Jewish scriptures and inherited traditions, and 'by doing this Mark created a new text from other texts, traces of which can be seen in his text'.[71] Sadly, Vorster passed away before he was able to explore this further. What he was nevertheless able to see was the seeds of a compositional approach to Mark's use of the Jewish scriptures in the pioneering work of Suhl.

The influence of Suhl can also be observed in two other works from the same period. Hugh Anderson echoes Suhl by noting that whilst Mark was 'liberally sprinkled with references to the Old Testament', in comparison to Matthew and Luke, there was a 'low incidence' of $\pi\lambda\eta\rho\sigma\tilde{\nu}$ phrases.[72] For Anderson, this signals Mark did not use scriptural material to demonstrate prophetic-fulfilment, but simply to show how Jesus conformed to the 'will of God witnessed to in Scripture'.[73] Suhl likewise appears to have influenced Donald Juel's study *Messianic Exegesis*.[74] For Juel, like Dibelius, the early Christian use of the Jewish scriptures began with the early kerygmatic assumption found in 1 Cor. 15:3-4: the life and death of Jesus happened 'in accordance with the scriptures'. This, in turn, led to a 'highly artful, even fanciful, history of interpretation'.[75] The early Christians, like their contemporaries in Qumran, viewed the scriptures as 'collections of sacred sentences and words, whose meaning were not bound to an immediate historical or literary context... [A]ncient exegetes were interested in uniting the world of text with their own.'[76] Everything in the scriptures was interpreted through the person of Jesus and everything about Jesus was told using the scriptures.[77] Thus, the life of Jesus was not 'told as a recitation of facts'.[78] Rather, early Christian exegesis moved from 'explanation to heightening the dramatic to the creation of

---

70. Vorster, 'The Production of the Gospel of Mark', 392.

71. Vorster, 'The Production of the Gospel of Mark', 394.

72. Hugh Anderson, 'The Old Testament in Mark's Gospel', in *The Use of the Old Testament in the New and Other Essays: Studies in Honor of William Franklin Stinespring*, ed. J. M. Efird (Durham, NC: Duke University Press, 1972), 280–306 (281).

73. Anderson, 'The Old Testament in Mark's Gospel', 297; compare with Suhl, *Die Funktion der alttestamentlichen Zitate*, 45, 65, 157–8.

74. Donald Juel, *Messianic Exegesis: Christological Interpretation of the Old Testament in Early Christianity* (Philadelphia, PA: Fortress, 1988).

75. Juel, *Messianic Exegesis*, 13.

76. Juel, *Messianic Exegesis*, 15.

77. Juel, *Messianic Exegesis*, 56–7.

78. Juel, *Messianic Exegesis*, 113.

1. *Introduction* 15

legends that sometimes [became] part of the exegetical tradition'.[79] But Juel, like Suhl and Vorster before him, does not push this idea further. In the final analysis, the most enduring legacy of the 'Suhl camp' is its scepticism towards schemas of prophetic fulfilment and thematic frameworks in the Gospel, and its insistence on the atomistic nature of Markan exegesis. However, its most important contribution is in raising two questions. First, by composing in the 'colours' of the Jewish scriptures, was Mark involved in the 'creation of legends' – or to put it another way, the invention of new material in the life of Jesus on the basis of the scriptures? Second, can this process be observed elsewhere in the literature of the Second Temple period?

The 'Dodd camp' continued: the 1990s to the present

The 1990s saw a return to Dodd's thematic approach. The 1992 publication of Joel Marcus' *The Way of the Lord* again brought the question of Mark's use of the Jewish scriptures to the forefront of Markan scholarship. Marcus sets out to examine the Christological titles used in the Gospel – Christ, Son of David, Son of Man and Son of God – through the use of the Jewish scriptures.[80] He identifies the composite scriptural citation (Exod. 23:20; Mal. 3:1; Isa. 40:3) attributed to Isaiah in the Markan prologue as the hermeneutical key to interpreting the Gospel.[81] The citation introduces the Isaianic theme of the 'way' (ὁδός), through which Mark presents the 'entire story' of the Gospel as the 'fulfilment of the prophecy of holy war victory announced by the prophet Isaiah'.[82] Again, the original literary context of the Isaianic passage has a role in the interpretation of the narrative, as it evokes the theme of the 'second exodus' as well as the 'wilderness, the way of the Lord, the enlightening of the blind, [and] the festal procession to Jerusalem'.[83] By focusing primarily on 'citation formulas ("as it has been written," etc.) and/or [passages] that contain

---

79. Juel, *Messianic Exegesis*, 40.

80. This is done through a selection of passages: Mk 1:2-3, 9-11; 9:2-8, 11-13; 12:10-11, 35-37; chs. 14–15 (Marcus, *The Way of the Lord*, 8).

81. Marcus, *The Way of the Lord*, 17. Here, Marcus is building on Frank J. Matera, 'The Prologue as the Interpretative Key to Mark's Gospel', *JSNT* 34 (1988): 3–20.

82. Marcus, *The Way of the Lord*, 196.

83. Marcus, *The Way of the Lord*, 24–6, 46. Marcus sees this contextual approach as indicative of the Markan hermeneutical method, 'The conjuring up of the larger context of a passage through the citation of a specific verse or two is, as we have seen, a consistent Markan practice, and this practice corresponds to a method of citation found in rabbinic literature' (199–200).

significant overlaps in vocabulary with Old Testament text', Marcus avoids some of the pitfalls of older thematic studies. At the same time, Marcus brings the Markan use of scriptural material into an extensive dialogue with other Second Temple literature. Whether one is persuaded by Marcus' broad claim that the misattributed citation in Mk 1:2-3 provides the thematic framework for the whole Gospel, his study offers a plausible case following a careful methodology and thoroughly grounded in the exegesis of the Second Temple period.

By drawing attention to Mark's use of Isaiah, Marcus prepared the way for the subsequent generation of scholarship.[84] His work was shortly followed by Richard Schneck's study of Isaiah in the first half of the Gospel.[85] Although Schneck does not think 'any NT author would ever attempt to use the Isaian corpus as a model or paradigm to be copied in composing a new writing for the first century CE', he nevertheless continues Marcus' thematic approach.[86] Schneck identifies repeated conceptual links between Isaiah and Mark 1–8. Again, this is best illustrated in the *Stichwort* citation of Mk 1:2-3: the passages are linked by the statement 'prepare the way', which introduces the theme of the exodus, which in turn evokes a much larger Isaianic context.[87] As with other studies in the Dodd mould, Schneck's identification of shared 'theological themes' between two or more passages can often seem arbitrary and self-fulfilling. To his credit, Schneck is aware of this: 'We are really moving from biblical exegesis into the area of biblical theology'.[88]

The focus on Isaiah is continued in Rikki Watts' *Isaiah's New Exodus and Mark*, which, though independent of Marcus, presents an intensification of his thesis.[89] For Watts, Isaiah's 'New Exodus' theme is the 'conceptual

---

84. On the other end of the spectrum, see Morna Hooker's influential study questioning the influence of the Isaianic 'servant songs', especially in Mark, *Jesus and the Servant: The Influence of the Servant Concept of Deutero-Isaiah in the New Testament* (London: SPCK, 1959); also in her brief article, 'Mark', in *It is Written: Scripture Citing Scripture: Essays in Honour of Barnabas Lindars, SSF*, ed. D. A. Carson and H. G. M. Williamson (Cambridge: Cambridge University Press, 1988), 220–30.

85. Richard Schneck, *Isaiah in the Gospel of Mark, I–VIII*, BIBALDS 1 (Vallejo: BIBAL, 1994).

86. Schneck, *Isaiah in the Gospel of Mark*, 3.

87. Schneck, *Isaiah in the Gospel of Mark*, 31–2, 34–5, 41–2, 246.

88. Schneck, *Isaiah in the Gospel of Mark*, 124.

89. The work is a revision of Watts' 1990 doctoral thesis at Cambridge University, thus preceding the 1992 publication of *The Way of the Lord* (see Watts, *Isaiah's New Exodus*, v).

framework' for the whole Gospel.[90] Once again, this is introduced in the opening citation, which, 'as part of the heading [is] programmatic for the prologue and therefore the whole Gospel'.[91] From then on, Mark builds on the 'three-fold structure' of the Isaianic New Exodus: the deliverance of the exiles, the way out of captivity and the triumphal arrival in Jerusalem.[92] Watts painstakingly details the many ways Mark's scriptural citations, allusions and motifs can be stretched to fit this thematic framework. Thus Watts concludes – one suspects by design – 'the Gospel's basic literary structure is consistent with the [Isaianic New Exodus] schema'.[93]

'The Old Testament in the New': historical criticism or biblical theology?

The turn of the millennium has seen a burgeoning interest in the use of the Jewish scriptures in early Christian writings, spurred on in large part by Richard Hays' influential study, *Echoes of Scripture in the Letters of Paul*.[94] David Allen has commented that the study of the 'Old Testament in the New' – as it is often called – is now widely 'viewed as a *specialism*' and should be regarded as a sub-discipline within New Testament studies.[95]

---

90. Watts, *Isaiah's New Exodus*, 370. Mark recognized in Isaiah the 'prophetic transformation of the past Exodus into the future hope of the [New Exodus]' (380–1).

91. Watts, *Isaiah's New Exodus*, 56.

92. Watts, *Isaiah's New Exodus*, 135.

93. Watts, *Isaiah's New Exodus*, 371.

94. Richard B. Hays, *Echoes of Scripture in the Letters of Paul* (New Haven, CT: Yale University Press, 1989). The Haysian approach is most commonly seen in published dissertations: Sylvia C. Keesmaat, *Paul and His Story: (Re)Interpreting the Exodus Tradition*, JSNTSup 181 (Sheffield: Sheffield Academic, 1999); Kelly D. Liebengood, *The Eschatology of 1 Peter: Considering the Influence of Zechariah 9–14*, SNTSMS 157 (Cambridge: Cambridge University Press, 2014); Sarah Harris, *The Davidic Shepherd King in the Lukan Narrative*, LNTS 558 (London: Bloomsbury, 2016); with some modifications in Christopher Beetham, *Echoes of Scripture in the Letter of Paul to the Colossians*, BibInt 96 (Leiden: Brill, 2008); Kelli S. O'Brien, *The Use of Scripture in the Markan Passion Narrative*, LNTS 384 (London: T&T Clark, 2010); the Haysian approach has also been applied to the Hebrew Bible, see Yohan Pyeon, *You Have Not Spoken What Is Right About Me: Intertextuality and the Book of Job*, SBL 45 (New York, NY: Lang, 2003).

95. David M. Allen, 'Introduction: The Study of the Use of the Old Testament in the New', *JSNT* 38 (2015): 3–16 (4). Likewise in the same volume of *JSNT* devoted to the 'OT in the NT', Leroy A. Huizenga comments, 'The study of "the Old Testament in the New Testament" has become an effective sub-discipline within biblical scholarship, with interest generated both by tradition descriptive historical-critical concerns regarding issues behind the text...literary and theoretical interest in how

18 *Writing with Scripture*

The sheer number of doctoral dissertations published in this area has led one scholar to liken it to 'a mechanized production line, with its own methodology and theological agendas'.[96] But the division between Dodd and Suhl is still palpable. This can be illustrated in two millennial studies on the use of the Jewish scriptures in the Gospel of Mark, one from the beginning of the period, and one more recent.

Thomas Hatina's 2002 monograph, *In Search of a Context*, offers a marked contrast to the maximalist Isaianic studies of the 1990s.[97] For Hatina, Mark's 'ideological point of view' can be found in the proclamation of the kingdom in Mk 1:14-15 and not in the Isaianic opening citation of Mk 1:2-3.[98] Thus, Mark interprets the Jewish scriptures through the prism of the 'realization of the kingdom of God' in the person of Jesus and the Markan community.[99] This can be seen in the ethical 'way' of the kingdom introduced by the citation in Mk 1:2-3 as well as the use of scriptural material in the various conflicts with those outside of the kingdom (i.e. Mk 4:11-12; 7:6-7; 11:9; 13:24-27). Though Hatina is critical of Suhl, and engages in a thematic study reminiscent of Dodd, he nevertheless follows Suhl by insisting on the atomistic nature of Markan exegesis.[100] He singles out Marcus for 'forcing too much of the context of the scriptural passage into the Markan context'.[101] This stems from a failure to realize 'atomistic exegesis [was] the norm in early Jewish interpretation'.[102] By noting the supreme role of the Markan context, Hatina is able to provide a model for understanding the use of the Jewish scriptures sensitive to Mark's narrative and its historical setting. Whilst Hatina does not entirely

---

texts function within the system of textuality and culture...and more normative and prescriptive theological and ecclesial interests' ('The Old Testament in the New, Intertextuality and Allegory', *JSNT* 38 [2015]: 17–35 [17]).

96. Paul Foster, 'Echoes without Resonance: Critiquing Certain Aspects of Recent Scholarly Trends in the Study of the Jewish Scriptures in the New Testament', *JSNT* 38 (2015): 96–111 (98).

97. See Hatina, *In Search of a Context*, 1–4.

98. *Pace* Marcus, Schneck and Watts.

99. Hatina, *In Search of a Context*, 90–2, 376.

100. See his evaluation of Suhl, *In Search of a Context*, 25–8. Commenting on Moo, Hatina notes, 'Seeking to explain the use of Scripture within a thematic framework provides a solid beginning in any enquiry on the function of allusions and quotations' (37).

101. Hatina, *In Search of a Context*, 42.

102. Hatina, *In Search of a Context*, 42, for support cites Juel, 'Review of Joel Marcus, *The Way of the Lord*', *JBL* 114 (1995): 147–50.

1. *Introduction*   19

avoid the procrustean issues inherent to thematic studies, there is surely some truth to the sweeping claim that 'all the quotations and allusions in Mark contribute in some way to Jesus' announcement, demonstration and establishment of the kingdom of God'.[103]

On the other side is the more typical approach of Richard Hays' 2016 study *Echoes of Scripture in the Gospels*.[104] Following his ground-breaking work on the Jewish scriptures in the Pauline epistles, Hays has turned his hand to the Gospels, devoting a sizable first chapter to the Gospel of Mark. For Hays, Mark's use of the Jewish scriptures is understood through the parabolic disclaimer in Mk 4:21-25, which serves as the 'hermeneutical directive for the Gospel as a whole'.[105] This means Mark's use of scripture is parabolic and elliptical, often gesturing 'toward wider contexts and implications that remain not quite overtly stated'.[106] Again, this is best seen in the – Hays thinks intentionally – misattributed citation of Exod. 23:20, Mal. 3:1 and Isa. 40:3 in Mk 1:2-3. Like Watts, Hays contends 'Mark's use of the Isaiah ascription here signals that the conceptual framework for his Gospel is the Isaianic new exodus'.[107] The conflated citation alludes to the larger contexts of each passage: the new exodus of Isaiah; the entry into the promised land of Exodus; and the impending judgment of Malachi.[108] Building on this intuitive approach, Hays proposes a labyrinth of quotations, allusions and echoes, some more perceptible than others and often offered with little argument besides the refrain, 'If anyone has ears to hear, let him hear'.[109] There is a convenience to this logic: say, if one is unpersuaded by Hays' assertion that a single word – παρελθεῖν in Mk 6:48 – identifies Jesus as the 'God of Israel', the fault must lie with the reader's deficient hearing and not Hays' argument.[110]

---

103. Hatina, *In Search of a Context*, 376.

104. Richard B. Hays, *Echoes of Scripture in the Gospels* (Waco, TX: Baylor University Press, 2016).

105. Hays, *Echoes of Scripture in the Gospels*, 101.

106. Hays, *Echoes of Scripture in the Gospels*, 16. Hays call this technique 'metalepsis' (11), following its use by John Hollander, *The Figure of Echo: A Mode of Allusion in Milton and After* (Berkeley, CA: University of California Press, 1981), 65.

107. Hays, *Echoes of Scripture in the Gospels*, 21.

108. Hays, *Echoes of Scripture in the Gospels*, 20–3.

109. See Hays' method in *Echoes of Scripture in the Gospels*, 23–4, 48–50, 52–3, 58, 69, 102.

110. Hays, *Echoes of Scripture in the Gospels*, 72. This results from Hays' decision to interpret παρελθεῖν exclusively in relation to LXX Exod. 33:17-23 (34:6), despite the fact the word occurs over a hundred times in the Septuagint.

20 *Writing with Scripture*

Hays does little to conceal his theological motivations in making this claim – that Mark presents Jesus as 'both the God of Israel and a human being not simply identical with the God of Israel'[111] – at one point bidding the attentive reader to go searching for clues of Jesus' divinity: 'Such attentiveness will not go unrewarded'.[112]

But if Hays is guilty of reading later theological developments into the text, he insists the same cannot be said for the early Christians. Echoing Dodd and Lindars, Hays believes the early Christians were innocent of 'consciously manipulating snippets of preexisting traditions to craft their own clever imaginative fictions'.[113] Rather, they merely listened to the words of 'Israel's Scripture', which, with 'its own voice', revealed the person of Jesus through an organic process of '"dialectical," rather than "heuristic" intertextuality'.[114] The Gospel writers 'patiently insist that it was precisely the actual teaching and actions of Jesus that lived in the community's memory and subsequently catalyzed a retrospective recognition of unforeseen, divinely scripted, figural linkages with Israel's scripture'.[115] Here Hays is developing an idea from an earlier book, which argues the early Christians unintentionally found in the Jewish scriptures an 'unexpected *foreshadowing* of the later story' of Jesus.[116] The problem is that this assumes the scriptural character of Jesus' life and the Christian character of the Jewish scriptures. It is telling that Hays begins his study by presupposing 'Israel's Scripture prefigures and illuminates the central character in the Gospel stories'.[117] In the final analysis, Hays' work on Mark's use of the Jewish scriptures – though it has no shortage of rich and insightful exegesis – suffers from a malady common to other works in the burgeoning 'Old Testament in the New' field: it is *biblical theology*

---

111. Hays, *Echoes of Scripture in the Gospels*, 78. Hays writes that whilst Mark 'shies away from overt ontological declarations' (62), his presentation of Jesus as the God of Israel maintains a 'distinction of roles and persons' (77).

112. Hays, *Echoes of Scripture in the Gospels*, 69.

113. Hays, *Echoes of Scripture in the Gospels*, 7.

114. Hays, *Echoes of Scripture in the Gospels*, 8, referencing *Echoes of Scripture in the Letters of Paul*, 176–7.

115. Hays, *Echoes of Scripture in the Gospels*, 360; a claim repeated and expanded upon in 'Figural Exegesis and the Retrospective Re-cognition of Israel's History', *BBR* 29 (2019): 32–48, esp. 44.

116. Richard B. Hays, *Reading Backwards: Figural Christology and the Fourfold Gospel Witness* (Waco, TX: Baylor University Press, 2014), 94, emphasis original.

117. Hays, *Echoes of Scripture in the Gospels*, 7; cf. 347–66, esp. 358–65.

1. *Introduction* 21

dressed up in the garb of historical criticism.[118] Hays appears to believe the early Christians were right to find Jesus in 'Israel's Scripture' because he was, in some sense, already there – a confessional claim which puts Hays in the company of Dodd, Lindars and Moo.[119]

This leads to the question hanging over studies of the 'Old Testament in the New' – namely, where does historical criticism end and biblical theology begin? The terminology of the 'Old Testament' implies an ontological relationship with the 'New', along with anachronistic canonical boundaries and a Christian theology of prophetic-fulfilment and supersession. It can often seem as if scholars see as much or as little of the Jewish scriptures in the Gospel of Mark as their (all too often confessional) assumptions will allow. Those who follow Dodd in identifying broad scriptural themes and hermeneutical keys are capable of finding traces of them nearly everywhere in the Gospel. These same scholars tend to believe the original literary context of a citation or allusion is the key to its interpretation, so the Gospel alludes to a much larger body of scriptural material than is referenced in the text itself. Scholars who, like Suhl, are sceptical of overarching frameworks tend to view Mark's use of the Jewish scriptures as ad hoc and atomistic, but offer little information beyond that. Both camps agree their task is identifying 'citations' or 'allusions' or 'echoes' drawn from the Jewish scriptures in order to determine their significance for the interpretation of the Gospel. Using Dimant's terminology, they have focused almost exclusively on the expositional use of scriptural material. This has led to countless discussions concerning the exegetical significance of the composite citation in Mk 1:2-3. Less theologically satisfying examples – like the use of Esther in Mk 6:23 – have failed to command the same attention and are usually omitted from the discussion altogether. One sympathizes with Willem Vorster's frustration some thirty years ago: 'Certain data beliefs and assumptions concerning the Gospel have become so dominant that very little progress has been made in the history of interpretation'.[120] He goes on, 'We still do not know exactly how [Mark] went about creating his story of Jesus – that is, how he made his Gospel'.[121]

---

118. Despite Hays' claim to the contrary, *Echoes of Scripture in the Gospels*, 6–7; compare with the overtly theological discussion on 363–6.

119. Dodd, *According to the Scriptures*, 130–3; Lindars, *New Testament Apologetic*, 33–4; Moo, *The Old Testament in the Gospel Passion Narratives*, 380–1.

120. Vorster, 'The Production of the Gospel of Mark', 386.

121. Vorster, 'The Production of the Gospel of Mark', 390.

The compositional use of the Jewish scriptures
in the Gospel of Mark

Previous compositional approaches: lectionary, midrash and mimesis

The question of whether Mark used the Jewish scriptures to *compose* the Gospel has, however, been taken up by a few authors. That Mark designed their Gospel to parallel scripture readings from early Jewish and Christian liturgies has been argued in one form or another by Philip Carrington and Michael Goulder, but at greatest length by John Bowman.[122] Bowman seeks to explain 'How and why the Gospel as a literary form came about'.[123] For Bowman, the answer is liturgical: a haggadic interpretation of the Exodus narrative 'provided the pattern not merely for the Last Supper, but for the whole of Mark's Gospel form'.[124] Thus Mark composed a 'New Exodus Haggadah', reflecting the liturgical practices of his day, which was 'parallel to the course of the first Exodus story'.[125] This explains the absence of prophetic-fulfilment formulae in the Gospel.[126] In its use of scriptural material, the Gospel is closer to the 'haggadic midrash' of later Jewish literature.[127] Whilst Bowman and his peers can be credited with attempting to situate Mark's use of the Jewish scriptures firmly within a Second Temple context, no easily datable evidence of Second Temple liturgical practices survives to corroborate the conclusions. It can often seem as if the hypothetical liturgical practices proposed by scholars take the form of whatever text is being discussed. How these scholars would go about proving the opposite – that Matthew *did not* compose their Gospel on the basis of the Jewish lectionary (Goulder), or that Mark *did not* pattern their Gospel after the Passover Haggadah (Bowman) – is not exactly clear. One suspects the arguments preclude falsification.

---

122. Philip Carrington, *The Primitive Christian Calendar: A Study in the Making of the Marcan Gospel* (Cambridge: Cambridge University Press, 1952); Carrington, *According to Mark: A Running Commentary on the Oldest Gospel* (Cambridge: Cambridge University Press, 1960); Michael D. Goulder, *Midrash and Lection in Matthew* (London: SPCK, 1974); Goulder, *The Evangelist's Calendar: A Lectionary Explanation of the Development of Scripture* (London: SPCK, 1978); John Bowman, *The Gospel of Mark: The New Christian Jewish Passover Haggadah*, SPB 8 (Leiden: Brill, 1965).

123. Bowman, *The Gospel of Mark*, 311.

124. Bowman, *The Gospel of Mark*, xiv.

125. Bowman, *The Gospel of Mark*, 111.

126. Bowman, *The Gospel of Mark*, 18–19, 25.

127. Bowman, *The Gospel of Mark*, 36–43, esp. 43.

Bowman's discussion of midrash leads to the second major compositional approach to the use of the Jewish scriptures in the Gospel. Following the application of the term to the Gospels by John Drury and Michael Goulder in the 1970s, the following decade saw a spate of studies attempt to understand the Gospel of Mark as a sort of 'midrash'.[128] J. Duncan M. Derrett proposed the Gospel is a 'gigantic midrash on scripture'.[129] The whole Gospel is framed by its use of Lamentations, Canticles and 1 Samuel, whilst Mark 1–12 parallels Exodus, Numbers and Joshua.[130] Derrett's methodology seems to consist of little more than the call-and-response, 'Can that also be found in Lamentations? Indeed it can.'[131] This ad hoc approach leads to more than a few confusing claims, such as that John the Baptist is both Balaam and an Egyptian whilst the Gerasene demoniac is Amalek, or that the Transfiguration is 'an attempt to link the dynamic interpretation of Lamentations with the Hexateuchal theme of the conquest of the Land'.[132] Derrett's eccentric approach is continued in Dale and Patricia Miller's study, which argues the Gospel is 'essentially midrashic', so that every single pericope can be traced back to a 'midrashic source'.[133] Thus Mark composed a 'life-of-Jesus narrative' out of a 'mass of details from the Jewish sacred literature'.[134] The midrashic sources for the Gospel are so named: 'James/Jacob, 1 John, 1 Peter, Romans, 1–2 Corinthians, Galatians, Hebrews, the Testaments of the Twelve Patriarchs, the Wisdom of Solomon, and 1–2 Maccabees, in addition to the entire canonical Jewish Bible'.[135] This yields perplexing results, such as the claim that Peter warming himself by the fire is a midrash on 1 Pet. 1:7 or the tearing of the temple curtain is a midrash on

---

128. John Drury, 'Midrash and Gospel', *Theology* 77 (1974): 291–6; Goulder, *Midrash and Lection in Matthew*.

129. J. Duncan M. Derrett, *The Making of Mark: The Scriptural Bases of the Earliest Gospel* (Shipston-on-Stour: P. Drinkwater, 1985), 38.

130. Derrett, *The Making of Mark*, 24. Curiously, but characteristically, Derrett refuses to engage with any prior scholarship because Markan scholars 'care nothing about Joshua, Lamentations, and Canticles' (4). One wonders why.

131. Derrett, *The Making of Mark*, 237.

132. Derrett, *The Making of Mark*, 46–7, 52–4, 101–2, quoted at 113.

133. Dale Miller and Patricia Miller, *The Gospel of Mark as Midrash on Earlier Jewish and New Testament Literature*, SBEC 21 (Lewiston, NY: Edwin Mellen, 1990), 385.

134. Miller and Miller, *The Gospel of Mark as Midrash*, 27.

135. Miller and Miller, *The Gospel of Mark as Midrash*, 386.

24 *Writing with Scripture*

Heb. 9:3 and *T. Lev.* 10:3.[136] Common to all these studies is their uncritical use of the term midrash.[137] The Gospel of Mark bears scant resemblance to any text that can be confidently identified as 'midrash', a contested term usually reserved for Rabbinic exegesis in the form of lemmata followed by commentary like the *Genesis Rabbah* and the *Mekhilta de-Rabbi Ishmael*, or homiletical discourses like the *Pirḳê de Rabbi Eliezer*.[138] What these scholars mean by 'midrash', however, appears to be little more than a creative use of scriptural material.[139]

A more restrained 'midrashic' approach is found in Wolfgang Roth's *Hebrew Gospel*.[140] For Roth, the Gospel of Mark follows the 'scriptural model' of 1 Kings 17–2 Kings 13.[141] Roth notes Jesus' sojourn in the wilderness and his call of the disciples in Mk 1:12-20 resembles Elijah's sojourn in the wilderness and his call of Elisha in 1 Kgs 19:4-21. He also notes the similarity of Jesus' feeding of the multitudes in Mk 6:35-44 and 8:1-9 with Elisha's feeding of the multitude in 2 Kgs 4:42-44. More general similarities are noted between the healing miracles of Elijah, Elisha and Jesus.[142] A guiding assumption for Roth is that Mark identifies

136. Miller and Miller, *The Gospel of Mark as Midrash*, 353, 365. The Millers' freewheeling methodology is on full display in this representative statement: 'Mark is likely to have assumed that Paul was referring to 1 Peter's midrashic paraphrase of Isa 53' (216).

137. See Philip Alexander's influential critique of Goulder, 'Rabbinic Judaism and the New Testament', *ZNW* 74 (1983): 237–46; Alexander, 'Midrash and the Gospels', in *Synoptic Studies: The Ampleforth Conferences of 1982 and 1983*, ed. Christopher M. Tuckett, JSNTSup 7 (Sheffield: JSOT Press, 1984), 1–18.

138. On the contested nature of the term in recent scholarship, see Carol Bakhos, 'Method(ological) Matters in the Study of Midrash', in *Current Trends in the Study of Midrash*, ed. Carol Bakhos, JSJSup 106 (Leiden: Brill, 2006), 161–88. On distinctive forms of Rabbinic midrash, see Günter Stemberger, *Midrasch: Vom Umgang der Rabbinen mit der Bibel. Einführung – Texte – Erläuterungen* (Munich: Beck, 2002), 22–3.

139. This criticism may also apply to the more recent article by Robert M. Price, 'New Testament Narrative as Old Testament Midrash', in *Encyclopedia of Midrash: Biblical Interpretation in Formative Judaism*, ed. Jacob Neusner, vol. 1 (Leiden: Brill, 2005), 534–74.

140. Wolfgang Roth, *Hebrew Gospel: Cracking the Code of Mark* (Oak Park, IL: Meyer-Stone Books, 1988).

141. Roth, *Hebrew Gospel*, xi.

142. Mk 5:21-43; 7:24-30; cf. 1 Kgs 17:17-24; 2 Kgs 4:18-37 (Roth, *Hebrew Gospel*, 5–7).

Jesus as Elisha to John's Elijah.[143] As Elisha surpassed Elijah's miracles by eight, so Jesus surpasses Elisha's miracles by eight.[144] To reach this number, Roth must operate under a generous definition of miracle: the cleansing of the Temple and the tearing of the curtain are counted as miracles of Jesus, whilst multiple miracles are enumerated as one (i.e. Mk 5:21-43).[145] Whilst many of Roth's parallels fail to convince, he nevertheless makes a compelling case that Mark used incidents from the Elijah–Elisha cycle to compose episodes in the Gospel. Roth wonders whether this should be compared to haggadic midrash or the Greco-Roman practice of literary imitation, ultimately settling for a poetic classification of the Gospel as 'patterned storytelling' based on 1 Kings 17–2 Kings 13.[146] But by invoking the *imitatio* of Roman writers, Roth introduces the third and most illuminating compositional approach to the use of the Jewish scriptures in the Gospel.

Building on the work of his supervisor Thomas Brodie, Adam Winn argues that Mark modelled their Gospel on the Jewish scriptures using the Greco-Roman practice of *mimesis* or *imitatio*.[147] Just as Virgil used the Homeric corpus when composing the *Aeneid*, so Mark used the Elijah–Elisha cycle of 1 and 2 Kings to compose episodes in his life of Jesus.[148] 'The methods of imitation and adaption used by Virgil in his composition of the *Aeneid* existed and were known in the ancient world at the time of Mark's composition', so '[Mark] likely would have been aware of the method of Virgilian imitation that is found in it'.[149] A mimetic relationship

143. Roth, *Hebrew Gospel*, 2 and *passim*.

144. Roth, *Hebrew Gospel*, 16.

145. Roth, *Hebrew Gospel*, 4–7, 16.

146. Roth, *Hebrew Gospel*, 123.

147. Adam Winn, *Mark and the Elijah–Elisha Narrative: Considering the Practice of Greco-Roman Imitation in the Search for Markan Source Material* (Eugene, OR: Wipf & Stock, 2010). See also Thomas L. Brodie, *The Crucial Bridge: The Elijah–Elisha Narrative as an Interpretive Synthesis of Genesis–Kings and a Literary Model for the Gospels* (Collegeville, MN: Liturgical, 2000); and the mimetic approach of Dennis R. MacDonald, *The Homeric Epics and the Gospel of Mark* (New Haven, CT: Yale University Press, 2000).

148. Winn, *Mark and the Elijah–Elisha Narrative*, 10. Similar observations have been made by Bas M. F. van Iersel, *Mark: A Reader-Response Commentary*, trans. W. H. Bisscheroux, JSNTSup 164 (Sheffield: Sheffield Academic, 1998), 65–7; and more recently by Heike Omerzu, 'Geschichte durch Geschichten. Zur Bedeutung jüdischer Traditionen für die Jesusdarstellung des Markusevangeliums', *EC* 2 (2011): 77–99, esp. 84–8.

149. Winn, *Mark and the Elijah–Elisha Narrative*, 12.

26   *Writing with Scripture*

can be detected when a later text features complex structural similarities as well as specific details found in an antecedent text.[150] Winn notes how the burial of Misenus (*Aen.* 6.156-325) is modelled on the burial of Elpenor (*Od.* 11.75), as they follow the same narrative structure – mourning, the cutting of logs for the pyre, the burning of bodies and the erection of a tomb – whilst including specific details like the setting by the sea and the oar to mark the grave.[151] Like Roth, Winn finds a mimetic relationship between Jesus' sojourn in the wilderness and the call of the disciples (Mk 1:12-20) and Elijah's sojourn in the wilderness and the call of Elisha (1 Kgs 19:4-21) as well as the feeding of the multitudes by Jesus (Mk 6:30-44; 8:1-10) and Elisha (2 Kgs 4:42-44). Not quite as strong are his arguments for a direct literary relationship between Jesus' healing of a leper (Mk 1:40-45) and Elisha's healing of Naaman's leprosy (2 Kgs 5:1-19), Jesus' conversation with the Syrophoenician woman (Mk 7:24-30) and Elijah's conversation with the widow of Zarephath (1 Kgs 17:7-16) and Jesus' three passion predictions and Peter's three denials (Mk 8:31-32; 9:31-32; 10:33-34; 14:66-72) and Elijah's three ascension predictions and Elisha's three affirmations of faith (2 Kgs 2:1-12).[152]

Winn succeeds in his task, however, as he puts it, of 'demonstrating the existence of a significant literary relationship between Mark's gospel and the Elijah–Elisha narrative'.[153] But unlike previous studies, Winn does not go so far as to posit that Mark's use of 1–2 Kings is the 'interpretive key' for understanding the Gospel. He cautions 'one must be careful in correlating a narrative's source material with a narrative's meaning or significance'.[154] The author of a work may not intend the reader to pick up on its use of source material or for that material to play a role in the interpretation of the new work. Rather, the material may 'simply serve as a pattern for constructing a new narrative or perhaps as a quarry from which to draw narrative building blocks'.[155] What Winn offers is a *compositional* approach, one which examines the way Mark uses the Jewish scriptures to

---

150. Winn, *Mark and the Elijah–Elisha Narrative*, 31–3. It can include the conflation of two or more stories as an imitative model, the reversal or diffusion (into multiple episodes) of the imitative model, the omission or alteration of certain details to fit the new narrative context, as well as the intensification of the imitative model (29–30).

151. Winn, *Mark and the Elijah–Elisha Narrative*, 31–2.

152. See Winn, *Mark and the Elijah–Elisha Narrative*, 72–112.

153. Winn, *Mark and the Elijah–Elisha Narrative*, 117.

154. Winn, *Mark and the Elijah–Elisha Narrative*, 117.

155. Winn, *Mark and the Elijah–Elisha Narrative*, 118.

1. Introduction   27

model new episodes and provide narrative details in a manner consistent with other texts in antiquity. One wonders, however, if there is a literary analogy closer to Mark's orbit than Virgilian mimesis – videlicet, works which also take the Jewish scriptures as their compositional model.

Scripturalization as a Compositional Technique

Mark Goodacre has noted that scholarship continues to be divided over the role of the Jewish scriptures in the Passion Narrative.[156] On the one hand, scholars agree the Passion Narrative is full of language drawn from the Jewish scriptures. But on the other hand, there is profound disagreement as to how much of the narrative originates from history and how much originates from scriptural reflection. Dominic Crossan characterizes this disagreement as between those who think the Passion Narrative is 'history remembered' and those – more critical scholars like himself – who think it is 'prophecy historicized'.[157] Goodacre, however, finds Crossan's binary too severe. Perhaps instead there was 'from the beginning...an intimate interaction between historical event and scriptural reflection, so that the tradition developed in light of Old Testament languages and models'.[158] Goodacre suggests this process 'might be described, to utilize an illuminating term from Hebrew Bible scholarship, as *scripturalization*'. So, in place of the cumbersome 'history remembered' and 'prophecy historicized', Goodacre offers the more subtle 'tradition scripturalized'.[159]

Goodacre borrows the idea of scripturalization from the work of Judith Newman.[160] Following the compositional use of scriptural elements identified by Dimant, Newman proposes scripturalization as one of the

---

156. Mark Goodacre, 'Scripturalization in Mark's Crucifixion Narrative', in *The Trial and Death of Jesus: Essays on the Passion Narrative in Mark*, ed. Geert van Oyen and Thomas Shepherd (Leuven: Peeters, 2006), 33–47; Goodacre, 'Prophecy Historicized or Tradition Scripturalized? Reflections on the Origins of the Passion Narrative', in *The New Testament and the Church: Essays in Honour of John Muddiman*, eds. John Barton and Peter Groves, LNTS 532 (London: T&T Clark, 2016), 37–51.

157. John Dominic Crossan, *The Birth of Christianity: Discovering What Happened in the Years Immediately After the Execution of Jesus* (Edinburgh: T. & T. Clark, 1998), 520–1.

158. Goodacre, 'Prophecy Historicized or Tradition Scripturalized?', 42.

159. Goodacre, 'Scripturalization in Mark's Crucifixion Narrative', 41; 'Prophecy Historicized or Tradition Scripturalized?', 42.

160. Judith H. Newman, *Praying by the Book: The Scripturalization of Prayer in Second Temple Judaism*, EJL 14 (Atlanta, GA: Scholars Press, 1999).

28   *Writing with Scripture*

ways in which the Jewish scriptures were used to compose prayers in the Second Temple period. She defines it as 'the reuse of biblical texts or interpretive traditions to shape the composition of new literature... the observable recontextualization of identifiable scriptural language'.[161] It encompasses 'clear references to biblical stories', as well as 'biblical wording without regard to its source', which may serve 'simply to provide a biblical "ring" to the composition'.[162] This distinguishes it from other uses of scriptural material such as the inner-biblical exegesis proposed by Michael Fishbane, since the 'reuse of scripture does not necessarily entail the presumed author's *conscious* interpretation of scripture'.[163] Newman draws attention to three scripturalized prayers: Neh. 9:5-37; Jdt. 9:2-14; 3 Macc. 2:2-20. These texts together show the scriptural development of prayer from the post-exilic era through the Second Temple era, with the compositional use of scriptural material eventually becoming 'an unquestioned literary convention' in later Jewish and Christian liturgies.[164]

The phenomenon of scripturalization might also be used to describe the reuse of scriptural material in other kinds of literature. These include the scripturalized laws of the *Damascus Document* and the *Community Rule*, the scripturalized hymns of the *Hodayot* and the *Psalms of Solomon* and the scripturalized apocalyptic of *1 Enoch* and *4 Ezra*. The term may equally apply to narrative literature like the Gospel of Mark. Some of the previous studies observed how Mark weaves inexplicit but identifiable scriptural language into the fabric of the narrative. This is seen in the unmarked use of scriptural language in isolated details like the darkness at noon in Mk 15:33, from Amos 8:9, or the offer of 'sour wine' to Jesus in Mk 15:36, from Ps. 69:21. It is also seen in episodes which appear to follow a scriptural model, like the forty-day sojourn of Jesus in the wilderness and the call of the disciples (Mk 1:12-20) and that of Elijah (1 Kgs 19:4-21), or the feeding of the multitudes by Jesus (Mk 6:35-44; 8:1-9) and Elisha (2 Kgs 4:42-44). May these all be considered examples of scripturalized narrative?

---

161. Newman, *Praying by the Book*, 12–13.

162. Newman, *Praying by the Book*, 13–14.

163. Newman, *Praying by the Book*, 13; cf. the 'taxemic form' of aggadic exegesis in Michael A. Fishbane, *Biblical Interpretation in Ancient Israel* (Oxford: Clarendon, 1985), 430.

164. Newman, *Praying by the Book*, 206.

Identifying Scripturalization

For Goodacre, scripturalization has the potential to describe how the early community couched the historical events of Jesus' life in the language of the Jewish scriptures.[165] But this analysis can go one step further: scripturalization can also describe the literary process by which Mark as an author used scriptural elements to compose and model episodes in their life of Jesus, creating scripturalized narrative.[166] That Mark used the Jewish scriptures in this way depends in large part on whether this practice can be identified in other works from the period. If it can be shown across a diverse group of texts that the Jewish scriptures were regularly used to compose new narrative, then it would be appropriate to speak of scripturalized narrative as a stylistic feature of Second Temple literature. Accordingly, this study will be divided into two parts: the first part will look at episodes drawn from five works dating to the Second Temple period which use the Jewish scriptures to construct new narratives. Special attention will be paid to how these texts use scriptural material to model new episodes and insert scriptural language into the narrative. Against the backdrop of these texts, the second part will examine five episodes in the Gospel of Mark where a scriptural model is evident or scriptural language appears as part of the narrative. Together, these two parts aim to show how the compositional use of the Jewish scriptures in the Second Temple period illuminates Mark's narrative use of scriptural material. And finally, returning to Crossan's dilemma, the Conclusion will consider what scripturalization means for the Gospel's tenuous relationship to history and whether it is possible to distinguish historical memory couched in the language of the scriptures from wholesale invention on the basis of the scriptures.

But first, how does one identify scripturalized narrative? The criteria offered by scholars for identifying scriptural allusions or echoes tend to focus on material of an expositional nature.[167] The influential criteria

---

165. Goodacre, 'Scripturalization in Mark's Crucifixion Narrative', 40, 46; 'Prophecy Historicized or Tradition Scripturalized?', 42–4.

166. The possibility of scripturalization in pre-Markan sources may be entertained, but it is not essential to this argument. Whether each scripturalized narrative was composed by a single Markan author, or was the result of redactional activity, the question is whether they are a feature of the Gospel. The name 'Mark' is adopted simply as a stand-in for the hypothetical author(s) of the final (surviving) form of the Gospel.

167. See the survey of criteria in Samuel Emadi, 'Intertextuality in New Testament Scholarship: Significance, Criteria, and the Art of Intertextual Reading', *CBR* 14 (2015): 8–23.

30 *Writing with Scripture*

offered by Hays, for example, ask whether a proposed echo thematically coheres with the work and contributes to the 'argument' developed by its author.[168] For narrative texts, this limits the discussion to allusions and echoes which seek to interpret an event or support an argument – an external voice brought into dialogue with the new work. It does not cover identifiable scriptural language which contributes little to the meaning of the work, like the words of Ahasuerus on the lips of Herod Antipas, 'even half of my kingdom' (Mk 6:23). A thoroughgoing compositional approach is necessary to identify scriptural language and models embedded into the fabric of a new text. Here Dale Allison's comments on identifying scriptural typology prove useful.

Allison begins by outlining six forms of typological allusion. Although the first form, 'explicit' typological comparison, belongs to Dimant's expositional use of scriptural elements, the other kinds fall under the compositional use. These include 'inexplicit citation or borrowing' where a text is 'dug up and translated without acknowledgement'; 'similar circumstances' where an event recalls 'another circumstantially like it'; 'key words or phrases' where 'one may dress up a story with the words of another that is like it and well known'; 'similar narrative structure' where one story is modelled on another; and 'word order, syllabic sequence, poetic resonance' where a text imitates the style of another.[169] The difference between scripturalization and typology lies in its purpose. For example, Allison uses typology to describe the extended assimilation of Jesus with Moses in the Gospel of Matthew with which the author drapes 'the Messiah in the familiar mantle of Moses'.[170] Scripturalization, on the other hand, is less considered. It is simply the use of a scriptural model or language, drawn from any number of sources, to aid the composition of a new work for any or no discernible purpose. Nevertheless, Allison's criteria for assessing typology can be used to identify scripturalization.

As a matter of common sense, Allison acknowledges a 'text can only allude to or intentionally recall another prior to it in time'.[171] At the same time, the proposed source must belong 'to a book or tradition which held some significance for its author'.[172] From here Allison proposes four criteria specific to typology: there must be a confluence of similar vocabulary and circumstances; the type must be prominent and easily identifiable

---

168. Hays, *Echoes of Scripture in the Letters of Paul*, 29–33.
169. Allison, *The New Moses*, 19–20.
170. Allison, *The New Moses*, 277; also 13.
171. Allison, *The New Moses*, 21.
172. Allison, *The New Moses*, 21–2.

in the source; the type must have been used in the composition of other works; and it must include unusual and uncommon features unlikely to have come from anywhere else.[173] With some modifications, these criteria can be adapted to the study of scripturalization. The identification of scripturalized narrative thus requires *a confluence of similar language and narrative details* that is best explained by positing a literary relationship. The proposed source must be *easily identifiable within its original literary context*, and so this study will focus primarily on self-contained episodes of a similar length.[174] Any analysis of a scripturalized narrative must show *similar compositional techniques can be identified elsewhere* – within the same work as well as in others. This is especially relevant if different texts use the same scriptural elements to compose narrative. That Mark composed new stories out of scriptural elements will thus appear all the more likely if the practice can be observed elsewhere, and it is to this question the study will now turn.

173. Allison, *The New Moses*, 22–3.

174. The decision to focus on episodes rather than entire narrative works is based on two factors: first, narrative works in Jewish antiquity are primarily episodic rather than continuous; second, whilst there is ample evidence of isolated episodes depending on a single scriptural model (i.e. Judith slaying Holofernes), the same cannot be easily said for narrative works in their entirety (i.e. the book of Judith).

2

SCRIPTURALIZED NARRATIVE IN
SECOND TEMPLE LITERATURE

This chapter looks closely at five works dating to the Second Temple period – the *Liber Antiquitatum Biblicarum*, the *Genesis Apocryphon*, 1 Maccabees, Judith and the *Testament of Abraham* – each of which features self-contained episodes where one or more scriptural source is clearly and repeatedly drawn on to supply language and details or give a coherent narrative structure to the story. Though these works by no means exhaust the relevant material from the period, they encompass the three languages of literary composition in Jewish antiquity – Hebrew, Aramaic and Greek – as well as multiple genres and divergent perspectives, from the dynastic propaganda of 1 Maccabees to the farcical *Testament*. If similar compositional techniques can be found across such variegated texts, it would be appropriate to consider scripturalized narrative a stylistic feature of Second Temple literature.

The Liber Antiquitatum Biblicarum

Although the *Liber Antiquitatum Biblicarum* – once wrongly attributed to Philo – appears to quote from and allude to the Jewish scriptures more widely than any other text of the so-called Rewritten Bible genre, there is almost no verbatim agreement between it and surviving texts of the scriptures. This is because the work survives in a Latin version one or two layers removed from the original. Consequently, the full extent of scriptural use in the work is no longer recoverable. The cross-references listed in Harrington's *OTP* translation are exhaustive, but do not distinguish between different types of scriptural use or varying degrees of verbal correspondence.[1] The list proposed by Lange and Weigold, in

---

1. Daniel J. Harrington, 'Pseudo-Philo', in *OTP*, II, 304–77.

2. Scripturalized Narrative in Second Temple Literature 33

their otherwise excellent volume, omits a significant number of parallels as their methodology does not account for the complicated issue of *LAB*'s original language.[2] The problem is that whilst *LAB* survives in twenty-one partial or complete Latin manuscripts, there are signs of a Hebrew and a Greek stage of production.[3] Most follow Cohn in supposing the 'style, the expressions, and the method of statement bear an entirely Hebrew character' – indicating a Hebrew *Vorlage*.[4] To this can be added proper names where the *vav* has been mistaken as part of the name,[5] as well as cumbersome phrases and out-of-place verbs that can be easily explained as misread Hebrew words or phrases.[6] Other peculiarities seem to point to a Greek layer behind the surviving Latin

---

2. Armin Lange and Matthias Weigold, *Biblical Quotations and Allusions in Second Temple Jewish Literature*, JAJSup 5 (Göttingen: Vandenhoeck & Ruprecht, 2011), 236–9; for methodology, see 17–19.

3. See the survey of mss. in Daniel J. Harrington, *Text and Biblical Text in Pseudo-Philo's Liber Antiquitatum Biblicarum* (Cambridge, MA: Harvard University Press, 1969), 20–4.

4. Leopold Cohn, 'An Apocryphal Work Ascribed to Philo of Alexandria', *JQR* 10 (1898): 311. Following Cohn is M. R. James, *The Biblical Antiquities of Philo*, TED 1 (London: SPCK, 1917; repr. New York, NY: Ktav, 1971), 28–9; Daniel J. Harrington, 'The Original Language of Pseudo-Philo's "Liber Antiquitatum Biblicarum"', *HTR* 63 (1970): 503–14; Charles Perrot, Pierre-Maurice Bogaert and Harrington, *Pseudo-Philon: Les Antiquités Bibliques: Tome II: Introduction Littéraire, Commentaire et Index*, SC 230 (Paris: Les Éditions du Cerf, 1976), 75–7; Howard Jacobson, *A Commentary on Pseudo-Philo's Liber Antiquitatum Biblicarum: With Latin Text & English Translation*, 2 vols., AGAJU 31 (Leiden: Brill, 1996), 1:215–22; cf. Louis H. Feldman, 'Prolegomenon', in James, *Biblical Antiquities*, xxv–xxvii, who cautions that the presence of Hebraisms and affinities with targumic tradition do not preclude a Greek original. Alexander Zeron raises the possibility of an Aramaic original, 'Erwägungen zu Pseudo-Philos Quellen und Zeit', *JSJ* 11 (1980): 38–52, which is dismissed in Harrington, 'Text and Biblical Text', 85–7; Jacobson, *Commentary*, 1:221–2. Significant portions of *LAB* appear in the medieval Hebrew *Chronicles of Jerahmeel*, which Moses Gaster believed represents the original Hebrew text of *LAB*, *The Chronicles of Jerahmeel Or, the Hebrew Bible Historiale*, OTFNS 4 (London: 1899; repr. New York, NY: Ktav 1971), xxx–xxxix; compare with Daniel J. Harrington, *The Hebrew Fragments of Pseudo-Philo's Liber Antiquitatum Biblicarum Preserved in the Chronicles of Jerahmeel*, TAT 3, Pseudepigrapha Series 3 (Missoula, MT: SBL, 1974).

5. Such as *Visui* from ישוי[ו] in Gen. 46:17 (*LAB* 8:13) and *Gedru Messe* from גתר ומש in Gen. 10:23 (*LAB* 4:9).

6. Listed in Jacobson, *Commentary*, 1:217–21.

34 *Writing with Scripture*

text, including transliterations of Greek words and misreadings which appear to originate in Greek.[7]

The simplest answer is the Latin text depends on a Greek translation of a Hebrew original. But this is complicated by the fact that Pseudo-Philo often follows readings adopted by the LXX over the MT.[8] One cannot rule out the possibility the LXX or VL was consulted at some stage of production, but the most likely explanation is Pseudo-Philo had access to alternate texts of the Hebrew scriptures featuring similar readings to the LXX – much like those found in the Dead Sea Scrolls.[9] Given Pseudo-Philo's tendency for paraphrastic quotations, however, there is little hope of reconstructing these lost texts. Taken together, these issues make identifying Pseudo-Philo's use of the Jewish scriptures a daunting task.

Pseudo-Philo's Use of the Jewish Scriptures: Primary and Secondary Scripture

Nevertheless, one can speak coherently of two broad categories of scriptural use in *LAB*. Pseudo-Philo loosely follows the outline of Genesis to 2 Samuel whilst making significant alterations to the narrative. Bruce Fisk has helpfully described the role of this narrative as the 'primary scripture'.[10] To take one example, *LAB* 14–19 roughly follows the narrative

7. Misreadings include *Mazia* from Μαδιαμ (18:13) and *Ionatha* from the Greek vocative Ιωναθα instead of the indeclinable nominative *Ionathas* (62:8); for more see James, *Biblical Antiquities*, 254. Transliterations include *paratecem* from παραθήκην (3:10); *ometoceam* from ὠμοτοκεία (9:2); *antecimunum* from ἀντικείμενος (45:6); for more see Harrington, 'Original Language', 506–8, and Jacobson, *Commentary*, 1:223–4.

8. Agreements with the LXX can be found in genealogies (i.e. *LAB* 1:2-22; LXX Gen. 5:4-32; cf. MT Gen. 5:4-32), names (i.e. Tubal in *LAB* 2:9; LXX and VL Gen. 4:22; instead of Tubal-Cain in MT Gen. 4:22; cf. *Jub.* 9:11; 1QapGen 12:12), the order of the commandments (*LAB* 11:10-11; LXX Exod. 20:13, 15; cf. MT Exod. 20:13-14) and narrative details, like the role of angels in the giving of the law (*LAB* 11:5; 30:5; cf. LXX Deut. 33:2). Though as Feldman notes, Pseudo-Philo sometimes agrees with the LXX, sometimes with the MT and sometimes with neither ('Prolegomenon', lii). Harrington notes a number of interesting parallels with the so-called Lucianic recension, esp. of 1 Samuel, 'The Biblical Text of Pseudo-Philo's "Liber Antiquitatum Biblicarum"', *CBQ* 33 (1971): 1–17, esp. 13–16.

9. Harrington proposes a distinct Palestinian Hebrew text, 'The Biblical Text of Pseudo-Philo's "Liber Antiquitatum"', 1–17.

10. Bruce N. Fisk, *Do You Not Remember? Scripture, Story and Exegesis in the Rewritten Bible of Pseudo-Philo*, JSPSup 37 (Sheffield: Sheffield Academic, 2001), 14–16, esp. nn. 6–7. The term could equally describe the primary compositional technique of 'Rewritten Bible' works like *Jubilees* and the *Genesis Apocryphon*.

of Numbers. It starts with the census in Numbers 1 (*LAB* 14:1-4), which leads to the sending of the twelve spies into Canaan (*LAB* 15; cf. Num. 13–14), the rebellion of Korah (*LAB* 16; cf. Num. 15–16), the budding of Aaron's rod (*LAB* 17; cf. Num. 17) and the oracles of Balaam (*LAB* 18; cf. Num. 22–24) before ending with the death of Moses (*LAB* 19), which is pieced together from Exodus, Numbers and Deuteronomy.

At the same time, Pseudo-Philo inserts analogous and unrelated scriptural material into the primary scriptural narrative, what Fisk calls 'secondary scripture'.[11] Returning to the Numbers narrative in *LAB* 14–19: the detail that the spies 'troubled the heart of the people' (*LAB* 15:1: *contribulaverunt cor populi dicentes*) reflects the words of Caleb in Josh. 14:8; the genealogy in *LAB* 15:3 depends on 1 Chronicles (2:51; 4:15; 7:20-27); God's speech in *LAB* 15:5-6 alludes to Genesis (1:9; 15:3) and Exodus (3:8; 14:22) whilst using the language of Ps. 18:9, 'I bent the heavens and came down' (*LAB* 15:6: *inclinavi celos et descendi*); the death of Korah (*LAB* 16:2-3) is tied to the death of Abel (Gen. 4:1-16), the Egyptian army (Exod. 14:27-28) and those who perished in the flood (Gen. 7:21-23); the budding of Aaron's rod (*LAB* 17:3) alludes to the rod of Jacob (Gen. 30:37-39); God's speech to Balaam (*LAB* 18:4-6) references the Aqedah (Gen. 18:7; 22:17), the covenant with Abraham (Gen. 18:7; 22:17) and Jacob wrestling the angel (Gen. 32:24-27); and Moses' speech (*LAB* 19) uses the language of Ps. 78:25 (*LAB* 19:5: 'You have eaten the bread of angels') and references the covenant with Noah (Gen. 9:13-15). The use of secondary scripture is consistent throughout *LAB*.

Pseudo-Philo has several distinct ways of using secondary scripture.[12] Sometimes the secondary scripture is taken from corresponding passages which refer to the same episode in the primary scriptural narrative. For example, when describing the crossing of the Red Sea in Exodus 14, it reads, 'God rebuked the sea and the sea was dried up' (*LAB* 10:5: *comminatus est Deus mari et siccatum est*), which comes from the description

---

11. Fisk defines it as 'Scripture from other, sometimes distant, contexts [inserted] into the biblical (or traditional) story, in the form of explicit citations (perhaps with fulfilment formulae), unmarked allusions, narrative flashbacks and biblical echoes' (*Do You Not Remember?*, 15).

12. See the discussion in Richard Bauckham, 'The Liber Antiquitatum Biblicarum of Pseudo-Philo and the Gospels as "Midrash"', in *Gospel Perspectives: Studies in Midrash and Historiography: Volume 3*, ed. R. T. France and David Wenham (Sheffield: JSOT, 1983), 35–40; Jacobson, *Commentary*, 1:224–41; Fisk, *Do You Not Remember?*, 16–33.

of the same event in Ps. 106:9, '[God] rebuked the sea and it became dry' (ויגער בים סוף ויחרב).[13] Secondary scripture may also come from analogous contexts, as when God declares in the flood he will destroy 'all things that grow on the earth' (*LAB* 3:3: *et omnia que germinate sunt in terra*), a phrase borrowed from the destruction of Sodom and Gomorrah, where God destroys 'what grew on the ground' (Gen. 19:25: וצמח האדמה). At the death of Joshua it reads that he 'drew up his feet into the bed' (*LAB* 24:5: *complicuit pedes suos in lectum*), which is lifted from the death of Jacob, who 'drew up his feet into the bed' (Gen. 49:33: ויאסף רגליו אל־המטה). The analogous secondary scripture may appear in a single isolated detail, like when the infant Moses is placed in an ark of pine wood (*LAB* 9:12), which reflects the gopher wood of Noah's ark (Gen. 6:14), instead of an ark of bulrushes (Exod. 2:3).[14]

The most distinctive use of secondary scripture in *LAB* is the creation of new episodes out of scriptural material.[15] This is done by using a scriptural episode as a model for a new one, or by weaving scriptural language and distinctive narrative details into the story. The first clear example of this is the rescue of Abram from the fiery furnace of the Chaldeans (*LAB* 6), which takes the construction of the Tower of Babel as its setting (Gen. 11:1-9), and the rescue of the three young men from the fiery furnace of the Babylonians (Dan. 3) as its model. The celebration following Joshua's erection of the altar at Gilgal (*LAB* 21:7-10) is a pastiche of various celebration scenes in the Jewish scriptures (2 Sam. 6; 1 Kgs 8; 1 Chron. 15–16).[16] The narrative of the judge Kenaz (*LAB* 25–28) and his successor Zebul (*LAB* 29) is fashioned entirely out of secondary scripture, including the sin of Achan (Josh. 7), Gideon's defeat of the Midianites (Judges 7) and the inheritance of the daughters of Zelophehad (Num. 27:1-11;

---

13. Pseudo-Philo often inserts the language of the Psalms into the primary narrative, for example, in *LAB* 11:15, which roughly follows Exod. 25, God calls the sanctuary a 'tabernacle of my glory' (*tabernaculum gloriae meae*), a phrase borrowed from Ps. 26:8.

14. Compare with Pesh. Exod 2:3. Both Perrot (*Pseudo-Philon*, 2:107) and Jacobson (*Commentary*, 1:424) think *pini* reflects ארז ("cedar") in the underlying Hebrew, though disagree as to its origin. But this too could reflect Gen. 6:14, as Rabbinic literature sometimes renders גפר as 'cedar': קדרוס (Gk. κέδρος) in *Tg. Onq.* on Gen. 6:14; ארז in *Midr. Tanḥ.* B *Noach* 5:6.

15. Many of which are listed by Jacobson, *Commentary*, 1:231–3; and Bauckham, under the heading 'Interpreting Scripture by Scripture', 'Pseudo-Philo and the Gospels as "Midrash"', 40–59.

16. As noted by Jacobson, *Commentary*, 1:232, and at 2:689.

2. *Scripturalized Narrative in Second Temple Literature* 37

36:1-12). Jael's assassination of Sisera (*LAB* 31) borrows a number of details from Judith's assassination of Holofernes (Jdt. 13). The figure of Aod the Midianite magician (*LAB* 34) is based on Moses' description of the false prophet (Deut. 13:1-4) among other passages. The rescue of seven righteous men from the fiery furnace of Jair (*LAB* 38) is again created out of the fiery furnace of Daniel 3. The episode where Phinehas dwells on a mountain, is nourished by an eagle, opens and shuts the skies and ascends to heaven from where he will one day return (*LAB* 48:1) is based on Elijah (1 Kgs 17; 2 Kgs 2; Mal. 4:5), though unlike the other examples, this may have its roots in the identification of Phinehas with Elijah (i.e. *Judg. Rab.* 16:1).[17]

Although scholarship has for the most part classified these episodes as examples of 'midrash' or 'midrashic' interpretation,[18] these terms reflect the closed canon and relatively stable textual tradition of a later period.[19]

---

17. So Robert Hayward, 'Phinehas – the Same is Elijah: The Origins of a Tradition', *JJS* 29 (1978): 22–34.

18. For example, Cohn, 'An Apocryphal Work', 314, 322; Feldman, 'Prolegomenon', ix; Renée Bloch, 'Écriture et traditions dans le judaïsme – Aperçus sur l'origine du Midrash', *CS* 8 (1954): 29; Geza Vermes, *Scripture and Tradition in Judaism: Haggadic Studies*, SPB 8 (Leiden: Brill, 1961), 88–90; Perrot, *Pseudo-Philon*, 2:22–8, esp. 27; Gary G. Porton, 'Defining Midrash', in *The Study of Ancient Judaism*, ed. Jacob Neusner (New York, NY: Ktav, 1981), 72; Michael Wadsworth, 'Making and Interpreting Scripture', in *Ways of Reading the Bible*, ed. Michael Wadsworth (Sussex: Harvester, 1981), 7–22. Cf. the more critical comments in Frederick J. Murphy, *Pseudo-Philo: Rewriting the Bible* (Oxford: Oxford University Press, 1993), 4–5; Eckhart Reinmuth, *Pseudo-Philo und Lukas: Studien zum Liber Antiquitatum Biblicarum und seiner Bedeutung für die Interpretation des lukanischen Doppelwerks*, WUNT 2/74 (Tübingen: Mohr Siebeck, 1994), 13–17; Stemberger, *Midrasch*, 22–3; and to an extent Fisk, *Do You Not Remember?*, 25–7. Bauckham and Fisk use the equivalent expression 'scripture interpreting scripture', see 'Pseudo-Philo and the Gospels as "Midrash"', 34, 59; *Do You Not Remember?*, 327.

19. Since Philip Alexander's influential critique of Michael Goulder, scholarship has sought to limit the definition of midrash, see 'Rabbinic Judaism and the New Testament', 237–46; 'Midrash and the Gospels', 1–18; also Arnold Goldberg, 'Die funktionale Form Midrasch', *FJB* 10 (1982): 1–45; and Porton, 'Defining Midrash', 55–92. This was partly in response to the all-encompassing definitions of Bloch, 'Écriture et Tradition', 9–34; 'Note méthodologique pour l'étude de la littérature rabbinique', *RScR* 43 (1955): 194–227; and Vermes, *Scripture and Tradition*. Some see midrash as an exclusively Rabbinic phenomenon; so Solomon Zeitlin, 'Midrash: A Historical Study', *JQR* 44 (1953): 21–36; Lieve Teugels, 'Midrash in the Bible or Midrash on the Bible? Critical Remarks about the Uncritical Use of a Term', in

It also runs the risk of mischaracterizing how the scriptures function for Pseudo-Philo. Whilst the episodes created out of scriptural material might be inspired by some exegetical difficulty – i.e. reading 'Ur' as 'fire' in Gen. 15:7 leads to Abram's rescue from a fiery furnace – they do not actively seek to explain the scriptural text to the reader, thereby acting as a sort of 'commentary'.[20] Instead, they are self-contained narratives that can be understood without consulting the scriptural sources.[21] The scriptural elements are unmarked and there is no distinction between primary and secondary scriptures, both are woven seamlessly into the new narrative.[22]

In some cases it is possible to explain what led the author to compose the scripturalized narrative. But in many cases one can only speculate. Pseudo-Philo might simply be using scriptural elements for aesthetic purposes, providing images, motifs, language or plot devices. Examining the theological significance of the scriptures at this point would be mostly

---

Bibel und Midrasch: zur Bedeutung der rabbinischen Exegese für die Bibelwissenschaft, ed. G. Bodendorfer and M. Millard, FAT 22 (Tübingen: Mohr Siebeck, 1998), 43–63. For a helpful survey of approaches see Timothy H. Lim, 'Origins and Emergence of Midrash in Relation to the Hebrew Bible', in Neusner, ed., *Encyclopedia of Midrash*, 2:595–612, esp. 595–9.

20. *Pace* Cohn, 'An Apocryphal Work', 314; Bauckham, 'Pseudo-Philo and the Gospels as "Midrash"', 34.

21. Four times Pseudo-Philo explicitly refers readers to an external scriptural text (*LAB* 35:7; 43:4; 56:7; 63:5), always in the form 'Are they not written in the book of Judges/Kings?' (*Nonne hec scripta sunt in libro Iudicum/Regnum?*), itself in imitation of the scriptural style (Josh. 10:13; 1–2 Kings *passim*; 2 Chronicles *passim*; Est. 10:2). For discussion see Reinmuth, *Pseudo-Philo und Lukas*, 111, 126. The formulae refer to material covered in the preceding narrative (*LAB* 35:7; 56:7) or material not covered in the present work (43:4; 63:5). At one point, the author invokes Judges after relating a puzzling story of Gideon pouring water on a rock which turns into fire and blood (35:7), which is unparalleled in Judges. As Reinmuth notes, the formulae are as much a sign of *LAB* supplementing the scriptural text as the scriptural text supplementing *LAB*.

22. As opposed to Rabbinic midrash, where the scriptural text for the most part appears as something external, marked by a lemma or an introductory formula. Midrash denotes a 'Klare Trennung von geoffenbartem Bibeltext und Auslegung', and as such, 'Diese simple Tatsache unterscheidet die klassischen Midraschim von den meisten vorabbinischen Schriften, die man gern als Midrasch bezeichnet, aber auch von vielen biblischen Schriften des Mittel-alters, die als Bibelerzählungen die literarische Form von Büchern wie den Biblischen Altertümers Pseudo-Philos wieder aufnehmen' (Stemberger, *Midrasch*, 22–3).

2. Scripturalized Narrative in Second Temple Literature

irrelevant.[23] With these considerations in mind, the following examines three scripturalized narratives: Abram and the fiery furnace (*LAB* 6); Jair and the fiery furnace (*LAB* 38); and Kenaz's rout of the Amorites (*LAB* 27).

Abram and the Fiery Furnace: LAB 6 and Daniel 3

Tales of Abram's deliverance from a fiery furnace of the Chaldeans are ubiquitous in Jewish and Islamic literature. The legend originates in the interpretation of Gen. 15:7, 'I am the LORD who brought you from Ur of the Chaldeans'.[24] As the Hebrew *Ur* (אוּר) may also mean 'fire', the verse was taken to imply Abram's rescue from fire. The same word-play was applied to the death of Abram's brother Haran in Gen. 11:28, 'Haran died before his father Terah in the land of his birth, in Ur of the Chaldeans'. The book of *Jubilees* contains an early attempt to explain both passages. Abram is shown burning the Chaldean house of idols, whilst his brother Haran dies in the flames attempting to save the idols.[25] Thus it reads, 'And [Haran] was burned in the fire and died in Ur of the Chaldees before Terah, his father' (*Jub.* 12:14).

The most widespread tradition, however, tells of Abram's rescue from a fiery furnace of the Chaldeans, having been thrown in for refusing to participate in idolatry. This tradition finds its earliest manifestation in *LAB* 6. Though it is never quoted, the episode appears to originate in the word-play on Gen. 15:7, combined with the rallying cry of the Babelites in Gen. 11:3, 'Come, let us make bricks, and burn them thoroughly'. Whilst these passages serve as the primary scriptural basis for the episode, the narrative takes its shape from the secondary scriptural source, the rescue of the three men from the fiery furnace in Daniel 3. The Chaldeans

---

23. As Newman notes, scripturalization 'does not necessarily entail the presumed author's *conscious* interpretation of scripture' (*Praying by the Book*, 13, emphasis original).

24. For the classic study see Geza Vermes, *Scripture and Tradition in Judaism: Haggadic Studies*, SPB 4 (Leiden: Brill, 1961), 85–90. Vermes sees an unbroken tradition of interpreting Gen. 15:7 with Dan. 3 from the 'midrash' of *LAB* 6 to the expanded medieval legend in *Sefer Ha-Yashar*. But by associating Abram's rescue from the furnace with the building of the tower of Babel, Pseudo-Philo represents a different tradition from that found in Rabbinic literature and later in *Yashar*. Whilst some Rabbinic exegesis associated Abram (*PRE* 24; *Gen. Rab.* 38:6) and Nimrod (*b. Abod. Zar.* 53b; *b. Hul.* 89a) with the building of the tower, Abram's rescue from the furnace is never associated with it.

25. This tradition can also be found in *Ap. Ab.* 5:1-14.

40 *Writing with Scripture*

demand all the people bake bricks in order to build a tower in the plain of Babylon. Twelve men – including Abram – refuse to do so. The twelve are brought before the Chaldean chieftains where they profess their worship of the one God, saying, 'Even if you throw us into the fire with your bricks, we will not join you' (*LAB* 6:4). Enraged, the chieftains sentence the men to be thrown into the furnace along with their bricks. In an intervening section with no parallel to Genesis 11 or Daniel 3, one of the chieftains Joktan lets the men escape, but Abram chooses to remain and face the fiery ordeal. When Abram is thrown into the fire God causes an earthquake that sends sparks of flame gushing out of the furnace which kill many bystanders – 83,500 to be exact. Abram, however, is unharmed by the flames and emerges from the furnace unscathed.

Whereas the setting of the episode is provided by Gen. 11:1-9 and the character and place names are drawn from Genesis 10–11, the narrative of Abram being rescued from a Babylonian fiery furnace for refusing to participate in idolatry is loosely, but unmistakably, modelled on Daniel 3. The tradition of explaining the rescue of Abram, as well as the death of Haran, with a Danielic 'fiery furnace' continues in Rabbinic literature. The best known iteration is found in the *Genesis Rabbah*, where Abram is brought before Nimrod by his father Terah for insulting idol-worship.[26] As before, Nimrod sentences Abram to be thrown into a fiery furnace. At the same time, Haran is given the choice to follow the faith of Nimrod and live or the faith of Abram and be thrown into the furnace. Haran, however, waits to see whether the fire harms Abram. Upon seeing the fire has no effect, Haran follows Abram into the furnace but 'his inwards were scorched and he died in his father's presence' – as in Gen. 11:28.

Beyond the 'fiery furnace' and the focus on idolatry, the Rabbinic legends show few other signs of Danielic influence.[27] Although Nimrod is cast in the role of Nebuchadnezzar, only in later medieval accounts does Nimrod closely resemble the Babylonian king.[28] Rabbinic exegetes

---

26. *Gen. Rab.* 38:13; also *Tg. Ps.-J.* on Gen. 11:28; *Frag. Tg.* on Gen. 11:27-28; *Midr. Teh.* 118:9; *ARN* A 33; *S. Eli. Rab.* 27.

27. Danielic elements are scarce or entirely absent in *Gen. Rab.* 34:9; 44:13; *Exod. Rab.* 23:4; *Cant. Rab.* 1:56; *b. Eruv.* 53a; *b. Pes.* 118a; *PRE* 26 188; *Tg. Neof.* on Gen. 11:31 and 15:7; *Tg. Ps.-J.* on Gen. 15:7; *Tg. Est.* I 5:14; *Tg. 2 Chron.* 28:3; *Pes. Rab.* 33:4; *Midr. Tanh.* B Toldot 4:1; also Jerome, *Qu. Hebr. Gen.* 43; Vg. Neh. 9:7. Haran is consumed by a fire from heaven in *Tg. Ps.-J.* on Gen. 11:28.

28. Contrary to Bauckham ('The Liber Antiquitatum Biblicarum of Pseudo-Philo and the Gospels as "Midrash"', 43), there is little evidence before the Middle Ages that Nebuchadnezzar directly influenced the depiction of Nimrod. One response of

2. Scripturalized Narrative in Second Temple Literature   41

nevertheless associated the furnace of Abram with the three young men. One tradition says the LORD 'smelled the savour of the Patriarch Abraham ascending from the fiery furnace; He smelled the savour of Hananiah, Mishael and Azariah ascending from the fiery furnace' (*Gen. Rab.* 34:9). Another says 'Michael descended and rescued Abraham from the fiery furnace...and when did Michael descend? In the case of Hananiah, Mishael, and Azariah' (*Gen. Rab.* 44:13).[29] Other traditions relate that an angel wished to intercede on Abram's behalf, but God desired to rescue Abram himself, as it reads 'I am the LORD *who* brought you [out of the fire] of the Chaldeans'.[30] In return, God promises the angel, 'You will have the merit of saving three of his descendants' (*b. Pes.* 118a and par.) – referring to Hananiah, Mishael and Azariah.

Only in much later traditions do Danielic elements feature as prominently as in Pseudo-Philo. The Qur'ān makes repeated references to the rescue of 'Ibrāhīm from a fiery furnace (21:51-71; 29:16-27; 37:83-99), to which later Islamic tradition adds a number of Danielic elements, including the burning of his shackles in the fire and the presence of an angelic being (cf. Dan. 3:25).[31] The most sustained application of Daniel 3 to the legend, however, occurs in medieval Jewish literature. The *Chronicles of Jerahmeel*, which knows Pseudo-Philo, narrates Abram's rescue from the furnace no fewer than four times, with the first version resembling *LAB* 6. Jerahmeel adds the detail that Nimrod heated the furnace for 'seven (whole) days' (*CJ* 34:12), which comes from Nebuchadnezzar heating the furnace 'seven times more than was customary' (Dan. 3:19).[32] The *Sefer Ha-Yashar* adds still more Danielic elements to the episode: the fire melts

---

Nimrod resembles Nebuchadnezzar (*Gen. Rab.* 38:13) and the demand that Abram worship Nimrod's idol (*b. Erub.* 53a) is similar to Nebuchadnezzar's demand in Dan. 3:1-7.

29. And also in *Cant. Rab.* 2:16; *b. Sanh.* 93a.

30. As in *b. Pes.* 118a; *Exod. Rab.* 18:5; *Midr. Tanḥ.* B *Toldot* 4:1; *Midr. Tanḥ.* B *Tetz.* 12:2; *CJ* 34:13. Conversely, *Cant. Rab.* 1:56 names Michael as Abraham's deliverer, which is denied in *Gen. Rab.* 44:13.

31. Isḥāq ibn Bishr 168b; Ibn Kathīr, *Tafsīr* 5:352; al-Mahlisī 12:42-46; Ibn 'Asākir 6:187-189. For discussion of the texts, see Shari L. Lowin, *The Making of a Forefather: Abraham in Islamic and Jewish Exegetical Narratives*, Islamic History and Civilization 65 (Leiden: Brill, 2006), 198.

32. R. Baḥya, writing contemporary to the *Chronicles*, comments on Lev. 10:2 that '[Nebuchadnezzar] had stoked the kiln for seven consecutive days' (Eliyahu Munk, *Torah Commentary of Rabbi Bachya Ben Asher*, 7 vols. [Jerusalem: Urim, 1998], 5:1603).

away Abram's bonds so he can walk around the furnace (*Yashar* 12:24-25; cf. Dan. 3:25); the servants who throw Abram into the furnace die in the flames (*Yashar* 12:26, 29-31; cf. Dan. 3:22); and the king and the royal court repent upon seeing Abram walk around the furnace unmolested (*Yashar* 12:27-32; cf. Dan. 3:27-28).

The convention of interpreting Abram's departure from Ur with the help of Daniel 3 has its roots in the Second Temple period. The 'fire of the Chaldeans' in Gen. 15:7 naturally leant itself to that other fire of the Chaldeans in Daniel 3, from which the conclusion was drawn: as God rescued the three young men, so God rescued Abram. Pseudo-Philo's extensive use of Daniel to shape the legend is nevertheless without parallel in antiquity. The table below details the primary and secondary scriptural sources which led to the creation of the episode.

LAB 6	Primary Scriptures	Secondary Scriptures
The Chaldeans settle in the plain of Babylon and come together to build a tower to the heavens and make a name for themselves lest they be scattered (6:1).	The Chaldeans settle in the plain of Shinar and come together to build a city and a tower to the heavens and make a name for themselves lest they be scattered (Gen. 11:2-4).	Nebuchadnezzar sets up the golden statue in the plain of Dura in the province of Babylon (Dan. 3:1).
The Chaldeans write their names on bricks and 'burn them with fire' (6:2).	The Chaldeans make bricks and 'roast them with fire' (LXX 11:3; cf. MT 11:3).	
All the people participate in the burning of the bricks (6:2-3).		All the people fall down and worship the golden statue Nebuchadnezzar has set up (3:7).
Twelve men – Abram, Nahor, Lot, Ruge, Tenute, Zaba, Armodat, Jobab, Esar, Abimahel, Saba, Aufin – refuse to burn bricks (6:3).	The names are drawn from the sons of Joktan: Elmodad, Eval, Ahimael, Saba, Uphir (LXX 10:26-29); and the descendants of Peleg (Fenech): Reu, Nahor, Abram, Lot (11:18-29).	Three men – Hananiah, Mishael and Azariah – refuse to worship the golden statue (3:12).

2. Scripturalized Narrative in Second Temple Literature
43

The Chaldeans accuse the twelve men of refusing to participate and bring them before the chiefs, where they are questioned (6:4).		The Chaldeans accuse the three men of refusing to participate and bring them before Nebuchadnezzar, where they are questioned (3:12).
The twelve men answer that they worship the Lord and will not throw bricks into the fire even if they are thrown into the fire (6:4).		The three men answer that they will not worship the golden statue even if the God whom they serve does not deliver them from the furnace (3:16-18).
The response of the twelve men angers the chiefs. The chiefs demand the twelve either throw bricks into the fire or be thrown into the fire themselves (6:5).		Nebuchadnezzar demands the three men either worship the golden statue or be thrown into a fiery furnace (3:15). The response of the men angers Nebuchadnezzar (3:19).
Joktan orchestrates the escape of eleven men, although Abram remains, whilst Fenech and Nimrod discover the men are missing (6:6-15).	The names are drawn from Genesis 10: Nimrod (10:8-10); Joktan (10:25-29); Fenech appears to reflect Peleg, the brother of Joktan (rendered φαλεχ in LXX 10:25; 11:16-19).	
Abram is thrown into the fiery furnace (6:16).		Hananiah, Mishael and Azariah are thrown into the fiery furnace (3:23).
God causes an earthquake that sends sparks of flame leaping out of the furnace (6:17).		Sparks of flame leap out of the overheated furnace (MT 3:22); the flames leap 49 cubits out of the furnace (θ' and LXX 3:47).
83,500 bystanders die in the flames (6:17).		Bystanders die in the flames (θ' and LXX 3:48); the guards who throw the three men into the furnace die in the flames (MT 3:22).

Abram emerges from the fiery furnace unscathed (6:17-18).	God brings Abraham out of the 'fire' of the Chaldeans (15:7).	Hananiah, Mishael and Azariah emerge from the fiery furnace unscathed (3:25-27).
Abram finds the eleven who escaped. The story ends with a brief note on the place-name 'Deli' (6:18).	The story ends with a brief note on the place-name 'Babel' (11:9).	

The influence of Daniel 3 on the episode is unmistakable: in the plain of Babylon, the people are told to join in wickedness under pain of death, but a few righteous men refuse to participate in the idolatrous scheme and are brought to trial where they profess their allegiance to the one God, upon which they are thrown into a fiery furnace, only to emerge unscathed whilst their tormentors die in the flames. The episode also features some of the distinctive vocabulary found in the Aramaic and Greek versions of Daniel: the 'fiery furnace' of *LAB* 6:16-18 (*caminus ignis*) no doubt reflects the 'fiery furnace' (Aram. אתון נורא; Gk. κάμινος τοῦ πυρός) of Dan. 3:6ff.;[33] the 'sparks of flame' (*scintillas flamme*) of *LAB* 6:17 reflects the 'sparks of flame' (שביב די נורא) of Dan. 3:22;[34] the phrase 'And it burned all those standing around in sight of the furnace' (*LAB* 6:17: *et combussit omnes circumstantes in conspectu camini*) seems to reflect 'And [it] burned those Chaldeans it found about the furnace' (LXX and θ′ Dan. 3:48: καὶ ἐνεπύρισεν οὓς εὗρε περὶ τὴν κάμινον τῶν Χαλδαίων); and the phrase 'And Abram came up out of the furnace' (*LAB* 6:18: *et surrexit Abram de camino*) resembles the exit of the three men who 'came up out from the fire' (Dan. 3:26: נפקין...מן־גוא נורא).[35] To this can be added

33. The phrase κάμινος τοῦ πυρός is unique to θ′ and LXX Dan. 3, and is not used for the more common words for 'furnace' or 'kiln' (כבשן, תנור, בור). The LXX renders כור as κάμινος (Deut. 4:20; Prov. 17:3; Isa. 48:10; Jer. 11:4; Ezek. 22:18-22) or χωνευτήριον (1 Kgs. 8:51; Prov. 27:21); תנור as κλίβανος (Gen. 15:7; Exod. 7:28; Lev. 2:4; 7:9; 11:35; 26:26; Hos. 7:4-7; Mal. 3:19; Ps. 21:10; Lam. 5:10); and כבשן as κάμινος (Gen. 19:28; Exod. 19:18) or καμιναία (Exod. 9:8, 10).

34. This probably reflects σπινθήρ in the underlying Greek. Where the LXX has σπινθήρ, the Vulgate has *scintilla* (Vg. Isa. 1:31; Wis. 2:2; 3:7; 11:18[19]; cf. *flamma ignis* at Vg. Dan. 3:22).

35. This could be further proof of Pseudo-Philo's knowledge of a lost Hebrew/Aramaic text featuring similar readings to the LXX, i.e. the hypothetical Palestinian text proposed by Harrington, 'The Biblical Text of Pseudo-Philo's "Liber Antiquitatum Biblicarum"', 16–17.

2. Scripturalized Narrative in Second Temple Literature   45

general similarities, including the setting of each episode in a plain of
Babylon[36] and the dialogue of the trial scenes.[37]

36. *LAB* 6:1 follows Gen. 11:2, but reads 'Babylon' (*Babilonis*) instead of
'Shinar' (שנער), a reading found in several Aramaic texts (1QapGen 21:23; *Tg. Onk.*
on Gen. 14:1; *Tg. Neof.* on Gen. 10:10; 11:2; 14:1, 9; cf. Josephus, *Ant.* 1.118-119;
LXX Dan. 1:2 similarly has βαβυλῶνα instead of Σεννααρ [cf. θ' Dan. 1:2]). The
reference to Babylon might also reflect the location of Nebuchadnezzar's golden
statue: 'He set it up on the plain of Dura in the province of Babylon' (Dan. 3:1).
Pseudo-Philo may have noticed the similarities between the tower of Babel and
the golden statue, both large structures built on the plain of Babylon demanding
the participation of all peoples (Gen. 11:1-6; Dan. 3:1-7). Philip Michael Sherman
notes a number of 'analogical correlations' between Gen. 11 and Dan. 3, see *Babel's
Tower Translated: Genesis 11 and Ancient Jewish Interpretation*, BI 117 (Leiden:
Brill, 2013), 131–40. Later interpreters with no knowledge of the Abraham-in-the-
furnace tradition associated Gen. 11 with Dan. 3, see the Old English of Boethius's
Consolation of Philosophy 35.4: 'This Nimrod ordered the building of a tower on
the field that was called Sennar, and in the nation that was called Deira [cf. Δεῖρα in
θ' Dan 3:1], very near the city which is now called Babylon' (*Se Nefrod het wyrcan
anne tor on þam felda þe Sennar hatte, and on þære ðiode þe Deira hatte swiðe
neah þære byrig þe mon nu hæt Babilonia*). Yair Zakovitch, 'The Exodus from Ur of
the Chaldeans: A Chapter in Literary Archaeology', in *Ki Baruch Hu: Ancient Near
Eastern, Biblical and Judaic Studies in Honor of Baruch Levine*, ed. Robert Chazan,
William Hallo and Lawrence Schiffman (Warsaw, IN: Eisenbrauns, 1999), 437, is of
the unusual opinion that 'the plain of Dura' (בקעה דורא) reflects the Abrahamic 'Ur'
(אור), as he believes the Abraham-in-the-furnace tradition served as the model for
the fiery furnace episode in Dan. 3, not the other way around. Why a tale featuring
three hitherto unknown young men would eventually become the better known story,
Zakovitch does not explain. There may be an additional connection to Dan. 3 in
the curious note that ends the episode: 'And they named that place by the name of
Abram and in the language of the Chaldeans "Deli", which means "God"' (*LAB* 6:18).
Whilst there is no record of a Chaldean Deli, the name appears to reflect the Assyrian
or Babylonian suffix *-ili* ('of God'), and so could refer to the Babylonian *Dûr-ili*,
meaning 'gate of God', from which *Dura* (דורא) may also be derived. Although
there is no reference to *Dûr-ili* outside of Assyrian and Babylonian records, Assyrian
literature identifies *Dûr-ili* with *Uruk*, the scriptural *Erech* (ארך), which according to
legend was built by Nimrod 'in the land of Shinar' (Gen. 10:10), see Jean-Vincent
Scheil, 'Cylindres et Légendes Inédits (avec trois planches)', *RA* 13 (1961): 5–25
(21). On problems with translating דורא, see Edward M. Cook, ' "In the Plain of the
Wall" (Dan 3:1)', *JBL* 108 (1989): 115–16.

37. In both episodes, the righteous men address the rulers with the protatic
*si/*הן (*LAB* 6:4; Dan. 3:17-18), and the rulers threaten the men in a conditional
construction (*LAB* 6:5; Dan. 3:15). On the distinctive use of protasis and the

There are of course significant differences between the two stories. The escape of the eleven men manufactured by Joktan (*LAB* 6:6-15) has no obvious parallel to Daniel 3.[38] Bauckham and Jacobson note Joktan's attitude is less like Nebuchadnezzar and more like Darius in Daniel 6. The role of Nebuchadnezzar, however, is still occupied by Fenech and, as in Rabbinic tradition, Nimrod (*LAB* 6:14; cf. 5:1). At the same time, Joktan is described in terms reminiscent of Reuben, as he 'sought how he might save them from the hands of the people' (*LAB* 6:6; cf. Gen. 37:22). Bauckham goes further to argue that the influence of Daniel 3 is obscured by the large number killed – 83,500 – by the exploding furnace, which may suggest Pseudo-Philo was not responsible for the inclusion of Danielic elements, and merely inherited them from earlier tradition.[39] But although MT Dan. 3:22 relates only the deaths of the guards, some rabbis calculate that four classes of Nebuchadnezzar's subjects died in the flames emitting from the furnace (i.e. *Exod. Rab.* 18:5).[40] At the same time, the

conditional construction in Dan. 3, see Tarsee Li, *The Verbal System of the Aramaic of Daniel: An Explanation in the Context of Grammaticalization*, SAIS 8 (Leiden: Brill, 2009), 118, 121.

38. There are, however, some similarities with Israel drinking water at Horeb (Exod. 17:6), and Elijah drinking from the brook of Cherith (1 Kgs 17:3-4) and hiding from the murderous Jezebel (1 Kgs 19:1-9).

39. So Bauckham, 'Pseudo-Philo and the Gospels as "Midrash"', 43. Bauckham makes a fair point that the sensational death toll may simply reflect 'Pseudo-Philo's habitual exaggeration of numbers'. To take two examples, Pseudo-Philo raises the number of Sisera's chariots from 900 (Judg. 4:3, 13) to 8,000 (*LAB* 30:3) and the number of Philistines slain by Samson from 3,000 (Judg. 16:27) to 40,000 (*LAB* 43:8). The number of dead could also reflect the rebellion of Korah (esp. Num. 16:35, 49), an episode with some parallels to *LAB* 6, as a large number are similarly consumed by an earthquake and fire (Num. 16:31-35; these also occur at the destruction of the tower of Babel in *b. Sanh.* 109a). The influence of Num. 16 on *LAB* 6 is, however, overstated by Murphy (*Pseudo-Philo*, 81–3, 161).

40. The Rabbis observed that Dan. 3:3 reads Nebuchadnezzar sent for the 'satraps, the prefects, and the governors, the counselors, the treasurers, the justices, the magistrates, and all the officials of the provinces', whereas in Dan. 3:27 he calls only for the 'satraps, the prefects, the governors, and the king's counselors'. The question then arises: what happened to the treasurers, justices, magistrates and officials? These, too, perished in the fire: 'When Gabriel came down to deliver Hananiah, Mishael, and Azariah, he ordered the fire to scorch all those who had thrown them in... Some say that four classes of governors died there; for at first it says: Then the satraps, the prefects, and the governors, the judges, the treasurers, the counsellors, the sheriffs, and all the rulers of the provinces, whilst at this point four are lacking, as it says: And the satraps, the prefects, the governors, and the king's ministers' (*Exod. Rab.* 18:5; also *b. Sanh.* 92b).

2. Scripturalized Narrative in Second Temple Literature   47

Greek versions of Daniel say the 'flame steamed forth above the furnace forty and nine cubits...and burned those Chaldeans it found about the furnace' (LXX and θ' Dan. 3:47-48: καὶ διεχεῖτο ἡ φλὸξ ἐπάνω τῆς καμίνου ἐπὶ πήχεις τεσσαράκοντα ἐννέα ... καὶ ἐνεπύρισεν οὓς εὗρε[ν] περὶ τὴν κάμινον τῶν Χαλδαίων).[41] Perhaps the enormous death toll reflects Pseudo-Philo's amalgam of Genesis 11 and Daniel 3 – given that all nations were involved in building the tower (*LAB* 6:1; Gen. 11:1), there would naturally be a large number 'standing around in sight of the furnace' (*LAB* 6:17).[42] In any case, Pseudo-Philo's tendency to embellish hardly diminishes the case for the direct influence of Daniel 3 on the episode, one in which the righteous are thrown into a fiery furnace by the Babylonians for refusing to participate in idolatry, only to emerge from the furnace unscathed whilst the tormentors die in the flames.[43]

Though the episode has its origins in the interpretation of Gen. 15:7, its purpose is not simply to explicate this passage, which is never quoted by Pseudo-Philo.[44] And whilst Gen. 11:1-9 provides the episode with its setting, and Genesis 10–11 with its names, it is the story of Daniel 3 that gives the narrative its shape. It may well be Pseudo-Philo inherited the Danielic story of Abram's rescue from a fiery furnace from tradition, but several features point to the original nature of this composition. Though the episode purports to narrate Abram's rescue from the Chaldeans (Gen. 11:31; 15:7; cf. *LAB* 16:18), those involved in the building of the tower come from all nations (*LAB* 6:1; Gen. 11:1) and are led by the descendants of Noah (*LAB* 5:1; 6:14). The narrative requires the building

---

41. The number 49 seems to reflect Nebuchadnezzar's command that the furnace be heated 'seven times more than was customary' (Dan. 3:19), seven-times-seven, an interpretation preserved in *Midr. Teh.* 28:2.

42. The inclusion of the earthquake may also reflect tradition comparing the furnaces of Abram and the three youths: rabbinic tradition relates the deadly sparks emitting from Nebuchadnezzar's furnace were caused by an angel (*b. Pes.* 118b; *Exod. Rab.* 18:5). As there is no angelic involvement in Abram's furnace (so *Gen. Rab.* 44:13; *b. Pes.* 118a; *Exod. Rab.* 18:5; *Midr. Tanḥ.* B *Toldot* 4:1; *Midr. Tanḥ.* B *Tetz.* 12:2; *CJ* 34:13), God causes the deadly sparks by other means, in this case an earthquake (i.e. Num. 16:31-35).

43. Although the building of the tower is not motivated by idolatry (Gen. 11:4), the response of the twelve men can only be read as a rejection of idolatry (*LAB* 6:4), likely under the influence of Dan. 3:16-18. See Frederick J. Murphy, 'Retelling the Bible: Idolatry in Pseudo-Philo', *JBL* 107 (1988): 275–87; *Pseudo-Philo*, 41–8; Fisk, *Do You Not Remember?*, 141–52; Jacobson, *Commentary*, 1:355–56; Sherman, *Babel's Tower Translated*, 135–40.

44. Later allusions to Abram's rescue from the furnace make no mention of Gen. 15:7 (*LAB* 23:5; 32:1).

48 Writing with Scripture

of two furnaces, the first in which Abram and the eleven refuse to throw their bricks (*LAB* 6:3-5), and the second built for the special purpose of burning Abram (6:16), in which the bricks are again thrown. Pseudo-Philo's decision to combine Abram's rescue from fire with the Babel episode results somewhat clumsily in two separate attempts to build the tower, the first which is thwarted by Abram's exploding furnace and the second where God confounds the builders (*LAB* 7; cf. Gen. 11:1-9). These sorts of superfluities – which appear throughout *LAB* – seem to be of the author's own doing.

That Pseudo-Philo was responsible for the inclusion of Danielic elements in the story is also indicated by the compositional use of Daniel elsewhere in the work. For example, the sons of Reuben, Gad and Manasseh answer Joshua with what appears to be a quotation of Dan. 2:22, 'He [God] himself knows what are in the hidden places of the abyss and the light abides with him' (*LAB* 22:3: *ipse scit que in occultis sunt abyssi, et lumen cum eo permanet*). Compare this with MT Dan. 2:22: 'He reveals deep and hidden things; he knows what is in the darkness, and light dwells with him' (הוא גלא עמיקתא ומסתרתא ידע מה בחשוכא ונהירא ונהורא עמה שרא). Harrington and Jacobson italicize the quote apart from *abyssi*, but this too may come from Dan. 2:22, as *abyssus* could have come from misreading βαθύς (as in θ' and LXX Dan. 2:22; cf. MT: אמיק) as βυθός, thus ἄβυσσος. The surest sign the author made direct use of Daniel 3, however, is in the presence of not one but two tales of righteous men delivered from fiery furnaces.

Jair and the fiery furnace: LAB 38 and Daniel 3

The judge Jair is given relatively short shrift in the Jewish scriptures, occupying a mere three verses (Judg. 10:3-5). Pseudo-Philo, however, creates a new narrative for Jair by combining Jair's rule with the following account of Israel's lapse back into Baal-worship (Judg. 10:6), for which the author holds Jair responsible.[45] The episode begins with Jair issuing the command, 'Everyone who will not sacrifice to Baal will

---

45. Compare with the positive description of Jair in Josephus (*Ant.* 5.254). Pseudo-Philo may have identified Jair with the Manassite who conquered towns in Gilead (Num. 32:41; Deut. 3:14; Josh. 13:30; 1 Kgs 4:13; 1 Chron. 2:22-23). *LAB* 38:4 confusingly reads 'I have raised you up from the land' (*levavi te de terra*; ms. Δ adds *Egipti*), echoing Exod. 20:2 etc., which, as Jacobson notes, would be 'chronologically preposterous' if referring to the Jair of Judg. 10:3-5 (*Commentary*, 2:943), unless the author believed Jair was the son of Manasseh, who, according to some Rabbis, survived the wilderness (*b. B. Bat.* 121b).

2. Scripturalized Narrative in Second Temple Literature   49

die' (*LAB* 38:1). Again, seven men refuse to obey the order.[46] The men are taken before Jair where they confront him, quoting the words of Deborah – actually the words of Joshua in Josh. 1:7-8 – and challenging him, 'And now if [Baal] is God as you say, let him speak as God and then we will sacrifice to him' (*LAB* 38:2).[47] Angered by this, Jair orders his servants to throw the men into a fire. But when they are thrown in, the angel Nathaniel comes and extinguishes the fire for the men whilst burning the servants of Jair (38:3). The angel then blinds the people, allowing the men to escape. When Jair arrives at the scene, he perishes in the fire along with a thousand men (38:4).

The episode features many of the same elements from Daniel 3 found in the rescue of Abram in *LAB* 6. Righteous men are saved from a fire after being thrown in for refusing to participate in idolatry at the behest of a wicked ruler. But elements from Daniel 3 absent in *LAB* 6 are present in the fire of Jair. For example, the fire burns the servants of Jair who threw the seven men into the fire (*LAB* 38:3) as the overheated furnace burns the servants of Nebuchadnezzar who threw the three men into the furnace (Dan. 3:22). The reason the fire harms the servants but not the seven men is because an angel intervenes, just as one with the 'appearance of a god' appears in Nebuchadnezzar's furnace (Dan. 3:25), a figure understood to be an angel at an early stage (LXX and θ' Dan. 3:46-50). Later tradition often assigned the role to Gabriel, who cools or repels the fire for the righteous yet burns the wicked.[48] However, the angel who rescues the seven men, Nathaniel 'who was in charge of fire' (*qui preest igni*), is unattested outside of *LAB*. Given that other angelic names in *LAB* originate in word-play, Ginzberg speculates the name may derive from *Atuniel* reflecting the Aramaic for 'furnace' (אתון).[49] Aside from the

---

46. The bizarre names of the seven men – Defal, Abiesdrel, Getalibal, Selumi, Assur, Ionadali, Memihel – appear to be corrupt or fictional (or both). Besides the number, there is no reason to associate them with the seven martyrs of 2 Macc. 7, *pace* James, *Biblical Antiquities*, 59, 187.

47. This appears to reflect the words of Elijah in 1 Kgs 18:24. Deborah's words might also reflect Deut. 5:32

48. See the discussion in Michael Wadsworth, *The Liber Antiquitatum Biblicarum of Pseudo-Philo: Doctrine and Scriptural Exegesis in a Jewish Midrash of the First Century A.D.*, 2 vols. (Oxford: Oxford University Press, 1975), 2:151–2.

49. Ginzberg, *Legends*, 6:202 n. 105. Other angels in *LAB* are similarly named, i.e. the angel of strength who bears up Kenaz's arms is called *Zeruel* (*LAB* 27:10) which presumably derives from זריע ('strength' or 'arm'), so Ginzberg, *Legends*, 6:183–4 n. 17. As Perrot notes (*Pseudo-Philon*, 2:185), Pseudo-Philo possesses 'la singulatiré de l'angélogie'.

50   *Writing with Scripture*

blinding of the bystanders, the role of Nathaniel is *mutatis mutandis* the same as Gabriel or Michael in traditions about Daniel 3.[50]

The angel's curious name might, however, have something to do with the creation of the episode. Like the furnace of Abram, the fire of Jair appears to originate in word-play. Judges 10:5 tersely states 'Jair died, and was buried in Kamon'. Here the Hebrew place-name קמון could be read as the Aramaic קמין, derived from the Greek καμίνος for 'furnace'.[51] This would explain the words of the angel to Jair, 'And in the fire in which you will die there you will have a dwelling place' (*et in quo igne morieris in eo habebis habitationem*). Thus Bauckham sees the sole purpose of the episode as explicating scripture: 'Once again, we notice that the story has not simply been created on the basis of Daniel 3. It has a [starting point] in the exegesis of Judges, and Dan 3 has been enlisted to help in the interpretation of Judges.'[52] Indeed, this is the purpose of all new episodes created out of scripture according to Bauckham: 'Pseudo-Philo is always commenting on and explaining the text of the biblical narrative... Other passages of Scripture are always utilized as a means of explaining *this* narrative.'[53]

It is curious then that neither the place-name Kamon nor the Latin for 'furnace' ever appear in the episode. Even if Nathaniel originates in אתון, it would not be readily associated with קמין. It could be the verbal connection that inspired the episode has been lost in translation.[54] But even still, the absence of a furnace (*caminus*/*fornax*) is puzzling given the episode clearly requires something like it, that is, a controlled fire in which men can be thrown. Whilst the decision to read Kamon (קמון) as a furnace (קמין) might explain how Daniel 3 became associated with Jair, no explicit signs of this exegesis survive in the text, making it difficult to

---

50. Indeed, *Jerahmeel* has Gabriel instead of Nathaniel (*CJ* 57:34); on the role of Gabriel repelling fire and burning the bystanders, see *b. Pes.* 118a; *b. Yom.* 21b; *Exod. Rab.* 18:5; *Midr. Teh.* 117:3.

51. So Ginzberg, *Legends*, 6:202 n. 104.

52. Bauckham, 'Pseudo-Philo and the Gospels as "Midrash"', 52.

53. Bauckham, 'Pseudo-Philo and the Gospels as "Midrash"', 59, emphasis original. Bauckham earlier states that 'LAB must be regarded as a kind of commentary on the biblical text' (34).

54. There is no sign of it in the Hebrew *Chronicles of Jerahmeel*, which following Jair's death unceremoniously reads, 'And Iair was buried in Qamon' (*CJ* 58:10). Whether or not *Jerahmeel* knew a Hebrew text of *LAB* (affirmed by Gaster, denied by Cohn and Harrington), it is significant that the Hebrew author of the only other surviving account of Jair's fiery death is wholly unaware of the word-play on Kamon/furnace.

2. Scripturalized Narrative in Second Temple Literature 51

see the episode as simply an explanatory note on Judg. 10:3-5. Instead, the episode presents a self-contained narrative which, though inspired by scriptural interpretation, does not attempt to explain this exegesis to the reader and can be understood without consulting the scriptural passage.[55] It would be a mistake to confuse the interpretation that inspired the episode with the purpose of the episode itself, especially when the text bears no signs of it. The tendency of some scholars to treat so-called pseudepigraphical works as little more than supplements to the Jewish scriptures reveals more about their own attitude towards the scriptures than those of Second Temple authors, like Pseudo-Philo.[56]

The purpose of the episode aside, there is no mistaking the direct influence of Daniel 3. A wicked leader commands idolatry, a small number of righteous men refuse, a confrontation between the men and the wicked leader ensues, and as punishment the men are thrown into fire, out of which an angel rescues them whilst burning their persecutors.

LAB 38	Primary Scriptures	Secondary Scriptures
Jair builds a sanctuary to Baal and demands the people sacrifice to Baal or die (38:1).	Jair is the judge of Israel (Judg. 10:3-5) and afterwards the Israelites return to Baal-worship (10:6).	Nebuchadnezzar builds a golden statue and demands the people worship it or be thrown into a fiery furnace (Dan. 3:1-7).
Seven men refuse to sacrifice to Baal (38:1).		Three men refuse to worship the statue (3:12).
The men answer Jair by quoting the words of Deborah and challenging Baal-worship (38:2).		The words of Deborah are borrowed from Josh. 1:7-8 and the challenge to Baal may reflect 1 Kgs 18:24.
Jair orders the men to be thrown into the fire for their blasphemy (38:3).		Nebuchadnezzar orders the men to be thrown into the fiery furnace (Dan. 3:19-21).

55. Pseudo-Philo likewise does not alert readers to the interpretation of the 'fire of the Chaldeans' (Gen. 15:7) which inspired Abram's rescue from the fiery furnace (*LAB* 6). On Pseudo-Philo's dependence on and independence from the scriptural text, see Reinmuth, *Pseudo-Philo und Lukas*, 14–17.

56. As insightfully observed by Mroczek, *The Literary Imagination*, 6–9, 120–1.

The angel Nathaniel extinguishes the fire for the men (38:3).		One with the 'appearance of a god' is with the men in the furnace (3:25). Tradition identifies this figure as Michael or Gabriel come to extinguish the fire.
Nathaniel burns the servants of Jair with fire (38:3).		The servants of Nebuchadnezzar are burned by the overheated furnace (3:22). In tradition, this is done by the angel (*b. Pes.* 118b; *Exod. Rab.* 18:5).
The angel lets the men escape from the fire by striking the people with blindness (38:3).		The men emerge from the fire unscathed (3:26). The blinding has no parallel.
Jair dies in the fire and the angel of the Lord tells him he will have his dwelling place in fire (38:4).	Jair dies and is buried in Kamon (10:5), which could be read as 'furnace' (Aramaic: קמין; from the Greek: καμίνος).	
The angel of the Lord demolishes the pillar of Baal, burns Baal and a thousand men who stand by (38:4).		In Greek Daniel 3, those standing by the fiery furnace die in the flames (θ' and LXX 3:48). The scene is also similar to 2 Kgs 10:26-27.

The fiery furnace of Daniel 3 would go on to be used frequently as a compositional model in late antiquity and into the Middle Ages. In early Christian literature, the unsuccessful attempts to burn Polycarp (*Martyrdom of Polycarp* 15–16) and Thecla (*Syr. Thecl.* 7–8) clearly reflect the language of Daniel 3.[57] The fantastic tales of incombustibility in later

---

57. On the reception of Dan 3 in early Christian literature, see Jan Willem van Henten, 'Daniel 3 and 6 in Early Christian Literature', in *The Book of Daniel: Composition and Reception*, ed. John J. Collins and Peter W. Flint, 2 vols., VTSup 83 (Leiden: Brill, 2001), 1:149–69. On its influence on the *Martyrdom of Polycarp* see van Henten, 'Zum Einfluß jüdischer Martyrien auf die Literatur des frühen

2. Scripturalized Narrative in Second Temple Literature

martyrologies are more explicitly indebted to Daniel 3, as angels rescue multiple saints from fiery furnaces as thousands of pagan bystanders die in the flames.[58] At the same time, Jewish tradition used Daniel 3 to describe historical persecutions, like the murder of three rabbis by a Christian mob in Blois – the rabbis were bound and thrown into fire, only for the fire to burn away their shackles (cf. Dan. 3:25), so the rabbis could be heard singing amidst the flames and saying, 'Behold we are in this fire but it has no power over us' (cf. Dan. 3:27).[59] Thus over time the miraculous rescue of the three young men from a Chaldean furnace became a template for similar legends, albeit ones in which the heroes ultimately suffer martyrdom, sometimes with their basis in history – like the martyrs of Blois – but more often not.[60] However, the custom of using Daniel 3 to compose new narrative has its origins in the Second Temple period with the scripturalized narratives of Abram and Jair.

Christentums. II: Die Apostolischen Väter', *ANRW* II.27 (1993): 700–723, esp. 723; Gerd Buschmann, *Das Martyrium des Polykarp: Übersetzt und Erklärt*, Kommentar zu den Apostolischen Vätern 6 (Göttingen: Vandenhoeck & Ruprecht, 1998), 294 n. 8; Jan M. Kozlowski, 'And He Saw His Pillow Being Consumed by Fire (*Martyrium Polycarpi* 5,2): A Proposal of Interpretation', *ETL* 85 (2009): 147–58, esp. 156.

58. For example, the martyrdoms of Acislus and Victoria (Angel Fábrega Grau, *Pasionario hispánico*, 2 vols., Monumenta Hispaniae Sacra, Serie Litúrgica 6 [Barcelona: Instituto P. Enrique Florez, 1953], 2:12–13), Christina the Astonishing (Jacobus de Voragine, *Legenda aurea: vulgo historia lombardica dicta; ad optimuorum liborum fidem*, ed. Theodor Graesse, 3rd ed. [Breslau: Gulielmum Koebner, 1890], 1:387), Karitas (Hrotsvit of Gandersheim, *Sapientia* 144-145), Euphemia of Chalcedon (PHG 619d) and Januarius (*Acta SS. Januarii Episc., Sosii, Festi etc.* [*Acta Sanctorum* 46:878]) – to name but a few.

59. For the texts see Abraham Habermann, *Sefer Gezerot Ashkenaz ve-Ẓarefat* (Jerusalem: Tarshish, 1945), 143 (English translation in Susan L. Einbinder, *Beautiful Death: Jewish Poetry and Martyrdom in Medieval France*, Jews, Christians, and Muslims from the Ancient to the Modern World 8 [Princeton, NJ: Princeton University Press, 2002], 52–3); and Einbinder, 'The Jewish Martyrs of Blois', in *Medieval Hagiography: An Anthology*, ed. Thomas Head (London: Routledge, 2000), 546. The burning of the shackles appears again in the poem of R. Hillel of Bonn (Einbinder, 'The Jewish Martyrs of Blois', 548). Interestingly, it can also be found in the tale of Abram's rescue from the furnace in the medieval *Yashar* 12:25.

60. As Einbinder notes, 'artistic shaping is not the same as fictionalization' (*Beautiful Death*, 10) – though, in some cases, it necessarily entails it. These examples and the transformation of Dan. 3 into a tale of martyrdom are explored in Nathanael Vette, 'The Many Fiery Furnaces of Dan 3: The Evolution of a Literary Model', *Biblical Interpretation* (forthcoming).

Kenaz and Gideon: LAB 27 and Judges 7

Whilst the fiery furnaces of Abram and Jair are rooted in the language of the primary scriptural narrative, albeit in a single word, the same cannot be easily said for the lives of Kenaz (*LAB* 25–28) and his successor Zebul (29). Kenaz, the father of Othniel, occupies all of five verses in the Jewish scriptures (Josh. 15:7; Judg. 1:13; 3:9, 11; 1 Chron. 4:13). Pseudo-Philo, however, devotes almost as much time narrating the career of Kenaz as is devoted to Moses and Joshua. Kenaz replaces Othniel as the first judge after Joshua just as he does in Josephus.[61] But whereas Josephus simply ascribes the career of Othniel to Kenaz, Pseudo-Philo features a long and illustrious career without any parallel in extant litera-ture.[62] In fact, Pseudo-Philo appears to be alone in their interest in this figure. The *Lives of the Prophets* mentions the cave of a certain Kenaz, 'who became judge of one tribe in the days of the anarchy'.[63] Rabbinic literature, on the other hand, has no interest in Kenaz beyond his relation to Caleb and Othniel.[64] Despite Ginzberg's brilliant suggestion, Kenaz should not be identified with the mysterious figure of Cethel, the master of precious stones, who so fascinated medieval authors.[65] Although Pseudo-Philo's reasons for narrating the life of Kenaz may no longer be recoverable, how the author went about composing this narrative is still perceptible in the text.[66]

For example, the first act in the life of Kenaz (*LAB* 25–26) draws on a wide variety of scriptural sources, most notably the sin of Achan (Josh. 7). After the death of Joshua, the Israelites 'inquired of the Lord and said, "Should we go up and fight against the Philistines?"' (*LAB* 25:1; cf. Judg.

---

61. Josephus, *Ant.* 5.182-184.

62. *Jerahmeel* repeats Pseudo-Philo's description of Kenaz with little variation (*CJ* 57).

63. *Liv. Pro.* 10:9. Charles C. Torrey speculates this once read 'the first who became judge' (*Lives of the Prophets: Greek Text and Translation*, SBLMS 1 [Philadelphia, PA: Society of Biblical Literature and Exegesis, 1946], 27–8).

64. See *b. Tem.* 16a, 'Now was Caleb the son of Kenaz?' (cf. *b. Sot.* 11b-12a). Exegetes clearly had difficulty reconciling Josh. 15:17 with Judg. 1:13 (see Rashi on Num. 32:12).

65. Ginzberg, *Legends of the Jews*, 6:181, n. 1. Dismissed in Feldman, 'Prole-gomenon', xiii–xiv, cx–xi. The description of Cethel as a 'Jewish philosopher' best fits a figure like the ninth-century Jewish astrologer Sahl ibn Bishr ben Habib, with whose works Cethel's treatise survives, rather than a quasi-biblical figure like Kenaz.

66. Jacobson rightly calls Pseudo-Philo's peculiar interest in Kenaz 'one of the great mysteries of LAB' (*Commentary*, 2:738).

2. *Scripturalized Narrative in Second Temple Literature*   55

1:1).[67] God responds by saying the Israelites must first eradicate sin from the camp, 'Cast lots among your tribes and every tribe that comes out in the lot will be set aside for another lot, and then you will know whose heart is pure and whose may be defiled' – which is the first of many details influenced by the sin of Achan in Joshua 7. The lot for Israel's next leader falls on Kenaz from the tribe of Caleb (*LAB* 25:2).[68] The new leader goes on to address the Israelite camp, quoting Moses and Joshua (*LAB* 25:3; cf. Deut. 28:14; Josh. 23:6), and vowing to burn those selected by the lot of sin. The lot of sin falls upon 6,110 Israelites (cf. Josh. 7:16-18), whom Kenaz imprisons 'until it should be known what should be done about them' (*LAB* 25:4; language lifted from Num. 15:34; Lev. 24:12).[69] Kenaz addresses the people again, quoting Moses (*LAB* 25:5; cf. Deut. 29:18), and consults the Urim and Thummim, which reveal that those selected by lot must confess their sins and be burned with fire.[70]

Kenaz encourages those selected to confess their sins like Achan did (*LAB* 25:7; cf. Josh. 7:19-21), which they promptly do, confessing to various sins that may not all seem of equal measure to the modern reader (*LAB* 25:8-14) – ranging from cannibalism (Zebulun) and child sacrifice (Ephraim) to curiosity about the authorship of the Torah (Benjamin). Those selected from the tribe of Naphtali confess to making idols after

---

67. The episode is not, as Bauckham argues, 'an interpretation of Judg 1:1-2' ('Pseudo-Philo and the Gospels as "Midrash"', 48). Rather, Pseudo-Philo utilizes the approximate language of Judg. 1:1 as the starting point for a very different narrative. Notably, in Judg. 1:1, the enemy is the Canaanites, not the Philistines. This is changed to the Amorites in *LAB* 27:1. The author may have chosen the Philistines because Judah is elsewhere associated with them (Judg. 15; 1 Sam. 17; 30:16; Ezek. 25:15) or because the towns given to Judah – Gaza, Ashkelon and Ekron – were in Philistine territory, as Bauckham brilliantly conjectures.

68. Pseudo-Philo's decision to focus on the tribe of Caleb instead of Judah would be confusing were the episode simply expanding on the exploits of Judah in Judg. 1:1-10, *pace* Bauckham ('Pseudo-Philo and the Gospels as "Midrash"', 48), who nevertheless makes the interesting observation that *Cant. Rab.* 4:7 identifies this Judah with Othniel, the son of Kenaz.

69. Pseudo-Philo seems to have forgotten Kenaz had already promised to burn them in the previous verse.

70. This was Kenaz's original plan (*LAB* 25:3). The high priest Eleazar, who dies before the book of Judges (Josh. 24:33), consults the Urim for Joshua in Num. 27:21, as he does for Kenaz. Kenaz's actions, here and elsewhere, recall 1 Sam. 14:36-46 where Saul consults the Urim and Thummim to sort the wicked before fighting the Philistines.

the manner of the Amorites which are hidden under the tent of Elas (*LAB* 25:9), as Achan confesses to the loot hidden in his tent (Josh. 7:21-22).[71] After them, the tribe of Asher confesses to housing seven golden idols of the Amorites along with precious stones (*LAB* 25:10).[72] The remainder of the narrative relates the fate of these stones, which are left over after those selected by lot are burned (*LAB* 26:2), as a 'great heap of stones' is all that remains after Achan is burned (Josh. 7:26). God vows to destroy the stones and replace them with twelve, one stone for each tribe of Israel (*LAB* 26:10-11), the description of which is borrowed entirely from Exod. 28:17-20.[73] God discloses to Kenaz that these stones will one day feature in Solomon's temple, and after it is destroyed they will be hidden, only to be revealed in the last days (*LAB* 26:12-15).[74]

Whilst the opening line of the episode is loosely based on Judg. 1:1 (*LAB* 25:1), the remaining narrative is wholly untethered to the account of Judges. The story of an Israelite leader's quest to uncover sin in the camp by casting lots from each tribe, after which the sinner is burned and stones are left over, is taken from Joshua's discovery of Achan's sin and its punishment (Josh. 7). Other details Pseudo-Philo takes from the Pentateuch, including the description of the stones (Exod. 28:17-20 in *LAB* 26:10-11), attributed quotes (i.e. Deut. 28:14 and Josh. 23:6 in *LAB* 25:3), unmarked scriptural language (i.e. Num. 15:34 and Lev. 24:12 in *LAB* 25:4), and obscure personal and place names (i.e. Gen. 2:11 in *LAB* 25:11 and 26:1). By using the scriptures as a template, Pseudo-Philo creates a colourful opening scene for this obscure judge.[75] But the clearest use of a scriptural model is reserved for the following episode.

---

71. The author's interest in the gods of the Amorites appears to come from Josh. 24:15 (also Judg. 6:10). A similar interest in the sins of the Amorites can be seen in *t. Shab.* 6:1-7:18.

72. The names of the 'seven sinful men' of the post-diluvian period who crafted these idols come from Gen. 10:6-8, though the names are corrupted (cf. *LAB* 4:6-7). The stones themselves come from 'the land of Havilah' (*de terra Evilath*), a reference to Gen. 2:11, which may also lie behind the River Fison (*LAB* 26:1; 27:15).

73. For a comparison of Pseudo-Philo's description of the stones with the MT, LXX, Philo, Josephus, Revelation and *Exod. Rab.*, see Feldman, 'Prolegomenon', cxiii.

74. Similar to the tradition of lost temple treasure in 2 Macc. 2:4-8; 2 Bar. 6:7-9; 4 Bar. 3:10. Pseudo-Philo confusingly calls Solomon *Iahel*, a name unattested elsewhere.

75. On the use of scripture in *LAB* 25–26, see Nathanael Vette, 'Kenaz: A Figure Created out of the Scriptures?', *JSP* 29 (2020): 245–59, esp. 248–51.

2. Scripturalized Narrative in Second Temple Literature   57

The episode begins with Kenaz going up to fight the Amorites (*LAB* 27:1), instead of the Philistines (cf. *LAB* 25:1).[76] In the first two days of fighting, Kenaz kills an extraordinary number of men (1,300,000). But when Kenaz rests with his wives and concubines on the third day, the army grumbles amongst themselves (*LAB* 27:2). In response, Kenaz commands his captains to arrest the detractors, who number 37, though only 35 are named, vowing to punish them once he has saved his people (*LAB* 27:3-4). To do this, Kenaz commands his captains to select three hundred men from the people, 'Go and choose from my servants three hundred men and horses of the same number' (*LAB* 25:3), which is the first of many details taken from the rout of the Midianites (Judg. 7).

Kenaz and the three hundred then go down to the Amorite camp by night (*LAB* 27:6), as Gideon and the three hundred approach the Midianite camp by night (Judg. 7:8-9). Kenaz takes 'trumpets in his hand' and gives the army instructions for battle (*LAB* 27:6), similar to Gideon who puts 'trumpets in the hands' of his soldiers and gives instructions for battle (Judg. 7:16-18). He instructs the three hundred, 'Stay here. I will go down alone to the Amorite camp. And if I blow the trumpet, you may come down; but if not, you are not to look for me there.' As he approaches the enemy camp, Kenaz overhears the Amorites talking (*LAB* 27:7), as Gideon overhears the conversation of the Midianites (Judg. 7:9-14). Kenaz prays that his sword will be recognized by the Amorites as the sign they will be delivered into his hands (*LAB* 27:7), as the Midianites recognize Gideon's sword as the sign they will be delivered into his hands (Judg. 7:14).[77] Clothed with the spirit of the Lord, Kenaz rises and draws his sword, leading the Amorites to exclaim, 'Is this not this the sword of Kenaz[?]' (*LAB* 27:9), as the Midianites exclaim, 'This is no other than the sword of Gideon' (Judg. 7:14).

Kenaz is again clothed in the spirit and 'changed into another man' (*LAB* 27:10), a phrase borrowed from the description of Saul (1 Sam. 10:6), and

---

76. There is no obvious reason for the change in the enemy's identity. The idols of the Amorites play a major role in the previous chapters (esp. *LAB* 25:9-12) and a minor role in the battle sequence (27:8), whereas the Philistines are not mentioned again until the rule of Elon (41:2-3). The gods of the Amorites are mentioned in connection with the Gideon episode (Judg. 6:10) on which *LAB* 27 is loosely modelled.

77. Earlier, Gideon asks for a sign the Midianites will be delivered into his hand, which God answers with the sign of the fleece (Judg. 6:36-40).

58 *Writing with Scripture*

begins slaying the Amorites with the help of the angel Ingethel.[78] The Lord blinds the Amorites so they begin slaying each other (*LAB* 27:10), as the LORD sets the Midianite's sword against his neighbour (Judg. 7:22). Another angel, Zeruel,[79] comes to strengthen Kenaz's hands in the midst of battle (*LAB* 27:10), as the LORD promises Gideon his 'hands shall be strengthened to attack the camp' (Judg. 7:11).[80] Kenaz is then unable to release his hand from his sword (*LAB* 27:11), a detail which is not drawn from Gideon, but from Eleazar ben Dodo, one of David's mighty men, whose 'hand clung to the sword' in battle against the Philistines (2 Sam. 23:10).[81] The following narrative (*LAB* 27:11-12) expands on this as Kenaz seeks to release his hand from the sword. When a fleeing Amorite tells Kenaz his hand can be released by slaying a Hebrew, Kenaz promptly slays the Amorite, which releases his hand from the sword.

The remainder of the episode concerns the punishment of the detractors from earlier in the narrative (*LAB* 27:15-16; cf. 27:3-4). The detractors reveal to Kenaz that they had participated in the Achan-inspired sins of *LAB* 25 – despite the fact 'all those who planned evil deeds' had already been uncovered and burned (*LAB* 26:5). In response, Kenaz burns the men in the River Fison (cf. Gen. 2:11), as he had done before. The episode concludes with the coda, 'And Kenaz ruled the people fifty-seven years, and there was fear among all his enemies all his days' (*LAB* 27:16) – which resembles the codas of the Deuteronomistic histories but especially 2 Chron. 20:29.[82]

---

78. Othniel is likewise clothed in the spirit (Judg. 3:10), as is Gideon (6:34), Jephthah (11:29), Samson (14:6, 19; 15:14), but here the description of Kenaz owes primarily to 1 Sam. 10:6.

79. The name *Zeruel* appears to be derived from זריע ('strength', 'arm'), so Ginzberg, *Legends*, 6:183–4 n. 17, probably in reference to the promise to Gideon in Judg. 7:11.

80. It is possible the interest in Kenaz's hands has its roots in the description of Othniel, son of Kenaz, whose 'hand prevailed over Cushan-rishathaim' (Judg. 3:10), although cheirological language (i.e. יד) is common to military accounts in the Jewish scriptures. A more likely source for the detail is Deut. 33:7, which says of Judah, 'strengthen his hands for him'. Although the scriptural Kenaz belongs to Judah, Pseudo-Philo mentions only the 'tribe of Caleb' (*LAB* 25:2). Nevertheless, it could be Deut. 33:7 put the author in mind of Judg. 7, which includes many references to the 'hand' (יד) of Gideon (Judg. 7:2, 7-11, 14-15), though once more, it is primarily the story of Gideon that has influenced the description of Kenaz.

81. Pseudo-Philo seems to have been drawn to 2 Sam. 23:10 by Judg. 7:11.

82. Also Josephus, *Ant.* 5.3.3.

2. *Scripturalized Narrative in Second Temple Literature* 59

LAB 27	Primary Scriptures	Secondary Scriptures
Kenaz selects three hundred men and horses to go down to the Amorite camp at night (27:5).		Gideon selects three hundred men to go down to the Midianite camp at night (Judg. 7:6-9).
Kenaz takes trumpets and goes down with the three hundred, delivering instructions on what to do if he blows the trumpets (27:6).		Gideon takes trumpets and jars and gives them to the three hundred, delivering instructions on what to do when he blows the trumpet (7:16-18).
Kenaz goes down to the camp alone (27:7).		Gideon goes down only with his servant Purah (7:10-11).
Kenaz prays for his sword to be a sign by which the Amorites recognize him, so he will know they have been 'delivered into [his] hands' (27:7).		For the Midianites, the 'sword of Gideon' is a sign God has delivered the Midianites 'into his hand' (7:14).
Kenaz overhears the Amorites saying 'Rise up, and let us fight against Israel. For we know that our sacred nymphs are there with them, and they will deliver them into our hands' (27:8; cf. 25:11).		Gideon overhears the conversation of the Midianites (7:13-14). The Amorite call to arms recalls Gideon's call to arms, 'Get up; for the LORD has given the army of Midian into your hand' (7:15; cf. *LAB* 36:2).
Kenaz is clothed with the 'spirit of the Lord' (27:9).	The 'spirit of the LORD came upon' Othniel (Judg. 3:10).	'The spirit of the LORD took possession of Gideon' (6:34).
The sword of Kenaz 'shone on the Amorites like a lightning bolt', leading them to exclaim, 'Is not this the sword of Kenaz[?]' (27:9).		The interpretation of the Midianite dream is 'This is no other than the sword of Gideon' (7:14).

Kenaz is 'clothed with the spirit of power and was changed into another man' (27:10).		Samuel tells Saul the 'spirit of the Lord will possess you, and you will be…turned into a different person' (1 Sam. 10:6).
The Lord strikes the Amorites with blindness so they slay one another (27:10).		'The LORD set every man's sword against his fellow and against all the army' (Judg. 7:22).
The angel Zeruel 'bore up the arms of Kenaz lest they should sink down' (27:10).	Othniel's 'hand prevailed over' Israel's enemies (3:10).	God promises Gideon 'afterward your hands shall be strengthened to attack the camp' (7:11). The Midianites are delivered into Gideon's 'hand' (7:7, 9, 14-15).
Kenaz's hand clings to his sword so he cannot release it (27:11).		Eleazar ben Dodo 'struck down the Philistines until his arm grew weary, though his hand clung to the sword' (2 Sam. 23:10).

Kenaz's rout of the Amorites is for the most part modelled on Gideon's rout of the Midianites. This is done by following the structure of Gideon's victory: the selection of the three hundred; the nighttime approach to the enemy camp; the instructions to the three hundred; the leader spying on the enemy; and God miraculously delivering the enemy into Gideon/Kenaz's hands. It also features memorable details from the scriptural model: the three hundred selected for battle; the trumpets; the overheard conversation; the 'sword of Gideon/Kenaz'; and the enemy slaying themselves. Scattered details appear to be drawn from the descriptions of Saul (1 Sam. 10:6) and Eleazar ben Dodo (2 Sam. 23:10). Here the use of scripture resembles the previous episode, which was primarily modelled on the sin of Achan and the description of the breastplate, whilst occasionally referencing other scriptural material. In both episodes, Pseudo-Philo takes great liberty with the scriptural model, radically departing from the underlying narrative at several key moments. This results in a somewhat awkward narrative, where Kenaz selects three hundred men in the manner of Gideon, only to go up against

2. Scripturalized Narrative in Second Temple Literature   61

the Amorite forces on his own like Eleazar ben Dodo – a sure sign the story is the author's own creation.[83]

Once more, there is no explicit connection to the description of Kenaz or Othniel in Judges. The fleeting mention of Othniel's hand prevailing in battle (Judg. 3:10) has not contributed to the description of Kenaz's hands in the same way as Gideon (esp. Judg. 7:11) and Eleazar ben Dodo (2 Sam. 23:10).[84] The episode is not simply 'an expansion of Judg 3:9-10'.[85] Nor is the figure of Gideon absorbed into Kenaz, as Pseudo-Philo later epitomizes the career of Gideon (*LAB* 35–36), including his rout of the Midianites (36:1-2). Rather, Pseudo-Philo has once more freely composed a new and independent episode in the life of this marginal figure using the scriptures as a model.

Despite the fitting conclusion to Kenaz's career (*LAB* 27:16), Pseudo-Philo adds two more episodes concerning the judge.[86] The first consists of a confusing vision granted to Kenaz before his death, in which he sees an upper and lower firmament formed out of a flame and a spring, wherein man is to dwell until the time is fulfilled (*LAB* 28:6-9). Unlike the narrative of Kenaz up to this point, this detail could be rooted in the language of Judges. Caleb, who is the brother of Kenaz (Josh. 15:17; Judg. 1:13; 3:9), gives to his daughter, Achsah, who is the wife of Othniel, the son of Kenaz (Josh. 15:17; Judg. 1:13), an inheritance of the 'upper springs and the lower springs' in the land of the Negeb (Josh. 15:19; Judg. 1:15). Almost none of this survives in *LAB*, however, as Kenaz is neither the brother of Caleb nor the father of Othniel.[87] The only detail carried over from the story of Achsah's inheritance is the reference to an upper

---

83. The author may have drawn this detail from God's promise to Gideon that he will strike down Midian 'as one man' (LXX Judg. 6:16: ὡσεὶ ἄνδρα ἕνα), despite the fact Gideon does not do this alone: the Midianites slay themselves, whilst the remainder are slaughtered by the Israelite army.

84. Pseudo-Philo may also have the promise to Judah in mind (Deut. 33:7).

85. Bauckham, 'Pseudo-Philo and the Gospels as "Midrash"', 49. As Jacobson notes (*Commentary*, 2:741), this is also the opinion of Azariah dei Rossi, *Meor Einayim*, ed. David Cassel (Warsaw, 1899), 4:85. There is no clear sign the prayer of Jabez (1 Chron. 4:10) has influenced the prayer of Kenaz (*LAB* 27:7), though Jabez was identified with Othniel in later literature (*b. Tem.* 16a; *Cant. Rab.* 4:7).

86. On the use of scripture in *LAB* 28–29, see Vette, 'Kenaz', 253–7.

87. Caleb is Kenaz's father (*LAB* 20:6) and Kenaz has no sons, leading to the division of his inheritance among his daughters under the leadership of Zebul (*LAB* 29:1-2).

62   *Writing with Scripture*

spring,[88] but even this has been transposed entirely to an apocalyptic vision, where it refers to the separation of the firmaments, an image apparently based on Gen. 1:6-9.[89]

The second is the short account of the judge Zebul (*LAB* 29), which acts as an epilogue to the life of Kenaz.[90] The first half of this chapter is devoted to the inheritance and marriage of Kenaz's daughters, arbitrated by Zebul, an episode which, aside from the strange names, appears to have been created entirely out of the inheritance and marriage of Zelophehad's daughters (Num. 27:1-11; 36:1-12), arbitrated by Moses. So concludes Pseudo-Philo's enigmatic life of Kenaz, a judge and a prophet so heroic that when Israel desires another leader, it is not Moses or Joshua they seek, but another Kenaz, 'Let all of us cast lots to see who it is who can rule as Kenaz did…a man who may free us from our distress' (*LAB* 49:1).

Instead of originating in tradition, the figure of Kenaz has been pieced together from a variety of episodes and figures in the Jewish scriptures.[91] That Pseudo-Philo often uses scriptural models at odds with one another indicates the composition is original. This can be seen in a few awkward sequences and some outright contradictions. Kenaz is selected to go up against the Philistines (*LAB* 25:1), as is Judah (Judg. 1:2, 18), but instead goes up against the Amorites (*LAB* 27:1), because they have corrupted Israel with idolatry (Josh. 24:15; Judg. 6:10). Kenaz promises to burn those selected by the lot (*LAB* 25:3), as Joshua burns Achan (Josh. 7:25), only to imprison those selected until 'it should be known what should

---

88. Bauckham's decision to treat the episode as an exegesis of Judg. 1:15 (par. Josh. 15:19) is, again, confusing ('Pseudo-Philo and the Gospels as "Midrash"', 49). A more explicit exegesis of the passage occurs in *b. Tem.* 16a, which interprets Achsah's request as concerning the Torah, so that Caleb responds, 'From him to whom all the secrets of the upper world and the nether world are revealed, ask food from him'.

89. *Gen. Rab.* 4:2 features a similar interpretation of Gen. 1:6-9, where a flame congeals the waters of the upper and lower heavens. *Midr. Tanḥ.* B *Terumah* 11 and *PRE* 4:1 likewise associate fire and solid water with the firmament of Gen 1:6-9.

90. Why Pseudo-Philo names Zebul the second judge after Joshua is again inscrutable. The position belongs to Ehud in scriptural chronology (Judg. 3:15-30), whilst Pseudo-Philo inexplicably gives the name Ehud (*Aod*) to a Midianite wizard (*LAB* 34). The name Zebul, on the other hand, comes from the ruler of Shechem who assisted Abimelech in suppressing the rebellion of Gaal (Judg. 9:28-41). Pseudo-Philo's account of Zebul, however, bears no resemblance to the description of either figure.

91. An argument made at length in Vette, 'Kenaz'.

2. Scripturalized Narrative in Second Temple Literature 63

be done about them' (*LAB* 25:4), as Moses does with the wood-gatherer (Num. 15:34) and blasphemer (Lev. 24:12). Kenaz selects three hundred to go up against the Amorites by night (*LAB* 27:5-6), like Gideon (Judg. 7:8), but instead he goes up to fight the Amorites alone (*LAB* 27:10-11), like Eleazar ben Dodo (2 Sam. 23:9-10). Kenaz prays for the Amorites to recognize him (*LAB* 27:7), as the Midianites recognize Gideon (Judg. 7:14), but is then 'changed into another man' (*LAB* 27:10), like Saul (1 Sam. 10:6). God confuses the Amorites so they slay themselves (*LAB* 27:10), as he does to the Midianites (Judg. 7:22), and yet Kenaz slays the Amorites single-handedly (*LAB* 27:10-11), like Eleazar ben Dodo (2 Sam. 23:9-10).[92]

Elsewhere Pseudo-Philo runs into similar problems when following a scriptural model. The author must create two towers of Babel in order to narrate Abram's rescue from the Daniel-inspired fiery furnace (*LAB* 6) and the dispersion of the nations (*LAB* 7). But whereas the rescue of Abram from fire has its origins in the interpretation of a particular passage (i.e. Gen. 15:7), the acts of Kenaz and Zebul do not appear to answer an exegetical query. What exactly led Pseudo-Philo to narrate the career of Kenaz will perhaps remain a mystery. But as it is, the figure of Kenaz has been created out of the descriptions of Joshua, Gideon, Saul, Eleazar ben Dodo and Zelophehad. As with the fiery furnaces of Abram and Jair, the author does not simply replicate the scriptural model, but uses it as a template to tell a new story, loosely following its structure whilst including distinctive elements from its narrative, to which additional scriptural language is added as well as flights of creative fancy.

Scripturalized narrative is not, however, Pseudo-Philo's preferred mode of using secondary scripture: this is reserved for drawing analogies between events (i.e. Josh. 23:14 in *LAB* 33:2), conflating descriptions of the same (i.e. Ps. 78:25 in *LAB* 19:5) or similar events (i.e. Gen. 42:8 in *LAB* 12:1), filling in the speech of characters (i.e. Isa. 53:7 in *LAB* 30:5; Jer. 1:6 in *LAB* 56:6) or narrative details (i.e. Gen. 49:33 in *LAB* 24:5;

---

92. To this can be added other inconsistencies: Kenaz resolves to burn those selected by lot (*LAB* 25:3), but then waits until God reveals those selected by lot should be burned (25:6); the tribes of Dan and Naphtali are not enumerated among those selected by the lot (25:4), despite having been selected by the lot (25:9); the nymphs are made by seven men, though only six are named (26:11); God announces lightning will burn the books along with the stones (26:3), but an angel burns them instead (26:8); 37 men join the revolt against Kenaz, though only 35 are named (27:4); Kenaz burns 'all those who planned evil deeds' (26:5), and yet some are still alive later in the narrative (27:15).

64   *Writing with Scripture*

Jdt. 13:7-9 in *LAB* 31:7).[93] Nevertheless the above episodes show Pseudo-Philo repeatedly drawing on scriptural models to compose new narrative, which may have its origins in exegesis (i.e. Abram and Jair), or simply owe to the creativity of the author (i.e. Kenaz).

The Genesis Apocryphon

The *Genesis Apocryphon* (1QapGen) was one of the first scrolls discovered at Qumran.[94] Whilst the unfortunate title chosen by its first editors implies a derivative status, there is no reason to suppose the covenanters at Qumran held it to be apocryphal.[95] Indeed, as Fitzmyer conjectures, 'One might conceivably argue that it was hidden away in Cave 1 precisely for [the opposite] reason'.[96] Consisting of 23 partially preserved columns, the Aramaic text roughly follows the narrative of Genesis 5–15, narrated mostly from the first person with three distinct narrative voices:

93. There is still the question of what inspired Pseudo-Philo's distinctive use of scripture. Reinmuth (*Pseudo-Philo und Lukas*, 118) thinks the author was governed by a principle of correspondence, 'Das Korrelationsprinzip setzt voraus, daß Ereignisse durch das Wirken Gottes so korreliert sind, daß sie im Verhältnis der einfachen oder reziproken (bzw. kontrapunktischen) Entsprechung zueinander stehen'. So too Murphy, who thinks Pseudo-Philo's association of similar scriptural episodes 'underlines the structure and interconnectedness of history, which in turn illustrates God's control of events' (Murphy, *Pseudo-Philo*, 59). Fisk, on the other hand, concludes Pseudo-Philo writes from 'a *hermeneutical* conviction that the key for unlocking Scripture's meaning is to be found *in Scripture*' (*Do You Not Remember?*, 327, emphasis original). Bauckham makes the similar claim that Pseudo-Philo is always 'interpreting scripture by scripture' ('Pseudo-Philo and the Gospels as "Midrash"', 34, 59). This may be true when applied to Pseudo-Philo's characterization of Moses and Joshua, impressively studied by Fisk (*Do You Not Remember?*, 264–313). But as the narratives of Kenaz and Zebul show, an exegetical purpose is not always present. In the final analysis, something as small as the intrusion of a detail from the death of Jacob in the death of Joshua (*LAB* 24:5; cf. Gen. 49:33) may be purely aesthetic.

94. J. A. Fitzmyer, *The Genesis Apocryphon of Qumran Cave 1 (1Q20): A Commentary*, 3rd ed., Biblica et Orientalia 18B (Rome: Editrice Pontificio Istituto Biblico, 2004), 13. Citations of the English and Aramaic text, unless stated otherwise, come from the recent critical edition by Daniel A. Machiela, *The Dead Sea Genesis Apocryphon: A New Text and Translation with Introduction and Special Treatment of Columns 13–17*, STDJ 79 (Leiden: Brill, 2009).

95. So Fitzmyer: 'For this word inevitably evokes its counterpart, a canonical book, and consequently introduces into Qumran literature a slight anachronism' (*The Genesis Apocryphon*, 16).

96. Fitzmyer, *The Genesis Apocryphon*, 16

2. *Scripturalized Narrative in Second Temple Literature* 65

Lamech, Noah and Abram. Aside from this novel mode of narration, the *Apocryphon* exhibits distinctive compositional and exegetical techniques in its treatment of the Genesis narrative.[97] This includes the author's decision to have Noah offer sacrifices before exiting the ark so as to provide purification for the earth (1QapGen 10:12-13; cf. Gen. 8:15-21), the omission of Noah's drunkenness in favour of a wine-fueled vision (1QapGen 12:13–15:21; cf. Gen. 9:18-27) and Abram's dream of the palm and the cedar as the pretext for his and Sarai's deception of Pharaoh (1QapGen 19:14-21; cf. Gen. 12:11-13).

In addition to the Genesis narrative, the *Apocryphon* shares material with *Jubilees* and the so-called Book of Noah portion of *1 Enoch*. This includes the entire section from cols. 2 to 5:27 which parallels the birth of Noah narrated in *1 Enoch* 106–107. The agreement with *Jubilees* can be seen in the descent of the watchers in the 'days of Jared' (1QapGen 3:3; *Jub.* 4:15), Enoch learning 'everything' from the angels (1QapGen 2:20-21; *Jub.* 4:21), Bitenosh/Betenos as Lamech's wife (1QapGen 2:3-5; *Jub.* 4:28), the description of the flood destroying 'man and cattle and beasts and birds and everything which walks / moves on the earth' (1QapGen 6:26; *Jub.* 5:2, 20), Noah's atoning sacrifice (1QapGen 10:13; *Jub.* 6:2), the timing of Noah's harvest (1QapGen 19:7-8; *Jub.* 13:8), Abram and Sarai's five-year sojourn in Egypt before her abduction (1QapGen 19:23; *Jub.* 13:11) and the unmarked quotation of Num. 13:22 in connection with their arrival in Egypt (1QapGen 19:9-10; *Jub.* 13:12).[98]

That there was a literary relationship between *Jubilees* and the *Apocryphon* is certain. Whilst the direction of this relationship has been a matter of debate – with some prominent scholars advocating for the *Apocryphon*'s priority – its tendency to make corrections to the Genesis narrative which are unparalleled in *Jubilees* effectively demonstrates its posteriority.[99] For example, in 1QapGen 10:13–11:1, Noah offers

---

97. Explored in greater detail by Moshe J. Bernstein, 'The Genesis Apocryphon: Compositional and Interpretive Perspectives', in *A Companion to Biblical Interpretation in Early Judaism*, ed. Matthias Henze (Grand Rapids, MI: Eerdmans, 2012), 157–79.

98. For a full list of agreements see the table provided by Daniel K. Falk, *The Parabiblical Texts: Strategies for Extending the Scriptures among the Dead Sea Scrolls*, LSTS 63 (London: T&T Clark, 2007), 31–5.

99. Among those advocating the priority of the *Apocryphon* is Vermes, who argues that the condensed narrative in *Jubilees* suggests its posteriority. See Geza Vermes, '2. The Genesis Apocryphon from Qumran', in Emil Schürer, *The History of the Jewish People in the Age of Jesus Christ*, rev. Geza Vermes, Fergus Millar and Martin Goodman (Edinburgh: T. & T. Clark, 1986), 3.1:318–25.

66 *Writing with Scripture*

the sacrifice before exiting the ark so as not to defile the land, whereas in Gen. 8:15-20 and *Jub.* 6:1-3 Noah exits the ark before the sacrifice; Noah's drunkenness is omitted in 1QapGen 12:13–15:21, whereas *Jub.* 7:6-7 mostly preserves Gen. 9:21-27; 1QapGen 20:22-23 explains how Pharaoh came to know Sarai was Abram's wife, whereas Gen. 12:18-19 and *Jub.* 13:13-15 offer no explanation; Abram tours the land in fulfilment of God's command in 1QapGen 21:13-20, whereas in Gen. 13:14-17 and *Jub.* 13:19-21, the command is left unfulfilled; and Abram returns the spoils of the king of Sodom in fulfilment of his pledge in 1QapGen 22:24-26, whereas in Gen. 14:22-23 and *Jub.* 13:28-29, the pledge is left unfulfilled.[100] What is more, the chronology shared between *Jubilees* and the *Apocryphon* seems to sit easily with the former's systematization of 'weeks' whilst posing problems for the latter: Sarai is held captive for an unusually long two years (1QapGen 20:16-19; cf. *Jub.* 13:11) and the narrative struggles to reconcile Abram and Sarai's seven-year sojourn in Egypt with the ten years of Gen. 16:3 (1QapGen 22:27-29; cf. *Jub.* 13:10-16).[101] At the same time, the *Apocryphon* appears to have adapted the Enochic material to suit its purposes: the exchange between Lamech and Bitenosh (1QapGen 2:3-18; cf. *1 En.* 106:1) serves as a model for Abram and Sarai's exchange (1QapGen 19:17-21) and Lamech's first-person narration fits the testamental character of the scroll.[102] The additional presence of Enochic language – 'watchers and holy ones' (1QapGen 2:1, 16, 20; *1 En.* 1:2; 10:1; 12:2); 'the great holy one' (1QapGen 2:14, 16; *1 En.* 1:3; 10:1) – and Abram's narration to the Egyptian princes from 'the book of the words of Enoch' (1QapGen 19:25, 29) makes the *Apocryphon*'s dependence on an Enochic source all but certain.[103] Whilst

---

100. James A. Kugel offers more arguments to this effect, see *A Walk Through Jubilees: Studies in the Book of Jubilees and the World of its Creation*, JSJSup 156 (Leiden: Brill, 2012), 312–23; as does J. C. VanderKam, *Jubilees 1–21*, Hermeneia (Minneapolis, MN: Fortress, 2018), 93–4.

101. Kugel, *A Walk Through Jubilees*, 330–2; cf. Ben Z. Wacholder, 'How Long did Abram Stay in Egypt?', *HUCA* 35 (1964): 43–56 (52–3), who thinks the *Apocryphon*'s less developed chronology indicates its priority.

102. This argument is expanded by George W. E. Nickelsburg, 'Patriarchs Who Worry About Their Wives: A Haggadic Tendency in the Genesis Apocryphon', in *George W. E. Nickeslburg in Perspective: An Ongoing Dialogue of Learning, Volume 2*, ed. Jacob Neusner and Alan J. Avery-Peck, JSJSup 82 (Leiden: Brill, 2003), 177–99.

103. Nickelsburg also sees the influence of an Enochic source on the *Apocryphon*'s account of Sarai's captivity (*Jewish Literature Between the Bible and the Mishnah* [Minneapolis, MN; Fortress Press, 2011], 176). Whilst Enochic material already

2. Scripturalized Narrative in Second Temple Literature 67

the Enochic source appears to be the primary source for columns 2–5, the remaining narrative tends to follow Genesis more closely than it does *Jubilees*, and certainly more so than the Enochic source. In this sense, to borrow a phrase from Pseudo-Philo scholarship, the Genesis narrative functions as the *primary scripture* for the *Apocryphon*.

The Compositional Use of the Jewish Scriptures in the Genesis Apocryphon

In its treatment of the Genesis narrative, the *Apocryphon* employs language and details from related and unrelated scriptural texts – in other words, *secondary scripture*. Some of this material owes to its sources. For example, *Jubilees* depicts the Patriarchs fulfilling the requirements of the law prior to Sinai, as does the *Apocryphon*: in his first sacrifice, Noah offers a goat (1QapGen 10:13; par. *Jub.* 6:2; cf. Num. 15:24-25), burns fat upon the fire (1QapGen 10:14; par. *Jub.* 6:3; cf. Lev. 4:19), pours out blood on the altar (1QapGen 10:15; cf. Lev. 4:18) offers turtledoves kneaded with oil (1QapGen 10:15-16; par. *Jub.* 6:3; cf. Num. 15:24) and salts the sacrifices (1QapGen 10:17; par. *Jub.* 6:3; cf. Lev. 2:13); the Noachide prohibition against consuming blood (Gen. 9:4) becomes the Levitical prohibition (1QapGen 11:17; cf. Lev. 7:26); and the harvesting of Noah's vineyard (Gen. 9:20-21) becomes the Levitical feast of the first-fruits (1QapGen 12:13-16; par. *Jub.* 7:2; cf. Lev. 19:23-25).[104] Again like *Jubilees*, the *Apocryphon* combines the post-diluvian mandate to Noah (Gen. 9:1-7) with the creation mandate in Gen 1:28 (1QapGen 11:16-17; par. *Jub.* 6:5-9) and mentions the building of Hebron (Num. 33:22) in connection with Egypt (1QapGen 19:9; par. *Jub.* 13:12).

appears in *Jubilees*, the presence of Enochic language in the *Apocryphon* absent in *Jubilees* suggests that the Enochic source and *Jubilees* were two independent sources for the *Apocryphon*.

104. A central belief of *Jubilees* is that the law is eternal and existed before Sinai (*Jub.* Title; 2:33; 3:14; 6:14; 13:25; 23:32; 32:10; 33:16; 49:17). It was this law the Patriarchs obeyed: 'And [Jacob] worshiped the LORD with all of his heart according to the commands which were revealed according to the division of the days of his generations' (*Jub.* 36:20). This is not always maintained consistently, however, as Reuben and Bilhah are excused because the law 'had not been revealed' (*Jub.* 33:16), and yet Bilhah avoids punishment because of the law (*Jub.* 33:1-9; cf. Lev. 20:11). But for the most part, the Patriarchs are shown upholding the law and instituting aspects of it themselves. For a redaction-critical explanation of these inconsistencies, see Michael Segal, *The Book of Jubilees: Rewritten Bible, Redaction, Ideology and Theology*, JSJSup 117 (Leiden: Brill, 2007), 73–82.

68   *Writing with Scripture*

Elsewhere, the use of secondary scripture appears to be original: Abram's dream of the palm and the cedar (1QapGen 19:14-15) borrows the language of Ps. 92:13;[105] the description of the Rephaim (1QapGen 21:18-29) is taken from Deut. 2:20; and the description of Helbon reflects Ezek. 27:18 (1QapGen 22:10; cf. MT and LXX Gen. 14:15; Josephus, *Ant.* 1.10.1). Somewhat less certain is Pharaoh's gift to Sarai of '[m]uch si[lver and g]old and much clothing of *fine linen and purple*' (1QapGen 20:31: בוץ וארגואן) reflecting Ahasuerus' gift to Mordecai of a 'great golden crown and a mantle of *fine linen and purple*' (Est. 8:15: בוץ וארגמן).

The *Apocryphon* also features a few passages which appear to be modelled more extensively on secondary scriptural material. Daniel Falk raises the possibility that the song of Hirqanos and the Egyptians extolling Sarai's beauty (1QapGen 20:2-8) is 'a midrash on the ideal Israelite wife from Prov. 31.10-31 combined with Song of Songs, inspired by Gen. 12.11 ("I know well that you are a beautiful woman")'.[106] As in Canticles, Hirqanos' song praises Sarai's face (1QapGen 20:2, 4; cf. Song 2:14), hair (1QapGen 20:3; cf. Song 4:1; 6:5), eyes (1QapGen 20:3; cf. Song 4:1; 6:5), nose (1QapGen 20:3; cf. Song 7:4), breasts (1QapGen 20:4; cf. Song 4:5; 7:3, 7-8) and thighs (1QapGen 20:6; cf. Song 7:1).[107]

---

105. The identification of Abram and Sarai with the palm and the cedar may have its origins in Ps. 92:14, 'In old age they still produce fruit' (עוד ינובון בשׂיבה; cf. Gen. 18:11-15). A similar exegesis occurs in *Gen. Rab.* 41:1. Noah is also identified with the cedar (1QapGen 14:9; *Gen. Rab.* 30:7). For its significance see John C. Reeves, *Jewish Lore in Manichaean Cosmogony: Studies in the Book of Giants Traditions*, Monographs of the Hebrew Union College 14 (Cincinnati, OH: Hebrew Union College, 1992), 99–100; Machiela, *The Dead Sea Genesis Apocryphon*, 95; Esther Eshel, 'The Dream Visions in the Noah Story of the Genesis Apocryphon and Related Texts', in *Northern Lights on the Dead Sea Scrolls: Proceedings of the Nordic Qumran Network 2003–2006*, ed. Anders Klostergaard Petersen et al., STDJ 80 (Leiden: Brill, 2009), 41–61. Falk also notes the lover and his beloved are represented by the cedar and palm in Song 5:15 and 7:7-8 (*The Parabiblical Texts*, 87), which is interpreted as a reference to Abraham in *Tg. Cant.* 7:9.

106. Falk, *The Parabiblical Texts*, 86.

107. The praise of Sarai's forehead, white complexion, arms, hands, palms, fingers and legs, are, however, unparalleled. At the same time, only the statement 'Her beauty *surpasses* (על[י]א)' that of all women' (1QapGen 20:7; cf. Prov. 31:29: עלית) offers any verbal correspondence with Prov. 31. It could be, instead of literary dependence, that these similarities simply reflect the shared *topos* in antiquity of extolling a woman's beauty.

2. Scripturalized Narrative in Second Temple Literature 69

Nickelsburg makes the intriguing case that Pharaoh taking Sarai as his wife (1QapGen 19–20) is modelled on the watchers taking the daughters of man as their wives (*1 En.* 6–11).[108] Whilst the verbal evidence for this is slim, the fact that during the episode Abram reads to the princes from 'the book of the words of Enoch' (לספר מלי חנוך) means it is not out of the realm of possibility. What is sure, however, is that the *Apocryphon* uses the similar account of Sara and Abimelech (Gen. 20) to refurbish the account in Gen. 12:10-20: the detail that Pharaoh Zoan was 'not able to approach her' (1QapGen 20:17) comes from Gen. 20:4, whereas Lot's language is borrowed from Gen. 20:7, 'Then he will pray over him so that he might live' (1QapGen 20:23).[109] Other details in the episode reflect the scriptural depiction of Egypt, as when Pharaoh sends for the 'wise men of Egypt and all the magicians' (1QapGen 20:18-19), an image found in the narratives of Joseph (Gen. 41:8) and Moses (Exod. 7:11).[110]

But by far the most extensive use of secondary scripture is found in the *Apocryphon*'s account of the Noachide covenant (1QapGen 11:11-19), wherein God's promise to Noah is modelled on the promise of land to Abram.

Noah and Abram (and Isaac): 1QapGen 11 and Genesis 13, 15 (and 26)

The *Apocryphon* is not alone in conflating the words of the creation mandate (Gen. 1:28-30) with the post-diluvian mandate (1QapGen 11:16-17).[111] Whilst Gen. 9:1 reads, 'Be fruitful and multiply, and fill the earth', the *Apocryphon* has '[Be fr]uitful and multiply, and fill the land. Rule over all of them' (1QapGen 11:16) – which reflects Gen. 1:28: 'Be fruitful and multiply, and fill the earth and subdue it; and have dominion over [every living thing]'. This reading is also preserved in the Septuagint (LXX Gen 9:1) and Philo (*Quaest. in Gen.* 2.56), but is notably absent in *Jubilees* (*Jub.* 6:5-6).[112] The tradition is itself suggested by the recapitulation of the creation saga already inherent

---

108. See the synoptic table in Nickelsburg, 'Patriarchs Who Worry About their Wives', 190.

109. Like Pseudo-Philo, the *Apocryphon* conflates similar episodes; see Bernstein, 'Compositional and Interpretive Perspectives', 173–5.

110. As observed by Bernstein, who also notes the magician's inability to perform (1QapGen 20:20) is similar to Exod. 9:11 ('Compositional and Interpretive Perspectives', 173).

111. Extensively discussed in Falk, *The Parabiblical Texts*, 54–64.

112. Though 'rule' does appear at *Jub.* 6:5 in the Ge'ez ms. 12.

70   *Writing with Scripture*

in the Hebrew text (MT Gen. 9:1-7).[113] The *Apocryphon* builds on this tradition by omitting the provision to eat meat in Gen. 9:2-3, preserving the vegetation-only diet of Gen. 1:29 (1QapGen 11:17).[114] But the *Apocryphon* does more than simply recapitulate the creation mandate, it also uses the Noachide covenant to anticipate the Abrahamic covenant, particularly God's promise of land to Abram (Gen. 13:14-17).

The account begins with Noah narrating in the first person, '[Then] I, Noah, went out and walked through the land, in its length and in its breadth' (1QapGen 11:11: [אדין] אנה נוח נפקת והלכת בארעא לאורכהא ולפותיהא).[115] This is borrowed from Gen. 13:17, where God commands Abram, 'Rise up, walk through the length and breadth of the land'. The language corresponds *mutatis mutandis* with Targums *Onkelos* and *Neofiti* on Gen. 13:17: 'through the land, in its length and in its breadth' (הל[יך]ק בארעא לארכה ולפתי[י]ה).[116] Having praised the LORD for the land, Noah continues: '[the LORD] a[ppeared] to me from heaven, speaking with me and saying to me, "Do not fear, O Noah! I am with you and with those of yours sons who will be like you forever"' (1QapGen 11:15). The language here merges two separate appearances of the LORD to Abram and Isaac: '[The] word of the LORD came to Abram in a vision, "Do not be afraid, Abram, I am your shield"' (Gen. 15:1); '[The] LORD appeared to [Isaac] and said, "I am the God of your father Abraham; do not be afraid, for I am with you"' (Gen. 26:24).[117] The *Apocryphon* conflates the theophanies again when God addresses Abram later in the narrative: 'And now do not fear; I am with you, and will be for you a support and strength; I am a shield over you, and a buckler for you against those stronger than you' (1QapGen 22:30-31).

In particular, the personal address to Noah – 'Do not fear, O Noah!' (1QapGen 11:15: אל תדחל יא נוח) – reflects the opening words of Abram's vision: 'Do not fear, Abram' (*Tgs. Onk.* and *Neof.* on Gen. 15:1: לא תדחל אברם).[118] The other details come from the appearance to Isaac – '[The

---

113. See especially Carol M. Kaminski, *From Noah to Israel: Realization of the Primaeval Blessing After the Flood*, JSOTSup 413 (London: T&T Clark, 2004).

114. This makes the command to abstain from blood awkward (1QapGen 11:6; cf. Gen. 9:3-4; *Jub.* 6:6-7).

115. My translation.

116. See also *Tg. Ps.-J.* on Gen. 13:17: 'through its length and through its breath' (לארכא ולפתיא). Compare with *b. B. Bat.* 15b; 16a; 100a; *b. Sanh.* 111a; *b. Sab.* 118a.

117. The passages also appear to be conflated in Isa. 41:10: 'Do not fear, for I am with you, do not be afraid, for I am your God; I will strengthen you, I will help you, I will uphold you with my victorious right hand'.

118. *Tg. Ps.-J.* on Gen. 15:1 simply reads 'do not fear' (לא תדחל).

2. *Scripturalized Narrative in Second Temple Literature* 71

LORD] appeared ([תחזי]א)...saying (אמר)...I am with you (עמך אנה)'
(1QapGen 11:15) – which parallels the targum: '[the *memra* of the LORD
was] revealed (אתגלי)...saying (אמר)...I am with you (עמך אנה)' (*Tg.
Neof.* on Gen. 26:24).[119] And God's promise to Isaac – 'I am with you'
(עמך אנה) – also finds its way into God's appearance to Abram later in the
Apocryphon (1QapGen 22:31; cf. Gen. 15:1).

1QapGen 11[120]	Primary Scriptures	Secondary Scriptures	1QapGen 21-22
Noah surveys the land (11:1-10).		Abram is commanded to survey the land (Gen. 13:14-17).	Abram surveys the land (21:10-12).
Noah went out and walked 'through the land, in its length and in its breadth' (והלכת בארעא לאורכהא ולפותיהא) (11:11).		God commands Abram to walk 'through the length and breadth of the land' (הל]י[ק בארעא לארכה ולפתי]י[ה) (*Tgs. Onk.* and *Neof.* on Gen. 13:17).	God commands Abram to walk and inspect the 'length and width' of the land (21:14).
The LORD 'appeared' ([תחזי]א) to Noah, 'saying' (אמר) (11:15).		The *memra* of the LORD was 'revealed' (אתגלי) to Abram, 'saying' (אמר) (*Tgs. Onk.* and *Neof.* on Gen. 26:24; cf. MT 15:1; 26:24).	'God appeared to Abram in a vision and said to him' (22:27).

119. The Hebrew text of Gen. 26:24 partially preserved in 4Q12 1:4 corresponds
with the MT. The Targums, especially Neofiti, substitute the Heb. ירא ('appear') and
its Ar. equivalent חזי ('appear') with גלי ('reveal') when it concerns divine action. See
Martin McNamara, *Targum and Testament Revisited: Aramaic Paraphrases of the
Hebrew Bible: A Light on the New Testament*, 2nd ed. (Grand Rapids, MI: Eerdmans,
2010), 147–53.

120. See also the detailed tables sans Aramaic parallels in Falk, *The Parabiblical
Texts*, 55–68, tables 5-9.

'Do not fear, O Noah' (אל תדחל יא נוח) (11:15).		'Do not fear, Abram' (לא תדחל אברם) (*Tgs. Onk.* and *Neof.* on Gen. 15:1; cf. MT and *Tgs.* on Gen. 26:24).	'And now do not fear' (22:30).
'I am with you' (11:15) (עמך אנה).		'I am with you' (עמך אנה) (*Tg. Neof.* on Gen. 26:24).	'For I am with you' (22:30).
'Be fruitful and multiply, and fill the land' (11:16).	'Be fruitful and multiply, and fill the earth' (Gen. 9:1; cf. 9:7).	'Be fruitful and multiply, and fill the earth' (1:28).	
'Rule over all of them' (11:16)		'Rule over' every living thing (1:28; cf. LXX 9:1).	
'Behold, I am giving to you… everything for food; that of the vegetation and herbs of the land' (11:16-17).	'Every moving thing that lives shall be food for you; and just as I gave you the green plants, I give you everything' (9:3).	'Behold, I have given you every plant yielding seed that is upon the earth, and every tree with seed in its fruit; you shall have them for food' (1:29).	
'But you shall not eat any blood' (11:17).	'You shall not eat flesh with its life, that is, its blood' (9:4).	'You shall not eat any blood' (Lev. 7:26).	

Whilst there is a common tradition associating the post-diluvian mandate with the creation mandate, the explicit association of the Abrahamic covenant with the promise of land to Noah is, by all accounts, unique to the *Apocryphon*.[121] On one level, it is consistent with the *Apocryphon*'s effort to elevate Noah's significance, having already recounted Noah's miraculous birth (1QapGen 2:1–5:27) and election because of his

121. Kaminski makes the interesting case that Genesis implicitly connects the promise to Abram with the post-diluvian mandate (*From Noah to Israel*, 92–110), though seems to be unaware the *Apocryphon* makes the same connection.

2. Scripturalized Narrative in Second Temple Literature   73

righteousness (6:1-6, 14-16, 23). But a remarkable bit of exegesis lies behind the association of Noah with Abram. God's appearance to Noah in col. 11 is followed by a dream (partially preserved in cols. 12–15) in which God reveals to Noah the land to be inherited by his descendants (cols. 16–17). The *Apocryphon* takes this description of the land from the division of the earth among the descendants of Noah narrated in *Jubilees* (8:10–9:13; cf. Gen. 10:2-31). Thus, Noah is shown receiving land from God for his descendants just like Abram (Gen. 12:7; 13:15; 15:18-21; 1QapGen 21:12).

The *Apocryphon* later has Abram tour the land given to Noah.[122] First he surveys the portion of Shem (*Jub.* 8:12-21; partially preserved in 1QapGen 16:16-25) from the River of Egypt to Lebanon and Senir, from the Great Sea to Hauran, from Gebal to Kadesh and from the Great Desert to the Euphrates. He then surveys the portion given to Shem's sons, especially Arpachshad (*Jub.* 9:2-6; partially preserved in 1QapGen 17:7-14), from the Gihon River to Mount Taurus, then along the Great Sea of Salt until the Euphrates River, and from there to Erythrean Sea and then back to where he started at the River Gihon. By having Abram survey the land given by Noah to Shem and his descendants, the *Apocryphon* is able to tie the Abrahamic covenant to the covenant given to Abram's forebears, tracing it through Arpachshad, Shem and, ultimately, to Noah. The promise of land to Abram then becomes a recapitulation of the promise to Noah. Abram inherits the land *because* it is his birthright as a descendant of Noah through Shem.

---

122. Many have noted the distinctive geography of the *Apocryphon* and *Jubilees*; i.e. Philip S. Alexander, 'Notes on the "Imago Mundi" of the Book of Jubilees', *JJS* 38 (1982): 197–213; Francis Schmidt, 'Naissance d'une geographe juive', in *Moïse géographe: Recherches sur les representations juives et chrétiennes de l'éspace*, ed. Alain Desreumaux and Schmidt (Paris: Vrin, 1988), 13–30; James M. Scott, *Geography in Early Judaism and Christianity: The Book of Jubilees*, SNTSMS 113 (Cambridge: Cambridge University Press, 2002), 23–43; Esther Eshel, 'The Imago Mundi of the Genesis Apocryphon', in *Heavenly Tablets: Interpretation, Identity and Tradition in Ancient Judaism*, ed. Lynn LiDonnici and Andrea Lieber, JSJSup 119 (Leiden: Brill, 2007), 111–31; Daniel A. Machiela, '"Each to His Own Inheritance": Geography as an Evaluative Tool in the Genesis Apocryphon', *DSD* 15 (2008): 50–66; Machiela, *The Dead Sea Genesis Apocryphon*, 105–30; Katell Berthelot, 'Casting Lots and Distributing Territories: The Hellenistic Background of the Book of Jubilees and the Genesis Apocryphon', in *Sibyls, Scriptures, and Scrolls: John Collins at Seventy*, ed. Joel Baden, Hindy Najman and Eibert J. C. Tigchelaar, JSJSup 175 (Leiden: Brill, 2017), 148–66.

74 *Writing with Scripture*

The inclusion of Abrahamic elements (Gen. 13:14-17; 15:1) in the account of Noah has its roots in this exegesis. Noah is modelled on Abram because they are beneficiaries of the same covenant. That this covenant also extends to Abram's descendants explains how elements from the story of Isaac (Gen. 26:24) find their way into the narratives of Noah (1QapGen 11:15) and Abram (1QapGen 22:30).[123] For the *Apocryphon*, the promise of land to Israel does not originate with Abram, but is traced through Isaac and Abram, all the way back to Arpachshad, the son of Shem, the son of Noah.[124] The scripturalized narrative in 1QapGen 11:11-17 reflects this by merging the descriptions of Abram and Isaac with Noah. The *Apocryphon* thus elaborately threads together four passages concerning the multiplication of offspring: the promise to Isaac (Gen. 26:24), the promise to Abram (15:1-6), the post-diluvian mandate (9:1-7) and the creation mandate (1:28-30). Just as *Jubilees* grounds the giving of the law long before Sinai, the *Apocryphon* is able to find a primordial origin for the promise of land to Israel, so for both, the adage applies: the older, the better.

1 Maccabees

There are understandably fewer references to the Jewish scriptures in 1 Maccabees than in the *Liber Antiquitatum Biblicarum* and the *Genesis Apocryphon*. The book purports to relate the events which transpired under the brutal reign of the Seleucid Antiochus IV Epiphanes and the early years of Hasmonaean leadership in the first half of the second century BCE. 1 Maccabees nevertheless cites the Jewish scriptures in a number of places, whilst also weaving unmarked scriptural elements into the narrative. There is, however, little verbal correspondence between the scriptural language in 1 Maccabees and any surviving text of the scriptures. This is because, although all existing manuscripts of 1 Maccabees can be traced back to a Greek text, the style and syntax appear to be distinctly Semitic in character, suggesting a Hebrew *Vorlage*[125] – a

---

123. The implications for Abram's descendants may have been explained following the lacuna in the final column (1QapGen 22:34).

124. That the *Apocryphon* associates Abram's inheritance with Shem's portion on the basis of *Jub.* 8:10–9:13, whilst *Jubilees* makes no such association, is further proof of its posteriority.

125. Noted almost a century ago by H. W. Ettelson, 'The Integrity of 1 Maccabees', *Transactions of the Connecticut Academy of Arts and Sciences* 27 (1925): 249–384. This has since been the view of all major commentaries, see Solomon

2. Scripturalized Narrative in Second Temple Literature 75

conclusion which is also suggested by the mention of a Hebrew book of the Maccabees by ancient witnesses.[126]

Differences between 1 Maccabees and the LXX often owe to the author's tendency for paraphrastic quotations. Consider the quotation in 1 Macc. 7:17 – 'The flesh of your saints and their blood they poured out around about Jerusalem, and there was none to bury them' (σάρκας ὁσίων σου καὶ αἷμα αὐτῶν ἐξέχεαν κύκλῳ Ιερουσαλημ, καὶ οὐκ ἦν αὐτοῖς ὁ θάπτων) – which no doubt reflects Ps. 79(78):2-3, but departs from the literal rendering of the Hebrew in the LXX: 'The flesh of your saints for the wild animals of the earth; they poured out their blood like water, around about Jerusalem, and there was no one to bury them' (τὰς σάρκας τῶν ὁσίων σου τοῖς θηρίοις τῆς γῆς· ἐξέχεαν τὸ αἷμα αὐτῶν ὡς ὕδωρ κύκλῳ Ιερουσαλημ, καὶ οὐκ ἦν ὁ θάπτων).[127] Other differences owe to the idiosyncrasies of the Greek translator.[128] When the Gentiles say, 'We will blot out the memory of them from among humans' (1 Macc. 12:53: ἐξάρωμεν ἐξ ἀνθρώπων τὸ μνημόσυνον αὐτῶν), the language comes from Deut. 32:26, which is rendered in the LXX, 'I will stop the memory of them from among humans' (παύσω δὴ ἐξ ἀνθρώπων τὸ μνημόσυνον αὐτῶν). In its *hiphil* form, שבת can refer to 'stopping' (cf. Hos. 2:11) and 'removing' (cf. Ps. 89:44), with the Greek translator of 1 Maccabees opting for the latter.[129]

Zeitlin, *The First Book of Maccabees*, with English translation of the text by Sidney Tedesche (New York, NY: Harper, 1950), 33–4; John C. Dancy, *A Commentary on 1 Maccabees* (Oxford: Blackwell, 1954), 8–9; Félix-Marie Abel and Jean Starcky, *Les Livres des Maccabées* (Paris: Cerf, 1961), 15; John R. Bartlett, *The First and Second Books of the Maccabees* (Cambridge: Cambridge University Press, 1973), 14–15; Jonathan A. Goldstein, *1 Maccabees: A New Translation with Introduction and Commentary*, AB 41 (Garden City, NY: Doubleday, 1976), 14–16; Klaus-Dietrich Schunck, ׳, JSHRZ 1/4 (Mohn: Gütersloh, 1980), 289.

126. Origen, quoted in Eusebius, *Hist. eccl.* 6.25.2; Jerome, *Prologus galeatus* (PL 28.593-604).

127. LXX, my translation.

128. A reconstructed Hebrew text is attempted by Günter Neuhaus, *Studien zu den poetischen Stücken im ersten Makkabäerbuch* (Würzburg: Echter-Verlag, 1974), 40–75.

129. See BDB *s.v.* שבת. The hortatory subjunctive ἐξάρωμεν in 1 Macc. 12:53 could conceivably come from the imperfect cohortative נשביתה, which better preserves the sense of the Hebrew in Deut. 32:26 than the future παύσω of the LXX. Although the LXX often translates שבת with παύω (LXX Gen. 8:22; 2 Kgs 23:5, 11; Isa. 14:4 etc.), ונשבתו is rendered as ἐξαρθήσεται in Ezek. 6:6, in what is arguably an analogous context to Deut. 32:26.

76 *Writing with Scripture*

At the same time, agreements with the LXX could be the result of so-called biblicisms. The phrase in 1 Macc. 1:39 – 'Her feasts were turned into mourning' – may reflect a common expression, rather than Amos 8:10 (cf. Tob. 2:6). The same might apply to the description of Antiochus' sin as a 'desolating sacrilege' (1 Macc 1:54: βδέλυγμα ἐρημώσεως; cf. Dan. 11:31).[130] And as Rappaport and others have observed, the author adopts an evidently 'biblical' style of narration.[131] This is perhaps most visible in the Deuteronomistic refrain appended to the career of Judas: 'Now the rest of the acts of Judas, and his wars and the brave deeds that he did, and his greatness, have not been recorded, for they were very many' (1 Macc. 9:22; also 16:23; cf. 1 Kgs. 11:41; 14:19 etc.). To this can be added the anachronistic descriptions of the surrounding nations as the scriptural 'sons of Esau' (1 Macc. 5:3, 65; cf. Obad. 17-21), 'Amon' (1 Macc. 5:6) and 'the Philistines' (5:66, 68).

The scriptural style of 1 Maccabees serves the propagandistic aims of the author. The Hasmonaean dynasty could not easily lay hold of the traditional means of validating their rule, in either Davidic or Zadokite descent. The author thus seeks to legitimize their rule using the Jewish scriptures.[132] Where hereditary ties were lacking, the author was able to

130. Although the 'desolating sacrilege' may have been a common idiom for the events of 15 Kislev, 167 BCE, the author is elsewhere aware of Danielic tradition (1 Macc. 2:59-60; cf. Dan. 3:1-30; 6:17-24). Whereas 'desolating sacrilege' is an unusual phrase, the general sentiment of the song of the Judaeans following the defeat of Gorgias, 'for he is good, for his mercy endures for ever' (1 Macc. 4:24), may have existed as a common refrain apart from the *hallel* (Ps. 118:1, 29: 'for he is good, his steadfast love endures forever'), also reflected in the psalm at the end of Hebrew ms. B of Sir. 51:12. Other potential biblicisms include 1 Macc. 1:15 (cf. 2 Kgs 17:17); 1:48 (cf. Lev. 20:25); 3:58 (cf. 2 Sam. 2:7); 3:58 (cf. Exod. 34:2); 4:25 (cf. 1 Sam. 14:23); 5:31 (cf. 1 Sam. 5:12).

131. Uriel Rappaport, 'A Note on the Use of the Bible in 1 Maccabees', in *Biblical Perspectives: Early Use and Interpretation of the Bible in Light of the Dead Sea Scrolls: Proceedings of the First International Symposium of the Orion Center for the Study of the Dead Sea Scrolls and Associated Literature, 12–14 May, 1996*, ed. Michael E. Stone and Esther G. Chazon, STDJ 28 (Leiden: Brill, 1998), 175–9. However, the 'biblical' style of 1 Maccabees is often asserted rather than shown, so Rappaport, 'It is common knowledge that 1 Maccabees follows the model of biblical historiography' (175).

132. This in addition to what may be described as more 'Hellenistic' modes of validation, such as those proposed by Martha Himmelfarb, '"He Was Renowned to the Ends of the Earth" (1 Maccabees 3:9)', in *Jewish Literatures and Cultures: Context and Intertext*, ed. Anita Norich and Yaron Z. Eliav, BJS 349 (Providence, RI: Brown Judaic Studies, 2008), 77–97.

2. Scripturalized Narrative in Second Temple Literature 77

establish a connection between the new Hasmonaean rulers and the righteous kings, prophets and conquerors of the Deuteronomistic histories. The Maccabean brothers are in this way depicted as the heirs to Israel's golden age.[133] The military and political triumphs of Judas, Jonathan and Simon are cut from the same literary cloth as those of Moses and David, a fact which was no doubt meant to catch the eye of early readers.[134] But the author of 1 Maccabees does more than just imitate the style of the scriptural histories – scriptural language is woven into the fabric of the narrative, in isolated narrative details and episodes based on scriptural models.

The Compositional Use of the Jewish Scriptures in 1 Maccabees

The narrative concerning Mattathias (1 Macc. 2) features both the *expositional* and *compositional* use of the Jewish scriptures. The former can be seen in Mattathias' opening speech, which refers to the suffering of scriptural Israel at the hands of the Gentiles (1 Macc. 2:7-13, esp. 2:9; cf. 2 Chron. 36:7-18; Jer. 52:17-23; Lam. 2:21) and the encomia in his farewell speech praising the heroes of Israel's past as recorded in the scriptures (1 Macc. 2:51-60; cf. Gen. 15:6; 22:1-19; 39:7-12; 41:39-45; Num. 13:30; 14:6-10, 24, 30; 25:11-13; 32:12; Josh. 24:25; 2 Sam. 7:1-17; 1 Kgs 19:10, 14; Dan. 3:1-30; 6:17-24).[135] At the same time, in

---

133. Tessa Rajak compares this to the 'rediscovered tradition' of Augustan Rome; see her 'Hasmonean Kingship and Tradition', in *The Jewish Dialogue with Greece and Rome: Studies in Cultural and Social Interaction*, ed. Tessa Rajak, AGAJU 48 (Leiden: Brill, 2001), 50.

134. Katell Berthelot is rightfully sceptical that Joshua was a model for the depiction of Judas; see her 'The Biblical Conquest and the Hasmonean Wars According to 1 and 2 Maccabees', in *The Books of the Maccabees: History, Theology, Ideology: Papers of the Second International Conference on the Deuterocanonical Books, Pápa, Hungary, 9–11 June, 2005*, ed. Géza G. Xeravits and József Zsengellér, JSJ 118 (Leiden: Brill, 2007), 46–8. That Judas is a 'second Joshua' and 'Joshua redivivus' is argued, respectively, by Goldstein, *I Maccabees*, 293; and Ernst Axel Knauf, 'Joshua Maccabeus: Another Reading of 1 Maccabees 5', in *'Even God Cannot Change the Past': Reflections on Seventeen Years of the European Seminar in Historical Methodology*, ed. Lester L. Grabbe, LHBOTS 663 (London: T&T Clark, 2018), 203–12, esp. 210.

135. On the use of the Jewish scriptures in the narrative of Mattathias, see Thomas Hieke, 'The Role of "Scripture" in the Last Words of Mattathias', in Xeravits and Zsengellér, eds., *The Books of the Maccabees*, 61–74; and in the same volume, Friedrich V. Reiterer, 'Die Vergangenheit als Basis für die Zukunft Mattathias' Lehre für seine Söhne aus der Geschichte in 1 Makk 2:52-60', 75–100.

78   *Writing with Scripture*

his slaying of the Jew at the altar in Modeïn (1 Macc. 2:23-26), Mattathias is explicitly compared to the scriptural Phinehas: 'Thus he burned with zeal for the law, as Phinehas did against Zimri the son of Salu' (2:26). But elements of the story of Mattathias also appear to be *modelled* on the story of Phinehas (Num. 25:6-13). A sin is committed before the 'eyes' (Num. 25:6: עיני; 1 Macc. 2:23: ὀφθαλμοί) of 'all' (כל; πᾶς) people, and having 'seen' (Num. 25:7: ראה; 1 Macc. 2:24: ὁράω) what took place, the righteous men slay the sinner.[136] The scripturalization could have been triggered by genuine parallels between the actions of the historical Mattathias and the scriptural Phinehas. For 1 Maccabees, however, the Phinehaic depiction serves a propagandistic function. By invoking the legacy of Phinehas, and particularly his 'zeal', the author is able to associate the Hasmonaeans with the 'perpetual priesthood' granted Phinehas on account of his zeal (Num. 25:11-13), an association which is later made explicit: 'Phinehas *our ancestor*, because he was deeply zealous, received the covenant of everlasting priesthood' (1 Macc. 2:54).[137]

Elsewhere 1 Maccabees explicitly associates the assembly of the congregation at Mizpah (1 Macc. 3:46) with the assembly at Mizpah under Samuel (1 Sam. 7:5-6), from which it borrows the phrase 'they fasted that day' (καὶ ἐνήστευσαν τῇ ἡμέρᾳ ἐκείνῃ).[138] Judas likewise tells the people not to fear but remember what befell Pharaoh at the Red Sea (1 Macc. 4:8-9) as Moses tells Israel not to fear but remember what the LORD did to Pharaoh (Deut. 7:18).

---

136. See Goldstein, *1 Maccabees*, 6–7. The use of scriptural material is also evident in 1 Macc. 2:25, 'And he tore down the altar', which likely reflects Exod. 34:13, 'You shall tear down their altars'.

137. As Elias Bickerman (*The God of the Maccabees: Studies on the Meaning and Origin of the Maccabean Revolt*, trans. Hoerst R. Moehring, SJLA 32 [Leiden: Brill, 1979], 20) notes, the detail that Judas 'turned away wrath from Israel' (1 Macc. 3:8) can also be seen as a reference to the scriptural Phinehas, as in Num. 25:10, '[Phinehas] has turned back my wrath from the Israelites'. On the significance of the Phinehaic Priesthood for the Hasmonaean dynasty, see Vasile Babota, *The Institution of the Hasmonean High Priesthood*, JSJSup 165 (Leiden: Brill, 2014), 269–84. The Phinehaic 'perpetual priesthood' could also lie behind the language of the appointment of Simon, 'And the Jews and their priests decided that Simon should be their leader and high priest for ever (ἀρχιερέα εἰς τὸν αἰῶνα)' (1 Macc. 14:41; cf. 16:24), although this comes with the confusing addendum, 'until a trustworthy prophet should arise' (also 1 Macc. 4:46; cf. Deut. 18:15-19). Some identify the 'trustworthy prophet' as John Hyrcanus; see Rudolf Meyer, 'προφήτης C', *TDNT* 6:815–16; David Aune, *Prophecy in Early Christianity and the Ancient Mediterranean World* (Grand Rapids, MI: Eerdmans, 1983), 375 n. 19.

138. Cf. LXX 1 Sam. 7:6b: καὶ ἐνήστευσαν ἐν τῇ ἡμέρᾳ ἐκείνῃ.

2. Scripturalized Narrative in Second Temple Literature

79

At other points, the author weaves unmarked scriptural language into the narrative, most often with details borrowed from the Mosaic law. When Judas appoints 'leaders of the people, in charge of *thousands and hundreds and fifties and tens*' (1 Macc. 3:55: χιλιάρχους καὶ ἑκατοντάρχους καὶ πεντηκοντάρχους καὶ δεκαδάρχους), the language is that of Exodus: 'Moses chose able men from all Israel and set them over the people [in] *thousands and hundreds and fifties and tens* (χιλιάρχους καὶ ἑκατοντάρχους καὶ πεντηκοντάρχους καὶ δεκαδάρχους)' (LXX Exod. 18:25).[139] When Judas says 'to those who were building houses, or were betrothed, or were planting vineyards, or were fainthearted, that each should return to his home, according to the law' (1 Macc. 3:56), the command is taken from Deut. 20:5-8. The detail that the Judaeans 'removed the defiled stones to an *unclean place* (τόπον ἀκάθαρτον)' (1 Macc. 3:56) follows Leviticus: 'The priest shall command that the stones in which the disease appears be taken out and thrown into an *unclean place* (τόπον ἀκάθαρτον)' (LXX Lev. 14:40). Likewise the detail that they 'took *unhewn stones* (λίθους ὁλοκλήρους)' and 'built a new altar' (1 Macc. 4:47) reflects Deuteronomy: 'You must build the altar of the LORD your God of *unhewn stones* (λίθους ὁλοκλήρους)' (LXX Deut. 27:6). Exodus lies behind the placing of a lampstand, altar of incense, table with bread and hanging curtains in the Temple (1 Macc. 4:49-51; cf. Exod. 25:30; 26:33; 40:4-5). It could be that Judas and his followers followed the Mosaic commands this scrupulously, but as it is, the language appears to owe directly to the Jewish scriptures, especially Deuteronomy.[140] The scene in 1 Maccabees 3–4 has, in this sense, been partly created out of the scriptures.

Elsewhere Deuteronomy appears to have influenced the detail that Bacchides built 'strong cities' (πόλεις ὀχυράς) with 'high walls and gates and bars' (τείχεσιν ὑψηλοῖς καὶ πύλαις καὶ μοχλοῖς) (1 Macc. 9:50), just as scriptural Israel's enemies had 'strong cities' (πόλεις ὀχυραί) with 'high walls, gates and bars' (τείχη ὑψηλά πύλαι καὶ μοχλοί) (LXX Deut. 3:5). Deuteronomy also supplies the language of the Gentile threat in 1 Macc. 12:53 (cf. Deut. 32:26).

---

139. My translation. See also Exod. 18:21; Deut. 1:15.

140. Though Berthelot ('The Biblical Conquest and the Hasmonean Wars', 49–53) notes the singular influence of Deuteronomy on 1 Maccabees, she questions whether the work possesses a 'Deuteronomistic ideology', writing 'that the [Deuteronomistic] issue of land (be it promised or holy) is secondary and almost lacking' (53). This appears to overlook the Deuteronomistic language in 1 Macc. 5:48: ἀπελθεῖν εἰς τὴν γῆν ἡμῶν. The phrase concerning Simon, 'He *extended the borders* (ἐπλάτυνεν τὰ ὅρια) of his nation' (1 Macc. 14:6), may too reflect the promise in Exodus, 'For I [the LORD] will cast out nations before you and *enlarge your borders* (πλατύνω τὰ ὅριά)' (LXX Exod. 34:24; cf. Deut. 19:8).

80 *Writing with Scripture*

Outside of the Pentateuch, the national lament following Judas' death, 'How is the mighty fallen' (1 Macc. 9:21: πῶς ἔπεσεν δυνατός), appears to come from David's lament for Saul and Jonathan, 'How the mighty are fallen' (LXX 2 Sam. 1:25, 27: πῶς ἔπεσαν δυνατοί). The song of praise for Simon (1 Macc. 14:4-15) features unmarked but nevertheless clear language from Zechariah and Micah: Zech. 8:12 in 1 Macc. 14:8; Zech. 8:4 in 1 Macc. 14:9; and Mic. 4:4 in 1 Macc. 14:12.

Through scripturalization, the author of 1 Maccabees is able to associate the Hasmonaean dynasty with the Phinehaic priesthood, whilst also signaling their obedience to the law. Unmarked scriptural language embedded in the narrative contributes to the 'biblical' presentation of the Maccabean heroes. Their triumphs are painted, and thus legitimized, with the same colours as the heroes of Israel's past. But the most sustained example of this compositional process can be seen in an episode modelled on a military conquest – one could say atrocity – credited to Moses.

Judas and Moses: 1 Maccabees 5:45-51 and Deuteronomy 2:26-36 (and 20:10-14)

Having 'gathered together all the Israelites in Gilead' (1 Macc. 5:45), Judas and the congregation 'came to Ephron', a 'very strong city on the road', where they 'could not go round it to the right or to the left; they had to go through it' (5:46). When Ephron shuts its gates to the Judaeans, Judas sends a peaceful message requesting safe passage, 'Let us pass through your land to get to our land. No one will do you harm; we will simply pass by on foot' (5:48). The Ephronites, however, reject this plea. This prompts Judas to encamp and wage war 'until the city was delivered into his hands' (5:50). Victorious, Judas 'destroyed every male by the edge of the sword', razing and plundering the city, so the Judaeans 'passed through the city over the slain' (5:51).

Judas' conquest of Ephron is modelled on Moses' defeat of Sihon, king of the Amorites, at Heshbon, an incident narrated several times (Num. 21:21-24; Deut. 2:26-36; Judg. 11:19-21), though it also resembles the Edomites' refusal of passage to Israel (Num. 20:14-21).[141] Of all these, the influence of Deut. 2:26-37 and Judg. 11:19-21 is most apparent. Moses sends terms of peace to Sihon, saying, 'Let us pass through your land to our country' (Judg. 11:19; par. Num. 21:22; Deut. 2:27), vowing that Israel will 'turn aside neither to the right nor to the left' (Deut. 2:27;

---

141. Dimant considers the episode an example of the 'compositional use [of] biblical elements' in a 'free narrative' ('Mikra in the Apocrypha and Pseudepigrapha', 406–7).

2. Scripturalized Narrative in Second Temple Literature 81

cf. Num. 20:17) – they will simply 'pass through on foot' (Deut. 2:28). Sihon, however, bars the Israelites from entering (Deut. 2:30; Judg. 11:20; par. Num. 21:23; cf. 20:20-21). In the ensuing battle, the LORD delivers Heshbon into Moses' hand (Deut. 2:31-33; Judg. 11:21; par. Num 21:24), so Israel puts to the sword every man, woman and child, leading to Moses' chilling admission, 'We left not a single survivor' (Deut. 2:34).

The incident at Heshbon offers a close parallel to the structure of 1 Macc. 5:45-48. Israel comes to a place where they cannot go around, leading them to request safe passage through the region so they can get to their land. When the request is denied, Israel conquers the region and puts its people to the sword. The parallels extend to distinct phrases, including the detail that the Judaeans 'could not go round it to the right or to the left' (1 Macc. 5:46: οὐκ ἦν ἐκκλῖναι ἀπ' αὐτῆς δεξιὰν ἢν ἀριστεράν), as Moses would 'not turn to the right or to the left' (LXX Deut. 2:27: οὐχὶ ἐκκλινῶ δεξιὰ οὐδὲ ἀριστερά; par. Num. 20:17).[142] To this can be added the request, 'Let us pass through your land to get to our land' (1 Macc. 5:48: διελευσόμεθα διὰ τῆς γῆς σου τοῦ ἀπελθεῖν εἰς τὴν γῆν ἡμῶν), from Moses' request, 'Let us pass through your land to our country' (Judg. 11:19: נעברה־נא בארצך עד־מקומי),[143] and 'Only [let us] pass by on foot' (1 Macc. 5:48: πλὴν τοῖς ποςὶν παρελευσόμεθα) from 'Only that I will pass by on foot' (LXX Deut. 2:28: πλὴν ὅτι παρελεύσομαι τοῖς ποσίν).[144]

The remainder of the episode (1 Macc. 5:49-51), however, departs from this model. Whereas Sihon is the one who wages war on Israel (Num. 21:23; Deut. 2:32; Judg. 11:20), it is Judas who encamps against and besieges Ephron (1 Macc. 5:49-50).[145] Although the LORD hands Sihon

---

142. The Septuagint is shown only to demonstrate the underlying Hebrew may be rendered similarly, a possible indication of verbal agreement in the original text. The Greek of 1 Macc. 5:45-51 is closest to MT Deut. 2:26-34 and MT Judg. 11:19-21. Note, however, the minor variant ושמאל at Deut. 2:27 in 4Q31 1:8.

143. The phrase also occurs in the incident at Edom (Num. 20:17). The Greek puts the request in the singular, 'I will pass through your land to my place' (LXX Judg. 11:19: παρελεύσομαι διὰ τῆς γῆς σου ἕως τοῦ τόπου μου).

144. My translation. The phrase also occurs at Edom (Num. 20:19). It appears the defeat of Sihon narrated in Deut. 2:26-36 conflates details from Num. 20:14-21 and 21:21-24, its source, a conclusion shared by John E. Harvey, *Retelling the Torah: The Deuteronomistic Historian's Use of Tetrateuchal Narratives*, JSOTSup 403 (London: T&T Clark, 2004), 16–21.

145. It is possible, however, the sequence where the Judaeans 'encamped' (παρενέβαλον) and 'made war' (ἐπολέμησεν) on the Ephronites reflects Judg. 11:20, where the Amorites 'encamped' (παρενέβαλεν) and 'made war' (ἐπολέμησεν) on the Israelites.

over to Israel (Deut. 2:30-31, 33, 36), there is no direct counterpart to the divine passive, 'And the city was delivered into [Judas'] hands' (1 Macc. 5:49). Whilst the defeat of Sihon 'by the edge of the sword' (Num. 21:24: לפי־חרב) parallels Judas' victory 'by the edge of the sword' (1 Macc. 5:51: ἐν στόματι ῥομφαίας),[146] Moses' pogrom is indiscriminate (Deut. 2:34; cf. Num. 21:24; Judg. 11:21), whereas Judas' is confined to 'every male' (πᾶν ἀρσενικόν).[147] And, although Moses plunders the Amorites (Deut. 2:35) as Judas does Ephron (1 Macc. 5:51), the razing (ἐκρίζόω) of Ephron has no parallel.

What accounts for these differences? It appears the author is no longer drawing on the defeat of Sihon (Deut. 2:26-30; Judg. 11:19-21), but on material elsewhere in Deuteronomy. Earlier in the narrative, Judas issues the command that 'those who were building houses, or were betrothed, or were planting vineyards, or were fainthearted, that each should return to home, according to the law' (1 Macc. 3:56), an order taken entirely from Deut. 20:5-8. In the same way, the actions of Judas at Ephron follow the laws concerning *ḥērem* in Deut. 20:10-14.[148] When Judas approaches Ephron, he offers 'terms of peace' (1 Macc. 5:48), as Israel is commanded to offer 'terms of peace' when they approach a city (Deut. 20:10-11). When Ephron rejects the terms, Judas wages war on the city (1 Macc. 5:49-50), as Israel is to wage war on cities that do not accept its terms of peace (Deut. 20:12). After this, 'the city was delivered into [Judas'] hands' (1 Macc. 5:50: καὶ παρεδόθη ἡ πόλις ἐν χειρὶ αὐτοῦ), as the LORD promises Israel, 'And the Lord your God will deliver [the city] into your hands' (LXX Deut. 20:12: καὶ παραδώσει αὐτὴν κύριος ὁ θεός σου εἰς τὰς χεῖρας σου). Judas then slaughters 'every male by the edge of the sword' (1 Macc. 5:51a: πᾶν ἀρσενικὸν ἐν στόματι ῥομφαίας), as Israel is to slaughter 'every male by the edge of the sword' (Deut. 20:13: את־כל־זכורה לפי־חרב). And finally, the Judaeans plunder Ephron (1 Macc. 5:51b), as Israel is instructed to do (Deut. 20:14).[149]

---

146. The LXX renders לפי־חרב as ἐν στόματι ῥομφαίας at Josh. 6:21 and 8:24 (cf. LXX Num. 21:24). On the use of the phrase, see Berthelot, 'The Biblical Conquest and the Hasmonean Wars', 48 n. 11.

147. As it is in 1 Macc. 5:28, 35.

148. A detailed discussion of the laws of *ḥērem* in the career of Judas Maccabeus can be found in Christophe Batsch, *La guerre et les rites de guerre dans le judaïsme du deuxième Temple*, JSJSup 93 (Leiden: Brill, 2005), 438–43. Note the minor variants in the text of Deut. 20:10-14 in 4Q38a 2/3:5-9.

149. The term used by 1 Macc. 5:51, σκῦλα, does not occur in the LXX but does in σ′ and θ′ Deut. 20:14.

2. *Scripturalized Narrative in Second Temple Literature* 83

1 Macc. 5:45-51	Deuteronomy and Judges
Judas and the Judaeans 'could not go round it *to the right or to the left*' at Ephron (5:46).	Moses and the Israelites 'will not turn *to the right or to the left*' through the region of the Amorites (Deut. 2:27).
The Ephronites deny the Judaeans entry (5:47).	The Amorites deny the Israelites entry (Deut. 2:30; Judg. 11:20).
Judas sends 'terms of peace' to Ephron (5:48).	Israelites must send 'terms of peace' to a city (Deut. 20:10).
'Let me pass through your land to get to our land' (5:48).	'Let me pass through your land to our country' (Judg. 11:19).
'We will simply pass by on foot' (5:48).	'Only allow me to pass through on foot' (Deut. 2:28).
Judas 'encamped' against the city and 'made war' on it (5:49-50).	The Amorites 'encamped' against the Israelites and 'made war' on them (Judg. 11:20). If a town rejects 'terms of peace', the Israelites are to besiege it (Deut. 20:12).
'The city was *delivered into his hands*' (5:50).	'When the Lord your God *gives into your hand...*' (20:13).
'He destroyed *every male by the edge of the sword*' (5:51).	The Israelites shall 'destroy *every male by the edge of the sword*' (20:13).
The Judaeans plundered the city (5:51).	The Israelites are instructed to plunder defeated cities (20:14).

The author of 1 Maccabees has crafted the narrative of Judas' conquest of Ephron by following two scriptural models: Moses' defeat of Sihon (Deut. 2:26-36; Judg. 11:19-21) and the laws of *ḥērem* (Deut. 20:10-14). From these models, the episode takes almost all the elements of its narrative, including verbatim or near verbatim phrases (Deut. 2:27 in 1 Macc. 5:46; Judg. 11:19 in 1 Macc. 5:48; Deut. 2:28 in 1 Macc. 5:48; Deut. 20:13 in 1 Macc. 5:51). Does this mean the episode has simply been created out of scripture with no basis in history? There are certainly reasons to doubt the veracity of 1 Macc. 5:45-51. The parallel account of the siege of Ephron in 2 Macc. 12:27-28 includes none of the above elements, aside from the large number slain.[150] Though there is no mention of an Ephron outside of 1 and 2 Maccabees, it is nevertheless

---

150. On the relationship of 1 and 2 Maccabees and the identity of the unknown towns in 1 Macc. 5, see Goldstein, *I Maccabees*, 293–305; Daniel R. Schwartz, *2 Maccabees*, CEJL (Berlin: W. de Gruyter, 2008), 418ff. For discrepancies between 1 Maccabees and Josephus, see Abel, *Les Livres des Maccabées*, xi–xv.

84 *Writing with Scripture*

possible a small skirmish took place there.[151] But the implausibility of Judas amassing a military force capable of waging the scale of warfare described in 1 Maccabees 5 (par. 2 Macc. 12) renders the entire episode doubtful.

The issue of historicity aside, the incident at Ephron contributes to the larger presentation of the Hasmonaean warriors as obedient to, and zealous for, the law.[152] The Maccabean brothers, especially Judas, are depicted as behaving κατὰ τὸν νόμον (1 Macc. 3:56; 4:47, 53; 15:21), carefully following its precepts (3:55-56; 4:42-53; 5:68).[153] Judas' fulfilment of the laws of *ḥērem* is a further demonstration of his law-abiding righteousness, rooted in Phinehaic zeal. To an extent, Judas also becomes *like* the law-giver, Moses. In a conflict that began over the law (1:41-64), Judas begins to fulfil the words of Mattathias (2:64-68), that under his leadership, the law returns to Israel (3:46-56; 4:42-59). Judas thus emerges as the Moses-like defender and restorer of the law. Once more, the author of 1 Maccabees subtly uses the Jewish scriptures to dress the Maccabean family in the garb of the heroes of old.

The scripturalized narrative in 1 Macc. 5:45-51 shows the compositional use of scriptural material occurs outside of the so-called Rewritten Bible, even to historical works. Like Pseudo-Philo and the *Apocryphon*, 1 Maccabees composes a new episode by following a scriptural model, inserting distinctive elements and phrases into its narrative. But whilst the siege of Ephron may well have its roots in a more modest historical event, the episode as it is in 1 Macc. 5:45-51 has been pieced together out of the scriptures, specifically Deut. 2:26-36, Judg. 11:19-21 and Deut. 20:10-14.[154]

---

151. Aryeh Kasher is optimistic about recovering the identity of the unknown towns, *Jews and Hellenistic Cities in Eretz-Israel: Relations of the Jews in Eretz-Israel with the Hellenistic Cities During the Second Temple Period (332 BCE–70 CE)*, TSAJ 21 (Tübingen: Mohr Siebeck, 1990), 58–90, esp. 79–80 on Ephron. Less optimistic is Seth Schwartz, 'Israel and the Nations Roundabout: 1 Maccabees and the Hasmonean Expansion', *JJS* 42 (1991): 16–38.

152. For example, 1 Macc. 2:21, 26-27, 42, 50, 64, 67-68; 3:5-6, 48; 13:3; 14:4, 29. For a full discussion of 1 Maccabees' views on the law, see Francis Borchardt, *The Torah in 1 Maccabees: A Literary Critical Approach to the Text*, DCLS 19 (Berlin: W. de Gruyter, 2014), 189–230.

153. At the same time, details from Deuteronomy appear throughout the narrative (Deut. 3:5 in 1 Macc. 9:50; Deut. 32:26 in 1 Macc. 12:53).

154. It could even be 1 Macc. 5:45-51 relies on a lost 'Rewritten Bible' work which had conflated details from Deut. 2:26-36 and Judg. 11:19-21 in narrating the defeat of Sihon.

2. Scripturalized Narrative in Second Temple Literature 85

Judith

Despite the remarkable, and at times transgressive, afterlife of the tale of Judith, it does not appear to have been widely known during the Second Temple period.[155] Whilst this silence may simply be an accident of history, it is not difficult to imagine why the seductive and deceitful murderess would have offended some sensibilities in Jewish antiquity.[156] And yet, the similarly subversive Esther, whilst encountering some resistance, did not suffer the same fate.[157] Perhaps the book of Judith struggled to gain acceptance on account of its manifold historical blunders.[158] The events are supposed to unfold as the Assyrians ruled from Nineveh (seventh century BCE), in between the twelfth and eighteenth years of Nebuchadnezzar's reign (593–587 BCE), who is wrongly called the 'king of Assyria' (Jdt. 1:1ff.), after the return of the Judaeans from captivity

155. In particular, the subversive paintings of Artemisia Gentileschi, *Judith Slaying Holofernes* (*c.* 1614–1620, Oil on canvas, Galleria degli Uffizi, Florence) and Gustav Klimt, *Judith I* (1901, Oil on canvas, Österreichische Galerie Belvedere, Vienna). See also the wide-ranging inter-disciplinary studies on the reception of Judith in Kevin R. Brine, Elena Ciletti and Henrike Lähnemann, eds., *The Sword of Judith: Judith Studies Across the Disciplines* (Cambridge: OpenBook Publishers, 2010).

156. That this was the reason for Judith's ancient unpopularity is argued by Solomon Zeitlin, 'Introduction: The Books of Esther and Judith: A Parallel', in *The Book of Judith: Greek Text with an English Translation, Commentary and Critical Notes*, ed. Morton S. Enslin, JAL 7 (Leiden: Brill, 1972), 1–37; Carey A. Moore, 'Why Wasn't the Book of Judith Included in the Hebrew Bible?', in *'No One Spoke Ill of Her': Essays on Judith*, ed. J. C. VanderKam, SBLEJL 2 (Atlanta, GA: Scholars Press, 1992), 61–71; Sidnie White Crawford, 'Esther not Judith: Why One Made It and the Other Didn't', *Bible Review* 18 (2002): 22–31. On the transgressive elements of the book Judith, see David A. de Silva, 'Judith the Heroine? Lies, Seduction, and Murder in Cultural Perspective', *BTB* 36 (2006): 55–61.

157. Addressed by Zeitlin, 'The Books of Esther and Judith'; Crawford, 'Esther not Judith'.

158. On the mysterious historical origins of Judith itself, see Deborah Levine Gera, *Judith*, CEJL (Berlin: W. de Gruyter, 2013), 26–44. The legend would eventually become associated with the celebration of Hanukkah, possibly by the time of Vg. Jdt. 16:31 (see Gera, 'The Jewish Textual Traditions', in Brine, Ciletti, and Lähnemann, eds., *The Sword of Judith*, 30–6). Judith's association with Hanukkah can be seen in the many medieval menorahs decorated with an armed Judith figure holding the head of Holofernes, esp. the impressive *Hanukkah Lamp with Armed Judith* (Italy, *c.* 1500–1700, Bronze, cast and engraved; New York, the Jewish Museum).

86   *Writing with Scripture*

(late sixth century BCE).[159] Thus, the short tale of Judith somehow spans two centuries and the reigns of three consecutive empires.[160] And yet, narratives of equal historical absurdity – like Daniel, Esther and the *Letter of Aristeas* – seem to have fared much better in the Second Temple period.[161] That these issues would be an obstacle for Judith's acceptance and not others suggests a problem with the question itself. Not only is the literary evidence from the period too meagre to ascertain if a work was 'accepted' or 'rejected', the terms themselves belong to a later period. The controversial status of Judith in the Second Temple period is, for the most part, a scholarly abstraction. But given the deafening silence, the effect is the same. Despite its affinities with works like Esther or Tobit, the book of Judith remains something of an outlier in the miscellanea of Second Temple literature.

159. Jdt. 1:1, 7, 11, 13; 2:1, 4; 4:1, 3; 5:19. If the names Holofernes and Bagoas refer to the mid-fourth-century BCE Persian officials Orophones and Bagoas (Diodorus Siculus, *Hist.* 16.47.3; 17.5.3; 31.19.2), then this would be a further violation of historical logic.

160. Few dispute this, though there is the odd ardent defender of Judith's historical plausibility; so Claus Schedl, 'Nabochodonosor, Arpakšad und Darius', *ZDMG* 115 (1965): 242–54. Carey A. Moore surveys various explanations of Judith's historical errors; see *Judith: A New Translation with Introduction and Commentary*, AB 40 (Garden City, NY: Doubleday, 1985), 52–6.

161. For some, Judith's absurdities are a sign the author intended it to be read as a kind of historical fiction; so André-Marie Dubarle, *Judith: Formes et sens des diverses traditions. Tome I: Études*, Analecta Biblica Investigationes Scientificae in Res Biblicas 24 (Rome: Institut Biblique Pontifical, 1966), 162–4; Enslin, *The Book of Judith*, 38; Moore, *Judith*, 76–85; Gera, *Judith*, 60; Lawrence M. Wills, *Judith*, Hermeneia (Minneapolis, MN: Fortress, 2019), 78–95; or as a 'legend' in Benedict Otzen, *Tobit and Judith*, Guides to Apocrypha and Pseudepigrapha (London: Sheffield Academic, 2002), 124–6. The label of historical fiction is also applied to the equally fabulous Daniel, Esther and *Letter of Aristeas*. There is, however, no evidence that these texts were read as fiction during the Second Temple period. A simpler explanation is that the authors merely suffered from a lack of adequate historical information. This surely lies behind the absurd detail in the *Pirkê de Rabbi Eliezer* that 'Pharaoh, king of Egypt [of Exod. 5–14] went and ruled in Nineveh [in the time of Jonah]' (*PRE* 43:9). That this may also explain the historical inaccuracies in Judith is explored in an unjustly overlooked article by Alan Millard, 'Judith, Tobit Ahiqar and History', in *New Heaven and New Earth: Prophecy and the Millenium. Essays in Honour of Anthony Gelston*, eds. Peter J. Harland and Robert Hayward, VTSup 77 (Leiden: Brill, 1999), 195–203. There is less to commend Ernst Haag's view (*Studien zum Buche Judith: Seine theologische Bedeutung und literarische Eigenart*, Trierer Theologische Studien 16 [Trier: Paulinus, 1963]) that Judith's historical inaccuracies are simply part of its theological agenda.

2. Scripturalized Narrative in Second Temple Literature 87

Nevertheless, like other works from the period, the book of Judith makes extensive use of the Jewish scriptures – though once more, this is not without its issues. Although most commentators have assumed the syntax and style of the Greek point to a Semitic *Vorlage*, recent scholarship has begun to entertain the possibility of a Greek original.[162] At any rate, verbatim agreement with any surviving text of the scriptures, be they Greek or Hebrew, is scarce. Even when the text corresponds with the LXX, it is not clear whether this owes to agreement in the respective underlying texts (see Hanhart's reconstruction of 'der ursprüngliche Text' of Judith) or the direct influence of the LXX on Judith.[163] Examples of this kind are Jdt. 9:7 (also 16:3) – 'You are the Lord who crushes wars; the Lord is your name' (σὺ εἶ κύριος συντρίβων πολέμους. κύριος ὄνομά σοι) – which is close to LXX Exod. 15:3: 'The Lord who crushes wars; the Lord is his name' (κύριος συντρίβων πολέμους, κύριος ὄνομα αὐτῷ); and Jdt. 5:13 – 'Then God dried up the Red Sea before them' (καὶ κατεξήρανεν ὁ θεὸς τὴν ἐρυθρὰν θάλασσαν ἔμπροσθεν αὐτῶν) – which is close to LXX Josh. 2:10: 'The Lord God dried up the Red Sea before you' (κατεξήρανεν κύριος ὁ θεὸς τὴν ἐρυθρὰν θάλασσαν ἀπὸ προσώπου ὑμῶν).[164]

162. All versions of the Judith tale, including medieval Hebrew legends and midrashim, can be traced back to the Greek text. For the most comprehensive study of the text, see Robert Hanhart, *Iudith*, Septuaginta Vetus Testamentum graecum auctoritate academiae scientiarum Gottingensis editum 8.4 (Göttingen: Vandenhoeck & Ruprecht, 1979). Compare with Dubarle (*Judith*, 7–97), who believes the medieval Hebrew mss. share a Semitic source with the early Latin Judith. Dubarle is influenced here by Jerome's confusing comments about a 'Chaldean', presumably Aramaic, original ('Preface to Judith', in *Biblia Sacra Iuxta Vulgatum Versionem*, ed. Robert Weber [Stuttgart: Deutsche Bibelgesellschaft, 1969], 691; discussed in Enslin [and Zeitlin], *Judith*, 45). The majority view favouring a Hebrew original is expressed by Enslin (and Zeitlin), *Judith*, 39–40; Moore, *Judith*, 66–7; Wills, *Judith*, 18–23; see also Otzen, *Tobit and Judith*, 137–41. A more balanced assessment of arguments for both a Semitic and Greek original is found in Gera, *Judith*, 79–97; favouring a Greek original is Toni Craven, *Artistry and Faith in the Book of Judith*, SBLDS 70 (Chico, CA: Scholars Press, 1983), 5.

163. On the possibility the author of Judith made use of the LXX, see Gera, *Judith*, 91–7. Alternatively, the loose similarities with the LXX could owe to a Semitic original depending, rather faithfully, on an alternate Hebrew scriptural tradition, a possibility entertained by Wills, *Judith*, 20. On the task of recovering the hypothetical lost Hebrew text of Judith, see Robert Hanhart, *Text and Textgeschichte des Buches Judith*, MSU 14 (Göttingen: Vandenhoeck & Ruprecht, 1979); and earlier, Frank Zimmerman, 'Aids for the Recovery of the Hebrew Original of Judith', *JBL* 57 (1938): 67–74.

164. LXX, my translation. On the first passage see Judith Lang, 'The Lord Who Crushes Wars: Studies on Judith 9:7, Judith 16:2, and Exodus 15:3', in *A Pious Seductress: Studies in the Book of Judith*, ed. Géza G. Xeravits, DCLS 14 (Göttingen: Vandenhoeck & Ruprecht, 2012), 179–87; on the second, Dubarle, *Judith*, 143.

88   *Writing with Scripture*

More often, unmarked scriptural language appears in the direct speech of characters, in forms dissimilar to the MT and the LXX. One example is Jdt. 8:16, where Judith prays, 'For God is not like man, to be threatened, nor like a human being, to be won over by pleading' (ὅτι οὐχ ὡς ἄνθρωπος ὁ θεὸς ἀπειληθῆναι οὐδ' ὡς υἱὸς ἀνθρώπου τῶν ἐχθρῶν ἡμῶν), which clearly quotes Num. 23:19, though differs from the literal rendering of the LXX: 'God is not to be deceived like man, nor is he to be threatened like a human being' (οὐχ ὡς ἄνθρωπος ὁ θεὸς διαρτηθῆναι οὐδὲ ὡς υἱὸς ἀνθρώπου ἀπειληθῆναι).[165] Elsewhere, scriptural language is present but barely recognizable, as in Jdt. 16:15 – 'For the mountains shall be shaken to their foundations with the waters; at your presence the rocks shall melt like wax' – which appears to reflect Mic. 1:4: 'Then the mountains will melt under him and the valleys will burst open, like wax near the fire, like waters poured down a steep place'. In many cases, however, scriptural language, if once present, is no longer identifiable.[166]

The book of Judith, nevertheless, makes clear references to scriptural narrative, particularly Achior's speech (Jdt. 5:5-21), which neatly summarizes key events in Israelite history up until the return from exile. To this can be added the references to the testing of Abraham, Isaac and Jacob (Jdt. 8:26; cf. Gen. 22:1-19; 28:5; 29:1-32:1), the rape of Dinah (Jdt. 9:2; cf. Gen. 34:1-31) and the creation myth (Jdt. 16:14; cf. Gen. 1:1-27). At the same time, the book features many proper place and character names found in the scriptures, though contrary to Scholz and Haag, this does not signal exegetical intent.[167] But by far the most prevalent use of the Jewish scriptures in the book of Judith is the compositional use of scriptural material, often concerning celebrated women of Israel's past, to shape the new narrative, a point first made by André-Marie Dubarle: 'Le genre littéraire de Judith se caractérise plutôt comme une broderie d'épisodes à couleur biblique sur un canevas de faits traditionnels beaucoup plus sobre'.[168]

---

165. LXX, my translation. With the use of ἀπειλέω, Jdt. 8:16 is closer to LXX Num. 23:19 than MT Num. 23:19.

166. The following may be considered examples of this kind: 2 Kgs 19:19 in Jdt. 9:14; Dan. 2:37-38 in Jdt. 11:7; Prov. 23:18 in Jdt. 13:19; Isa. 66:24 in Jdt. 16:17.

167. Scholz and Haag believe Judith symbolically develops the scriptural portrait of Nebuchadnezzar; see Anton Scholz, *Das Buch Judith – eine Prophetie* (Würzberg: Leo Woerl, 1885), 33–48; Haag, *Studien zum Buche Judith*, 71–8. Although Judith appears to know Jonah (Jon. 3:8 in Jdt. 4:9, 12), the mention of 'the great city of Nineveh' (Jdt. 1:1) need not be a reference to it (Jon. 1:2; 3:2; 4:11), as similarly superlative descriptions of Nineveh can be found elsewhere (Xenophon, *Anabasis* 3.4.10; Strabo, *Geog.* 16.1-3).

168. Dubarle, *Judith*, 164.

2. Scripturalized Narrative in Second Temple Literature

The Compositional Use of the Jewish Scriptures in Judith

The author of Judith often draws narrative details from similar episodes in the Jewish scriptures. For example, upon learning of the threat posed by Holofernes, the Israelites fast and cry out to God, clothing all the inhabitants of Israel, including cattle, in sackcloth (Jdt. 4:9-12). Whilst putting on sackcloth, fasting and crying to God are hardly rare occurrences in the scriptures,[169] the strange image of cattle clothed in sackcloth brings to mind the lament of Nineveh in the book of Jonah (Jon. 3:6-9). There, the Ninevites are commanded to fast and put on sackcloth (Jon. 3:7-8) and to do likewise with their cattle. It is here the language of Judith most resembles Jonah: where Jonah reads 'And the people and cattle put on sackcloth, and they cried out earnestly to God' (LXX Jon. 3:8: καὶ περιεβάλοντο σάκκους οἱ ἄνθρωποι καὶ τὰ κτήνη, καὶ ἀνεβόησαν πρὸς τὸν θεὸν ἐκτενῶς), Judith has 'They even surrounded the altar with sackcloth and cried out in unison, [praying] earnestly to the God of Israel' (Jdt. 4:12: καὶ τὸ θυσιαστήριον σάκκῳ περιέβαλον καὶ ἐβόησαν πρὸς τὸν θεὸν Ισραηλ ὁμοθυμαδὸν ἐκτενῶς).

Judith's anticipatory prayer (Jdt. 9:2-14) and her song of victory following the defeat of the Assyrians (16:2-17) borrow details from the Song of the Sea following Israel's defeat of the Egyptians (Exod. 15:1-20): 'They are exalted, with their horse and rider' (Jdt. 9:7; cf. Exod. 15:1, 21); 'You are the Lord who crushes wars; the Lord is your name' (Jdt. 9:7; 16:3; cf. LXX Exod. 15:3); Judith and Miriam sing 'with tambourines' (Jdt. 16:3; cf. Exod. 15:20).[170] Exodus also appears to lie behind the complaint of the Bethulians in two medieval Hebrew mss. of the Judith legend which might reflect an early reading of Jdt. 7:16: 'It is better for us to | go into captivity (B) | serve our God under the hand of the King of Assur (C) | than to die of thirst' – compare with Exod. 14:12 (17:3):

---

169. Neh. 9:1; Est. 4:1-4; Pss. 35:13; 69:10-11; Isa. 58:5; Dan. 9:3; Joel. 1:13-14.

170. See also Jdt. 15:12-13. Further parallels are noted by Claudia Rakel, *Judit – über Schönheit, Macht und Widerstand im Krieg: Eine feministisch-intertextuelle Lektüre*, BZAW 334 (Berlin: W. de Gruyter, 2003), 250–2; Larry Perkins, ' "The Lord is a Warrior" – "The Lord Who Shatters Wars": Exodus 15:3 and Judith 9:7; 16:2', *BIOSCS* 40 (2007): 121–38; Lang, 'The Lord Who Crushes Wars'. See also Dubarle, *Judith*, 142–3; Newman, *Praying by the Book*, 146–8; Claudia Rakel, ' "I Will Sing a New Song to my God": Some Remarks on the Intertextuality of Judith 16.1-17', in *Judges: A Feminist Companion to the Bible*, ed. Athalya Brenner (Sheffield: Sheffield Academic, 1999), 38–44; Moore, *Judith*, 192, 256–7; Gera, *Judith*, 312–13, 448–50; Wills, *Judith*, 286–7. On the broader phenomenon of scripturalized prayer in Judith (esp. 9:2-14), see Newman, *Praying by the Book*, 117–54.

90　　　　　　　　　　*Writing with Scripture*

'It would have been better for us to serve the Egyptians than to die in the wilderness'.[171]

Above all, the author of Judith is fond of drawing phrases and narrative details from the tales of scriptural women.[172] As Ruth declares to Naomi, 'Your God [shall be] my God' (LXX Ruth 1:16: ὁ θεός σου θεός μου), so Holofernes, in a moment of irony, declares to Judith, 'Your God shall be my God' (Jdt. 11:23: ὁ θεός σου ἔσται μου θεός). At the same time, the Ammonite general Achior echoes the words of another woman, Rahab: 'Then God dried up the Red Sea before them' (Jdt. 5:13; cf. Josh. 2:10). It is perhaps no coincidence the Achior, like Rahab, eventually becomes part of Israel himself (Jdt. 14:10; cf. Josh. 6:25).[173] And as already noted, Judith leading Israel in a victory song (15:12-13; 16:2-17) resembles the songs of Miriam (Exod. 15:20-21) and Deborah (Judg. 5).[174]

There are also intriguing, if somewhat harder to detect, parallels with the other *femme fatale* of Second Temple literature, Esther. Judith and Esther are women famed for their beauty, who single-handedly save the Jewish people from an existential threat posed by one Gentile man, using deceit and seduction to sway a weak-willed ruler at a banquet.[175] Additions C and D to LXX Esther reveal an even closer semblance

---

171. Exod. 14:12 is used similarly in *LAB* 9:14. The variant at Jdt. 7:16 is discussed by Dubarle, *Judith*, 143. Dubarle is convinced that similarities between the medieval Hebrew mss. and the Vulgate point to an early Hebrew version of Judith, possibly used by Jerome (see 20–47). As many commentators have noted, this is difficult to prove; see Gera, *Judith*, 21–2. For a more sympathetic view, see Otzen, *Tobit and Judith*, 138–9.

172. As noted by André Lacocque, *The Feminine Unconventional: Four Subversive Figures in Israel's Tradition* (Minneapolis, MN: Fortress, 1990), 35; Otzen, *Tobit and Judith*, 74–7; Gera, *Judith*, 51–2; Wills, *Judith*, 270.

173. Compare Jdt. 14:10, 'When Achior saw all that the God of Israel had done, he believed firmly in God. So he was circumcised, and joined the house of Israel, remaining so to this day', with Josh. 6:25, 'But Rahab the prostitute, with her family and all who belonged to her, Joshua spared. Her family has lived in Israel ever since.' Later interpreters would likewise associate Rahab's deliverance with belief, 'By faith (πίστις) Rahab the prostitute did not perish' (Heb. 11:31; also *1 Clem.* 12; cf. Jas. 2:25), as in Jdt. 14:10, '[Achior] believed (πιστεύω) firmly in God'.

174. On the relationship of the songs of Miriam and Deborah, see Alan J. Hauser, 'Two Songs of Victory: A Comparison of Exodus 15 and Judges 5', in *Directions in Biblical Hebrew Poetry*, ed. Elaine R. Follis, JSOTSup 40 (Sheffield: JSOT, 1987), 265–84.

175. There is, however, no sign the story of Judith as a whole was composed with Esther in mind, *pace* Paul Haupt, 'Purim', *Beiträge zur Assyriologie* 6 (1906): 1–53, esp. 7.

2. Scripturalized Narrative in Second Temple Literature   91

between the two. There, Esther takes off her splendid attire and puts on garments of mourning (LXX Est. 14:1-2), covering her head with ashes (and dung!). She then prays to God for help (14:3-19), after which she takes off the garments of mourning and 'arrayed herself in splendid attire' (περιεβάλετο τὴν δόξαν αὐτῆς), and then, 'majestically adorned' (γενηθεῖσα ἐπιφανής), Esther brings her two 'maids' (ἄβραι) to go before the king, Ahasuerus (15:1-6). Likewise, Judith, before she prays to God for help, takes off the sackcloth and covers her head with ashes (Jdt. 9:1). After this she puts away the sackcloth, bathes and 'arrayed herself in her gayest apparel' (ἐνεδύσατο τὰ ἱμάτια τῆς εὐφροσύνης αὐτῆς), and, having 'made herself very beautiful' (ἐκαλλωπίσατο σφόδρα), she brings her 'maid' (ἄβρα) to go before Holofernes (10:1-5). Whilst there is little by way of verbal correspondence,[176] the shared structure of the episodes raises the possibility one served as the model for the other.[177] Favouring the priority of Judith is Carey Moore, who notes that Esther's actions in Additions C and D do not contribute to the broader narrative, whereas Judith 9–10 are crucial to the development of the narrative, which suggests LXX Esther is more likely derivative.[178] On the other hand, Linda Day notes some of the Judith-like elements in LXX Esther are already 'indirectly suggested' in the Hebrew text of Esther, so they may not be as extraneous to the narrative as Moore suggests.[179]

One other detail, however, suggests the priority of Judith in the case of a literary relationship. Curiously, Esther prays, 'And your servant has not eaten at Haman's table, and I have not honoured the king's feast or drunk the wine of his libations' (LXX Est. 14:17). An astute reader of Esther knows, however, that she dines with Ahasuerus and Haman at least two times (Est. 5:5-8; 6:14–7:1).[180] The detail better reflects Judith,

---

176. The responses of Ahasuerus and Holofernes to Esther and Judith, respecp tively, are in one place similar (Jdt. 11:1; LXX Est. 15:9): 'Take courage' (θάρσησον/ θάρσει).

177. Explored by Zeitlin, 'The Books of Esther and Judith', 15–21; Moore, *Judith*, 195–7, 212–16; Gera, *Judith*, 299–300; Wills, *Judith*, 279. Charl Pretorius Van der Walt postulates a similar *Sitz im Leben* for the two works, 'The Prayer of Esther (LXX) and Judith Against Their Social Backgrounds: Evidence of a Possible Common "Grundlage"?', *JSem* 17 (2008): 194–206.

178. Moore, *Judith*, 215.

179. Linda Day, *Three Faces of a Queen: Characterization in the Books of Esther*, JSOTSup 186 (Sheffield: Sheffield Academic, 1995), 222–5, esp. 224.

180. A fact which troubled many ancient interpreters; see Aaron Koller, *Esther in Ancient Jewish Thought* (Cambridge: Cambridge University Press, 2014), 118–19, 136–8, 193.

92 *Writing with Scripture*

who rebuffs Holofernes' offer of a table with food and wine, saying, 'I cannot eat it, lest it be an offense' (Jdt. 12:1-2). By borrowing this detail from Judith, the author of the Greek additions may have wished to correct Esther's behavior. Indeed, the entire prayer scene (LXX Est. 14:1–15:5) could be an effort to infuse Esther with some of Judith's piety.[181] If so, then Esther's prayer (LXX Est. 14–15) might be regarded as a scripturalized narrative, loosely modelled on Judith 9–10.[182]

A further parallel between Esther and Judith exists in the Old Latin. When the Israelites learn of Holofernes' threat, they pray for God 'not to give up their infants as prey and their wives as booty, and the cities they had inherited to be destroyed, and the sanctuary to be profaned and desecrated to the malicious joy of the Gentiles' (Jdt. 4:12: τοῦ μὴ δοῦναι εἰς διαρπαγὴν τὰ νήπια αὐτῶν καὶ τὰς γυναῖκας εἰς προνομὴν καὶ τὰς πόλεις τῆς κληρονομίας αὐτῶν εἰς ἀφανισμὸν καὶ τὰ ἅγια εἰς βεβήλωσιν καὶ ὀνειδισμὸν ἐπίχαρμα τοῖς ἔθνεσιν). A remarkably similar prayer appears in the Old Latin of Esther, this time on the lips of the Israelites upon learning of Haman's threat: 'Do not give your children over to captivity, nor our wives to rape, nor to destruction…and do not give over our inheritance into disgrace, such that enemies [gentiles] would dominate us' (VL Est. 3:15: *non des filios tuos in captiuitatem neque uxores nostras in uiolationem neque in perditionem…et non des haereditatem nostram in infamiam ut hostes (gentes) dominentur nostri*).[183] Once more, the direction of this literary relationship is difficult to determine. The Old Latin likely depends on an earlier lost Greek text of Esther,[184] but whether this

---

181. That Judith was composed as a corrective to Esther, see David Daube, 'Judith', in *The Collected Works of David Daube*. Vol. 3, *Biblical Law and Literature*, ed. Calum M. Carmichael (Berkeley, CA: Robbins Collection, 1992), 849–70. Also Zeitlin, 'The Books of Esther and Judith', 14. For a comparison of Esther and Judith, see Sidnie White Crawford, 'Esther and Judith: Contrasts in Character', in *The Book of Esther in Modern Research*, ed. Crawford and Leonard J. Greenspoon (London: A. & C. Black, 2003), 61–76.

182. The Greek Additions also appear to have influenced Josephus' account of Esther's prayer (*Ant.* 11.232-234), as observed by Feldman, 'Hellenizations in Josephus' Version of Esther', *Transactions and Proceedings of the American Philological Association* 101 (1970): 143–70.

183. English translation from Simon Bellman and Anathea Portier-Young, 'The Old Latin Book of Esther: An English Translation', *JSP* 28 (2019): 267–89 (277).

184. Suggested over a century ago by Lewis Bayles Paton, who concluded the additions to VL Esther (including 3:14-15) 'bear internal evidence of being translated from a Greek original' (*A Critical and Exegetical Commentary on the Book of Esther*,

2. Scripturalized Narrative in Second Temple Literature   93

text pre-dates the Greek of Judith is unknown. It is nevertheless further evidence of an early tendency to conflate details in the tales of Esther and Judith, a practice which is continued in the medieval Hebrew versions of the Judith legend.[185]

But whilst the prayer and song of Judith brings to mind Miriam, Deborah and Esther, it is with the murder of Holofernes that she most resembles a scriptural heroine: the tent-dwelling assassin Jael.

Jael and Judith (and Jael again): Judith 10–16 and Judges 4–5 (and LAB 31)

Jael's grisly assassination of Sisera takes place during the military campaign of the prophetess Deborah and her general Barak against the Canaanites (Judg. 4:1-16, 23-24). Jael, who is introduced as the wife – *lit.* woman – of Heber the Kenite (4:17), invites the enemy of Israel, the Canaanite general Sisera, into her tent, where she offers him drink and covers him up with a 'blanket' (*hapax* שׂמיכה) (4:18-19). Once Sisera is asleep, Jael drives a tent peg into his temple with a hammer, killing him (4:21). Jael then comes out to meet Barak and shows him the fallen enemy (4:22), and thus fulfills Deborah's prophecy to Barak: Sisera will be given 'into the hand of a woman' (4:9). After the Canaanites are defeated, Deborah and Barak lead Israel in a song, in which they praise Jael, 'of tent-dwelling women most blessed' (5:24), and retell the episode, adding that the slain Sisera sank and fell and 'lay still at [Jael's] feet' (5:27).[186]

Like Jael, Judith is introduced late in the narrative as the wife of Manasseh (8:1-2; cf. Judg. 4:17), and her story is appended by a song led by a woman (Jdt. 16:2-17; cf. Judg. 5). But the influence of the Jael episode is most apparent in Judith 10–13 (esp. 12:10–13:10). Judith makes herself beautiful to entice the enemy of Israel, the Assyrian general Holofernes (Jdt. 10:4; 12:15). Aroused by her appearance, Holofernes invites Judith into his tent with the hopes of engaging in sexual intercourse (12:11-16). Judith then drinks with Holofernes until he falls asleep

---

ICC 19 [Edinburgh: T. & T. Clark, 1908], 40–1). Ditto Bickerman, who considers VL Esther one of 'four Greek texts of Esther'; see 'Notes on the Greek Book of Esther', *PAAJR* 20 (1950): 101–33.

185. See the legends surveyed by Dubarle, esp. ms. C (*Judith*, 161).

186. The mention of Jael's 'feet' (רגל) could imply sexual intercourse. See the euphemistic usage in Deut. 28:57; Judg. 3:24; Ruth 3:7; 1 Sam. 24:4; 2 Sam. 11:8; Isa. 7:20; Ezek. 16:25. For this interpretation of Judg. 5:27; see *b. Hor.* 10b; *b. Naz.* 23b; *b. Yeb.* 103a.

94   *Writing with Scripture*

inebriated, leaving them alone in the tent (12:17–13:2). Once Holofernes is asleep, Judith cuts off his head and pushes his body onto the floor, taking the canopy from his bed and placing his head in a bag (13:6-10). Judith then returns to her hometown of Bethulia, where she presents the leaders with Holofernes' head along with the canopy, announcing, 'The Lord has struck [Holofernes] down by the hand of a woman' (13:15). When Holofernes' head is presented to Achior, he praises Judith, saying, 'Blessed are you in every tent of Judah!' (14:7). After the Assyrians are defeated, Judith leads Israel in a song of praise, extolling the victory won 'by the hand of a woman' (16:5).

That the author of Judith knew Judges is evident from Achior's report: '[The Israelites] drove out before them the Canaanites, the Perizzites, the Jebusites, the Shechemites, and all the Gergesites, and lived there a long time' (Jdt. 5:16). The list of conquered nations comes from Josh. 3:10, except for the unusual inclusion of the Shechemites, which reflects the defeat of Shechem narrated in Judg. 9:22-57.[187] Judith's slaying of Holofernes also appears to take several phrases directly from Judges 4–5: the defeat of Holofernes comes 'by the hand of a woman' (Jdt. 9:10; 13:15; 16:5: ἐν χειρὶ θηλείας) as Sisera falls 'into/by the hand of a woman' (MT Judg. 4:9: בְּיַד־אִשָּׁה; LXX: ἐν χειρὶ γυναικός); Achior praises Judith, saying 'Blessed are you in every tent of Judah' (Jdt. 14:7: εὐλογημένη σὺ ἐν παντὶ σκηνώματι Ιουδα), as Deborah praises Jael, 'Of women in the tent may she be blessed' (LXX Judg. 5:24: ἐκ γυναικῶν ἐν σκηνῇ εὐλογηθείη). But the use of Judges 4–5 is most apparent in the narrative of a woman who, on her own, faces the general of Israel's enemy by enticing him into a tent and kills him by striking him in the head once he has fallen asleep after drinking. All this would seem to confirm the conclusion of Sidnie White Crawford: '[It is] plain the author of Judith used the story of Jael and Deborah in Judges 4 and 5'.[188]

The two heroines are, of course, not identical. Whilst Jael invites Sisera into her tent (Judg. 4:18), it is Holofernes who acts as the host to Judith (Jdt. 10:20; 12:5, 10-16). Whilst Jael gives Sisera a skin of milk to drink (Judg. 4:19) and curds to eat (5:25), Holofernes gets drunk on his own

---

187. The Shechemites are referenced again at Jdt. 9:2-4.

188. Sidnie White Crawford, 'In the Steps of Jael and Deborah: Judith as Heroine', in VanderKam, ed., *No One Spoke Ill of Her*, 5–16 (5). See also Fokkelein van Dijk-Hemmes, 'Gezegende onder de vrouwen: een moeder in Israël en een maagd in de kerk', in *'t Is kwaad gerucht, als zij neit binnen blijft: Vrouwen in oude culturen*, ed. van Dijk-Hemmes, Tekst en Maatschappij (Utrecht: HES, 1986), 123–47. There is less to commend the strange conclusion of J. Edgar Bruns that 'Judith is none other than the [same] Jael of Judges 4–5' ('Judith or Jael?', *CBQ* 16 [1954]: 12–14).

2. Scripturalized Narrative in Second Temple Literature 95

supply of wine (Jdt. 12:13–13:2), which Judith drinks with him (12:17-19). Whilst Jael's weapon of choice is a tent peg (Judg. 4:21-22; 5:26), Judith beheads Holofernes with his own sword (Jdt. 13:8; 16:9). Whilst Jael is liable to the charge of sexual impropriety (so *b. Hor.* 10b; *b. Naz.* 23b; *b. Yeb.* 103a; cf. *Lev. Rab.* 23:10), Judith goes out of her way to absolve herself of the charge: 'I swear that it was my face that seduced him to his destruction, and that he committed no sin with me, to defile and shame me' (Jdt. 13:16).[189] To this can be added many details which are absent in the story of Jael, including the maid (Jdt. 8:10, 33; 10:2, 5, 10, 17; 12:15, 19; 13:3, 9), the servants (especially Bagoas: 12:10-15; 14:14-18), the banquet (12:10–13:1) and the duration of Judith's stay at the enemy camp (12:7, 10). Unlike Judith, who prays before entering the enemy camp (9:2-14; also 12:8) and from inside Holofernes' tent (13:4-5, 7), Jael is not a pious figure. And whilst there is no direct parallel to the 'canopy' (κωνώπιον) of Holofernes' bed, which plays so central a role in Judith's revelation to the Bethulian elders (13:9, 15), it may be intended to reflect the *hapax legomenon* שמיכה in Judg. 4:18, as Crawford brilliantly speculates.[190]

These differences did not, however, prevent one ancient reader from seeing Jael in the person of Judith. In Pseudo-Philo's account of Jael (*LAB* 31), it is Judith who becomes the model for Jael. Before Sisera

189. This may be an attempt to distance Judith from Jael's impropriety; so Colleen M. Conway, *Sex and Slaughter in the Tent of Jael: A Cultural History of a Biblical Story* (Oxford: Oxford University Press, 2016), 29–30. If so, it was not entirely effective, since, as Dubarle shows, later accounts depict Judith sleeping with Holofernes (*Judith*, 134). The theme of defilement is continued in the reference to the rape of Dinah (Jdt. 9:2-5; cf. Gen. 34) and the name of the – probably fictitious – town of Bethulia, from Hb. בתלה, 'virgin', which explains Holofernes' attempt to penetrate the narrow pass into Bethulia (Jdt. 4:7); see William Loader, *The Pseudepigrapha on Sexuality: Attitudes towards Sexuality in Apocalypses, Testaments, Legends, Wisdom, and Related Literature* (Grand Rapids, MI: Eerdmans, 2011), 213–14.

190. The *hapax* may also lie behind κώδιον in Jdt. 12:15, see Crawford, 'In the Steps of Jael and Deborah', 9–10. Philip Esler argues, to the contrary, that these 'significant disparities…prevent us from regarding Jael as a central model for Judith' ('"By the Hand of a Woman": Culture, Story and Theology in the Book of Judith', in *Social Scientific Models for Interpreting the Bible: Essays by the Context Group in Honor of Bruce J. Malina*, ed. Bruce J. Malina and John J. Pilch, BibInt 53 [Leiden: Brill, 2001], 77). That Jael was not Judith's only model is noted by Jan Willem van Henten, 'Judith as Alternative Leader: A Rereading of Judith 7–13', in *A Feminist Companion to Esther, Judith and Susanna*, ed. Athalya Brenner (London: T&T Clark, 1995), 224–52, esp. 224.

arrives, Jael 'adorned herself with jewelry' (*ornavit se ornamento*), to which the author adds, 'now the woman was very beautiful in appearance' (*LAB* 31:3: *mulier autem erat bone specie valde*) – just as Judith '[dressed] herself in all her woman's finery' (Jdt. 12:15) and was 'beautiful in appearance' (Jdt. 8:7). When Jael invites Sisera into her tent, he sees 'roses scattered on the bed' and desires her for a wife (*LAB* 31:3) – as Holofernes desires to sleep with Judith (Jdt. 12:12, 16; also 11:22-23). When Sisera asks for a drink, Jael mixes wine with milk so he becomes drunk and falls asleep (*LAB* 31:4-6) – as Holofernes drinks wine until he falls asleep (Jdt. 12:20; 13:2).[191] Once Sisera is asleep, Jael takes a stake in her left hand and prays for a sign, that when she pushes him off the bed onto the ground he will not wake (*LAB* 31:7) – as Judith pushes Holofernes' body off the bed (Jdt. 13:9). When Sisera does not wake, Jael prays 'Strengthen in me today, Lord, my arm on account of you and your people and those who hope in you' (*LAB* 31:7) – as Judith prays, 'Give me strength today, O Lord God of Israel!' (Jdt. 13:7). With his dying breath, Sisera complains of his fate at the hands of a woman (like Abimelech in Judg. 9:54), leading Jael to exclaim, 'Go, boast before your father in hell and tell him that you have fallen *into the hands of a woman* (*in manus mulieris*)' (*LAB* 31:7). When Barak arrives at the scene, he remembers the words of Deborah's prophecy, '*Into the hand of a woman* (*in manum mulieris*) Sisera will be handed over' (*LAB* 31:9; cf. 31:1). Barak then cuts off Sisera's head and sends it, perversely, to his mother with the message, 'Receive your son, whom you hoped to see coming back with spoils' (*LAB* 31:9) – so that like Holofernes (Jdt. 13:8), Sisera is also beheaded.

Judith 10–16	Judges 4–5	*LAB* 31
Judith 'was beautiful in appearance' (8:7; also 10:4).		Jael 'was very beautiful in appearance' (31:3).
Judith adorns herself with all kinds of jewelry before meeting Holofernes (10:3-4; also 12:15).		Jael 'adorned herself with jewelry' before meeting Sisera (31:3).

---

191. The use of *dissolvo* implies drunkenness in *LAB* 31:5-7; cf. 31:4, where it implies exhaustion, from עיף (Judg. 4:21). Pseudo-Philo may have been led to conflate the words of Sisera, 'I am thirsty' (Judg. 4:19: כי צמאתי), with the words of Esau, 'I am weary' (Gen. 25:30: כי עיף אנכי), by the use of עיף in Judg. 4:21.

2. Scripturalized Narrative in Second Temple Literature
97

Holofernes invites Judith into his tent (12:5, 13).	Jael invites Sisera into her tent (4:18).	Jael invites Sisera into her house (31:3).
Holofernes desires to sleep with Judith (12:12, 16).		Sisera desires to marry/sleep with Jael (31:3).
Judith drinks wine with Holofernes until he becomes drunk (12:20; 13:2).	Jael gives Sisera milk to drink (4:19; also curds in 5:25).	Jael gives Sisera wine mixed with milk to drink so that he becomes drunk (31:6).
Because of the wine, Holofernes falls asleep in the tent with Judith (13:2).	After drinking, Sisera falls asleep in the tent with Jael (4:19, 21).	Because of the wine mixed with milk, Sisera falls asleep in the house with Jael (31:6).
Judith takes Holofernes' sword and approaches the bed (13:6-7).	Jael takes a tent peg and a hammer in her hand and approaches Sisera (4:21).	Jael takes a stake in her left hand and approaches Sisera (31:7).
Judith prays, 'Give me strength today, O Lord God of Israel!' (13:7).		Jael prays, 'Strengthen in me today, Lord' (31:7).
Judith strikes Holofernes' neck twice with the sword and cuts off his head (13:8).	Jael drives the tent peg into Sisera's temple (4:21; 5:26).	Jael takes the stake and hammers it into Sisera's temple (31:7). Barak cuts off Sisera's head (31:9).
Judith 'rolled [Holofernes'] body off the bed' (13:9).	Sisera sinks and falls at Jael's feet (5:27).	Jael 'pushed [Sisera] onto the ground from the bed' (31:7).
Judith shows Holofernes' decapitated head to the leaders of Bethulia (13:15) and Achior (14:6).	Jael shows Sisera's body to Barak (4:22).	Jael shows Sisera's body to Barak (31:9). Barak sends Sisera's decapitated head to Sisera's mother (31:9).
Achior praises Judith, 'Blessed are you in every tent of Judah!' (14:7).	Deborah praises Jael, 'of tent-dwelling women most blessed' (5:24).	
Victory is won 'by the hand of a woman' (prophesied in 9:10; repeated in 13:15; 16:5).	Deborah prophesies Sisera will fall 'into the hand of woman' (4:9).	Sisera falls 'into the hand of a woman' (31:1, 7, 9).

Pseudo-Philo was no doubt prompted by the inherent similarities in the Jael and Judith stories to conflate the two figures.[192] This is characteristic of Pseudo-Philo's tendency to conflate similar figures and events: the destruction of Sodom (Gen. 19:25) becomes the destruction of the flood (*LAB* 3:3); the rod of Jacob (Gen. 30:37-39) becomes the rod of Aaron (*LAB* 17:3); the death of Jacob (Gen. 49:33) becomes the death of Joshua (*LAB* 24:5); and, even in the Jael episode, the words of Esau (Gen. 25:30) become the words of Sisera (*LAB* 31:4; cf. Judg. 4:19). In the same way, the actions of Judith and Holofernes become those of Jael and Sisera. Rather than modelling the new on the old, like Judas Maccabeus and Moses (1 Macc. 5:45-51), Pseudo-Philo has modelled an old story on one purporting to come from more recent history, like the story of Abram and the fiery furnace of Daniel (*LAB* 6).

But why the author of Judith modelled their heroine on Jael in the first place is as mysterious as the book itself.[193] Was Judith wholly a product of the author's imagination, pieced together out of Jael, Deborah, Miriam and other scriptural heroines, or was a pre-existing legend over time given elements of the Jael story? Here there can be no certainty, other than that the author Judith made use of Judges 4–5 when composing the story. If the book of Judith was meant to be read as historical fiction – which is doubtful – then it would be an example of a knowingly fictional character fashioned, in part, out of the Jewish scriptures. As no sign of the author's intent survives, and the events are narrated in the historiographical style, it is more appropriate to consider the book of Judith as *pseudo-history* – which is a statement of fact, rather than intention.[194] The events described in Judith did not happen, not least because in some cases they would be

192. Bauckham raises the interesting possibility that Pseudo-Philo was also influenced by 'midrashic developments' in the Jael story ('Pseudo-Philo and the Gospels as "Midrash"', 50). Feldman details some of these developments, including Jael's beauty and the role of wine ('Prolegomenon', cxxii).

193. On the lingering question of the book's purpose, see Moore, *Judith*, 76–7.

194. The term *pseudo-history* is borrowed from Lionel Pearson, who uses it to describe the fabricated history of the Messenians as recounted in Pausanias (*Descr.* 4.6) in 'The Pseudo-History of Messenia and Its Authors', *Historia: Zeitschrift für Alte Geschichte* (1962): 397–426. On applying this term to Second Temple literature, see Katherine M. Stott, 'Ezra's "Lost Manuscripts": Narrative Context and Rhetorical Function', in *The One Who Reads May Run: Essays in Honour of Edgar W. Conrad*, ed. Roland Boer, Michael Carden and Julie Kelso, LHBOTS 553 (London: T&T Clark, 2012), 96–106, esp. 102–5. Gera notes the stylistic similarities between Judith and Greek historical writings (*Judith*, 60–78).

2. Scripturalized Narrative in Second Temple Literature

impossible. The author nevertheless presents them as if they did. What historical or legendary sources the author used to compose this story, if any, are lost.[195] The only surviving sources are the Jewish scriptures.[196] Though the scriptures do not explain every aspect of the story, a scripturalized episode lies at the heart of the *pseudo-historical* tale: the slaying of an enemy general in a tent 'by the hand of a woman'.

The Testament of Abraham

On the use of the Jewish scriptures in the *Testament of Abraham*, its translator, E. P. Sanders, has written, 'Almost nothing of the Old Testament appears [in the *Testament*] except the obvious references to Abraham in Genesis'.[197] One would be forgiven, then, for wondering what the humorous, if not mildly irreverent, *Testament* is doing alongside much better-known works in a discussion about the use of the Jewish scriptures in the Second Temple period.[198] To date, only one monograph has attempted to show the use of the scriptures outside of Genesis in the *Testament*, and it has been met with strong criticism.[199] Recent work by Dale Allison has, however, called Sanders' assessment into question.[200] Drawing on Allison's work, this final section explores a scripturalized narrative in the most unlikely of places: the comical *Testament of Abraham*.

195. *Pace* Mark Stephen Caponigro, 'Judith, Holding the Tale of Herodotus', in VanderKam, ed., *No One Spoke Ill of Her*, 47–59. Otzen surveys a number of proposed literary sources (*Tobit and Judith*, 74–80).

196. As noted by Gera, *Judith*, 56.

197. E. P. Sanders, 'Testament of Abraham', in *OTP*, I, 879.

198. At times, the *Testament* verges on comedy. The archangel Michael, who is supposed to be the 'commander-in-chief', is often found crying (*T. Ab.* A 3:9-10; 5:10, 14) over his failure to complete his one simple task (4:6; 8:1-3; 15:14-15). Abram, on the other hand, is deceitful, disobedient and obdurate to the end. Unwilling to obey God and die – apparently unsatisfied with his ample 995 years – he resorts to tricking God and Michael, until God fatally tricks him in return. But perhaps the most laughable scene is Michael's attempt to get some privacy from Abraham by pretending to urinate (4:5), despite the fact that angels neither eat nor drink (4:10).

199. Phillip B. Munoa, *Four Powers in Heaven: The Interpretation of Daniel 7 in the Testament of Abraham*, JSPSup 28 (Sheffield: Sheffield Academic, 1998); see the critical review by Michael E. Stone, 'Review of Munoa, *Four Powers in Heaven*', *JQR* 90 (1999): 235–37.

200. Dale C. Allison Jr., 'Job in the Testament of Abraham', *JSP* 12 (2001): 131–47; Allison, *Testament of Abraham*, CEJL (Berlin: W. de Gruyter, 2003).

100   *Writing with Scripture*

But first, a brief note on the textual history of the *Testament* is necessary. The work survives in two variant Greek recensions, one longer (A) and one shorter (B).[201] Whilst the longer recension is usually thought to preserve the original, the style of the Greek appears to be later and both recensions include Christian interpolations.[202] The most probable explanation is that the two Christian recensions independently relied on a Greek original composed by a Jewish author, the scriptural and traditional style of which is best reflected in the longer recension.[203]

The longer recension nevertheless preserves little of the terse scriptural report of Abraham's death (Gen. 25:7-11). Instead, the narrative follows the archangel Michael as he appears by the oak at Mamre to inform Abraham of his impending death, with the hope he will amicably forfeit his soul (*T. Ab.* 1:4-7). Michael, however, grows fond of Abraham and loses the courage to break the bad news (2:1–5:14). Abraham's fate is only revealed when Sarah uncovers Michael's angelic identity (6:1–7:11). Abraham attempts to forestall Michael from completing his task, cleverly asking to be taken on a cosmic tour to see all things in creation (9:2-6). On their heavenly journey, Michael and Abraham observe a number of eschatological scenes (10:1–14:14).[204] In one, Abraham demands punishment for certain sinners, only to intervene on their behalf when he sees the terrible judgment scene (14:1-15). When Michael and Abraham return home from their journey, Death is there to take Abraham's soul (16:6-15).

---

201. On the Greek mss., see Allison, *Testament*, 4–7. On the Coptic, Arabic, Ethiopic, Slavonic and Romanian mss. and their relationship to the Greek recensions, see 8–11.

202. See Allison, *Testament*, 15–27. Favouring the longer recension is M. R. James, *The Testament of Abraham: The Greek Text Now First Edited with an Introduction and Notes*, TS 2/2 (Cambridge: Cambridge University Press, 1892), 49; George H. Box, *The Testament of Abraham: Translated from the Greek Text with Introduction and Notes* (London: SPCK, 1927), xii–xv; George W. E. Nickelsburg, 'Structure and Message in the Testament of Abraham', in *Studies on the Testament of Abraham*, ed. George W. E. Nickelsburg, SACS 6 (Missoula, MT: Scholars Press, 1976), 85–93; Sanders, 'Testament of Abraham', 872. Favouring the shorter recens sion is Nigel Turner, *The Testament of Abraham: A Study of the Original Language, Place of Origin, Authorship, and Relevance* (London: University of London, 1953), 48–100, 194–257; Francis Schmidt, *Le Testament grec d'Abraham: Introduction, edition critique des deux recensions grecques, traduction*, TSAJ 11 (Tübingen: Mohr-Siebeck, 1986), 115–24.

203. So Allison, *Testament*, 24–7. The following discussion will focus on the longer recension (hereafter *T. Ab.*).

204. Abraham also tours the heavens in *LAB* 18:5; 23:6; *Ap. Ab.* 19-21.

2. Scripturalized Narrative in Second Temple Literature   101

Abraham continues to resist, however, until Death deceives him with a kiss, at which point he dies and ascends to heaven (20:8-15).

Despite its departure from the Genesis narrative, the *Testament* borrows several phrases, almost verbatim, from LXX Genesis 18–25. God blesses Abraham 'as the stars of heaven and as the sand by the seashore' (*T. Ab.* 1:5: ὡς τὰ ἄστρα τοῦ οὐρανοῦ καὶ ὡς τὴν ἄμμον τὴν παρὰ χεῖλος τῆς θαλάσσης), as he does in LXX Gen. 22:17: ὡς τοὺς ἀστέρας τοῦ οὐρανοῦ καὶ ὡς τὴν ἄμμον τὴν παρὰ τὸ χεῖλος τῆς θαλάσσης. Michael appears by 'the oak of Mamre' (*T. Ab.* 2:1: τὴν δρῦν τὴν Μαβρήν),[205] as the three men appear to Abram before τῇ δρυὶ τῇ Μαμβρή (LXX Gen. 18:1).[206] And Abraham addresses 'Isaac his son, "My beloved son"' (*T. Ab.* 4:1: Ἰσαὰκ τὸν υἱὸν αὐτοῦ υἱέ μου ἀγαπητέ), as does the angel in LXX Gen. 22:11-12: Ἰσαὰκ τὸν υἱὸν αὐτοῦ...υἱοῦ σου τοῦ ἀγαπητοῦ.[207]

As with other works, the *Testament* also draws secondary material from elsewhere in the Jewish scriptures, weaving unmarked scriptural language into the narrative. Abraham prays, 'You have given to me according to my heart and have fulfilled all my plans' (*T. Ab.* 9:4: ἔδωκάς μοι κατὰ τῆς καρδίας μου καὶ πᾶσαν τὴν βουλήν μου ἐπλήρωσας), which *mutatis mutandis* reflects LXX Ps. 19:5: 'May he give to you according to your heart and may he fulfil all your plans' (δώη σοι κατὰ καρδίαν σου καὶ πᾶσαν τὴν βουλήν σου πληρώσαι).[208] In the same prayer, Abraham prays, '[All] shudder and tremble before your power' (*T. Ab.* 9:5: [πάντα] φρίττει καὶ τρέμει ἀπὸ προσώπου δυνάμεώς σου), which appears to be borrowed verbatim from *Pr. Man.* 4: 'All shudder and tremble before your power' (πάντα φρίττει καὶ τρέμει ἀπὸ προσώπου δυνάμεώς σου).[209] The three curses Abraham calls down on the sinners likewise follow scriptural models: upon his request, wild beasts 'came out...of the forest' (ἐξῆλθον...ἐκ τοῦ δρυμοῦ) and devoured the first group of sinners (*T. Ab.* 10:5-6), as when Elisha curses the children and bears 'came out...of the forest' (ἐξῆλθον... ἐκ τοῦ δρυμοῦ) to kill them (LXX 2 Kgs 2:24). For the next group, 'the earth opened up and swallowed them' (*T. Ab.* 10:10: ἐδιχάσθη ἡ γῆ καὶ κατέπιεν αὐτούς), as in the rebellion of Korah, 'the earth opened and swallowed [the men of Korah]' (LXX Num. 16:32: ἠνοίχθη ἡ γῆ καὶ

---

205. Also *T. Ab.* 1:2; 6:4; 16:7; 20:11.

206. Cf. LXX Gen. 13:18; 14:13

207. Also LXX Gen. 22:2-3, 9, 16.

208. My translation. See Allison, 'Job in the Testament of Abraham', 133–34; *Testament*, 207.

209. Allison brilliantly notes this phrase also occurs in *Gk. Apoc. Ezra* 7:7; *Apos. Con.* 8.7.5; and Ps.-Chrysostom, *Prec.* (PG 64.1065) (*Testament*, 207–8).

κατέπιεν αὐτούς).[210] And for the last group, 'fire came down from heaven and consumed them' (*T. Ab.* 10:12: κατῆλθεν πῦρ ἐκ τοῦ οὐρανοῦ καὶ κατέφαγεν αὐτούς; cf. 10:11), as on Elijah's command, 'fire came down from heaven and consumed [the captain and his fifty men]' (LXX 2 Kgs 1:10: κατέβη πῦρ ἐκ τοῦ οὐρανοῦ καὶ κατέφαγεν αὐτόν).

The *Testament* also appears to be influenced by contemporary traditions concerning the death of Moses, preserved in much later texts.[211] In particular, Abraham's confrontation with Death (*T. Ab.* 16–20) is strikingly similar to Moses' confrontation with Death (esp. *Deut. Rab.* 11:10; *Sifre* Deut. 305:5):[212] God sends Death/Sammael from heaven to fetch the hero (*T. Ab.* 16:1-6; cf. *Deut. Rab.* 11:10; *Sifre* Deut. 305:5); the hero resists Death/Sammael (*T. Ab.* 16:16; 19:2-4; 20:4-5; cf. *Deut. Rab.* 11:10; *Sifre* Deut. 305:5); Death/Sammael returns to heaven and reports on his failure (*Deut. Rab.* 11:10; *Sifre* Deut. 305:5; cf. Michael in *T. Ab.* 4:6-11; 8:1-12; 15:11-15); God sends Death/Sammael a second time (*Deut. Rab.* 11:10; *Sifre* Deut. 305:5; cf. Michael in *T. Ab.* 4:7–5:1; 8:4–9:1); God instructs the hero that all men must die (*T. Ab.* 8:9; cf. *Deut. Rab.* 11:8; *Sifre* Deut. 339:1); the hero has a vision of everything in creation (*T. Ab.* 10–14; cf. *Sifre* Deut. 357:1-27); the divine name protects the hero from death (*T. Ab.* 17:11; cf. *Deut. Rab.* 11:5, 10); the hero dies with a kiss (*T. Ab.* 20:8-9; cf. *Deut. Rab.* 11:10); the hero is taken to heaven (*T. Ab.* 20:12, 14; cf. *Deut. Rab.* 11:10).[213]

---

210. Allison, *Testament*, 226. Allison notes the verbal agreement with LXX Num. 16 is closer in some mss. of the shorter recension (B, E, F, G 12:7). The fate of the men of Korah is used as a model for other scenes of divine judgment: *LAB* 6:17; 26:1; Rev. 12:16; *b. Sanh.* 109a.

211. Noted by Samuel E. Loewenstamm, 'The Testament of Abraham and the Texts Concerning Moses' Death', in Nickelsburg, ed., *Studies in the Testament of Abraham*, 219–25; Esther Glickler-Chazon, 'Moses' Struggle for his Soul: A Prototype for the Testament of Abraham, the Greek Apocalypse of Ezra, and the Apocalpse of Sedrach', *The Second Century: A Journal of Early Christian Studies* 5 (1985/86): 151–64. Less convinced is Ludlow, *Abraham Meets Death*, 50–4; compare with the critical note in Allison, *Testament*, 26 n. 52. The Death of Moses tradition also appears to have influenced *Gk. Apoc. Ezra* 6:3–7:14; so Chazon, 'Moses' Struggle with Death', 158–62; Allison, *The New Moses*, 64–5.

212. Also *Deut. Rab.* 11:5, 8; *Sifre* Deut. 339:1; 357:1-27; *Petirat Moshe* in Jellinek, *BHM* 1.115-129. Rella Kushelevsky has collected many of the relevant texts in *Moses and the Angel of Death*, STML 4 (New York, NY: Peter Lang, 1995).

213. See the extensive list in Allison, *Testament*, 24–5. For an overview of traditions of Moses' death, see Loewenstamm, 'The Death of Moses', in Nickelsburg, ed., *Studies in the Testament of Abraham*, 185–217.

2. Scripturalized Narrative in Second Temple Literature   103

The narrative of Abraham's struggle with death in the *Testament* has no obvious starting point in the Jewish scriptures and appears to be without parallel in antiquity.[214] Speculation about Moses' death is, on the other hand, widely attested and has a plausible basis in the scriptures: the rebuke in Deut. 3:23-29 and the ambiguity of Deut. 34:1-6.[215] All of this suggests the priority of the Death of Moses tradition and its subsequent influence on the *Testament*.[216] Moses is not, however, the only scriptural figure who appears to have influenced the depiction of Abraham in the *Testament*.

Abraham and Job: Testament of Abraham *4–15 and LXX Job 1–2*

Explaining why he cannot break the news of Abraham's death, the archangel Michael tells God, 'Because I have not seen upon earth a man like him – merciful, hospitable, righteous, truthful, God-fearing, refraining from every evil deed' (*T. Ab.* 4:6: ὅτι οὐκ εἶδον ἐπὶ τῆς γῆς ἄνθρωπον ὅμοιον αὐτοῦ, ἐλεήμονα, φιλόξενον, δίκαιον, ἀληθινὸν, θεοσεβῆ, ἀπεχόμενον ἀπὸ παντὸς πονηροῦ πράγματος). Michael's description of Abraham is borrowed entirely from the description of Job in the Septuagint: 'That there is none like him on the earth, a man blameless, truthful, God-fearing, refraining from every evil deed' (LXX Job 1:8: ὅτι οὐκ ἔστιν κατ'αὐτὸν τῶν ἐπὶ τῆς γῆς ἄνθρωπος ἄμεμπτος, ἀληθινός, θεοσεβής, ἀπεχόμενος ἀπὸ παντὸς πονηροῦ πράγματος).[217] Michael later repeats this description, as he refuses to bring Abraham's soul, because 'There is no man like unto

---

214. There are, however, Islamic traditions concerning Abraham's struggle with the Angel of Death that bear a striking resemblance to the *Testament*. These are detailed in Stephen R. Burge, *Angels in Islam: Jalāl al-Dīn al-Suyūṭī's al-Ḥabā'ik fī akhbār al-malā'ik*, Culture and Civilization in the Middle East (London: Routledge, 2012), 135–6. It is unclear whether these traditions owe directly to the *Testament* or suggest a wider tradition of Abraham's conflict with Death.

215. On the scriptural origins of the Death of Moses tradition, see Allison, *Testament*, 26 n. 53; also Loewenstamm, 'The Death of Moses', 185. On the mythic character of Moses in antiquity, see again Loewenstamm, 'The Testament of Abraham', 219–24.

216. Allison notes the parallels with the Death of Moses tradition are stronger in the longer recension of the *Testament* and appear to be a feature of the original Jewish text (*Testament*, 26–7).

217. Also LXX Job 1:1: καὶ ἦν ὁ ἄνθρωπος ἐκεῖνος ἀληθινός, ἄμεμπτος, δίκαιος, θεοσεβής, ἀπεχόμενος ἀπὸ παντὸς πονηροῦ πράγματος; 2:3: ὅτι οὐκ ἔστιν κατ' αὐτὸν τῶν ἐπὶ τῆς γῆς ἄνθρωπος ἄκακος, ἀληθινός, ἄμεμπτος, θεοσεβής, ἀπεχόμενος ἀπὸ παντὸς κακοῦ. See Allison, 'Job in the Testament of Abraham', 138.

104   *Writing with Scripture*

him on earth, not even Job, the wondrous man' (*T. Ab.* 15:15: οὐκ ἔστιν ἄνθρωπος ὅμοιος αὐτοῦ ἐπὶ τῆς γῆς, οὐ κἂν Ἰὼβ ὁ θαυμάσιος ἄνθρωπος).[218]

Allison notes, however, that the *Testament*'s use of Job goes far beyond the borrowing of a phrase.[219] The author also appears to have modelled elements of the narrative on the first two chapters of Job, again in the Greek. Each narrative begins by praising a 'righteous' (δίκαιος) hero (*T. Ab.* 1:1; cf. LXX Job 1:1). This hero then becomes the subject of a discussion between God and a heavenly being (*T. Ab.* 1:4-7; cf. LXX Job 1:6-12), where his wealth is said to result from God's blessing (εὐλογέω). God gives the heavenly being instructions concerning the hero (*T. Ab.* 1:6-7; cf. Job 1:12). A messenger/angel (ἄγγελος) then speaks to the hero (*T. Ab.* 2:1; cf. LXX Job 1:14, 16-18), as the hero remains unaware of the heavenly plot. The heavenly being, however, fails in his task (*T. Ab.* 4:5-6; cf. Job 1:20-22), appearing in heaven for a second time (*T. Ab.* 4:5; cf. Job 2:1-2), where the hero is praised, '[there is none] on earth like him etc.' (*T. Ab.* 4:6; cf. LXX Job 2:3). God once more sends the heavenly being (*T. Ab.* 4:7-8, 10-11; cf. Job 2:6), only for him to fail again in his task (*T. Ab.* 7:12; cf. Job 2:10). The author of the *Testament* returns to this model later in the work, where Michael 'refrain[s] from touching' (φείδομαι τοῦ ἅψασθαι) Abraham because 'there is no man on earth like him, not even Job' (*T. Ab.* 15:14-15; cf. LXX Job 1:8; 2:3)[220] – with Michael's refusal to 'touch' (ἅπτω) Abraham finding its roots in God's command to Satan concerning Job, 'But do not touch him' (LXX Job 1:12: ἀλλὰ αὐτοῦ μὴ ἅψῃ).[221]

***Testament of Abraham* A 1–15**	**LXX Job 1–2**
Abraham is introduced as a 'righteous' man (1:1).	Job is introduced as a 'righteous' man (1:1).
God and Michael discuss Abraham's fate in heaven (1:4-7).	God and Satan discuss Job's fate in heaven (1:6-12).
Abraham's prosperity is the result of God's 'blessing' (1:5).	Job's prosperity is the result of God's 'blessing' (1:10).

218. Allison notes the agreement is even closer in Alexandrinus: LXX Job 1:8 A: οὐκ ἔστιν ἄνθρωπος ὅμοιος αὐτῷ (also LXX Job 2:3 A; cf. *T. Ab.* 15:15a: οὐκ ἔστιν ἄνθρωπος ὅμοιος αὐτοῦ). See Allison, 'Job in the Testament of Abraham', 137; *Testament*, 316–18. This variant is also found in mss. 161, 248 and in the margin of Syro-hex. at Job 1:8.

219. Allison, 'Job in the Testament of Abraham', 139–40; *Testament*, 128–30.

220. Allison, *Testament*, 316–18.

221. Compare the following table with the more extensive parallels in Allison, 'Job in the Testament of Abraham', 139; *Testament*, 129.

God sends Michael with instructions concerning Abraham (1:6-7).	God sends Satan with instructions concerning Job (1:12).
An angel (Michael) comes to Abraham bearing bad news (2-7).	Messengers (ἄγγελοι) come to Job bearing bad news (Job 1:14, 16-18).
Michael initially fails in his objective (4:5-6).	Satan initially fails in his objective (1:20-22).
Michael appears in heaven a second time (4:5).	Satan appears in heaven a second time (2:1-2).
Michael says to God, 'I have not seen upon earth a man like [Abraham]... truthful, God-fearing, refraining from every evil deed' (4:6).	God says to Satan, 'There is none like [Job] on the earth...truthful, God-fearing, refraining from every evil deed' (1:8; cf. 1:1; 2:3).
God sends Michael a second time (4:7-8, 10-11).	God sends Satan a second time (2:6).
Again, Michael fails in his objective (7:12).	Again, Satan fails in his objective (2:10).
Michael refuses to touch Abraham (15:14-15).	God commands Satan not to touch Job (1:12).
Michael says, 'there is no man like [Abraham] on earth, not even Job, the wondrous man' (15:15).	God says, 'there is none like [Job] on the earth' (1:8; 2:3).

The *Testament* is not, however, the only work in antiquity to conflate the figures of Job and Abraham. The Gemara states Satan spoke to God, 'Lord of the world, I have surveyed the whole world and found none so faithful as your servant, Abraham' (*b. B. Bat.* 15b; cf. Job 1:8; 2:3). Satan also speaks the words of Eliphaz the Temanite to Abraham on his way to the *Aqedah*: 'If we try to commune with you, will you be grieved?... Behold you have instructed many, and you have strengthened weak hands. Your words have held up him who was falling, and you have strengthened feeble knees. But now it is come upon you, and you faint... But should not your fear be your confidence?' (*b. Sanh.* 89b; cf. Job 4:2-6).[222] Abraham responds to Satan also with the words of Eliphaz, 'Remember, I pray you, whoever perished, being innocent' (cf. Job 4:7). Upon seeing his

222. In a later collection, Eliphaz contrasts Job with Abraham, 'Are your works like those of Abraham? He was tried in ten trials and endured all of them, but you have only been in one trial' (*Midr. Tanh.* [Buber] *Vay.* 8:2; cf. *ARN* A 7). Interestingly, as Allison observes (*Testament*, 317–18), Job complains of his friends, 'These ten times you have cast reproach upon me' (Job 19:3), the same number of trials faced by Abraham (*Jub.* 17:26-28; *m. Abot* 5:3; *Gen. Rab.* 56:11). At the same time, Joseph faces 'ten trials' in *T. Jos.* 2:7; on the significance of the repetition of 'ten', see *Pirkei Avot* 5:1-6.

106   *Writing with Scripture*

words have no effect, Satan once more quotes Eliphaz, 'Now a thing was secretly brought to me' (cf. Job 4:12) – referring to the ram which would be provided in Isaac's place. And although there are few verbal parallels, Job 1–2 probably lies behind Mastema's accusation against Abraham in *Jubilees* (17:15-16; par. 4QpsJub[a] 2:1-2), which serves as the pretext for the *Aqedah* (*Jub.* 17:17-8:13).[223]

The Rabbis were, at the same time, fond of comparing Abraham and Job, often at Job's expense.[224] Delcor and Weinberg see in the *Testament* a similar effort to elevate Abraham above Job, particularly in the statement, 'There is no man like unto [Abraham] on earth, not even Job, the wondrous man' (*T. Ab.* 15:15).[225] That this was meant as a critique of Job is, however, far from certain, as Allison notes, 'this is a way of exalting Abraham, not denigrating Job'.[226] Alternatively, Allison has proposed the similitude of Job and Abraham in the *Testament* functions as a *synkrisis*, through which the lives of Abraham and Job are contrasted for the benefit of the reader.[227] The readers of the *Testament*, according to Allison, were probably 'expected to espy the parallels between Abraham and Job', though the parallels were likely intended more for enjoyment than edification.[228] As a device, however, *synkrisis* aims at revealing the character of a person by way of direct comparison, a method most associated with Plutarch's *Parallel Lives*.[229] The explicit comparison of

223. Allison, *Testament*, 318; cf. Jacques T. A. G. M. van Ruiten, *Abraham in the Book of Jubilees: The Rewriting of Genesis 11:26–25:10 in the Book of Jubilees 11:14–23:8*, JSJSup 161 (Brill: Leiden, 2012), 212–14.

224. For example, *b. B. Bat.* 16a; *y. Sot.* 20c; *y. Ber.* 14b; *Gen. Rab.* 49:9; *Deut. Rab.* 11:3; *Midr. Teh.* 26:2; *ARN* A 7. One notable exception is the pronouncement of R. Yoḥanan: 'What is said about Job is more impressive than what is said about Abraham' (*b. B. Bat.* 15b).

225. Mathias Delcor, *Le Testament d'Abraham: Introduction, traduction du texte grec et commentaire de la recension grecque longue, suivi de la traduction des Testaments d'Abraham, d'Isaac et de Jacob d'après les versions orientales*, SVTP 2 (Leiden: Brill, 1973), 76; Joanna Weinberg, 'Job versus Abraham: The Quest for the Perfect God-Fearer in Rabbinic Tradition', in *The Book of Job*, ed. W. A. M. Beuken, BETL 114 (Leuven: Peeters, 1994), 291 – both of whom argue the author of the *Testament of Abraham* may have had the *Testament of Job* in their sights. The *Testament of Job* itself appears to reflect legends concerning Abraham, see Ginzberg, *Legends*, 5:383 n. 10.

226. Allison, 'Job in the Testament of Abraham', 145.

227. Allison, 'Job in the Testament of Abraham', 140–4; *Testament*, 129, 317.

228. Allison, 'Job in the Testament of Abraham', 146.

229. See the influential article by Friedrich Focke, 'Synkrisis', *Hermes* (1923): 327–68.

2. Scripturalized Narrative in Second Temple Literature   107

Job and Abraham in *T. Ab.* 15:15 would meet this criterion. As for the unmarked use of Job elsewhere in the *Testament*, it is harder to say. It is possible the transparent allusions to Job in the words of Michael (*T. Ab.* 4:6; 15:15) were intended as a cue for identifying other parallels in the work. But as it is, the only thing certain is that the author of the *Testament* modelled scenes and borrowed phrases from a Greek text of Job.

As to what drew the author to Job in the first place, it is possible to speculate. It was perhaps Job's experience with a secret, and initially unsuccessful, heavenly plot that recommended it as a model to the author.[230] Job 1–2 thus provided fertile material with which to narrate Abraham's struggle with Michael and the Angel of Death. At the same time, this narrative has its origins in the Death of Moses tradition, wherein Satan/Sammael/Death travels between heaven and earth in an unsuccessful bid to fetch Moses' soul (preserved in *Deut. Rab.* 11:10; *Sifre* Deut. 305:5). It could be that this bi-worldly narrative, in turn, put the author of the *Testament* in mind of the bi-worldly narrative of Job 1–2.[231]

In any case, the *Testament of Abraham* features a scripturalized narrative in which Michael plays the role of Satan to Abraham's Job. Michael's unsuccessful attempt to take Abraham's soul is modelled, at least in part, on Satan's unsuccessful attempt to induce Job to curse God. From this, Michael borrows, almost verbatim, language from the heavenly scenes of Greek Job 1–2. For a work sometimes considered marginal to the literature of the Second Temple period, the *Testament* exhibits many of the same stylistic features as other works, particularly in its compositional use of scriptural elements to shape a new narrative about a well-known figure. At least in this respect, the *Testament of Abraham* is hardly an exception to the literary conventions of the Second Temple period.

Summary

The scripturalized narratives surveyed so far encompass the three languages of literary composition in the Second Temple period – Hebrew, Aramaic and Greek – as well as multiple genres, from scriptural rewriting

---

230. Allison, 'Job in the Testament of Abraham', 145–6. Allison also lists general similarities that may have prompted the association, see 'Job in the Testament of Abraham', 140–3; *Testament*, 317–18.

231. Two texts in the Death of Moses tradition, *Deut. Rab.* 11:10 and *Sifre* Deut. 305:5, reference material in Job (12:10 and 28:23, respectively). It is possible the association of these figures lies behind the detail that Moses (*Deut. Rab.* 11:10), Job (*T. Job* 52:8) and Abraham (*T. Ab.* 20:8-9) each succumbed to death with a kiss.

108 *Writing with Scripture*

to (pseudo-)historiography, and subjects historical and legendary. All of these works feature self-contained episodes that have been created, for the most part, out of scriptural elements. The stylistic similarities between these heterogenous works can be explained by two distinct, but closely related, compositional techniques.

First, *a new episode may be modelled in whole or in part on a scriptural episode.* Thus the fiery furnace of Daniel 3 serves as the model for the fiery furnaces of Abram (*LAB* 6) and Jair (*LAB* 38). Gideon's rout of the Midianites with the three-hundred (Judg. 7) serves as the model for Kenaz's rout of the Amorites with the three-hundred (*LAB* 27). The promise of land to Abram (Gen. 13–15) serves as a model for the promise of land to Noah (1QapGen 11). Moses' siege of Sihon (Deut. 2:26-36; Judg. 11:19-21) serves as a model for Judas Maccabeus' siege of Ephron (1 Macc. 5:45-51). Jael's assassination of Sisera in a tent (Judg. 4:17-22) serves as the model for Judith's assassination of Holofernes in a tent (Jdt. 10–13; reversed in *LAB* 31). The secret heavenly plot against Job (LXX Job 1–2) serves as a model for the secret heavenly plot against Abraham (*T. Ab.* 1–4; 15:14-15). None of these examples simply replicates the scriptural model in its entirety, instead adapting it to suit the new demands of the narrative, sometimes following it only loosely. Nevertheless each episode preserves distinct elements from its model, clearly indicating its source – be it the miraculous rescue from a fiery furnace, the mass slaughter of the inhabitants of a city that denies peaceful passage or the murder of an enemy general in a tent with a blow to the head. In some cases these elements are traditional, arising from the interpretation of the passage which serves as the model, such as the presence – or absence – of angels in the fiery furnaces. But above all, the source is indicated by phrases and narrative details lifted, sometimes verbatim, from the scriptural model, which leads to the second compositional technique.

Narrative details or phrases may be inserted into the new episode. Sometimes these details, whilst not always verbatim, reflect the distinctive vocabulary of the scriptural model, like the 'sparks' (*scintillas*) emitting from the 'fiery furnace' (*camino ignis*) of Abram (*LAB* 6:16-18; cf. Dan. 3:22) or the 'sword of Kenaz/Gideon' (*LAB* 27:9; cf. Judg. 7:14). At the same time, phrases may be lifted directly from the model: Noah walks 'through the land, in its length and in its breadth' (1QapGen 11:11; cf. Gen. 13:17); the Judaeans cannot go around Ephron 'to the right or to the left' (1 Macc. 5:46; cf. Deut. 2:26), so they ask, 'Let us pass through your land to get to our land [and] pass by on foot' (1 Macc. 5:48; cf. Judg. 11:19; Deut. 2:27-28), but when they are denied, the Judaeans 'destroyed every male by the edge of the sword' (1 Macc. 5:51; cf. Deut. 20:13);

2. Scripturalized Narrative in Second Temple Literature   109

Judith's victory is won 'by the hand of a woman' (Jdt. 9:10; 13:15; 16:5; cf. Judg. 4:9); and Michael says of Abraham, 'I have not seen upon earth a man like him – merciful, hospitable, righteous, truthful, God-fearing, refraining from every evil deed' (*T. Ab.* 4:6; cf. LXX Job 1:8; 2:3).

The subject of a scripturalized narrative is usually an individual from sacred history, either well-known (Abram; Noah) or obscure (Kenaz; Jair), though they may also be historical (Judas Maccabeus) or pseudo-historical (Judith). Sometimes the scripturalized narrative is triggered by exegesis: the 'Ur/fire' (אור) of the Chaldeans in Gen. 15:7 becomes the 'fiery furnace' of the Chaldeans; the place-name 'Kamon' (קמון) in Judg. 10:5, read as 'furnace' (קמין), becomes the fire of Jair. Elsewhere, it reflects the ideology of the work: Judas behaves 'according to the law' (1 Macc. 3:56; 4:47, 53), and thus besieges Ephron like Moses (Deut. 2:26-36; Judg. 11:19-21) according to the rules of *ḥērem* (Deut. 20:10-14). In many cases, however, the scripturalized narrative has no obvious explanation, and may owe simply to the creativity of the author – like Kenaz, Judith and Abraham in the *Testament*.

Nevertheless each work features new compositions that take a scriptural episode as their primary model, from which narrative details and phrases are drawn. That these compositional techniques can be found across such disparate works suggests scripturalized narrative is a stylistic feature of Second Temple literature. The question then follows, can the characteristics of scripturalized narrative seen here also be observed in the earliest surviving Gospel, the one attributed to Mark?

3

SCRIPTURALIZED NARRATIVE IN THE GOSPEL OF MARK

This chapter looks at five episodes from the Gospel of Mark in which scriptural elements serve as a model for the narrative: Jesus' sojourn in the wilderness and the call of the first disciples (Mk 1:12-20); the two feedings of the multitude (6:35-44; 8:1-9); the execution of John the Baptist (6:21-28); and the crucifixion of Jesus (15:21-41). Each is a self-contained episode of a comparable length that is modelled primarily, though not exclusively, on one scriptural source.[1] The compositional use of scriptural elements in these five episodes will be compared with the scripturalized narratives surveyed in the previous chapter, along with other relevant texts from the period.

Jesus and Elijah in Mark 1:2-20

The Gospel of Mark begins with a citation of the Jewish scriptures, and from then on, the scriptures are often in view, though there are few other citations. Given the pride of place given to the scriptures in the opening citation, scholars have tended to see the Markan prologue, including John's baptism and Jesus' sojourn in the wilderness, as indicative of Mark's hermeneutical approach to the scriptures, and therefore programmatic for the Gospel as a whole. Language that depends on the Jewish scriptures often plays an outsize role in the minds of interpreters, so that fleeting reminiscences of scriptural passages become clues that unlock hidden meanings, often informed by passages the author never cites – a

---

1. Because of their significance, additional comments will be made about the use of scripture in the narratives surrounding Jesus' sojourn in the wilderness and crucifixion: the prologue (Mk 1:2-11) and Passion Narrative (chs. 14–15). This is not necessary for the execution of John and the feeding of the multitudes as they follow each other in the Markan chronology.

3. Scripturalized Narrative in the Gospel of Mark   111

technique sometimes called *metalepsis*. That Mark intended any of this is far from certain. To the contrary, the prologue shows an author primarily concerned with the immediate demands of their narrative, untroubled by the precise wording of their sources, and creative in their application of them. Mark is nourished by the language of scripture more than the substance of it. There is little uniformity or method in their use of scriptural language, although the author occasionally gestures to larger themes, or ideas taken up later in the work. If there is one subject that ties together the scriptural language in the prologue, it is the figure of Elijah, who is traditionally equated with John the Baptist, though he is not the only figure who resembles the Tishbite.

Mark and Malachi: Mark 1:2-3 and Malachi 3:1

The shadow of Elijah hangs over the beginning of Mark's Gospel. Nearly all commentators see in the opening citation a veiled reference to Elijah, 'See, I am sending my messenger ahead of you, who will prepare your way' (Mk 1:2: ἰδοὺ ἀποστέλλω τὸν ἄγγελόν μου πρὸ προσώπου σου, ὃς κατασκευάσει τὴν ὁδόν σου). This, to be sure, closely resembles Mal. 3:1: 'See, I am sending my messenger to prepare the way before me' (הנני שלח מלאכי ופנה־דרך לפני). Since later in Malachi, Elijah (אליה) is said to appear before the day of the Lord (Mal. 4:5; LXX Mal. 3:22), the figure in Mal. 3:1 has often been identified as Elijah.[2] By referencing Mal. 3:1, so the argument goes, Mark is subtly introducing a prophecy of the coming of Elijah, who is later identified as John the Baptist (Mk 1:6; 9:13).[3]

---

2. Most have followed Calvin (*Harmony of the Gospels* 1.119) in thinking the redactional purpose of Mal. 4:5 is to identify the figure in Mal. 3:1. So Otto Eissfeldt, *The Old Testament: An Introduction*, trans. P. R. Ackroyd (New York, NY: Harper & Row, 1965), 441–2; Andrew E. Hill, *Malachi: A New Translation with Introduction and Commentary*, AB 25D (New York, NY: Doubleday, 1998), 363–6. The first explicit association of Elijah with the figure of Mal. 3:1 in Jewish literature is in *PRE* 29:18 (cf. *Deut. Rab.* 4:11). For further discussion, see Marcus Öhler, *Elia im Neuen Testament: Untersuchungen zur Bedeutung des alttestamentlichen Propheten im frühen Christentum*, BZNW 88 (Berlin: W. de Gruyter, 1997), 2–6.

3. Most recently argued in Hays, *Echoes of Scripture in the Gospels*, 20–4. See the classic formulation in Walter Wink, *John the Baptist in the Gospel Tradition*, SNTSMS 7 (Cambridge: Cambridge University Press, 1968), 2–8. See also the commentaries: Ernst Lohmeyer, *Das Evangelium des Markus* (Göttingen: Vandenhoeck & Ruprecht, 1953), 11; Rudolf Pesch, *Das Markusevangelium*, 2 vols., HTKNT (Freiburg: Herder, 1976–77), 1:77–8; Joachim Gnilka, *Das Evangelium nach Markus*, 2 vols., EKK 2 (Zurich: Benziger, 1978), 1:44; Robert A. Guelich, *Mark 1–8:26*, WBC 34A (Dallas, TX: Word, 1989), 11; Joel Marcus, *Mark: 1–8: A New Translation with Introduction and Commentary*, AB 27 (New York, NY: Doubleday, 2000), 142.

This interpretation runs into two problems, however. The first is that Mal. 3:1 is not the only possible source for the citation in Mk 1:2. Malachi itself appears to be quoting another passage, Exod. 23:20, which in the LXX reads, 'And see, I am sending my messenger before you in order to guard you on the way' (καὶ ἰδοὺ ἐγὼ ἀποστέλλω τὸν ἄγγελόν μου πρὸ προσώπου σου, ἵνα φυλάξῃ σε ἐν τῇ ὁδῷ).[4] In the context of the Exodus passage, the messenger (Hb.: מַלְאָךְ; Gk: ἄγγελος) is the angel sent ahead of the Israelites in the wilderness. The Israelites are to listen to it, and thereby listen to the voice (φωνή) of the LORD (LXX Exod. 23:21-22). This voice in the wilderness brings to mind the following verse in Mark – 'The voice of one crying out in the wilderness: "Prepare the way of the Lord, make his paths straight"' (Mk 1:3: φωνὴ βοῶντος ἐν τῇ ἐρήμῳ· ἑτοιμάσατε τὴν ὁδὸν κυρίου, εὐθείας ποιεῖτε τὰς τρίβους αὐτοῦ) – which is *mutatis mutandis* a quotation of LXX Isa. 40:3. But the object of the verb in Mk 1:2 is in the second person (πρὸ προσώπου σου...τὴν ὁδόν σου), in agreement with LXX Exod. 23:20 (πρὸ προσώπου σου...σε ἐν τῇ ὁδῷ), whereas the object in Mal. 3:1 is in the first person (LXX: πρὸ προσώπου μου). At least on its surface, a comparison of the passages favours LXX Exod. 23:20 over LXX Mal. 3:1 as the source for Mk 1:2.

Mark 1:2	LXX Exod. 23:20	LXX Mal. 3:1	LXX Mal. 3:22
<u>ἰδοὺ ἀποστέλλω τὸν ἄγγελόν μου πρὸ προσώπου σου, ὃς κατασκευάσει τὴν ὁδόν σου</u>	Καὶ <u>ἰδοὺ ἐγὼ ἀποστέλλω τὸν ἄγγελόν μου πρὸ προσώπου σου</u>, ἵνα φυλάξῃ σε ἐν τῇ ὁδῷ.	<u>ἰδοὺ ἐγὼ</u> ἐξαποστέλλω <u>τὸν ἄγγελόν μου</u>, καὶ ἐπιβλέψεται <u>ὁδὸν πρὸ προσώπου</u> μου	καὶ <u>ἰδοὺ ἐγὼ ἀποστέλλω</u> ὑμῖν Ηλιαν τὸν Θεσβίτην πρὶν ἐλθεῖν ἡμέραν κυρίου τὴν μεγάλην καὶ ἐπιφανῆ

But as the above table shows, the second clause of Mk 1:2 differs considerably from LXX Exodus and LXX Malachi. On the one hand, the use of the second person favours the Exodus passage, whilst on the other, the accusative ὁδὸν is closest to LXX Mal. 3:1.[5] The verb κατασκευάζω in Mk 1:2 is, however, unparalleled in LXX Exod. 23:20 (φυλάσσω) and LXX Mal. 3:1 (ἐπιβλέπω). It is here that a case can be made for Mal. 3:1. As in Mk 1:2, the verb in LXX Mal. 3:1 appears in the future indicative.[6]

---

4. My translation. On the use of Exod. 23:20 in Mal. 3:1, see David L. Petersen, *Late Israelite Prophecy: Studies in Deutero-prophetic Literature and in Chronicles*, SBLMS 23 (Atlanta, GA: Scholars Press, 1977), 42–3.

5. Cf. the dative in LXX Exod. 23:20.

6. Cf. the aorist subjunctive in LXX Exod. 23:20.

3. Scripturalized Narrative in the Gospel of Mark

Given their similar form, the unusual choice of κατασκευάζω in Mk 1:2 might conceivably owe to the Hebrew of Mal. 3:1.[7] When the verb פנה ('to make clear') appears in the *piel* – as it does in Mal. 3:1 – the LXX tends to favour ἑτοιμάζω (LXX Gen. 24:31; LXX Isa. 40:3) or ὁδοποιέω (LXX Ps. 79:10; LXX Isa. 62:10).[8] Only in one place does the LXX render the verb in the third person as ἀποσκευάσαι (LXX Lev. 14:36). Significantly, the same verb (ἀποσκευάζω) appears in the translation of σ′ Mal. 3:1.[9] Whilst this shows some precedent for translating פנה with -σκευάζω verbs – though not κατασκευάζω – it is equally possible פנה was misread as בנה ('to build'), which the LXX renders as κατασκευάζω (LXX Num. 21:27).

If the verb in Mk 1:2 originates from פנה in the *piel*, however, then it provides an additional connection to the following citation from Isa. 40:3, which shares with Mal. 3:1 the phrase, 'prepare the way' (פנה[-]דרך). In both passages, the preparation precedes the coming of the LORD (Isa. 40:3-5; Mal. 3:1, 5).[10] This could have led Mark or their source to conflate the passages. But whatever verbal similarities exist in the Hebrew are not on display here, as the citation of Isa. 40:3 in Mk 1:3 follows the LXX in translating פנה as ἑτοιμάζω. At the same time, the use of the second person in Mk 1:2 better suits the context of Exod. 23:20. Whilst it is possible Mark or their source consciously weaved the Hebrew of Mal. 3:1 into a citation of LXX Exod. 23:20, the wording could also owe to a Greek variant of Exod. 23:20 which was influenced at some stage by the language of Mal. 3:1, or a variant of Exod. 23:20 completely unrelated to Mal. 3:1.[11]

Even if one were to grant that Malachi lies somewhere behind the citation in Mk 1:2, the second problem remains: Mark attributes the entire citation to Isaiah, 'As it is written in the prophet Isaiah' (Mk 1:2a: καθὼς

---

7. The verb in MT Exod. 23:20b, שמר ('to guard'), bears no relation to κατασκευάζω.

8. Also rendered as καθαρίζω (LXX Isa. 57:14) and λυτρόω (LXX Zech. 3:15). On the other hand, the ἐπιβλέπω of Mal. 3:1b is anomalous in the *piel* (though common fοι the *qal*: i.e. LXX Num. 12:10; LXX Judg. 6:14; LXX 1 Sam. 13:17; LXX Hag. 1:9; LXX Mal. 2:13; also *hiphil*: LXX Nah. 2:9).

9. Cf. ἑτοιμάσει in θ′ Mal. 3:1.

10. On the use of Isa. 40:1-5 in Second Temple literature, see Klyne R. Snodgrass, 'Streams of Tradition Emerging from Isaiah 40:1-5 and their Adaption in the New Testament', *JSNT* 8 (1980): 24–45.

11. It could also be Mark or their source inherited the unusual form of the citation (and the mistaken attribution to Isaiah) from a pre-existing *testimonia* source, see Fitzmyer, ' "4Q Testimonia" and the New Testament'.

114

Writing with Scripture

γέγραπται ἐν τῷ ᾿Ησαΐᾳ τῷ προφήτῃ). In an effort to cover up what appears to be a glaring mistake, some scholars have opted for the inventive solution that Mark is using a figure of speech in order to introduce readers to the Isaianic 'hermeneutical key' for the Gospel.[12] And yet, Mk 1:2a leaves little doubt Mark understood the source of the citation in 1:2b-3 to be Isaiah. The absence of the formula and the omission of Isa. 40:3 in Mt. 11:10 and Lk. 7:27 suggests Mark's early readers perceived it as an error.[13] At this point, the path to seeing Mk 1:2 as a clear reference to Elijah in Malachi becomes increasingly perilous. It could be that Isa. 40:3, Exod. 23:20 and Mal. 3:1 (as interpreted by Mal. 4:5) were so intertwined in contemporary exegesis that an allusion to one was seen as an allusion to all.[14] In that sense, each was understood to be, in effect, a prophecy of Elijah's coming. But as it is, there is no clear sign Isa. 40:3 or Exod. 23:20 were independently associated with the coming of Elijah.[15] Although Mal. 4:5 (LXX 3:22) was likely inserted as a redactional comment on Mal. 3:1, the first explicit declaration in Jewish literature that the 'messenger' in Mal. 3:1 should be identified with 'Elijah' in Mal. 4:5 comes much later in *PRE* 29:18 (cf. *Deut. Rab.* 4:11).[16] It would seem then that if the citation in Mk 1:2-3 functions as an allusion to Elijah in Malachi, it is because

---

12. Matera, 'The Prologue as the Interpretative Key to Mark's Gospel'; Marcus, *The Way of the Lord*, 20–2; Watts, *Isaiah's New Exodus*, 88–90; compare with the more judicious comments in Steve Moyise, 'Is Mark's Opening Quotation the Key to his Use of Scripture?', *IBS* 20 (1998): 146–58.

13. Cf. Mt. 3:3; Lk. 3:4. It seems more likely that the separation of Isa. 40:3 from the Exod. 23:20 and Mal. 3:1 conflation owes to the editorial activity of Matthew (and Luke), given the misattribution in Mk 1:2, rather than the independent attestation of *Q, pace* W. D. Davies and D. C. Allison Jr., *The Gospel According to Saint Matthew, Volume 1: Introduction and Commentary on Matthew I–VII*, ICC (London: T&T Clark, 1988), 294.

14. Exod. 23:20 is associated with Mal. 3:1 in *b. Seder* 61a; *Exod. Rab.* 32:9; *Deut. Rab.* 11:19; with Mal. 4:6 in *Exod. Rab.* 3:4. Jacob Mann, *The Bible as Read and Preached in the Old Synagogue*, 2 vols. (Cincinnati, OH: Jewish Publication Society, 1940), 1:479, argues the two passages were read together in a liturgical setting. Stendahl, *The School of St. Matthew*, 51–2, asserts without evidence that the three texts were associated in oral tradition.

15. Elijah is absent in the use of Isa. 40:3 in 1QS 8:13-15; 4QTanh 1:6-9; *ALD* 2:5; likewise in the use of Exod. 23:20 in *b. B. Kam.* 93a; *Tg. Ps.-J.* on Deut. 1:33; *Midr. Tanh. Mish.* 17:7-8. The angel in Exod. 23:20 is identified as מטטרון in *b. Sanh.* 38b; *3 En.* 10:4-5. The coming of Elijah (Mal. 3:1; 4:5) is associated with Isa. 40:4 in *Deut. Rab.* 4:11 and Isa. 42:1 in *Midr. Teh.* 42:5.

16. Cf. the messenger in Mal. 3:1 is identified as Judah in *Midr. Tanh. Vay.* 10:1-2.

Mark elsewhere identifies John as Elijah (Mk 9:13), in which case the 'messenger' in 1:2 is also incidentally Elijah who is to come.[17]

But when scholars simply state that, for Mark, John is Elijah, they appear to be reading the clarity of Matthew (11:14: αὐτός ἐστιν Ἠλίας; also 17:13) into Mark's more paradoxical account.[18] In the discussion in Mk 9:11-13, the disciples ask concerning the coming of Elijah. Jesus responds saying 'Elijah has come, and they did to him whatever they pleased, as it is written about him' (9:13). Whilst John is not mentioned, the detail that 'they did to him whatever they pleased' is best seen as a reference to John, who suffers at the 'pleasure' of the Herodian family in 6:17-29 (esp. 6:19, 25). However, the disciples' question about the coming of Elijah makes little sense in the broader context of the passage, as it comes directly after Elijah himself appears on the mount of Transfiguration with Jesus and Moses (9:4). As Strauss drily notes: 'so klingt dieß ganz, wie wenn etwas vorangegangen wäre, woraus sie hätten abnehmen müssen, Elias werde nicht erscheinen, und gar nicht, wie wenn sie eben von einer Erscheinung desselben herkämen'.[19] The Transfiguration and the following discourse appear to imagine two different Elijahs: Elijah as himself, a heavenly being (9:4; cf. 15:35) and Elijah as John the Baptist (9:13; cf. 1:6). No effort appears to have been made to harmonize these identifications. On the question of Elijah's identity, Mark is evasive.[20]

And yet, in both passages in which Elijah explicitly appears – as himself and as John – Malachi lurks in the background. The appearance of Elijah with Moses seems to reflect the pairing of the two figures in contemporary eschatological expectation, which may be traced to their appearance together in Mal. 4:4-6 (LXX Mal. 3:22-24). The influence of

---

17. For the interesting opinion that the messenger of Mk 1:2-3 should be identified with Jesus and not John, see Mary Ann Tolbert, *Sowing the Gospel: Mark's World in Literary-Historical Perspective* (Minneapolis, MN: Fortress, 1996), 239–48; Paul Katz, 'Wie einer der Propheten? Das biblische Markusevangelium als Darbietung eines "Vorevangeliums"', *TZ* 58 (2002): 46–60.

18. See the survey of scholarship in Vette, 'Who is Elijah in the Gospel of Mark?', in *Reading the Gospel of Mark in the Twenty-First Century*, ed. Geert Van Oyen, BETL 301 (Leuven: Peeters, 2019), 799–810, esp. 799. The comments of Silvia Pellegrini apply, 'Die traditionelle Interpretation liest Mk, als ob er Mt wäre, d.h. mit – für Mk – illegitimen Voraussetzungen', *Elija – Wegbereiter des Gottesohnes: Eine textsemiotische Untersuchung im Markusevangelium*, HBS 26 (Freiburg: Peterson, 2000), 382.

19. Strauss, *Das Leben Jesu*, 2:284.

20. See Vette, 'Who is Elijah in the Gospel of Mark?', 808–10.

116 *Writing with Scripture*

Malachi is even more evident in Mk 9:12 – 'Elijah is indeed coming first to restore all things' (Ἠλίας μὲν ἐλθὼν πρῶτον ἀποκαθιστάνει πάντα) – wherein Elijah 'restores' as he does in LXX Mal. 3:23: 'who *will restore* (ἀποκαταστήσει) the heart of the father to his son and the heart of a man to his neighbour'.[21] Whether or not the verb ἀποκαθίστημι owes to the direct literary influence of LXX Mal. 3:23, the eschatological outlook of Malachi has clearly influenced Mark's presentation of Elijah at this point. Given the influence of Malachi here, one cannot rule out the possibility that Mal. 3:1 and 4:5 also lie behind the citation in Mk 1:2-3. But even if one were to grant the direct influence of Malachi, the purpose of the opening citation is not to identify John as Elijah, but to introduce John the Baptist (Mk 1:4), whose primary function is to introduce Jesus (1:7-8). In the final analysis, the garbled citation of LXX Isa. 40:3 and LXX Exod. 23:20 (and possibly Mal. 3:1), which is misattributed to Isaiah, is, above all, a prophecy concerning the coming of the Lord. Any reference to Elijah, if intended, is secondary to this aim.

Elijah and John: Mark 1:6 and 2 Kings 1:8

By contrast, there can be little doubt that Elijah is in view in Mk 1:6 (par. Mt. 3:4): 'Now John was clothed with camel's hair, *with a leather belt around his waist* (καὶ ζώνην δερματίνην περὶ τὴν ὀσφὺν αὐτοῦ)'.[22] This matches the description of Elijah in LXX 2 Kgs 1:8: 'and wearing a leather belt around his waist' (καὶ ζώνην δερματίνην περιεζωσμένος τὴν ὀσφὺν αὐτοῦ). Elijah's appearance is apparently so distinguishing that on this description alone, Ahaziah is able to identify him, 'This is Elijah the Tishbite'. Here the scriptural material is used in a fundamentally different way than in the opening citation. Mark 1:2-3 is a marked citation separated from the ensuing narrative or argument with a clear interpretive aim (7:6-7, 10; 10:6-8, 19; 11:17; 12:10-11, 26, 29-33, 36; 14:27). Occasionally an argument is supported with references to scriptural sources without citing them – sometimes the source is clear (1:44; 2:25-26; 10:4; 13:14), at other times less so (9:12-13; 14:21, 49). This type of scriptural language belongs to Dimant's category of *expositional* scriptural use. Elsewhere, unmarked scriptural language appears in the direct speech of characters whilst nonetheless resembling a citation (1:11;

---

21. My translation. Cf. *Sir.* 48:10, where it is Elijah's task 'to turn the heart of the father to the son, and to restore the tribes of Jacob' (ἐπιστρέψαι καρδίαν πατρὸς πρὸς υἱὸν καὶ καταστῆσαι φυλὰς Ιακωβ).

22. ζώνην δερματίνην etc. is omitted from Mk 1:6 in mss. D it[a, b, d] vg[ms].

3. Scripturalized Narrative in the Gospel of Mark

4:12; 9:7, 48; 11:9; 13:24-25; 14:62; 15:34). And in Mk 1:6, the unmarked scriptural language appears as part of the narrative. These examples fall under the *compositional* use of the Jewish scriptures. Scriptural elements have become re-contextualized as part of the narrative or direct speech of characters. But like the *expositional* examples, the *compositional* use of scriptural language can still have an interpretive function – and Mk 1:6 is one such case. Since Mark appears to identify Elijah with John elsewhere (Mk 9:13), the description of his appearance is not accidental. It could be that Mark's readers are, like Ahaziah, meant to identify Elijah by the description of his appearance alone.

That being said, Elijah's hair and leather belt are hardly his most enduring attributes in the literature of the period. Only Josephus – whose account (*Ant.* 8.13.4–9.2.2) more or less repeats the scriptural narrative – mentions them in his description of Elijah (*Ant.* 9.2.1). Elsewhere, descriptions of the 'historical' Elijah tend to focus on his miracles or ascension (i.e. Sir. 48:2-5; 1 Macc. 2:58; *Liv. Pro.* 21:4-15; *4 Ezra* 7:109; *Gk. Apoc. Ezra* 7:6; *Ques. Ezra* A 40; Lk. 4:25-26). At the same time, Mk 1:6 differs from the portrait in 2 Kgs 1:8: John is 'clothed with camel's hair' (ἐνδεδυμένος τρίχας καμήλου), whereas Elijah is described as a 'hairy man' (LXX 2 Kgs 1:8: ἀνὴρ δασύς).[23] Regarding this deviation from the scriptural description, the opinion of Craig Evans is typical: 'The reference to camel's hair points to independence of the Old Testament description, which argues further for the historicity of the Synoptic portrait of John'.[24] It is indeed hard to see how Mark's description of 'camel's hair' could have originated in the description of Elijah, though it is a non-sequitur to conclude the detail must therefore be historical.[25]

---

23. Elsewhere, Elijah is said to wear a 'sheep skin' (μηλωτή) mantle (LXX 1 Kgs 19:13, 19; 2 Kgs 2:8, 13-14; cf. 'ram's skin' [עורו של איל] in *PRE* 31:13).

24. Craig A. Evans, 'The Baptism of John in a Typological Context', in *Dimensions of Baptism: Biblical and Theological Studies*, ed. Stanley E. Porter and Anthony R. Cross, JSNTSup 234 (London: Sheffield Academic, 2002), 48–9; see the similar comments in Robert H. Gundry, *Mark: A Commentary on His Apology for the Cross, Chapters 1–8* (Grand Rapids, MI: Eerdmans, 2000), 44. Cf. J. P. Meier finds no reference to Elijah in the reference to hair, see *A Marginal Jew: Rethinking the Historical Jesus, Volume 2: Mentor, Message, and Miracles* (New York, NY: Doubleday, 1994), 47.

25. Joan Taylor notes the description of John is reminiscent of Josephus' description of his teacher, Bannus (*Life* 11). Taylor speculates, 'When Josephus refers to Bannus wearing what trees provided, he may well have been referring to the camel's hair that stuck to the branches' (*The Immerser: John the Baptist within Second Temple Judaism* [Grand Rapids, MI: Eerdmans, 1997], 35).

The Hebrew of 2 Kgs 1:8 reads literally 'man [of] hair' (אִישׁ בַּעַל שֵׂעָר), with the *nomen regens* בַּעַל equivalent in function to a genitive preposition.[26] It is unlikely someone familiar with Hebrew would have mistaken בַּעַל – which as a common noun refers to a 'master' or 'husband' – with גמל ('camel'). But one can imagine a possible misreading in Aramaic where בַּעַל is rendered בעלא in the emphatic state.[27] In this case, בעלא could have been misread as בעוא (Syr. ܒܥܘܐ), a noun referring to the soft hair on a camel's belly.[28] The same noun occurs in the description of John in the Old Syriac mss. of Mt. 3:4: ܠܒܘܫܐ ܕܒܥܘܐ ܕܓܡܠܐ ('clothing of *ba'wa* from a camel').[29] Given the grammatical function of בַּעַל in 2 Kgs 1:8, however, it would likely be rendered as it is in *Tg. 2 Kgs* 1:8 (בעיל) and not in the emphatic state (בעלא). Alternatively, בעוא could conceivably have come from סערא, the Aramaic equivalent of the Hebrew שֵׂעָר. Torrey speculates ܒܥܘܐ ܕܓܡܠܐ (Aram. בעוא דגמלא ['*ba'wa* of a camel']) in the Old Syriac may have arisen from סערא דגמלא (camel's hair) in a lost Aramaic text of the Gospel.[30] To take Torrey's argument in another direction, perhaps Mark's τρίχας καμήλου (Mk 1:6; par. Mt. 3:4) resulted from a misreading of סערא as בעוא in an Aramaic text of 2 Kgs 1:8.[31] This was then, at a later date, translated back to ܒܥܘܐ in the Old Syriac of the Gospels. However, the fact that the word *ba'wa* is not

---

26. BDB calls it a 'noun of relation'; cf. Gen. 37:19; 49:23; Exod. 24:14; Prov. 29:22 etc. Compare also with the description of Esau as a 'hairy man' (Gen. 27:11: אִישׁ שֵׂעָר).

27. So 1QapGen 20:23, 25; *Tg. Ps.-J.* on Gen. 20:3; Lev. 21:3-4; Num. 5:29; *Tg. Onk.* on Exod. 21:3; Syr. *Sir.* 4:10.

28. For the definition of ܒܥܘܐ, see Jessie Payne Smith, *A Compendious Syriac Dictionary* (Oxford: Oxford University Press, 1902; repr. ALR; Eugene, OR: Wipf & Stock, 1999), 50; Francis Crawford Burkitt, *Evangelion Da-Mepharreshe, Volume 2: Introduction and Notes* (Cambridge: Cambridge University Press, 1904; repr. 2014), 81; Carl Brockelmann, *Lexicon Syriacum*, 2nd ed. (Halle: Max Niemeyer, 1928), 83.

29. syr[cur] Matt 3:4; syr[s] Matt 3:4; Ephrem, *Commentary on the Diatessaron* 1.17 (L. Leloir, *Saint Éphrem: Commentaire de l'Évangile Concordant Texte Syriaque (Manuscrit Chester Beatty 709) Folios Additionnels*, CBM 8 [Leuven: Peeters, 1990], 20); Isho'dad of Merv, *Commentary on Matthew* 14a (Margaret Dunlop Gibson, *The Commentaries of Isho'dad of Merv: Bishop of Ḥadatha (c. 850 A.D.): In Syriac and English*, 5 vols. [Cambridge: Cambridge University Press, 1911], 2:38): ܗܢ ܐܦܪܝܡ ܒܠܚܘܕ ܡܪܐ ܒܥܘܐ ('Mar Ephraim alone calls it *ba'wa*'); cf. *ba'wa* does not appear in Pesh. Mt. 3:4 (par. Mk 1:6): ܠܒܘܫܗ ܕܗܘܐ ܕܣܥܪܐ.

30. Torrey, *Documents of the Primitive Church* (New York, NY: Harper & Brothers, 1941), 257.

31. Cf. סערן in *Tg. 2 Kgs* 1:8.

3. Scripturalized Narrative in the Gospel of Mark 119

attested prior to the Old Syriac manuscripts – which could be as late as the fourth century CE[32] – urges caution.

A simpler explanation is that the inclusion of κάμηλος reflects the location of John's ministry. On this point, the description of John eating 'locusts and wild honey' (ἀκρίδας καὶ μέλι ἄγριον) has no parallel in the career of Elijah, who instead eats 'bread and meat' (לחם ובשׂר) brought to him by ravens (1 Kgs 17:6), 'a cake baked on hot stones' (עגת רצפים) brought to him by an angel (1 Kgs 19:6), water 'from the wadi' (1 Kgs 17:6: מן־הגחל) and 'a jar of water' (1 Kgs 19:6: צפחת מים).[33] As James Kelhoffer correctly observes, 'Despite the attempts of certain scholars, a connection with Elijah or, more broadly, a "biblical" origin for John's *diet* [is not] readily discerned'.[34] Rather, John's unusual diet is better explained by his location 'in the wilderness' (Mk 1:4: ἐν τῇ ἐρήμῳ), where locusts and raw honey are some of the only available food. The same could be said for the inclusion of κάμηλος.[35] If so, τρίχας καμήλου might be an 'ecotype' of the description of Elijah in 2 Kgs 1:8 – to borrow a term from folklore studies which describes how an idea can become acculturated into a new physical environment.[36] The *topos* of the 'wilderness' (Mk 1:4: ἐν τῇ ἐρήμῳ) in the description of John does, however, reflect the citation of Isa. 40:3 in the previous verse (Mk 1:3: ἐν τῇ ἐρήμῳ). In view of this, the paraphernalia of John's ministry – the camel's hair, the locusts, the honey – may be, albeit indirectly, scriptural in origin.[37]

---

32. Kurt Aland and Barbara Aland, *The Text of the New Testament: An Introduction to the Critical Editions and to the Theory and Practice of Modern Textual Criticism*, trans. Erroll F. Rhodes (Grand Rapids, MI: Eerdmans, 1987), 189–90.

33. See the text-critical note on 1 Kgs 17:6 in Dominique Barthélemy, *Critique textuelle de l'Ancien Testament I*, OBO 50/1 (Fribourg: Éditions Universitaires; Göttingen: Vandenhoeck & Ruprecht, 1982), 368–9.

34. James A. Kelhoffer, *The Diet of John the Baptist: "Locusts and Wild Honey" in Synoptic and Patristic Interpretation*, WUNT 176 (Tübingen: Mohr Siebeck, 2005), 5, emphasis original.

35. Cf. Clement of Alexandria (*Instr.* 2.11), who regards John's clothing of camel's hair and diet as a sign of frugality.

36. See the influential study by Carl W. von Sydow, 'Geography and Folk-Tale Oicotypes', in *C. W. von Sydow, Selected Papers on Folklore*, ed. L. Bødker (Copenhagen: Rosenkilde & Bagger, 1948), 44–55. This is certainly not the case in Sulipicius Severus (*Life of Martin* 10 [FC 7.117]), where the disciples of Martin of Tours are said to be 'dressed in camel's hair', hardly reflecting the environment of the Loire Valley. That monks sought to emulate the appearance of the Baptist, however, is suggested by the gift of Sulpicius in Paulinus of Nola, *Epist.* 29.1 (CSEL 29.251).

37. Kelhoffer, *The Diet of John the Baptist*, 122.

Other Elijah Parallels in Mark 1:4-11

Another connection to Elijah may be found in the location of John's baptizing, 'in the River Jordan' (Mk 1:5: ἐν τῷ ᾽Ιορδάνῃ ποταμῷ; also 1:10).[38] That this was also the scene of Elijah's departure from Elisha (LXX 2 Kgs 2:7: ἐπὶ τοῦ Ιορδάνου) has led some to conclude the Markan scene envisages a similar prophetic succession: as Elisha succeeds Elijah, so Jesus succeeds John.[39] Several similarities exist between the two episodes in addition to the location at the Jordan: the description of the prophet's mantle (LXX 2 Kgs 2:8, 13-14: μηλωτή; cf. Mk 1:6: τρίχας καμήλου); the two men cross (2 Kgs 2:8) or enter (Mk 1:9-10) the Jordan river; the spirit (πνεῦμα) rests (LXX 2 Kgs 2:15: ἐπαναπαύομαι) or descends (Mk 1:10: καταβαίνω) on one of the men; the intrusion of the extraterrestrial location, 'heaven' (LXX 2 Kgs 2:11; Mk 1:10-11: οὐρανός); and the invocation of fatherhood (2 Kgs 2:12: πάτερ πάτερ; Mk 1:11: σὺ εἶ ὁ υἱός μου). Despite these general similarities, there is no verbal agreement between the passages. Moreover, there are notable differences: Elisha and Elijah miraculously cross over the Jordan (2 Kgs 2:8; also 2 Kgs 2:14; cf. Exod. 14:21-22), whereas Jesus is baptized by John in the Jordan (Mk 1:9); Elisha receives Elijah's spirit (2 Kgs 2:9, 15), whereas Jesus receives a spirit from heaven (Mk 1:10); Elisha addresses Elijah as 'father' (2 Kgs 2:12), whereas the voice from heaven addresses Jesus as 'son' (Mk 1:11). And the most remarkable detail of 2 Kgs 2:8-12, the ascension of Elijah to heaven in a chariot of fire, has no parallel in Mk 1:4-11.

Although there is no clear sign 2 Kgs 2:8-12 has influenced John's baptism of Jesus in the Jordan, the possibility of its more general influence on the Markan episode is an open question. The parallel between Elisha

---

38. On the significance of this location, see Jeremy M. Hutton, 'Topography, Biblical Traditions, and Reflections on John's Baptism of Jesus', in *Jesus Research: New Methodologies and Perceptions: The Second Princeton-Prague Symposium on Jesus Research Research, Princeton 2007*, ed. J. H. Charlesworth and Brian Rhea (Grand Rapids, MI: Eerdmans, 2014), 149–77. Cf. *b. Ḥag.* 25a, where Elijah purifies the road from Galilee to Judea in the messianic age – an image which may more readily apply to Jesus in the Gospel.

39. See Roth, *Hebrew Gospel*, 9–10; Joel Marcus, *John the Baptist in History and Theology*, Studies on Personalities of the New Testament (Columbia, SC: University of South Carolina, 2018), 88–9. A clearer example of the succession-model in 2 Kgs 2:8-12 is found in Ambrose, *Epist.* 15.8-9 (PL 16.957). As Barthélemy notes, the repetitiveness of the narrative surrounding 2 Kgs 2:14 is not the result of corruption but is intended to amplify the traits of Elijah in Elisha (*Critique textuelle de L'Ancient Testament I*, 379).

3. Scripturalized Narrative in the Gospel of Mark   121

succeeding Elijah (2 Kgs 2:9-15) and Jesus succeeding John (Mk 1:7-8, 14) deserves consideration. For Mark, however, this should be amended: Jesus does not so much succeed John, as John precedes Jesus (Mk 1:2-3). Despite further parallels between the miracles of Elisha and the miracles of Jesus – from the general: Mk 1:40-42; cf. 2 Kgs 5:9-14; Mk 5:35-43; cf. 2 Kgs 4:18-37; Mk 16:4-8; cf. 2 Kgs 13:20-21; to the specific: Mk 6:35-44; 8:1-9; cf. 2 Kgs 4:42-44 – the figure of Elisha appears to be of little interest to Mark, who does not mention him. There is also no indication that anyone in that period expected the eschatological return of Elisha. According to Mark, popular expectation identified Jesus with either Elijah, one of the prophets or John himself raised from the dead (6:4-16; 8:28). In Mk 1:4-11, at least, the scriptural account of Elisha is of much greater relevance to the person of John than the person of Jesus. It is, after all, Elisha who instructs Naaman, 'Go, wash in the Jordan seven times' (2 Kgs 5:10). When Naaman follows Elisha's command, the LXX reads, 'And Naaman went down and *baptized* (ἐβαπτίσατο) himself *in the Jordan* (ἐν τῷ Ιορδάνῃ) seven times according to the word of Elisha' (LXX 2 Kgs 5:14).[40] Again, there is no sign Mark themselves connected the activity of John at the Jordan with the episode of Elisha and Naaman in 2 Kgs 5:9-14.[41] But the possibility that this scriptural episode informed the consciousness of the historical John cannot be easily dismissed.

The question of whether the figure of Elijah influenced Mk 1:4-11 more generally also deserves to be explored further. Whilst some have seen in John's proclamation – 'The one who is more powerful than I is coming after me' (Mk 1:7: ἔρχεται ὁ ἰσχυρότερός μου ὀπίσω μου) – an allusion to Elijah, there is no clear indication Mk 1:7-8 relies on the language of Malachi or any other known passage concerning Elijah.[42] Nor is it clear that Mk 1:7-8 has been influenced by some contemporary expectation of Elijah as the messianic forerunner, an idea which does not appear in any definite form prior to Christian literature.[43] When the coming of Elijah

---

40. The verb βαπτίζω appears three other times in the LXX: it is used to describe Judith's bath before meeting Holofernes (Jdt. 12:7) and ritual cleansing after touching a corpse (Sir. 34:25); note also the metaphorical use in LXX Isa. 21:4.

41. The loose similarities with the Naaman episode do not contribute to the characterization of John as Elijah, *pace* Evans, 'The Baptism of John in a Typological Context', 49.

42. Cf. J. A. T. Robinson, 'Elijah, John and Jesus: An Essay in Detection', *NTS* 4 (1958): 263–81, esp. 270; Pesch, *Das Markusevangelium*, 1:83; Marcus, *Mark: 1–8*, 157.

43. See the back-and-forth in the *Journal of Biblical Literature* between Morris M. Faierstein, 'Why do the Scribes Say that Elijah Must Come First?', *JBL* 100

122 *Writing with Scripture*

is addressed by Jesus directly in 9:11-13, messianic expectation does not feature explicitly in the disciples' question, 'Why do the scribes say that Elijah must come first?' (9:11). The question follows a discussion concerning the resurrection in 9:9-10, although it is also not clear the question is prompted by an association of Elijah with the eschatological resurrection of the dead.[44] In all likelihood, 9:11 simply envisages Elijah preceding the 'day of the LORD' (Mal 4:5), the eschatological event *par excellence* to which all others are related, including the resurrection of the dead and the coming of the messiah. For its part, Mk 9:9-13 reveals nothing specific about the event Elijah is supposed to precede. And yet, Jesus' answer implies that Elijah's coming precedes the present moment in the narrative, and by extension, the Son of Man (himself). For Mark, John the Baptist has influenced the depiction of Elijah as much as, if not more than, Elijah has influenced the depiction of John. If Elijah precedes the Messiah, it is because John precedes Jesus, and not the other way around. Rather than reflecting contemporary expectation of Elijah as the precursor to the Messiah, the germ of the idea is encountered for the first time in Mk 1:2-11. And it is this idea, as interpreted by Matthew (11:13-14; 17:10-13), that would eventually grow into the later Christian concept of Elijah as the messianic forerunner, first articulated explicitly by Justin Martyr (*Dial.* 49.1).

Other Uses of the Jewish Scriptures in Mark 1:2-11

Aside from the opening citation and the reference to the 'leather belt', Mk 1:11 is the only other instance in the prologue where a scriptural source is certain.[45] But again, identifying the source is no easy task. The words spoken by the heavenly voice – 'You are my son, the beloved; with you I am well pleased' (σὺ εἶ ὁ υἱός μου ὁ ἀγαπητός, ἐν σοὶ εὐδόκησα) – are definitely

---

(1981): 75–86; D. C. Allison Jr., 'Elijah Must Come First', *JBL* 103 (1984): 256–8; and J. A. Fitzmyer, 'More About Elijah Coming First', *JBL* 104 (1985): 295–6. The earliest indisputable evidence of this idea in Jewish literature may be found in *b. Shab.* 118a; *b. Erub.* 43a-b. Cf. *b. Ket.* 77b, where Elijah is said to prepare the way before R. Levi.

44. Although this association is implied elsewhere: Sir. 48:10-11; *m. Sot.* 9:15.

45. Less certain is the allusion to Gen. 1:2 in the dove of Mk 1:10, in light of *b. Hag.* 15a (cf. *Tg. Cant.* 2:12; *b. Ber.* 3a): Adela Yarbro Collins, *Mark: A Commentary*, Hermeneia 55 (Minneapolis, MN: Fortress, 2007), 148; Camille Focant, *The Gospel According to Mark: A Commentary*, trans. L. R. Keylock (Eugene, OR: Pickwick, 2012), 46–7. That the 'tearing' (σχίζω) of the heavens is a reference to Pss. 18:9; 144:5 or Isa. 64:1 is also uncertain, but it may allude to the 'tearing' (σχίζω) of the Temple curtain at the crucifixion (Mk 15:38), a scene which bears many similarities

3. Scripturalized Narrative in the Gospel of Mark 123

scriptural in origin. The first clause contains a clear reference to LXX Ps. 2:7 – 'You are my son' (υἱός μου εἶ σύ) – a passage which is elsewhere associated with messianic expectation.[46] The origin of the appellation 'the beloved', however, is obscure. Whilst the common adjective 'beloved' (Hb. ידיד; Gk. ὁ ἀγαπητός; Aram. חביב) was often used to describe filial or divine–human relations[47] – or perhaps both in the case of Mk 1:11 – many have suspected a scriptural source. It could have its roots in the interpretation of Ps. 2:7, which is expanded in the Targum: 'You are as beloved to me as a son to a father' (*Tg. Ps.* 2:7: חביב כבר לאבא).[48] Another possibility is that it comes from a famous passage concerning sonship, the *Aqedah*, in which Isaac is repeatedly referred to as '[Abraham's] beloved son' (LXX Gen. 22:2: τὸν υἱόν σου τὸν ἀγαπητόν; also Gen. 22:12, 16).[49]

Alternatively, the addition of ὁ ἀγαπητός could reflect Isa. 42:1, the source for the final clause of the heavenly pronouncement. Mark's language – 'with you I am well pleased' (ἐν σοὶ εὐδόκησα) – departs from the MT and the LXX – 'my soul has accepted him' (προσεδέξατο αὐτὸν ἡ ψυχή μου) – but is close to Theodotion, Symmachus and the Targum.[50]

to the baptism, so Stephen Motyer, 'The Rending of the Veil: A Markan Pentecost?', *NTS* 33 (1987): 155–7; David Ulansey, 'The Heavenly Veil Torn: Mark's Cosmic *Inclusio*', *JBL* 110 (1991): 123–5.

46. Acts 13:33; Heb. 1:5; *b. Suk.* 52a; *Midr. Teh.* 2:9; cf. the possible allusion in 1Q28a 2:11-12; 4 Ezra 7:28. The suggestion of Wilhelm Bousset, *Kyrios Christos: Geschichte des Christusglaubens von den Anfängen des Christentums bis Irenaeus* (Göttingen: Vandenhoeck & Ruprecht, 1913; rev. ed. 1921), 57 n. 2, and Joachim Jeremias ('παῖς θεοῦ', *TDNT* 5:700–709) that Mk 1:11 originally read ὁ παῖς μου (following Isa. 42:1) finds little support elsewhere in the Gospel, where the language is absent. Though there is no explicit exegesis of Ps. 2 in the Gospel, the twin titles 'Christ' and 'Son of God', and their association with Jews and Gentiles, respectively, may have their origin in the interpretation of the psalm.

47. See Deut. 33:12; Pss. 60:4 (LXX 59:7); 108:6 (LXX 107:7); 127:2 (LXX 126:2); Bar. 4:16; *1 En.* 91:4; *Jub.* 19:27; *LAB* 53:2; *T. Jos.* 1:2; *Ap. Ab.* 9:6; *T. Ab.* A 1:6.

48. Note, however, the uncertain date of the Targum. David M. Stec dates the composition between the fourth and sixth century CE (*The Targum of Psalms: Translated, with a Critical Introduction, Apparatus, and Notes*, Aramaic Bible 16 [London: T&T Clark, 2004], 2).

49. See, for example, Carl R. Kazmierski, *Jesus, the Son of God: A Study of the Markan Tradition and its Redaction by the Evangelist* (Wurzburg: Echter, 1979), 53–6. The Christian interpolator of the *Testament of Levi* apparently saw an allusion to Abraham and Isaac in the scene (*T. Levi* 18:6-7).

50. σ′ and θ′ Isa. 42:1b both have εὐδοκέω in place of the LXX's προσδέχομαι, whilst the form is similar to *Tg. Isa.* 42:1 (cf. 41:8-9; 43:10): 'my Memra has been

124   *Writing with Scripture*

The Isaianic text it is closest to, however, is Mt. 12:18-21, which cites the passage in full (Isa. 42:1-4). There Isa. 42:1 reads, 'Here is my servant, whom I have chosen, my beloved, with whom my soul is well pleased' (Mt. 12:18a: ἰδοὺ ὁ παῖς μου ὃν ἡμέτισα, ὁ ἀγαπητός μου εἰς ὃν εὐδόκησεν ἡ ψυχή μου). It could be Matthew and Mark both reflect a variant reading of Isaiah 42 with the addition of ὁ ἀγαπητός.[51] The similar addition of ὁ ἀγαπητός in α' Isa. 41:8 suggests the appellation was associated with the Servant Songs.

In any case, the Isaianic text of Mt. 12:18-21 confirms the *bat ḳōl* at Jesus' baptism in Mk 1:11 contains a confusing, but discernible, reference to Isa. 42:1. The context of the baptism strengthens the allusion. The 'spirit descending' (πνεῦμα...καταβαῖνον) evokes the clause following Isa. 42:1b: 'I have put my spirit on him' (LXX Isa. 42:1c: ἔδωκα τὸ πνεῦμά μου ἐπ' αὐτόν).[52] The author of the tradition in Mk 1:9-11 could have been led to Isa. 42:1 by the description of the spirit descending on Jesus' baptism, or, conversely, the description of the baptism may have been influenced by the language of Isa. 42:1f. What is not clear is that the scriptural sources of the *bat ḳōl* signal exegetical intent. As tempting as it may be to view Mk 1:11 as the announcement of the Davidic Messiah (Ps. 2:7) who is to be sacrificed (Gen. 22:2 etc.) as the servant (Isa. 42:1), the primary function of the heavenly voice is not the identification of the scriptural source, but the *phonic* source, which is heaven (οὐρανός). In the context of Mk 1:4-11, the voice functions, not as an explicit scriptural interpretation of the narrative – like the editorial citation of Mk 1:2-3 – but as a divine imprimatur of Jesus' privileged status, especially in relation to John (cf. in relation to Elijah and Moses in Mk 9:7).[53] The conflated allusion in Mk 1:11 in this way resembles other instances in Second Temple literature

---

pleased' (דאתרעי ביה מימרי). On the latter see Bruce D. Chilton, *A Galilean Rabbi and His Bible* (London: SPCK, 1984), 128–30. In favour of the allusion in some form or another are Dennis E. Nineham, *Saint Mark*, Pelican Gospel Commentaries (Harmondsworth: Penguin, 1963), 62; Pesch, *Das Markusevangelium*, 1:92; Gnilka, *Das Evangelium nach Markus*, 1:50; Guelich, *Mark 1–8:26*, 34; cf. Morna D. Hooker, *The Gospel According to St Mark* (London: A. & C. Black, 1991), 47.

51. Another possibility is Matthew was influenced by Mark's use of the term (also at 9:7; 12:6), though the form of the citation in Mt. 12:18 differs from other Matthaean parallels to Mk 1:11 (Mt. 3:17; 17:5).

52. See Steichele, *Der leidende Sohn Gottes*, 131–3.

53. Compare with Thomas R. Hatina, 'Embedded Scripture Texts and the Plurality of Meaning: The Announcement of the "Voice from Heaven" in Mk 1.11 as a Case Study', in *Biblical Interpretation in Early Christian Gospels, Volume 1: The Gospel of Mark*, ed. Hatina, SSEJC 16 (London: T&T Clark, 2006), 81–99, esp. 98–9.

3. Scripturalized Narrative in the Gospel of Mark   125

where language from the Psalms and the Servant Songs is attributed to God but repurposed in different narrative contexts.[54]

In the final analysis, however, Mk 1:11 is one of three instances in the prologue (1:2-11) that clearly relies on a scriptural source – the others being 1:2-3 and 1:6. In each case, the scriptures function differently: Mk 1:2-3 is an editorial marked citation (albeit incorrectly) of LXX Exod. 23:20, LXX Isa. 40:3 and possibly Mal. 3:1, which aims to interpret the ensuing narrative (Mk 1:4-11); Mk 1:6 weaves unmarked language from LXX 2 Kgs 1:8 into the narrative description of John's attire and so equates him with Elijah (cf. Mk 9:13); and Mk 1:11 ascribes unmarked language from Ps. 2:7 and Isa. 42:1 to a heavenly voice to signal Jesus' privileged status. The opening citation of Mk 1:2-3 appears as something external to the narrative (i.e. an *expositional* use of scriptural elements) whereas the scriptural language of Mk 1:6 and 1:11 is embedded into the narrative or direct speech of characters (i.e. a *compositional* use). Whilst these three passages do not exhaust all potential scriptural references in the prologue (i.e. 2 Kgs 2:8-12; 5:9-14; Pss. 18:9; 144:5; Gen. 22:2), they account for 44 of the 175 words in Mk 1:2-11, so at least one quarter of the opening narrative depends on the language of the Jewish scriptures. Though scholars have a tendency to see a far greater hermeneutical significance in these three passages than is perhaps there, the prologue shows that scriptural language is an indispensable feature of Mark's writing, whether or not the reader is supposed to identify the source. With the high rate of scriptural language in Mk 1:2-11 in the background, we will now turn to the use of the Jewish scriptures in the following section, the sojourn of Jesus in the wilderness and the call of the disciples (Mk 1:12-20).

Jesus and Elijah: Mark 1:12-20 and 1 Kings 19

The narrative of Mk 1:12-20 finds Jesus leaving the Jordan, driven by the spirit 'into the wilderness' (1:12: εἰς τὴν ἔρημον). Jesus stays 'in the wilderness forty days' (1:13: ἐν τῇ ἐρήμῳ τεσσεράκοντα ἡμέρας), where he is tempted by Satan and is 'with the wild beasts; and the angels waited on him' (μετὰ τῶν θηρίων, καὶ οἱ ἄγγελοι διηκόνουν αὐτῷ). After John is arrested, Jesus begins proclaiming the 'good news of God' (εὐαγγέλιον τοῦ θεοῦ) in Galilee (1:14-15). Then, passing along the sea of Galilee, Jesus calls Simon and Andrew as they are casting nets, saying, '*Come after me* (δεῦτε ὀπίσω μου) and I will make you fish for people' (1:17) – and

---

54. For example, Ps. 85:10 in *1 En.* 11:2; Ps. 114:4 in *1 En.* 51:4; Ps. 18:9 in *LAB* 15:6 and 23:10; Ps. 116:15 in *LAB* 40:4; Isa. 40:15 in *LAB* 7:3 and 12:4; Isa. 51:1 in *LAB* 23:4; Isa. 45:21-22 in *Sib. Or.* 8.377; Isa. 45:21 in *T. Ab.* A 8:7.

126   *Writing with Scripture*

they immediately leave their nets and 'followed him' (1:18: ἠκολούθησαν αὐτῷ). Farther along, Jesus calls James and John as they are mending their nets, and they immediately leave their father Zebedee with the servants in the boat and 'followed after him' (1:20: ἀπῆλθον ὀπίσω αὐτοῦ).

As commentators have long noted, the sequence of Jesus' sojourning in the wilderness and then calling the disciples closely resembles Elijah's sojourn in the wilderness and his call of Elisha in 1 Kings 19.[55] Following his confrontation with Jezebel, Elijah flees 'into the wilderness' (LXX 1 Kgs 19:4: ἐν τῇ ἐρήμῳ) where he despairs of his life before the LORD. There he falls asleep under a plant until an 'angel' (ἄγγελος) twice awakens him (LXX 19:5-7) and provides him with food and water for his journey 'forty days and forty nights' (LXX 19:8: τεσσαράκοντα ἡμέρας καὶ τεσσαράκοντα νύκτας) to Horeb. Following the revelation at Horeb (19:11-18), Elijah finds Elisha plowing twelve yoke of oxen and throws his mantle over him (19:19). Elisha then leaves the oxen and 'ran after' (LXX 19:20: κατέδραμεν ὀπίσω) Elijah, saying, 'I will kiss my father *and I will follow after you*' (LXX 19:20: καὶ ἀκολουθήσω ὀπίσω σου). Having slaughtered the oxen for the people, '[Elisha] arose and went after Elijah and served him' (LXX 19:21: καὶ ἀνέστη καὶ ἐπορεύθη ὀπίσω Ηλιου καὶ ἐλειτούργει αὐτῷ).

That 1 Kings 19 served as a compositional model for Mk 1:12-20 is seen in the shared narrative details and sequence of the sojourn in the wilderness followed by the call of the disciple(s).[56] In both narratives, a prophetic figure goes 'into the wilderness' for 'forty days [and nights]', where he is ministered to by 'angels/an angel'. Following a revelation from God, the prophetic figure finds men/a man at work, where he calls them and, leaving their work and father, they 'follow after' him. The two narratives share vocabulary: the location 'in the wilderness' (Mk 1:13; LXX 1 Kgs 19:4: ἐν τῇ ἐρήμῳ); the duration of 'forty days' (Mk 1:13; LXX 1 Kgs 19:8: τεσσαράκοντα ἡμέρας); the 'angels/angel' (Mk 1:13;

---

55. Farrer, *A Study in Mark*, 60–3; Paul Katz, 'Jesus als Vorläufer des Christus: Mögliche Hinweise in den Evangelien auf Elia als den "Typos" Jesu', *TZ* 52 (1996): 225–35 (229); Van Iersel, *Mark*, 65, 102; Marcus, *Mark: 1–8*, 167–71; Dale C. Allison, 'Behind the Temptations of Jesus: Q 4:1-13 and Mark 1:12-13', in *Authenticating the Activities of Jesus*, ed. Bruce D. Chilton and Craig A. Evans (Leiden: Brill, 2002), 202–3; Johannes Majoros-Danowski, *Elija im Markusevangelium. Ein Buch im Kontext des Judentums*, BWANT 180 (Stuttgart: Kohlhammer, 2008), 163–76; Winn, *Mark and the Elijah–Elisha Narrative*, 71–6; Mary Ann Beavis, *Mark*, Paideia (Grand Rapids, MI: Baker Academic, 2011), 38–9; Omerzu, 'Geschichte durch Geschichten', 85.

56. As Winn, *Mark and the Elijah–Elisha Narrative*, 75–6.

3. Scripturalized Narrative in the Gospel of Mark

LXX 1 Kgs 19:7: ἄγγελοι/ἄγγελος); as well as distinctive narrative details: the call of the disciples/Elisha in the midst of work (Mk 1:16, 19; 1 Kgs 19:19); the disciples/Elisha leaving their work to 'follow after' Jesus/ Elijah (Mk 1:18, 20; LXX 1 Kgs 19:20); the disciples/Elisha leaving their father to follow Jesus/Elijah (Mk 1:20; LXX 1 Kgs 19:20).

Mark 1:12-20	1 Kings 19
The Spirit sends Jesus 'into the wilderness' (ἐν τῇ ἐρήμῳ) (1:13).	Elijah flees 'into the wilderness' (ἐν τῇ ἐρήμῳ) (LXX 19:4).
Jesus is in the wilderness 'forty days' (τεσσαράκοντα ἡμέρας) (1:13).	Elijah is in the wilderness 'forty days' (τεσσαράκοντα ἡμέρας) and nights (LXX 19:8).
Jesus is tested by the Satan (1:13).	Elijah despairs of his life (19:4; Phinehas/Elijah is 'tested' [*probo*] in *LAB* 48:1).
Jesus is with the wild animals and 'angels' (ἄγγελοι) minister to him (1:13).	An 'angel' (ἄγγελος) feeds Elijah (LXX 19:5-7; ravens feed Elijah in 17:4-6).
Jesus sees the four disciples at work (1:16, 19).	Elijah comes upon Elisha at work (19:19).
Jesus calls them from their work, saying 'Come after me' (δεῦτε ὀπίσω μου) (1:17).	Elijah throws his mantle on Elisha (19:19).
The disciples leave their work and father and 'followed after' (ἠκολούθησαν/ἀπῆλθον ὀπίσω) Jesus (1:18, 20).	Elisha says he will 'follow after' (ἀκολουθήσω ὀπίσω) Elijah once he has kissed his father. Elisha leaves his work and 'followed after' (ἐπορεύθη ὀπίσω) Elijah (LXX 19:20-21).

Jesus and Elijah in the Wilderness: Mark 1:12-13 and 1 Kings 19:4-8

Although Elijah is the only individual in the Jewish scriptures to sojourn in the wilderness for forty days with angelic support, most studies on Mk 1:12-13 have associated Jesus' sojourn with Israel's forty years in the wilderness led by an angel.[57] There are obvious differences in the subject

57. Robert H. Lightfoot, *History and Interpretation in the Gospels* (London: Hodder & Stoughton, 1935), 65–6; Rudolf Schnackenburg, 'Der Sinn der Versuchung Jesu bei den Synoptikern', *ThQ* 132 (1952): 306–7; André Feuillet, 'L'episode de la tentation d'après l'Evangile selon Saint Marc (1,12-13)', *EstBíb* 19 (1960): 49–73; Jeffrey B. Gibson, *The Temptations of Jesus in Early Christianity* (London: T&T Clark, 2004), 63; cf. C. E. B. Cranfield, *The Gospel According to St. Mark*,

128   *Writing with Scripture*

(Israel/Jesus), the duration (years/days) and the function of the angel (vanguard/servant). But the language of *temptation* – which is absent in 1 Kings 19 – is abundant in the Exodus tradition. In Jewish literature, the language of 'temptation/testing' (MT: בנה/נסה; LXX: πειρασμός/πειράζω; δοκιμή/δοκιμάζω) is usually reserved for the incident at Meribah, where Israel tempts the LORD.[58] Elsewhere the LORD tests (πειράζω) Israel by vowing to rain down bread upon them, 'that I will test them whether they will walk by my law or not' (LXX Exod. 16:4: ὅπως πειράσω αὐτοὺς εἰ πορεύσονται τῷ νόμῳ μου ἢ οὔ). In LXX Exod. 20:20, Moses explains to the Israelites, 'For in order to test you God has come to you' (ἕνεκεν γὰρ τοῦ πειράσαι ὑμᾶς παρεγενήθη ὁ θεὸς πρὸς ὑμᾶς). But where the testing of an individual is concerned, the most common example is Abraham at the *Aqedah*,[59] though God is also known to test righteous persons.[60]

However, Jesus is tempted not by God but Satan, which has no parallel in the Exodus narrative or related traditions. And yet, one of Mark's early readers clearly associated Jesus' temptation with Israel's experience in the wilderness. In Matthew's expansion of Mark's temptation narrative (Mt. 4:1-11), it reads that Jesus 'fasted forty days and forty nights' (4:2: καὶ νηστεύσας ἡμέρας τεσσεράκοντα καὶ νύκτας τεσσεράκοντα) – alluding to Moses' forty-day fast on Sinai/Horeb.[61] When the devil tempts Jesus, he responds by alluding to the incident at Meribah: 'Again it is written, "You shall not tempt the Lord your God"' (Mt. 4:7: πάλιν γέγραπται· οὐκ

CGTC (Cambridge: Cambridge University Press, 1959), 57; Hooker, *The Gospel According to St. Mark*, 49; Ernest Best, *The Temptation and the Passion: The Markan Soteriology*, 2nd ed., SNTSMS 2 (Cambridge: Cambridge University Press, 1990), 5. Birger Gerhardsson, on the other hand, argues the Markan temptation abbreviates a longer tradition, preserved in Mt. 4:1-11 (*The Testing of God's Son (Matt. 4:1-11 & Par): An Analysis of an Early Christian Midrash* [Lund: Gleerup, 1966], 10–11). The reverse seems to be the case: Mt. 4:1-11 is an expansion of Mk 1:12-13. Even less convincing is the smorgasbord of allusions in Ardel B. Caneday, 'Mark's Provocative Use of Scripture in Narration: "He Was with the Wild Animals and Angels Ministered to Him"', *BBR* 9 (1999): 19–36.

58. Exod. 17:7; Deut. 6:16; 9:22; 33:8; Pss. 78:18, 41; 81:7; 95:8-9; 106:14; 4QTest 15; Heb. 3:8-9; cf. Ps. 81:7, where it is the LORD who tests the Israelites at Meribah.

59. Gen. 22:1; 1 Macc. 2:52; Jdt. 8:25; Sir. 44:20; *Jub.* 17:16-18; Heb. 11:17.

60. 1 Chron. 29:17; Job 23:10; Pss. 17:3; 26:2; 139:23; Prov. 17:3; Qoh. 3:18; Jer. 11:20; 12:3; Sir. 2:1; 11QT 54:12; 4QCatena 2:10; *Ps. Sol.* 16:14; 1 Thess. 2:4; cf. *T. Mos.* 9:4.

61. Par. Lk. 4:1-13. The scriptural expansions in the longer temptation narrative are more characteristic of Matthew's scriptural expansions of Mark than Luke's.

3. Scripturalized Narrative in the Gospel of Mark — 129

ἐκπειράσεις κύριον τὸν θεόν σου).[62] Jesus' words are a verbatim citation of LXX Deut. 6:16: 'You shall not tempt the Lord your God' (οὐκ ἐκπειράσεις κύριον τὸν θεόν σου) – which concludes, 'as you tempted in the temptation' (ὃν τρόπον ἐξεπειράσασθε ἐν τῷ πειρασμῷ). Two other responses of Jesus to Satan appear to be drawn from Deuteronomy (Mt. 4:4; cf. LXX Deut. 8:3; Mt. 4:10; cf. Deut. 6:13). This suggests some of Mark's early readers saw in Jesus' temptation an allusion to Moses' and Israel's experience in the wilderness.

It is noteworthy details from Moses' forty-day fast also appear in another narrative modelled on 1 Kgs 19:4-8.[63] In the *Apocalypse of Abraham*, a text roughly contemporary with Mark, the character of Abraham describes meeting an angel: 'And we went, the two of us alone together, forty days and nights. And I ate not bread and drank no water, because (my food) was to see the angel who was with me, and his discourse with me was my drink. We came to God's mountain, glorious Horeb' (*Ap. Ab.* 12:1-3).[64] Like 1 Kgs 19:4-8, the *Apocalypse* has a journey of 'forty days and nights' to Horeb (cf. 1 Kgs 19:8) and the appearance of an angel who provides – in this case, metaphorical – food and drink for the journey (cf. 1 Kgs 19:6, 8).[65] However, the detail that Abraham 'ate not bread and drank no water'

---

62. My translation.

63. Moses' forty-day sojourn clearly lies behind the forty-day seclusion of Ezra (*4 Ezra* 14:23, 36, 44-45), so Allison, *The New Moses*, 62–5.

64. On the dating of the *Apocalypse of Abraham* relative to 70 CE, see James R. Mueller, 'The *Apocalypse of Abraham* and the Destruction of the Second Jewish Temple', in *The Society of Biblical Literature 1982 Seminar Papers*, ed. Kent Harold Richards, SBLSP 21 (Chico, CA: Scholars Press, 1982), 343–7.

65. The flight of Elijah in 1 Kgs 19:1-8 may have influenced *Mart. Ascen. Isa.* 2:7-11, where Isaiah and the prophets flee from their persecutors to a 'mountain in a desert place' (2:8; see also the description of their clothing and diet in 2:10-11); and *LAB* 6:7-12, where the eleven righteous men flee from their persecutors for thirty days in the mountains and they drink 'water flowing from rocks' (6:9; cf. 1 Kgs 17:4; Exod. 17:6; Isa. 33:16). The journey of Zosimus in the *History of the Rechabites* recalls 1 Kgs 19:6-8, where, having fasted for forty years (*Hist. Rech.* 1:1, 4), Zosimus meets an angel: 'Then I left the cave, and traveled with the angel (for) forty days' (2:1). The description of Zosimus is similar to the descriptions of later desert-dwelling ascetics, who are either modelled on or modelled themselves after Elijah (Athanasius, *Vita. Ant.* 7.37 [PG 26.853]; Jerome, *Epist.* 58.5 [PL 22.583]; John Cassian, *Conf.* 18.6 [NPNF 11.481]). To take one example, with the help of angels, Abba Serapion goes on a thirty-day journey to see Mark the hermit, who lives on a mountain where he is ministered to and fed by angels (*Vita S. Marco Atheniensi* 4-5,13). He is also said to have hairs growing on his entire body so 'all [his] members were covered' (*Vita S. Marco Atheniensi* 8; cf. 2 Kgs 1:8). See also the description of Shenoute of Atripe

130   *Writing with Scripture*

is borrowed verbatim from Moses' forty-day fast on Sinai/Horeb (Exod. 34:28; Deut. 9:9, 18). Interestingly, once Abraham arrives at Horeb, he is tempted by Azazel (*Ap. Ab.* 13:3-14), who appears as an unclean bird (cf. Gen. 15:11; Lev. 11:13-19).[66] The association of Moses and Israel in the wilderness with the experience of Elijah in 1 Kings 19 is natural, when one considers that 1 Kgs 19:4-18 itself was likely modelled on the experience of Moses on Sinai/Horeb.[67]

Then again, the testing/tempting of Jesus might reflect the experience of Elijah in 1 Kings 19. Whilst the language of 'testing' (Hb.: בחן/נסה; Gk: πειράζω/δοκιμάζω) does not appear, Elijah is in some sense tested: following the threats of Jezebel, he is 'afraid' (LXX 19:3: ἐφοβήθη) and flees for his life (ἀπῆλθεν κατὰ τὴν ψυχὴν ἑαθτοῦ) into the wilderness, where he despairs, begging the LORD for death: 'Take my life away from me' (LXX 19:4: λαβὲ δὴ τὴν ψυχήν μου ἀπ' ἐμοῦ). At Horeb, Elijah restates his despair to the LORD, saying, 'They destroyed your altars and killed your prophets by the sword, and I alone am left, and they seek my life to take it' (LXX 19:10, 14). One text contemporary to Mark uses the language of 'testing' (Lt. *probo*) to describe Elijah's anguish. In the *Liber Antiquitatum Biblicarum* (*LAB* 48:1), Elijah appears under the guise of Phinehas (*LAB* 48:1). God tells Phinehas/Elijah to dwell on a mountain, saying, 'and you will not come down to mankind until the time arrives *and you will be tested in that time* (*et proberis in tempore*)' – alluding to the deeds of Elijah during the reign of Ahab. It is difficult to know what Hebrew or Greek verb lies behind *probo* in *LAB* 48:1, but the Vulgate sometimes has *probo* where the LXX has πειράζω (i.e. Exod. 20:20 for Hb. נסה; Dan. 12:10 for Hb. צרף).[68] Whilst it is possible that both the 'testing' of Israel

---

(*Life of Shenoute* 10). For more Elijianic descriptions of ascetics, see Kristi Upson-Saia, 'Hairiness and Holiness in the Early Christian Desert', in *Dressing Judeans and Christians in Antiquity*, ed. Kristi Upson-Saia, Carly Daniel-Hughes and Alicia J. Batten (London: Routledge, 2014), 155–72. At other times, the model is Elijah's first sojourn in the wilderness (1 Kgs 17:2-7), as when Jerome relates that ravens brought bread to Paul of Thebes for sixty years (*Vita Paul* 10 [PL 23.25]; cf. 1 Kgs 17:6). Countless other examples show the image of Elijah in the wilderness (1 Kgs 17:2-7; 19:4-8) continued to inspire scripturalized narratives beyond Mk 1:12-13; see David T. M. Frankfurter, *Elijah in Upper Egypt: The Apocalypse of Elijah and Early Egyptian Christianity* (Minneapolis, MN: Fortress, 1993), 65–74.

66. Elsewhere, the *Apocalypse* describes Azazel's ability to tempt the righteous (*Ap. Ab.* 13:11) and Adam and Eve (22:5–23:13).

67. See Allison, *The New Moses*, 41–4.

68. Most often, *probo* appears for δέχομαι, from which δοκιμάζω is derived. Ambrose (*Epist.* 63.28 [PL 16.1257]) says in the wilderness 'the Lord was training [Elijah] to the perfection of virtue' (*Dominus ad virtutis erudiebat perfectionem*).

3. *Scripturalized Narrative in the Gospel of Mark* 131

and Elijah have influenced the temptation of Jesus in Mk 1:13, neither tradition appears to associate the testing in the wilderness with the wiles of Satan.

The 'wild animals' (θηρίον) of Mk 1:13 also have no direct parallel in the Exodus and Elijah traditions. Whilst some following Pesch have seen the inclusion of the 'wild animals', along with Satan, as an allusion to Genesis 2–3,[69] the animals might also recall Elijah's first sojourn in the wilderness. In 1 Kgs 17:2-7, God sends Elijah to the Wadi Cherith 'which is before the Jordan' (LXX 17:3: τοῦ ἐπὶ προσώπου τοῦ Ιορδάνου), saying to him, 'I will command my ravens to feed you there' (LXX 17:4: τοῖς κόραξιν ἐντελοῦμαι διατρέφειν σε ἐκεῖ).[70] It is unlikely, however, that Mark's θηρίον substitutes for 'ravens' (ערבים/κόρακες), since the word is rarely used as a substitute for birds (cf. Arist., *Birds* 69-70) and never for ravens. But there is some confusion over the identity of Elijah's creaturely helpers in *LAB* 48:1, where God says to Phinehas/Elijah, 'I will command *my eagle* (*aquile mee*) and he will nourish you there'.[71] The command concerns the period of time before Phinehas/Elijah returns to humanity to shut and open the heavens (1 Kgs 17:1) and so presumably does not refer to Elijah's sojourn by the Wadi Cherith. The syntax is nevertheless borrowed almost verbatim from 1 Kgs 17:4. At any rate, it is unlikely the 'wild animals' of Mk 1:13 reflect 1 Kgs 17:4-6. But it is worth noting a clear reference to scriptural material, like the 'leather belt around his waist' in Mk 1:6 (cf. LXX 2 Kgs 1:8), can be accompanied by an incongruous detail that nevertheless preserves something of the scriptural reference ('camel's hair' [τρίχας καμήλου]; cf. 'hairy man' [איש בעל שׂ ער/ἀνὴρ δασύς]). The fact remains, however, that the detail concerning Elijah's creaturely helpers does not come from 1 Kgs 19:4-8, but 1 Kgs 17:2-7. The episode in 1 Kgs 17:2-7 does share some general similarities with Mk 1:12-13: the 'word of the Lord' (LXX 17:2: ῥῆμα κυρίου) sends Elijah eastward to the Wadi Cherith 'which is before the Jordan'

---

69. Pesch, 'Anfang des Evangeliums Jesu Christi. Eine Studie zum Prolog des Markusevangeliums (Mark 1,1-15)', in *Die Zeit Jesu: Festschrift für Heinrich Schlier*, ed. Günther Bornkamm and Karl Rahner (Freiburg: Herder, 1970), 130–3; Pesch, *Das Markusevangelium*, 1:94–6; Petr Pokorny, 'The Temptation Stories and Their Intention', *NTS* 20 (1974): 120–2; Best, *The Temptation and the Passion*, 6–7; Ulrich Mell, 'Jesu Taufe durch Johannes (Markus 1,9-15) – zur narrative Christologie vom neuen Adam', *BZ* 40 (1996): 161–78; Marcus, *Mark: 1–8*, 169–71; Focant, *The Gospel According to Mark*, 44; cf. William Lane, *The Gospel According to Mark*, NICNT 2 (Grand Rapids, MI: Eerdmans, 1974), 61 n. 79.

70. Cf. *2 Bar.* 77:24; *Liv. Pro.* 21:13; Josephus, *Ant.* 8.13.2.

71. Baruch compares an eagle to the ravens of 1 Kgs 17:4-6 (*2 Bar.* 77:18-26).

132 *Writing with Scripture*

(LXX 17:3: τοῦ ἐπὶ προσώπου τοῦ Ιορδάνου), as in Mk 1:12, the 'spirit' (πνεῦμα) sends Jesus away from the Jordan (1:9: εἰς τὸν Ἰορδάνην) into the wilderness. Moreover, the events in Elijah's life are sometimes conflated or re-ordered in contemporary literature (Sir. 48:1-8; *Liv. Pro.* 21:4-15; *LAB* 48:1). In this sense, it is possible that the author of Mk 1:12-13 incorporated elements from each of Elijah's sojourns in the wilderness (1 Kgs 17:2-7; 19:4-8). Then again, perhaps a simpler explanation is that the presence of 'wild animals' (θηρίον) is another instance of 'eco-typing' – in other words, it simply owes to Jesus' location 'in the wilderness' (ἐν τῇ ἐρήμῳ; cf. Mk 1:4-6).[72]

Attempts to discount the influence of 1 Kgs 19:4-8 on Jesus' sojourn in the wilderness based on the absence of 'and forty nights' (καὶ τεσσαράκοντα νύκτας) as in 1 Kgs 19:8 are unconvincing.[73] The redundant 'and nights' ([ו]לילה/καὶ νύκτας) is often omitted from similar occurrences of 'forty days': i.e. the 'forty days and nights' of Noah (Gen. 7:4, 12; 'and nights' omitted: Gen. 7:17; 8:6; Josephus, *Ant.* 1.3.5; Philo, *Ques. Gen.* 2.33; *b. Yom.* 76a); the 'forty days and nights' of Moses (Exod. 24:18; 34:28; Deut. 9:9 etc.; 'and nights' omitted: Josephus, *Ag. Ap.* 2.25; *Ant.* 3.7; Philo, *Mos.* 2.14; *Alleg. Interp.* 3.48; *Ques. Ezra* A 39; Clement, *Misc.* 3.7.1; *m. Taan.* 4:6; *b. Shabb.* 89a; *b. Yom.* 4b; 76a; *b. Taan.* 8a; *b. Menah.* 99b; *PRE* 46:1-6). Later literature also omits 'and nights' from Elijah's sojourn in the wilderness: in the *Sifre* to Deut. 2:2 it reads, 'Is it not a journey [of] forty days in line with what is said concerning Elijah?' Similarly, Irenaeus has 'Fasting those forty days, like Moses and Elias' (*Adv. Haer.* 3.22.2); as does Tertullian, 'For forty days Moses and Elias fasted, and lived upon God alone' (*Res.* 61). Returning to Jesus, the Matthaean version adds καὶ νύκτας τεσσεράκοντα (Mt. 4:2; par. Lk. 4:2) clearly under the influence of Moses in Exod. 34:28 (and par.). Whilst no early Greek mss. of Mark include 'and forty nights', Origen attributes the following to the Gospel: 'Mark has the following: "And he was in the desert forty days and forty nights tempted by Satan, and he was with the wild beasts; and the angels ministered to him"' (*Comm. Jo.* 10.1: ὁ δὲ Μάρκος· Καὶ ἦν, φησὶν, ἐν τῇ ἐρήμῳ τεσσαράκοντα ἡμέρας καὶ τεσσαράκοντα νύκτας, πειραζόμενος ὑπὸ τοῦ σατανᾶ· καὶ ἦν μετὰ τῶν θηρίων, καὶ οἱ ἄγγελοι διηκόνουν αὐτῷ).[74] The Vulgate at Mk 1:13 similarly reads 'forty

---

72. In *T. Naph.* 8:4, angels help the pious whilst devils and wild animals flee.

73. *Pace* Ernst Haenchen, *Der Weg Jesu* (Berlin: Töpelmann, 1966), 64; Hermann Mahnke, *Die Versuchungsgeschichte im Rahmen der synoptischen Evangelien. Ein Beitrag zur frühen Christologie*, BBET 9 (Frankfurt: Lang, 1978), 25; Öhler, *Elia im Neuen Testament*, 135 n. 142.

74. Likewise Eusebius, *Theo.* 3.55.

3. Scripturalized Narrative in the Gospel of Mark 133

days and forty nights' (*quadraginta diebus, et quadraginta noctibus*).[75] Whether the addition of 'and nights' in Origen and the Vulgate points to an early variant of Mk 1:13 not witnessed in the early Greek mss. or, as is more likely, the influence of Mt. 4:2, the general point stands that 'and nights' can be omitted from otherwise unambiguous references to 1 Kgs 19:8, as it may be included in otherwise unambiguous references to Mk 1:13.[76]

There is, however, no clear sign 1 Kings 19 has influenced the proclamation of the kingdom in Mk 1:14-15. Favouring the allusion, Adam Winn has argued that 1 Kgs 19:15-18 and Mk 1:14-15 reflect 'parallel proclamations about the kingdom of God' – in the sense that Elijah's task of anointing Hazael, Jehu and Elisha and Jesus' announcement that the 'kingdom of God has come near' (ἤγγικεν ἡ βασιλεία τοῦ θεοῦ) both concern the establishment of divine rule over human affairs.[77] To this, one can add other loose similarities: Elijah is tasked with anointing kings (LXX 1 Kgs 19:15-16: βασιλέα) whilst Jesus announces the kingdom (Mk 1:15: βασιλεία) of God and is himself anointed (1:9-11); Elijah receives a revelation at Horeb (1 Kgs 19:9-14) whilst Jesus' proclamation of 'good news of God' (Mk 1:14: τὸ εὐαγγέλιον τοῦ θεοῦ) implies a revelation from God; Elijah retreats into the wilderness following the violent threats of Jezebel (1 Kgs 19:2) and twice entreats God concerning the Israelites, who have 'killed your prophets with the sword' (LXX 1 Kgs 19:10, 14: τοὺς προφήτας σου ἀπέκτειναν ἐν ῥομφαίᾳ), whilst Jesus emerges from the wilderness following the arrest of John (Mk 1:14) who is later beheaded (6:27). As Mk 1:14-15 and 1 Kgs 19:15-18 both fall between their respective 'wilderness' and 'call' narratives, it is tempting to see them as equivalent episodes despite their obvious differences. But the more natural conclusion is that Mark has simply deviated from the scriptural model. Other scripturalized narratives similarly deviate from their model. For example, in the episode of Abram in the fiery furnace (*LAB* 6), Abram and eleven righteous men are arrested for refusing to commit idolatry (6:1-5) as in Dan. 3:1-18, and then Abram is thrown into the fiery furnace but comes to no harm (*LAB* 6:16-18) as in Dan. 3:19-27. But in the intervening section (*LAB* 6:6-15), the narrative departs from this model and instead relates a long and confusing episode in which the eleven righteous men escape into the mountains. Mark 1:12-20 features a similar sort of

---

75. Also Augustine, *Harm.* 16.33.

76. Some mss. later than the eighth century include καὶ τεσσαράκοντα νύκτας (Lᶜ 33 M).

77. Winn, *Mark and the Elijah–Elisha Narrative*, 73–6.

134 *Writing with Scripture*

scripturalized intercalation, with the scripturalized narratives of Jesus in the wilderness (1:12-13) and the call of the disciples (1:16-20) placed either side of Jesus' inaugural proclamation of the kingdom in Galilee, a pivotal moment which acts as the fulfilment of the words of John in 1:7-8, and indeed the ἀρχὴ τοῦ εὐαγγελίου of 1:1.[78]

The Call of the Disciples and Elisha: Mark 1:16-20 and 1 Kings 19:19-21

As early as Chrysostom (*Hom.* 14.3), commentators have noted the similarity of the call narratives in Mk 1:16-20 and 1 Kgs 19:19-21.[79] In both episodes, the prophet comes upon the man/men as they are working, places his mantle upon him/calls them and the man/men leave their work/ father and follow after the prophet. Each episode features a disciple leaving their work and family to 'follow after' (ἀκολουθέω...ὀπίσω) their master: Jesus sees Simon and Andrew working and says, 'Follow after me' (Mk 1:17: δεῦτε ὀπίσω μου), at which point they leave their nets and 'followed him' (1:18: ἠκολούθησαν αὐτῷ).[80] Likewise, Jesus sees James and John, and after he calls them, they leave their father and 'followed after him' (1:20: ἀπῆλθον ὀπίσω αὐτοῦ). In 1 Kgs 19:19-21, Elijah comes upon Elisha working and throws his mantle over him, at which point

78. See the helpful discussion in Hatina, *In Search of a Context*, 102–14.

79. Discussed in modern scholarship at least since Strauss, *Das Leben Jesu*, 1:525–6, who comments, 'Könnte es sich klarer, als durch diesen Zug, verrathen, wie die ganze Erzählung bei Matthäus und Markus nur eine überbietende Nachbildung der A.T.lichen ist' (526). See the more recent comments in Anselm Schulz, *Nachfolgen und Nachahmen*, StANT 6 (Munich: Kösel, 1962), 100–103; Eduard Schweizer, *Das Evangelium nach Markus*, NTD 1 (Göttingen: Vandenhoeck & Ruprecht, 1967), 22; Rudolf Pesch, 'Berufung und Sendung, Nachfolge und Mission: Eine Studie zu Mk 1,16-20', *ZKT* 91 (1969): 1–31, esp. 9–18; *Das Markusevangelium*, 1:109–14; Gnilka, *Das Evangelium nach Markus*, 1:74–5; Marcus, *Mark: 1–8*, 183; Roger D. Aus, 'Jesus' Calling the First Four Disciples in Mark 1:16-20 and Judaic Traditions on Elijah's Calling Elisha as his Disciple in 1 Kgs 19:19-21', in *Stilling the Storm: Studies in Early Palestinian Judaic Traditions*, ed. Aus (Binghamton, NY: Global Publications, 2000), 89–135; D. C. Allison Jr., *The Intertextual Jesus: Scripture in Q* (Harrisburg, PA: Trinity Press International, 2000), 142–3; Winn, *Mark and the Elijah–Elisha Narrative*, 74–5; Focant, *The Gospel According to Mark*, 59; cf. the sceptical remarks in Gundry, *Mark*, 70; Öhler, *Elia im Neuen Testament*, 158.

80. Jesus' command (Mk 1:17: δεῦτε ὀπίσω μου) also agrees verbatim with Elisha's command to the Arameans (LXX 2 Kgs 6:19: δεῦτε ὀπίσω μου), but as there are no other links to this passage, it is likely a coincidence (cf. Pesch, 'Berufung und Sendung', 15). Aus' theory that the number of twelve disciples reflects the twelve oxen of Elisha is a little too clever ('Jesus' Calling the First Four Disciples', 96–7).

3. Scripturalized Narrative in the Gospel of Mark 135

Elisha says, 'I will kiss my father and *will follow after you*' (LXX 1 Kgs 19:20: ἀκολουθήσω ὀπίσω σου), after which he 'went after Elijah' (19:21: ἐπορεύθη ὀπίσω Ἠλιου).

The circumstantial differences between the two call narratives are characteristic of scripturalized narratives. Returning to Pseudo-Philo, whilst the fiery furnace narratives of Abram and Jair are both modelled on Daniel 3, *LAB* 6 has twelve men sentenced to the furnace for refusing to build the tower of Babel, and *LAB* 38 has seven sentenced for refusing to worship Baal in Israel, whereas Daniel 3 has three sentenced for refusing to worship Nebuchadnezzar in Babylon. In the same way, the differences in location, vocation and number of the disciples in Mk 1:16-20 and 1 Kgs 19:19-21 reflect their respective narrative contexts (i.e. the fishermen reflect the Galilaean context of Mk 1:14-39). As Pesch observes, 'Die Ortsangabe "am Meer" ist durch den Beruf der beiden Brüderpaare bedingt, wie 1 Kön 19,19 das Ochsengespann auf dem Acker den Beruf des Elisha symbolisierte; die Angabe verändert den Charakter der "idealen Szene" nicht, erlaubt aber den Ausbau eines tragfähigen, an Ortsangaben orientierten Erzählfadens'.[81]

Others have sought to contrast the immediacy (εὐθύς) and severity of the disciples' response in Mk 1:16-20 with Elisha's request to bid farewell to his father (LXX 1 Kgs 19:20; cf. MT 19:20 adds 'and mother').[82] But as Roger Aus observes, the language of immediacy also occurs in Josephus' version of Elisha's calling: 'Thereupon Elisha immediately began to prophesy, and, leaving his oxen, followed Elijah' (*Ant.* 8.13.7: ὁ δ' Ἐλισσαῖος εὐθέως προφητεύειν ἤρξατο καὶ καταλιπὼν τοὺς βόας ἠκολού-θησεν Ἠλίᾳ).[83] Note also the severity of Elisha's response in the later *Seder Eliyahu Rabbah*: 'At once Elisha left all that he owned and ran after [him]' (*S. Eli. Rab.* 32: מיד הניח אלישע את כל אשר לו וירץ אחריו).[84]

The immediacy and severity scholars attribute to the Markan call narratives (1:16-20; 2:14) is much better reflected in Matthew and Luke.[85] The

---

81. Pesch, *Das Markusevangelium*, 1.110.

82. Arguing against the influence of 1 Kgs 19:19-21 on this basis are Gundry, *Mark*, 70; Öhler, *Elia im Neuen Testament*, 158; James R. Edwards, *The Gospel According to Mark*, Pillar New Testament Commentary (Grand Rapids, MI: Eerdmans, 2002), 50.

83. Aus, 'Jesus' Calling the First Four Disciples', 117–21.

84. Instead of bidding farewell to his parents, Elisha immediately 'renounced ownership of all that he had, indeed he salted his entire field so that it became barren' (*S. Eli. Rab.* 32).

85. So Aus, 'Jesus' Calling the First Four Disciples', 123–4.

discourse concerning the would-be disciples (Mt. 8:18-22; Lk. 9:47-62) appears to be influenced by both Mk 1:16-20 and 1 Kgs 19:19-21.[86] The second would-be disciple says to Jesus, '[Lord,] first let me go and bury my father' (Mt. 8:21: ἐπίτρψόν μοι πρῶτον ἀπελθεῖν καὶ θάψαι τὸν πατέρα μου; Lk. 9:59: [κύριε,] ἐπίτρεψόν μοι ἀπελθόντι πρῶτον θάψαι τὸν πατέρα μου). This resembles Elisha's request to Elijah, especially as it appears in LXX 1 Kgs 19:20: 'I will kiss my father and will follow after you' (καταφιλήσω τὸν πατέρα μου καὶ ἀκολουθήσω ὀπίσω σου). Whereas Elijah appears to grant Elisha's request (LXX 1 Kgs 19:20; Josephus, *Ant.* 8.7), Jesus denies the request of the would-be disciple (Mt. 8:22; Lk. 9:60). Luke includes a third would-be disciple, who says, 'I will follow you, Lord; but let me first say farewell to those at my home' (Lk. 9:61: ἀκολουθήσω σοι, κύριε· πρῶτον δὲ ἐπίτρεψόν μοι ἀποτάξασθαι τοῖς εἰς τὸν οἶκόν μου). Whilst the disciples' request already resembles that of Elisha (1 Kgs 19:20-21), Jesus' answer makes it more pronounced: 'No one who puts a hand to the plow and looks back is fit for the kingdom of God' (Lk. 9:62: οὐδεὶς ἐπιβαλὼν τὴν χεῖρα ἐπ' ἄπορτον καὶ βλέπων εἰς τὰ ὀπίσω εὔθετός ἐστιν τῇ βασιλείᾳ τοῦ θεοῦ). This recalls the vocation of Elisha when Elijah calls him, 'he was plowing with oxen' (LXX 1 Kgs 19:19: ἠροτρία ἐν βουσίν). The 'hand to the plow' (τὴν χεῖρα ἐπ' ἄπορτον) of Lk. 9:62 also functions as a metaphor for discipleship in the same way 'casting a net' (ἀμφιβάλλω) does in Mk 1:16: as Jesus says, 'Follow me and I will make you *fish for people*' (1:17: ἁλιεῖς ἀνθρώπων).

In addition to influencing the episode of the would-be disciples, the call of Elisha is associated with another call narrative: Phannias ben Samuel, the last high priest before the destruction of the Temple, is said to have been called to the high priesthood whilst he was 'ploughing, as it says concerning Elisha' (*t. Yom.* 1:6: חורש כמה שנאמר באלישע; cf. 1 Kgs 19:19).[87] But more often it is the relationship of Elijah and Elisha that served as a model for teacher–disciple relationships: Paphnutius writes that Abba Isaac 'poured water on [the] hands' of his teacher Abba Aaron, 'as the great Elisha did for the prophet Elijah' (Paphnutius, *Hist.* 10b; cf.

---

86. See the studies of H. J. Blair, 'Putting One's Hand to the Plough: Luke ix.62 in the Light of 1 Kings xix.19-21', *ExpTim* 79 (1967–68): 342–3; Öhler, *Elia im Neuen Testament*, 156–62; Richard A. Horsley, 'Prophetic Envoys for the Renewal of Israel: Q 9:57-10:16', in *Whoever Hears You Hears Me: Prophets, Performance, and Tradition in Q*, ed. Richard A. Horsley and Jonathan A. Draper (Harrisburg, PA: Trinity Press International, 1999), 240–1; Allison, *The Intertextual Jesus*, 143–4.

87. For additional examples see Aus, 'Jesus' Calling the First Four Disciples', 98.

3. Scripturalized Narrative in the Gospel of Mark 137

2 Kgs 3:11);[88] and Ambrose models the bishop Acholius on Elijah and his successor Anysius on Elisha, 'Like Elijah [Acholius] was carried up to heaven… For at the very moment when he was being taken up, he let fall so to speak the vestment which he wore, and invested with it holy Anysius his disciple, and clothed him with the robes of his own priesthood' (*Epist.* 15.8-9 [PL 16.957]; cf. 2 Kgs 2:11-14).

This association of Elijah and Elisha with teacher–disciple relationships may offer a clue as to what prompted the author to compose a scripturalized narrative modelled on 1 Kings 19. Contemporary and later Jewish texts describe Elisha as Elijah's 'disciple' ($\mu\alpha\theta\eta\tau\eta\varsigma$ in Josephus, *Ant.* 8.13.7; 9.2.2; 9.3.1; תלמיד in *Mek.* 13:19; *b. Sot.* 13a; 49a; *b. San.* 105b; *S. Eli. Rab.* 17) and call Elijah his 'lord' or 'rabbi' (אדוני in *Mek.* 13:19; אדני in *PRE* 33:8; אדין in 4Q481a 3:4?; רבי in *Tg. 2 Kgs* 2:12; רבו in *Mek.* 13:19; *t. Sot.* 4:8; 12:5).[89] Likewise, Jesus has 'disciples' ($\mu\alpha\theta\eta\tau\alpha\iota$ in Mk 2:15-16, 23; 3:7 etc.) and he is called 'lord' ($\kappa\nu\rho\iota\varsigma$ in 7:28) and 'rabbi' ($\dot{\rho}\alpha\beta\beta\iota/\rho\alpha\beta\beta\sigma\nu\nu\iota$ in 9:5; 10:51; 11:21; 14:45).[90] That Jesus gathered his own disciples appears to have been a widely known tradition (1 Cor. 15:5; Rev. 21:14)[91] and it may have been this fact alone

88. Tim Vivian, *Histories of the Monks of Upper Egypt; and the Life of Onnophrius by Paphnutius* (Kalamazoo, MI: Cistercian Publications, 1993), 26.

89. On the possible relationship between 4Q481a 3:4 and 2 Kgs 2:12, see Ariel Feldman, *The Dead Sea Scrolls Rewriting Samuel and Kings: Texts and Commentary*, BZAW 469 (Berlin: W. de Gruyter, 2015), 154–5. Compare with *Tg. 2 Kgs* 2:12, where the Hebrew אבי אבי has been replaced with רבי רבי; and *PRE* 33:8, where Elisha calls Elijah 'my lord' (יאדני).

90. The medieval *Ma'aseh Torah* relates that Elijah had four disciples: Elisha, Micah, Obadiah and Jonah (Jellinek, *BHM* 2:95; Ginzberg, 6:343). Parts of this tradition belong to an earlier age: Obadiah as disciple of Elijah (*Liv. Pro.* 9:2); Jonah as son of the Zarephathite woman (*Liv. Pro.* 10:6; *PRE* 33:2); cf. Jonah as disciple of Elisha (*S. Olam. Rab.* 19). Other texts envisage a large number of disciples for Elijah (*Tg. Ps.-J.* on Deut. 34:3; *Cant. Rab.* 4.11; *Lam. Rab.* 4.25; cf. Elisha: *b. Ket.* 106a; *Tg. Ps.-J.* on Deut. 34:3). Elisha's disciple, Gehazi, on the other hand, becomes the archetypical wicked disciple in later literature (esp. *b. Sot.* 47a; *b. Sanh.* 107b; *y. Sanh.* 10:2 [29b]; compare with the remarkably similar episodes in Mk 9:42; 10:13-16).

91. The enumeration of twelve disciples appears to have been widely known and likely dates to Jesus' ministry, see Robert P. Meye, *Jesus and the Twelve: Discipleship and Revelation in Mark's Gospel* (Grand Rapids, MI: Eerdmans, 1968), 192–209; J. P. Meier, 'The Circle of the Twelve: Did it Exist During Jesus' Public Ministry?', *JBL* 116 (1997): 635–72; and most recently in D. C. Allison Jr., *Constructing Jesus: Memory, Imagination, and History* (Grand Rapids, MI: Baker Academic, 2010), 67–76.

138   *Writing with Scripture*

that led the author of Mk 1:12-20 to compose a scripturalized narrative in which Jesus calls his disciples in the manner of Elijah: emerging from a forty-day sojourn in the wilderness to call his disciples from their work and families to follow after him. The structure for this episode is provided by 1 Kgs 19:4-8, 19-21. In this way, Mk 1:12-20 resembles two other Markan episodes modelled on a scene from the Elijah–Elisha cycle, this time from the career of Elisha: the multiplication of loaves at Gilgal (2 Kgs 4:42-44).

Jesus and Elisha: Mark 6:35-44, 8:1-9 and 2 Kings 4:42-44

In Mk 6:30-34, Jesus and the disciples are attempting to escape into the wilderness in order to rest, when a large crowd follows them. Jesus has compassion for the crowds, because they are 'like sheep without a shepherd' (6:34: ὡς πρόβατα μὴ ἔχοντα ποιμένα). As evening approaches, the disciples ask Jesus to send the crowds away so they might buy something to eat (6:35-36). But Jesus tells them, 'You give them [something] to eat' (6:37: δότε αὐτοῖς ὑμεῖς φαγεῖν). The disciples respond with disbelief, asking, 'Are we to go and buy two hundred denarii worth of bread, and give it them to eat?' (6:37). Jesus asks, 'How many loaves have you?' – to which the disciples answer, 'Five, and two fish' (6:38). Jesus then orders the crowds to sit on the green grass in groups of hundreds and fifties (6:39-40). Jesus takes the five loaves and two fish, offers a blessing, and then breaks the bread and gives it to the disciples who set it before the people, along with the two fish. Then a miracle occurs: 'all ate and were filled' (6:42: ἔφαγον πάντες καὶ ἐχορτάσθησαν) – whilst some was left over, as the disciples collect twelve baskets full of broken bread and fish (6:43). The episode concludes by noting, 'Those who had eaten the loaves numbered five thousand men' (6:44: καὶ ἦσαν οἱ φαγόντες [τοὺς ἄρτους] πεντακισχίλιοι ἄνδρες). The miracle occurs a second time in Mk 8:1-9. Again, a great crowd comes before Jesus without anything to eat (8:1). Jesus tells the disciples, 'I have compassion for the crowd' (8:2). If the crowds go away hungry, so Jesus argues, they will faint (8:3). Again, the disciples respond with disbelief, 'How can one feed these people with bread here in the desert?' (8:4). Jesus asks how many loaves the disciples have, and they answer, 'seven' (8:5). Jesus then orders the crowd to sit, and having given thanks, he breaks the bread and gives it to the disciples, who distribute it to the crowds. Jesus does the same with a few small fish. Again, a miracle takes place: '[the crowds] ate and were filled' (8:8: ἔφαγον καὶ ἐχορτάσθησαν) – leaving seven baskets of broken pieces. This time the size of the crowd is enumerated at 'about four thousand [people]' (ἦσαν δὲ ὡς τετρακισχίλιοι).

3. Scripturalized Narrative in the Gospel of Mark
139

Both episodes appear to be modelled in part on the miracle of Elisha in 2 Kgs 4:42-44.[92] The setting is provided by 2 Kgs 4:38, 'When Elisha returned to Gilgal, *there was a famine in the land*' (והרעב בארץ). Having already performed one feeding miracle in 4:38-41, Elisha receives 'twenty loaves of barley and fresh ears of grain' (4:42: שׂערים־לחם עשׂרים וכרמל). Elisha says to his servant – presumably Gehazi (cf. 4:12, 25; LXX 4:41) – 'Give it to the people and let them eat' (4:42: תן לעם ויאכלו). But his servant responds with disbelief, 'How can I set this before a hundred people?' (4:43: מה אתן זה לפני מעה איש). Elisha repeats, 'Give it to the people and let them eat', adding, 'For thus says the LORD, "*They shall eat and have some left*"' (4:43: אכל והותר). The servant then sets the food before the hundred men, and as Elisha prophesied, 'they ate, and had some left' (4:44: ויאכלו ויותרו). As with 1 Kings 19 in Mk 1:12-20, the episodes in 6:35-44 and 8:1-9 follow *mutatis mutandis* the structure of 2 Kgs 4:42-44, whilst incorporating distinctive narrative details: a small amount of food, including loaves, is brought to the prophet (Mk 6:38; 8:5; cf. 2 Kgs 4:42); the prophet tells his disciples/servant to give it to the people so they may eat (Mk 6:37; cf. 2 Kgs 4:42); the disciples/servant respond with disbelief (Mk 6:37; 8:4; cf. 2 Kgs 4:43); the prophet persists despite the disbelief of the disciples/servant (Mk 6:38; 8:5; cf. 2 Kgs 4:43); the prophet invokes heaven/the LORD (Mk 6:41; 8:6-7; cf. 2 Kgs 4:43); the food is set before the people (Mk 6:41; 8:6-7; cf. 2 Kgs 4:44); a large number of people eat (Mk 6:42, 44; 8:8-9; cf. 2 Kgs 4:44); some food is left over (Mk 6:43; 8:8; cf. 2 Kgs 4:44).

Jesus' command to the disciples in Mk 6:37 – 'You give them [something] to eat' (δότε αὐτοῖς ὑμεῖς φαγεῖν) – echoes the command of Elisha to his servant in 2 Kgs 4:42 (and v. 43): 'Give to the people and let them eat' (תן לעם ויאכלו).[93] A more literal rendering of the Hebrew is found

---

92. The only full-length study on the literary relationship is Roger D. Aus, *Feeding the Five Thousand: Studies in the Judaic Background of Mark 6:30-44 par. and John 6:1-15*, Studies in Judaism (Lanham, MD: University Press of America, 2010). See also the valuable comments in Alkuin Heising, *Die Botschaft der Brotvermehrung*, SBS 15 (Stuttgart: Kohlhammer, 1966), 17–20; Winn, *Mark and the Elijah–Elisha Narrative*, 82–4. Others simply note the parallels: Strauss, *Das Leben Jesu*, 2:233–4; Pesch, *Das Markusevangelium*, 1:354; Davies and Allison, *Matthew*, 2:482; Marcus, *Mark: 1–8*, 415–16; John R. Donahue and Daniel J. Harrington, *The Gospel of Mark*, SP 2 (Collegeville, MN: Liturgical, 2002), 208; Yarbro Collins, *Mark*, 320; Focant, *The Gospel According to Mark*, 258–9. Cf. the sceptical comments in Michael Labahn, *Offenbarung in Zeichen und Wort*, WUNT 2/17 (Tübingen: Mohr Siebeck, 2000), 163–4.

93. The words of Elisha's command also appear in new contexts in *b. Men.* 66b; *b. Sanh.* 12a.

in LXX 4:42(43): δότε τῷ λαῷ καὶ ἐσθιέτωσαν. Both Mark and the LXX agree in using the second-person plural imperative δότε ('you all give'). The singular ὁ λαός in the LXX, however, better reflects the singular עָם of 2 Kgs 4:42 – although the LXX is capable of rendering עָם as αὐτοῖς (LXX Exod. 20:20; LXX Num. 14:19; LXX Josh. 6:7) as in Mk 6:37.[94] At the same time, whilst Mark's use of the infinitive φαγεῖν would more naturally follow לֶאֱכֹל – as it does in LXX 2 Kgs 4:8, 40 – rather than the jussive וְיֹאכְלוּ of 2 Kgs 4:42, the LXX can also render וְיֹאכְלוּ as φαγεῖν (LXX 2 Chron. 28:15). Nevertheless, given the equivalent function of the command at this stage in the narrative, there is good reason to think Jesus' words in Mk 6:37 have their origin in 2 Kgs 4:42. The detail in Mk 6:41 and 8:6 that the disciples 'set [the food] before' (παρατίθημι) the people seems to reflect the language of 2 Kgs 4:44, where the servant 'set [the food] before them' (וַיִּתֵּן לִפְנֵיהֶם). Whilst the detail is absent in LXX 2 Kgs 4:44, the LXX translates the only other instance of לִפְנֵיהֶם וַיִּתֵּן (Gen. 18:8) with παρατίθημι. And whilst Mk 8:8 uses the noun περίσσευμα ('left over') for the abundance of loaves, it may reflect the food 'left over' (MT: יָתַר; LXX: καταλείπω) in 2 Kgs 4:43-44, as the verb יתר can be translated as περισσεύω (LXX 1 Sam. 2:36; α' Gen. 49:4; α' and θ' Deut. 30:9; α', σ' and θ' Isa. 4:3 etc.), the noun יִתְרָה as περίσσευμα (α' Isa. 15:7) and יִתְרוֹן as περισσεία (LXX Eccl. 1:3; 2:11, 13; 3:9; 5:8, 15; 6:8; 7:11-12; 10:10-11; α' Lev. 8:25).[95]

Mark 6:35-44; 8:1-9	2 Kgs 4:42-44
The people have nothing to eat (8:1-2; cf. 6:35-36).	There was a famine in the land (4:38).
Jesus tells the disciples, 'You give them something to eat' (6:37).	Elisha tells his servant, 'Give it to the people and let them eat' (4:42).
The disciples respond with disbelief (6:37; 8:4).	The servant responds with disbelief (4:43).
Jesus persists despite the disbelief (6:38; 8:5).	Elisha persists despite the disbelief (4:43).
A small amount of food (including loaves) is brought to Jesus (6:38; 8:5).	A small amount of food (including loaves) is brought to Elisha (4:42).
Jesus invokes heaven (6:41; cf. 8:6).	Elisha invokes the Lord (4:43).

94. Mark favours the personal pronoun to the point of being unclear (i.e. 9:13). Compared to Matthew and Luke, Mark rarely uses λαός (Mk 7:6; 14:12).

95. Aus likewise notes וְיוֹתִרוּן in *Tg. 2 Kgs* 4:43 (*Feeding the Five Thousand*, 112). It may also be compared to LXX Ruth 2:14: 'She ate and was satisfied and had some left over' (ἔφαγεν καὶ ἐνεπλήσθη καὶ κατέλιπεν).

The food is set before a large group of people (6:41; 8:6-7)	The food is set before a large group of people (4:44).
A large number of people eat (6:42, 44; 8:8, 9).	A large number of people eat (4:44).
Some food is left over (6:43; 8:8).	Some food is left over (4:44).

The number of those fed by each miracle differs considerably: from the 'hundred men' (LXX 2 Kgs 4:43: ἑκατὸν ἀνδρῶν) of Elisha's miracle to the 'five thousand men' (Mk 6:44: πεντακισχίλιοι ἄνδρες) and 'about four thousand' (8:9: ὡς τετρακισχίλιοι) of Jesus' miracles. Some have interpreted the great disparity between the numbers of those fed as a sign of Jesus' superiority to Elisha.[96] But since the Gospel makes no mention of Elisha, this is probably not the intention. It is noteworthy that the number of men fed by Elisha is inflated in later literature: the Gemara relates a lesson based on the story of a man who brought 'a basket of small fish' (גילדני דבי גילי) to R. Anan, which is compared to the gift of first fruits to Elisha, from which he is said to have fed 2,200 sages – a number arrived at by multiplying each barley loaf by a hundred, along with two meals of first fruits and corn (*b. Ket.* 105b-106a; cf. the distribution of the *omer* in Exod. 16:16).[97] More generally, scripturalized narratives tend to inflate the numbers of their scriptural source: whilst only a few guards are burnt in Dan. 3:22, Pseudo-Philo has 83,500 (*LAB* 6:17) and one thousand (*LAB* 38:4) burnt bystanders; whilst only Achan is uncovered in the lot of sin (Josh. 7:16-26), Kenaz uncovers 6,110 sinners (*LAB* 25:4).

As with the four fishermen of Mk 1:16-20, the differences between the two feeding miracles of Jesus and 2 Kgs 4:42-44 owe primarily to the demands of the Markan narrative. The inclusion of the fish (Mk 6:38, 41, 43; 8:7) reflects the setting by the sea of Galilee: the first feeding takes place by the sea, as Jesus and the disciples arrive at the place by boat (6:32), and immediately after, the disciples depart across the sea to Bethsaida (6:45); whilst prior to the second feeding miracle, Jesus 'went by way of Sidon towards the Sea of Galilee, in the region of Decapolis' (7:31), and immediately after, he leaves with the disciples across the sea to

---

96. See Strauss, *Das Leben Jesu*, 2:234; Pesch, *Das Markusevangelium*, 1:354–5; Roth, *Hebrew Gospel*, 37; Aus, *Feeding the Five Thousand*, 148; M. Eugene Boring, *Mark: A Commentary*, NTL (Louisville, KY: Westminster John Knox, 2006), 185; Robert H. Stein, *Mark*, BECNT (Grand Rapids, MI: Baker Academic, 2008), 317–318.

97. Noted in Aus, *Feeding the Five Thousand*, 147. Compare with *S. Eli. Zut.* 173 (Braude and Kapstein, 412).

142 *Writing with Scripture*

Dalmanutha (8:10). These areas are significant for the interpretation of the feeding miracles within the Gospel: as commentators have noted, whilst the first miracle occurs ostensibly in a Jewish region, the second occurs in the predominantly Gentile region of the Decapolis. This distinction probably lies behind Jesus' cryptic comment to the disciples concerning the number of baskets of broken pieces: twelve for the five thousand and seven for the four thousand (Mk 8:17-21).[98] If the 'twelve' is intended as a symbol for the Jews, and the 'seven' for gentiles – though this is somewhat speculative[99] – the two episodes may be intended to show the mission of Jesus and the disciples extends, not just to Galilee and Judea, but to the gentile Decapolis as well.[100] As with other scripturalized narratives, the narrative setting of Mk 6:35-44 and 8:1-9 takes precedence over the scriptural model. In this way, the distinctive elements of the episodes – the circumstances leading to the miracles (6:35-37; 8:1-3), the geographical setting (6:35; 8:4), the inclusion of fish (6:38, 41; 8:7) and even the number of baskets (6:43; 8:8) – each reflect their respective Markan contexts.

Other differences owe to the influence of scriptural material beyond 2 Kgs 4:42-44.[101] Jesus' statement concerning the crowds in Mk 6:34 that

98. So Guelich, *Mark 1–8:26*, 405; Gundry, *Mark*, 396–7; Ben Witherington III, *The Gospel of Mark: A Socio-Rhetorical Commentary* (Grand Rapids, MI: Eerdmans, 2001), 235–6; especially Kelly R. Iverson, *Gentiles in the Gospel of Mark: 'Even the Dogs Under the Table Eat the Children's Crumbs'*, LNTS 339 (London: T&T Clark, 2007), 67–74.

99. The seven 'Hellenists' of Acts 6:3 are often cited here, but the significance of the number is uncertain (cf. Acts 19:14; Jn 21:2). The number is associated with Gentiles in later Jewish literature: seven reflects the number of Noachide commandments (*b. Avod. Zar.* 22a), the seven Canaanite nations (who represent 'all nations' in *b. Yev.* 23a; cf. *b. Avod. Zar.* 36b) and in *Midr. Tanh.* B *Tzav* 1:1 it reads that Balaam, 'an advocate for the nations of the world', offered seven altars to God in contrast to the twelve cakes of Israel. It is likely the number of baskets in the Markan feeding miracles reflects the same enumeration.

100. As the Lukan Jesus notes, the miracles of Elisha (and Elijah) also extended to gentiles (Lk. 4:27), see Jeffrey S. Siker, '"First to the Gentiles": A Literary Analysis of Luke 4:16-30', *JBL* 111 (1992): 73–90. The shift from predominantly Jewish regions to the mixed Decapolis, may also signal the movement's early success in the region, in contrast to predominantly Jewish areas, or even the location of the Markan community.

101. The reference to 'the green grass' (τῷ χλωρῷ χόρτῳ) may contain an allusion to Ps. 23:2, so D. C. Allison Jr., 'Psalm 23 (22) in Early Christianity: A Suggestion', *IBS* 5 (1983): 132–7, esp. 134 – though such a fleeting allusion better fits

3. Scripturalized Narrative in the Gospel of Mark 143

they are 'like sheep without a shepherd' (ὡς πρόβατα μὴ ἔχοντα ποιμένα) clearly reflects the words of Moses in Num. 27:17: 'like sheep without a shepherd' (כצאן אשר אין־להם רעה).[102] And there may be other allusions to Moses in the episode. The detail that the crowds were organized into 'groups of hundreds and of fifties' (Mk 6:40: πρασιαὶ κατὰ ἑκατὸν καὶ κατὰ πεντήκοντα; cf. Lk. 9:14) may reflect the groups of 'thousands, hundreds, fifties and tens' in the wilderness (Exod. 18:21, 25; Deut. 1:15), which served as the model for similar groups of 'thousands, hundreds, fifties and tens' (1 Macc. 3:55; 1QS 2:21-22; CD 13:1-2; 1QM 4:1-4; 4QM^a Frags. 1-3:10; 1QSa 1:29–2:1; cf. 'thousands and hundreds' in 11QT^a 42:15; 'hundreds and fifties' in 4QPsJoshua^a Frag. 3 2:6-7).[103] As commentators have noted, other details may connect Jesus' two feeding miracles with the feeding of *manna* in the wilderness (Exod. 16:4-36; Num. 11:6-9; cf. Num. 11:31-35):[104] the Israelites are fed 'in the wilderness' (LXX Exod. 16:32: ἐν τῇ ἐρήμῳ) as Jesus' miracles occur in the 'wilderness' (Mk 6:31-32, 35: ἔρημον τόπον; 8:4: ἐρημίας); the *manna* is identified as 'bread' (ἄρτος) in LXX Exod. 16:4-36 (also LXX Deut. 8:3; LXX Pss. 77:24; 104:40; LXX Neh. 9:15) as Jesus also multiplies 'bread' (ἄρτος);[105] the meat or the *manna* was sent in the evening (Num. 11:9; cf. *manna* in the morning in Exod. 16:8, 12) as Jesus feeds at a 'late hour' (Mk 6:35: ἤδη ὥρα); the Israelites ate and were 'filled' (ἐμπίπλημι in LXX Pss. 77:29; 104:40; LXX Neh. 9:25; πίμπλημι in LXX Exod. 16:12) as the crowds ate and were 'filled' (Mk 6:42; 8:8: χορτάζω); and, as Dale Allison notes, at

Pseudo-Philo's use of scripture than Mark's. Attempts to see Isa. 40 or Ezek. 34 in the narrative fail to convince, *pace* Paul Owen, 'Jesus as God's Chief Agent in Mark's Christology', in *Mark, Manuscripts, and Monotheism: Essays in Honor of Larry W. Hurtado*, ed. Dieter Roth and Chris Keith, LNTS 528 (London: Bloomsbury, 2016), 40–58, esp. 54–6.

102. See the similar use of Num. 27:17 in Jdt. 11:19, where it refers to Holofernes' siege of Judah.

103. Noted in Allison, *The New Moses*, 239. Aus' solution is, again, too clever: 2 Kgs 4:1 has been read in light of 1 Kgs 18:4, 13, 'hundred prophets...fifty to a cave' (*Feeding the Five Thousand*, 44).

104. See Larry W. Hurtado, *Mark*, NIBC (Peabody, MA: Hendrickson, 1989), 100–102; William Richard Stegner, *Narrative Theology in Early Christianity* (Louisville, KY: Westminster John Knox, 1989), 53–81; Witherington, *The Gospel of Mark*, 217; cf. Marcus, *Mark: 1–8*, 407 (cf. 419–21).

105. Allison suggests the similar feeding miracles of Exod. 16 and Num. 11 'would not have been recognized by our spiritual forebears as doublets' (*The New Moses*, 239). To the contrary, the two episodes are conflated in LXX Ps. 104:40, where the quails bring 'bread of heaven' (ἄρτον οὐρανοῦ).

144   *Writing with Scripture*

least one tradition has the Israelites eating fish in the wilderness (*Sifre* to Num. 95:1; cf. Mk 6:38-43; 8:7).[106]

Whether or not these details were intended to recall Israel in the wilderness, others apparently saw in the feeding of the five and four thousand allusions to Moses and Israel. Whilst the Matthaean version does not include the clearest Mosaic parallels from Mk 6:30-44 (Num. 27:17; Exod. 18:21, 25?), it includes the number of men with the addendum, 'besides women and children' (Mt. 14:21; 15:38), which may reflect Exod. 12:37: 'six hundred thousand men on foot, *besides children*' (לבד מטף).[107] Even more so, the Johannine feeding of the five thousand associates the episode directly with the experience of Israel in the wilderness. Here, the feeding miracle serves as the introduction to the 'bread of life' discourse, where the crowd tells Jesus, 'Our ancestors ate the manna in the wilderness; as it is written, "He gave them bread from heaven to eat"' (Jn 6:31: οἱ πατέρες ἡμῶν τὸ μάννα ἔφαγον ἐν τῇ ἐρήμῳ, καθώς ἐστιν γεγραμμένον· ἄρτον ἐκ τοῦ οὐρανοῦ ἔδωκεν αὐτοῖς φαγεῖν) – alluding to LXX Ps. 77:24.[108] Jesus goes on to compare the 'bread of life' which prevents death to the *manna*: 'Your ancestors ate the manna in the wilderness, and they died' (Jn 6:49: οἱ πατέρες ὑμῶν ἔφαγον ἐν τῇ ἐρήμῳ τὸ μάννα καὶ ἀπέθανον).[109] At the same time, the Johannine feeding of the five thousand also strengthens the association with the miracle of Elisha, by including details not found in the Markan episodes.[110] The bread is described as 'barley loaves' (Jn 6:9, 13: ἄρτους κριθίνους) as the man from Baal-shalishah brings 'barley loaves' (LXX 2 Kgs 4:42: ἄρτους κριθίνους). Likewise, a 'boy' (παιδάριον) supplies the food in Jn 6:9 as Gehazi, 'the boy' (LXX 2 Kgs 4:41: τὸ παιδάριον), distributes the food in 2 Kgs 4:43. It is quite possible John was led to further scripturalize the episode under the direct influence of Mk 6:35-44.[111] In any case, the Johannine version shows the feeding of the five/four thousand tradition was associated with 2 Kgs 4:42-44 at an early stage.

Returning to Mark, the feeding miracles of Mk 6:35-44 and 8:1-9 also share with 2 Kgs 4:42-44 themes of scarcity and abundance common in

106. Allison, *The New Moses*, 239.

107. Expanded in *Midr. Tanh.* B *Bo* 9:1: '[besides] little ones and women' (קטנים ונשים).

108. Cf. Wis. 16:20.

109. Cf. Jn 6:32.

110. As noted in Alkuin Heising, 'Exegese und Theologie der Alt- und Neutestamentlichen Speisewunder', *ZKT* 86 (1964): 80–96, esp. 91–2.

111. Aus is alone in seeing multiple allusions to 1 Sam. 9–10 in Jn 6:1-15 (*Feeding the Five Thousand*, 47–67).

3. Scripturalized Narrative in the Gospel of Mark

antiquity.[112] Barley bread was often seen as a sign of scarcity or poverty (Josephus, *Ant.* 5.220; *War* 5.427; *t. Ber.* 4:11; *Sifre* to Num. 89:1; *b. Ber.* 39b; *b. Erub.* 81a; *b. Avod. Zar.* 39b). This is perhaps best illustrated by the Rabbinic comparison of the wealthy R. Ḥisda with the poor Babba Rabba: 'At Rabbah's house all they had was barley bread for human beings, and even that they didn't have' (*b. Moed Kat.* 28a). The mention of 'baskets' (κόφινοι) in Mk 6:43 and 8:8 likewise reflects notions of abundance, as having bread in one's basket was seen as a sign of satiety: 'For one who has "bread in his basket" is not so hungry as one who does not have bread in his basket' (*m. Yom.* 6:5). The saying also forms the basis of a *baraita* of R. Eliezer the Great which parallels some synoptic material: 'Whoever has a piece of bread in his wallet [or basket] and says, "What shall I eat tomorrow" is only one of those of little faith' (*b. Sot.* 48b; cf. Mt. 6:25-31; 16:8 and par.).

It is perhaps no surprise these themes of scarcity and abundance resurface in other texts modelled on 2 Kgs 4:42-44.[113] Rabbinic commentators associated the miracle of Elisha with the distribution of the *omer* (עומר/עמר) in Exod. 16:18, and the *omer* of the first fruits in Lev. 2:14 and 23:9-14 (*t. Sanh.* 2:9; *b. Keth.* 105b; *S. Eli. Zut.* 2).[114] Both 2 Kgs 4:42-44 and Exod. 16:18 appear to be in view in a miracle during the high priesthood of Shimon HaTzaddik, where a blessing was sent upon the two loaves and shewbread of the *omer*, so that 'some of [the priests] ate and were sated, while others ate and left bread over' (*b. Yom.* 39a).[115] Christian literature, on the other hand, combined the miracles of Elisha and Jesus. For example, Gregory (*Dial.* 2.21) writes that 'during a time of famine' (cf. 2 Kgs 4:38), Benedict's monastery had nearly run out of bread, so

---

112. See the discussion in Richard I. Pervo, 'Panta Kiona: The Feeding Stories in the Light of Economic Data and Social Practice', in *Religious Propaganda and Missionary Competition in the New Testament World*, ed. Lukas Bormann (Leiden: Brill, 1994), 163–94.

113. Whilst it is not modelled on 2 Kgs 4:42-44, the multiplication of loaves in the oven of the wife of R. Hanina ben Dosa occurs despite the fact there was no bread in her house (*b. Taan.* 25a).

114. See Aus, *Feeding the Five Thousand*, 6–9; Michael A. Daise, *Feasts in John: Jewish Festivals and Jesus' 'Hour' in the Fourth Gospel*, WUNT 2/229 (Tübingen: Mohr Siebeck, 2007), 105–12.

115. A similar episode appears in the *Acts of John*, where the Pharisees invite Jesus and the disciples to a banquet (cf. Lk. 7:36) and set a loaf before each of them, 'and [Jesus] would bless his own and divide it amongst us; and from that little piece each of us was filled, and our own loaves were saved intact, so that those who invited him were amazed' (*Acts John* 93 [ANT 318]).

146　　　　　　　　　　*Writing with Scripture*

that 'only fives loaves could be found to set before the community' (cf. Mk 6:38, 41 and par.). But Benedict announces to the hungry monks, 'Tomorrow you will have more than you need' (cf. 2 Kgs 4:43) – and the next day, two hundred measures of flour appeared at the gates of the monastery. Gregory relates a similar story (*Dial.* 3.37) concerning Lawrence, that 'because of the famine there was no bread' (cf. 2 Kgs 4:38), until Lawrence discovers a miraculous loaf of bread with which he feeds a large number of men. Afterwards, 'when they had all taken their fill, the fragments were gathered up [and] they amounted to more than the original loaf' (cf. Mk 6:43; 8:8 and par.). Lawrence continued feeding the men this way for ten days, so that 'each meal thus seemed to be a multiplication of bread'. Palladius also narrates that when the monk Elias had run out of bread, he discovered three loaves, with which he was able to feed twenty men 'to satiety' and have one loaf left over (*Hist. Laus.* 51).[116]

Whereas Elijah served as the model for Jesus' forty-day sojourn in the wilderness and his call of the disciples, it is the figure of Elisha who appears to lie behind the feeding miracles of Mk 6:35-44 and 8:1-9. Of the two feeding miracles, the influence of 2 Kgs 4:42-44 is more pronounced in the first (Mk 6:35-44) rather than the derivative second miracle (8:1-9).[117] Whilst many of Jesus' miracles elsewhere resemble those of Elisha – the raising of children, the healing of lepers – Elisha does not appear to be a significant figure for Mark (cf. Elijah in 1:6; 6:15; 8:28; 9:4-5, 11-13; 15:35-36).[118] There is little reason to think Mark portrays Jesus as Elisha to John's Elijah: Jesus is also modelled on Elijah (1:12-13, 16-20) and Elijah is not always identified with John (9:2-8; cf. 9:13). It is not clear what prompted the author to select 2 Kgs 4:42-44 as the model for the feeding miracles of Jesus. The multiplication of food was a common feature of miracle-working traditions in antiquity and, at least in Jewish tradition,

---

116. W. K. Lowther Clarke, *The Lausiac History of Palladius* (London: SPCK, 1918), 160. Likewise, in *Hist. mon.* 8.46 (Normal Russell, *Lives of the Desert Fathers*, CSS 34 [Kalamazoo, MI: Cistercian Publications, 1980], 77), the monk Apollo miraculously multiplies bread to feed hungry men.

117. *Pace* Angelika Seethaler, 'Die Brotvermehrung – Ein Kirchenspiegel?', *BZ* 34 (1990): 108–9.

118. On the similarities between the miracles of Jesus and Elisha, see Raymond E. Brown, 'Jesus and Elisha', *Perspective* 12 (1971): 85–104. Lorne R. Zelyck has recently argued that the fragmentary (and early) *Egerton Gospel* contains an episode in which Jesus performs a miracle by the Jordan modelled on Elisha's purification of water in 2 Kgs 2:19-22 (the parallel is even closer to Josephus, *War* 4.460-464), 'Elisha Typology in Jesus' Miracle on the Jordan River (Papyrus Egerton 2,2v.6-14)', *NTS* 62 (2015): 1–8.

3. Scripturalized Narrative in the Gospel of Mark

none was better known than the multiplication of loaves by Elisha.[119] In this sense, the author may have been led to the well-known miracle in 2 Kgs 4:42-44 by the reputation of Jesus as a miracle-worker. At the same time, Mark shows a fondness for drawing on the Elijah–Elisha cycle (Mk 1:6; cf. LXX 2 Kgs 1:8; Mk 1:12-13, 16-20; cf. 1 Kgs 19:4-8, 19-21), which itself features similar conflict-oriented miracle stories narrated in an episodic style. But whilst some commentators have seen the influence of the Elijah–Elisha cycle elsewhere in Mark, in none of the proposed episodes does one find verbal and structural parallels comparable to the description of John's attire, Jesus' forty-day sojourn in the wilderness, call of the disciples and the two feeding miracles.[120] Indeed, one episode often thought to contain allusions to Elijah's conflict with Ahab and Jezebel bears a much greater resemblance to the Greek text of Esther: the execution of John the Baptist (Mk 6:17-29).[121]

119. See the many parallels outside of Jewish and Christian tradition in Hendrick van der Loos, *The Miracles of Jesus* (Leiden: Brill, 1965), 625–7. For the significance of Mk 6:35-44 in a Hellenistic context, see Angela Standhartinger, ' "And All Ate and Were Filled" (Mark 6.42 par.): The Feeding Narratives in the Context of Hellenistic-Roman Banquet Culture', in *Decisive Meals: Dining Politics in Biblical Literature*, ed. Nathan MacDonald, Luzia Sutter Rehman and Kathy Ehrensperger, LNTS 449 (London: T&T Clark, 2012), 62–82.

120. See the proposed parallels in Roth, *Hebrew Gospel*, 5–9 and *passim*; Brodie, *The Crucial Bridge*, 86–95; Winn, *Mark and the Elijah–Elisha Narrative*, 72–112.

121. Elijah has a contentious relationship with King Ahab and his wife, Jezebel, who wants (θέλω) to kill him; John also has a contentious relationship with 'king' Antipas and his wife, Herodias, who wants (θέλω) to kill him. Since John is identified as Elijah elsewhere (Mk 1:6; 9:13), so the argument goes, John's altercation with Antipas and Herodias must be modelled on 1 Kgs 18–21. There are, of course, considerable differences: Herodias is successful in her bid to kill John, whereas Jezebel is spectacularly unsuccessful (Elijah never dies). But, as the earlier examples show, writers were capable of straying from their scriptural models when it suited them. Scholars are probably right to see shades of Ahab and Jezebel in Antipas and Herodias, as John plays the role of Elijah, though this can be overstated: e.g. David M. Hoffeditz and Gary E. Yates, 'Femme Fatale Redux: Intertextual Connection to the Elijah/Jezebel Narratives in Mark 6:14-29', *BBR* 15 (2005): 199–221; Regina Janes, 'Why the Daughter of Herodias Must Dance (Mark 6.14-29)', *JSNT* 28 (2006): 443–67. And yet, except for Herodias' 'wish' (θέλω) to kill John, the influence of 1 Kings on the narrative is not as pervasive as Esther. There is, however, an overlooked parallel in the Animal Apocalypse of *1 Enoch* describing a prophetic sheep who 'escaped alive, and fled away' (cf. 1 Kgs 18:3-8) before God 'caused him to ascend' (*1 En.* 89:52; cf. 2 Kgs 2:11). This Elijianic sheep 'cried aloud to the sheep, and they *wanted to kill him*' (*1 En.* 89:52) – compare with the description of Herodias, who 'wanted to kill him' (ἤθελεν αὐτὸν ἀποκτεῖναι), that is, John.

148 *Writing with Scripture*

Antipas and Ahasuerus: Mark 6:21-28 and Esther

When the daughter of Herodias dances and pleases Herod Antipas and those banqueting with him, he tells her, 'Ask me for whatever you wish, and I will give it' (Mk 6:22: αἴτησόν με ὃ ἐὰν θέλῃς, καὶ δώσω σοι). He then solemnly swears, 'Whatever you ask me, I will give you, even half of my kingdom' (6:23: ὅ τι ἐάν με αἰτήσῃς δώσω σοι ἕως ἡμίσους τῆς βασιλείας μου). Commentators have long noted that Antipas' question appears to be borrowed from a famous episode in Jewish literature where a young girl pleases a king, although the passage is usually omitted from studies on Mark's use of the scriptures. The Persian king Ahasuerus repeatedly asks Esther, 'What is it, [Queen] Esther? What is your request? It shall be given you, even to the half of my kingdom' (MT Est. 5:3: מה־לך אסתר המלכה ומה־בקשתך עד־חצי המלכות וינתן לך; LXX: τί θέλεις, Εσθηρ, καὶ τί σού ἐστιν τὸ ἀξίωμα; ἕως τοῦ ἡμίσους τῆς βασιλείας μου καὶ ἔσται σοι).[122]

Beyond noting the similarity with either the MT or the LXX, commentators have rarely dwelt on the role of Esther in the episode of John's execution.[123] Some have even been sceptical of a relationship between Antipas' question and Esther in the first place, countering that the oath of 'up to half' was proverbial in antiquity.[124] The oath does bear some

---

122. Also MT and LXX Est. 5:6; 7:2; cf. 9:12.

123. The Esther parallel is omitted from studies devoted to the use of the Jewish scriptures in the Gospel (Suhl, Marcus, Watts, Hays) and some commentaries (Goguel, Hurtado, Trocmé). See the brief comments in H. B. Swete, *The Gospel According to St Mark* (London: Macmillan, 1905), 119; Cranfield, *The Gospel According to St. Mark*, 212; Vincent Taylor, *The Gospel According to St. Mark*, 2nd ed. (London: Macmillan, 1966), 315; Schweizer, *Das Evangelium nach Markus*, 75; Pesch, *Das Markusevangelium*, 1:339; Hugh Anderson, *The Gospel of Mark*, NCB (London: Oliphants, 1976), 169; Gnilka, *Das Evangelium nach Markus*, 1:250; Hooker, *The Gospel According to St Mark*, 161; Guelich, *Mark 1–8:26*, 332; Marcus, *Mark: 1–8*, 401–2; Donahue and Harrington, *The Gospel of Mark*, 202; Yarbro Collins, *Mark*, 309–10. See the more detailed comments in Eugene LaVerdiere, *The Beginning of the Gospel: Introducing the Gospel According to Mark, Volume 1* (Collegeville, MN: Liturgical, 1999), 164–8; James G. Crossley, 'History from the Margins: The Death of John the Baptist', in *Writing History, Constructing Religion*, ed. James G. Crossley and Christian Karner (Aldershot: Ashgate, 2005), 147–61; Crossley, *Jesus and the Chaos of History: Redirecting the Life of the Historical Jesus* (Oxford: Oxford University Press, 2015), 149–56. The only study entirely devoted to the use of Esther in Mk 6:17-29 is Roger D. Aus, *Water into Wine and the Beheading of John the Baptist*, BJS 150 (Atlanta, GA: Scholars Press, 1988), 39–74.

124. Harold W. Hoehner, *Herod Antipas: A Contemporary of Jesus Christ* (Grand Rapids, MI: Zondervan, 1980), 151; Neil R. Parker, *The Marcan Portrayal of the*

3. Scripturalized Narrative in the Gospel of Mark   149

resemblance to LXX 1 Kgs 13:8, where the man of God promises Jeroboam, 'If you give me half your house, I will not go in with you' (ἐάν μοι δῷς τὸ ἥμισυ τοῦ οἴκου σου, οὐκ εἰσελεύσομαι μετὰ σοῦ). One also finds similar language in the promise of Achilles to Phoenix, son of Amyntor, 'Be thou king even as I am, and share the half of my honour' (Homer, *Il.* 9.616: ἴσον ἐμοὶ βασίλευε καὶ ἥμισυ μείρεο τιμῆς).[125] Then again, the wording of Mk 6:23 provides one of the closest – though often overlooked – instances of verbal correspondence between the Gospel of Mark and the LXX. A closer look at the passage, however, reveals a much greater resemblance to another Greek text of Esther: the so-called Alpha-text.[126]

Here, the verbal similarities between Mk 6:21-28 and Esther extend beyond the phrasing of Antipas' question to the narrative setting in which the question takes place. Both LXX and Est. A 2:9 describe Esther as a 'young girl' (κοράσιον) who 'pleases' (ἤρεσεν), as the 'young girl' (κοράσιον) dances and 'pleases' (ἤρεσεν) Antipas.[127] But the similarities with the Alpha-text become most apparent when Mk 6:21-28 is compared with the scene in which Haman is executed (Est. A 7:1-12; cf. MT Est. 7:1-10): at a 'banquet' (συμπόσιον; cf. Est. A 5:5: δεῖπνον), Ahasuerus 'vows' (ὤμοσεν) to Esther with an 'oath' (ὅρκος), promising 'up to half of my kingdom' (ἕως [τοῦ] ἡμίσους τῆς βασιλείας μου).[128] In response, Esther asks the king to spare her life and the lives of her people (7:3-4), before singling out Haman as the man who had been conspiring against

---

"Jewish" Unbeliever: A Function of the Marcan References to Jewish Scripture, Studies in Biblical Literature 79 (New York, NY: Lang, 2008), 15; Focant likewise emphasizes the differences, *The Gospel According to Mark,* 247, 251.

125. To this can be added the promise of Zacchaeus, 'Look, half of my possessions, Lord, I will give to the poor' (Lk. 19:8: ἰδοὺ τὰ ἡμίσιά μου τῶν ὑπαρχόντων, κύριε, τοῖς πτωχοῖς δίδωμι). A similar promise also occurs in *PRE* 50:6 whilst narrating Est. 3:1-11, where Haman asks Ahasuerus, 'If it please the king, accept half of my wealth and give me power over [the Jews]' (אם על המלך טוב קח החצי מממוני ותן לי רשות עליהם).

126. As given in Robert Hanhart, *Esther,* Septuaginta Vetus Testamentum Graecum Auctoritate Academiae Letterarum Goettengensis editum 8/3 (Göttingen: Vandenhoeck & Ruprecht, 1966); on the relationship of Esther A to the LXX and MT, see Karen H. Jobes, *The Alpha-Text of Esther: Its Character and Relationship to the Masoretic Text,* SBLDS 153 (Atlanta, GA: Scholars Press, 1996).

127. The language is uncommon for Mark: the episode has two of the four instances of κοράσιον (cf. 5:41-42), one of two instances of δεῖπνον (cf. 12:39), and the only instance of the relatively common verb ἀρέσκω and the likewise common nouns ἥμισυς and ὅρκος. See Lohmeyer on the distinctive vocabulary, *Markus,* 117–18.

128. Δεῖπνον also appears in the 'Old Greek' of Est. 7:9 in mss. *b* 108.

150   *Writing with Scripture*

the Jews (7:5-6). Haman is then hanged at the orders of the king (7:9-10). Likewise, it is at a 'banquet' (δεῖπνον) where Antipas 'vows' (ὤμοσεν) with 'oaths' (ὅρκοι) to the daughter of Herodias, 'even half of my kingdom' (ἕως ἡμίσους τῆς βασιλείας μου). Under the influence of Herodias, the girl responds by asking for the head of John the Baptist (6:24-25). The king then orders John to be beheaded (6:27-28). Most significantly, there is verbatim agreement between the Alpha-text and the Markan episode in the promise of 'even half of my kingdom' (Est. A 5:3, 6 [7:2]: ἕως ἡμίσους τῆς βασιλείας μου; Mk 6:23: ἕως ἡμίσους τῆς βασιλείας μου), with both omitting the genitive article found in LXX Est. 5:3; 7:2 (ἕως τοῦ ἡμίσους τῆς βασιλείας μου). Given these repeated and conspicuous formal and verbal similarities, it appears the author of Mk 6:21-2 drew upon the execution of Haman in Est. 7:1-10, as well as details elsewhere in Esther (2:9; 5:3, 6), using a text resembling the Alpha-text. The author thereby composed a banquet scene in which a king offers half of his kingdom to a young girl who instead requests the death of one man.

But the similarities between Mk 6:21-28 and Esther go even further than the Greek Alpha-text. As Roger Aus has meticulously detailed, the Markan episode not only parallels the so-called canonical text(s) of Esther, but also traditional expansions of the Esther narrative.[129] Of these, the most significant are the later Rabbinic commentaries of the Talmudic tractate *Megillah*, the *Pirḳê de Rabbi Eliezer*, the two Esther targumim and the *Esther Rabbah*.[130] As the daughter of Herodias dances at Herod's banquet (Mk 6:21), so dancing is associated with the banquets of Ahasuerus: *PRE* 49:12 notes it was customary for the harem to be brought in 'naked, playing and dancing' (ערוה משחקות ומרדות), but when Queen Vashti refused to do so, she was 'slain' (שתשחט). A similar association of dancing and the death of Vashti is found in *b. Meg.* 11b, 'Along came Satan and danced between them and killed Vashti' (בא שטן וריקד ביניהן והרג את ושתי). Alternatively, in *Tg. Est.* II on 2:8, it says Esther would

---

129. See Aus, *Water into Wine*, 39–74.

130. The medieval commentaries marshalled by Aus (*Abba Gorion*, *Yalkut Shimoni* and the later compilation of *Aggadat Esther*) are too late to be of value. However, over a century ago Jacob Reiss raised the possibility that the Esther targumim depend on the lost Targum Rabbati, which itself depends on the lost Midrash Rabbati ('Das Targum Scheni zu dem Buche Esther', *MGWJ* 25 [1876]: 398–406). One similarly wonders whether the extensive shared features of the medieval commentaries owe to (an) earlier lost midrashic collection(s). See the survey in Myron B. Lerner, 'The Works of Aggadic Midrash and the Esther Midrashim', in *The Literature of the Sages: Second Part*, ed. Shmuel Safrai et al. CRINT 2.3 (Assen: Royal Van Gorcum, 2006), 176–227.

3. Scripturalized Narrative in the Gospel of Mark   151

not 'dance' (מרקדן) like the gentile girls of the harem.[131] Whilst dancing women may be found in other royal banquet scenes (i.e. Josephus, *Ant.* 12.187-189), there is one parallel that is unlikely to be a matter of coincidence: *Tg. Est.* I on 1:19 and 1:21 relates that Vashti was beheaded on the recommendation of Memucan, who said, 'Let the king decree her head be cut off' (ית מימר מלכא אחשורוש דגזר).[132] Similarly, whilst *PRE* 49:12 only mentions that Vashti was 'slain' (שתשחט), the verb שחט can carry the meaning of throat-cutting or beheading.[133] However, the most uncanny parallel is found in *Est. Rab.* 4:9, where Memucan advises the king, 'I shall put her head on a platter' (ואני מכניס את ראשה בדיסקוס). The deed is done in *Est. Rab.* 4:11, as it reads, 'He made the decree, and he brought in her head on a platter' (גזר והכניס ראשה בדיסקוס).[134] This, of course, recalls the gruesome scene in the Markan episode where the young girl asks for 'the head of John the Baptist on a platter' (Mk 6:25: ἐπὶ πίνακι τὴν κεφαλὴν Ἰωάννου τοῦ βαπτιστοῦ). Following this, 'immediately the king sent a soldier of the guard with orders to bring John's head. He went and beheaded him in the prison, brought his head on a platter and gave it to the girl' (6:27-28).[135]

The *Rabbah*, which bears no other signs of Christian influence, is unlikely to have gleaned this detail from the Gospel of Mark, whilst the fact the 'head on a platter' appears in both texts alongside or as part of Esther material suggests something more than serendipity.[136] Far and away the most plausible explanation is that Mk 6:21-28 and *Est. Rab.* 4:9-11, though centuries apart, witness to a tradition extant in the first

131. As the daughter dances before 'those reclining' (Mk 6:22: συνανάκειμαι) so Ahasuerus' harem dances before 'those reclining' in the seventh-century *Panim Aherot* B (Buber, 59), as noted by Aus, *Water into Wine*, 51–2.

132. Compare also the perplexity of Antipas (Mk 6:20) with the 'confusion' of Ahasuerus (*Tg. Est.* I on 1:10), again noted in Aus, *Water into Wine*, 42–4.

133. Jastrow, *s.v.* שחט.

134. Aus notes the Hebrew דיסקוס in *Esther Rabbah* is a loan-word from the Greek δίσκος, compare with the Latin *discus* ('platter') of Vg. Mk 6:28 (*Water into Wine*, 63).

135. Note also the unusual inclusion of ספקלטור (from the Latin *speculator*) in *Tg. Est.* II on 5:3, where the executioner brings Esther before the king, compared with Mk 6:27, where a σπεκουλάτωρ brings the head of John the Baptist on a platter (*speculator* in Vg. Mk 6:27); so Aus, *Water into Wine*, 60–1.

136. *Pace* the influential comments in George W. Buchanan, 'The Use of Rabbinic Literature for New Testament Research', *BTB* 7 (1977): 112. If the allusion-happy Christian commentators of late antiquity were unable to espy the Esther parallels in Mk 6:21-28 (par. Mt. 14:6-11), one wonders how the author(s) of the *Rabbah* would have been able to do so.

century CE which included the grisly image of a 'head on a platter' as part of the retelling of the Esther narrative.[137] Thus, in addition to modelling the episode on a Greek version of Esther resembling the Alpha-text, the author of Mk 6:21-28 appears to have incorporated this traditional elaboration of the Esther narrative into the new story.[138] By including traditional material along with the scriptural model, Mk 6:21-28 resembles other scripturalized narratives: the episode of Abram in the fiery furnace in *LAB* 6, although clearly depending on Daniel 3, reflects a tradition concerning Gen. 15:7 found in later Rabbinic interpretation; the same applies to the identification of Phinehas with Elijah in *LAB* 48:1; and the *Testament of Abraham* reflects the traditional comparison of Abraham and Job, as well as the legendary death of Moses.

Mk 6:21-28	Esther Traditions
Antipas throws a 'banquet' (δεῖπνον) (6:21).	Esther throws a 'banquet' (δεῖπνον in A 5:5; LXX 7:9 *b* 108; cf. συμπόσιον in A 7:12[9]).
A 'young girl' (κοράσιον) dances and 'pleases' (ἤρεσεν) the king (6:22).	Esther is described as a 'young girl' (κοράσιον) who 'pleases' (ἤρεσεν) (LXX and A 2:9).
Antipas 'vows' (ὤμοσεν) to the girl with 'oaths' (ὅρκους) (6:23, 26).	Ahasuerus 'vows' (ὤμοσεν) to Esther with an 'oath' (ὅρκου) (A 7:7).
Antipas tells the girl to ask for anything she wants, 'up to half of my kingdom' (ἕως ἡμίσους τῆς βασιλείας μου) (6:23).	Ahasuerus tells Esther to ask for anything she wants, 'up to half of my kingdom' (ἕως ἡμίσους τῆς βασιλείας μου) (A 5:3, 6; cf. A 7:2; LXX 5:3, 6; 7:2).
The girl asks instead for the head of John the Baptist (6:24-25).	Esther instead singles out Haman the Assyrian (7:3-6).
Antipas orders the execution of John (6:27).	Ahasuerus orders the execution of Haman (7:9-10).
John the Baptist's head is brought in on a platter (6:25, 28).	Queen Vashti's head is brought in on a platter (*Est. Rab.* 4:9, 11; cf. *Tg. Est.* I on 1:19, 21).

137. That a first-century and sixth-century CE text might reflect a shared tradition is not without precedent: i.e. Mt. 7:3-5, *b. Arak.* 16b and *b. Bat.* 15b each reflect a common saying concerning the 'Mote and the Beam'.

138. This renders Aus' theory of an Aramaic *Vorlage* for Mk 6:17-29 unlikely (*Water into Wine*, 71). A text composed in Greek (i.e. Josephus' *Antiquities*; cf. *Ant.* 20.263; *Ag. Ap.* 1.50) may independently attest traditions found in much later Hebrew and Aramaic literature, as recently argued in Tal Ilan and Vared Noam, eds., *Josephus and the Rabbis*, 2 vols. (Jerusalem: Yad Ben-Zvi, 2017 [Hebrew]).

3. Scripturalized Narrative in the Gospel of Mark 153

It is not immediately clear what prompted the scripturalization of John's death with material from Esther. The episode is, of course, riddled with historical issues. The text wrongly calls Antipas 'king' (Mk 6:14, 22, 25-27: βασιλεύς) instead of 'tetrarch' (cf. Mt. 14:1: τετραάρχης) and names Herodias' first husband Philip (Mk 6:17) instead of Herod II (Josephus, *Ant.* 18.109-110, 136). The narrative itself also strains credulity, as Joan Taylor notes, 'Antipas did not, in fact, have a kingdom; he had a tetrarchy, and this was not really his to give away freely to his young stepdaughter'.[139] But whilst on the death of John the more sober account of Josephus (*Ant.* 18.116-119) is to be preferred, it nevertheless shares several important details with Mk 6:17-29:[140] Herod arresting John; Herod's fear concerning John; an – albeit loose – association of Herod's marriage to Herodias with the death of John; and, finally, John's execution at the orders of Herod. On other points, however, they do not agree: whilst in the Markan episode, John opposes Herod's marriage to Herodias, in Josephus, Herod fears the political threat posed by John. Although Josephus mentions Salome, the daughter of Herodias from her marriage to Herod II (*Ant.* 18.136), he makes no mention of the dancing daughter, the birthday banquet or the beheaded prophet. At the same time, Josephus names the site of John's execution as the Herodian palace at Machaerus in Peraea, whereas Mark seems to imagine a Galilaean setting: 'Herod on his birthday gave a banquet for his courtiers and officers and for the leaders of Galilee' (Mk 6:21).[141] Herod may well have ordered John's head to be brought from Peraea to Galilee, but the 'immediacy' (εὐθύς) of the order in Mk 6:27 implies John's severed head was served to Herodias on a platter at the same banquet. In the final analysis, the distinctive narrative details of the Markan episode have a legendary quality to them.

---

139. Taylor, *The Immerser*, 246–7. It could even be Mark imagines Antipas as a 'king' with a 'kingdom' under the influence of Esther; so S. Anthony Cummins, 'Integrated Scripture, Embedded Empire: The Ironic Interplay of "King" Herod, John and Jesus in Mark 6.1-44', in Hatina, eds., *Biblical Interpretation in Early Christian Gospels*, 1:45.

140. On the comparative reliability of the account of Josephus, see Michael Tilly, *Johannes der Taüfer und die Biographie der Propheten: Die synoptische Taüfer- überlieferung und das jüdische Prophetenbild zur Zeit des Taüfers*, BWANT 137 (Stuttgart: Kohlhammer, 1994), 57; and recently, Marcus, *John the Baptist in History and Theology*, 99. For a complementary view of the accounts, see Craig A. Evans, 'Josephus on John the Baptist and Other Jewish Prophets of Deliverance', in *The Historical Jesus in Context*, ed. Amy-Jill Levine, D. C. Allison Jr. and J. D. Crossan (Princeton, NJ: Princeton University Press, 2006), 55–63.

141. Cf. Hoehner, *Herod Antipas*, 148, needlessly speculates a Galilaean 'deputation' may have been sent to Peraea.

154 *Writing with Scripture*

Because of this, some have speculated the story in Mk 6:17-29 originated with some of the Baptist's followers.[142] But the episode also bears signs of Christian influence, with the placing of John in a tomb in v. 29 acting as an *inclusio* to the claim that Jesus was John raised from the dead (6:14-16), whilst in the same breath prefiguring the empty tomb of Jesus (16:4-6).[143] The Esther material in the episode, therefore, could very well be the result of Markan compositional or editorial activity, rather than simply a feature of a pre-Markan source. In any case, one may venture some possible reasons Mark or their source may have had for infusing the narrative of John's death with details from Esther. Whilst the function of the Esther material in Mk 6:21-28 is certainly not typological – in which case, it would make John the Baptist Haman the Assyrian, which hardly seems plausible – it could serve an ironic function. Mark, ever the ironist, flips the logic of the Esther narrative on its head: whereas in Esther the righteous are vindicated by executing the wicked at a banquet, in Mark, it is the wicked who are vindicated by executing the righteous at a banquet.[144] Alternatively, it could serve as a polemic against the Herodian dynasty. By modelling Antipas' court after the orgiastic banqueting of the court of the gentile king Ahasuerus, the episode may invoke the Esther material as an invective against the Idumean Herodian dynasty, whose Jewish identity had always been suspect.[145] Then again, it is equally possible the author never intended readers to pick up on the Esther parallels in the first place. It is noteworthy that Matthew, one of Mark's closest readers, excises Antipas' promise of 'even half of my kingdom' from their version of the episode (Mt. 14:1-12). Perhaps Mark or their source simply found in Esther a suitable model for a scene in a royal court. There is at least one other example in Jewish literature where an episode is modelled on the banquets of Ahasuerus.

1 Esdras relates that king Darius 'gave a great banquet' (1 Esdr. 3:1: ἐποίησεν δοχὴν μεγάλην) for his household and 'for all the nobles of Media

---

142. Rudolf Bultmann, *The History of the Synoptic Tradition*, trans. John Marsh, 2nd ed. (Oxford: Blackwell, 1968), 301; Pesch, *Das Markusevangelium*, 1:343; Lane, *The Gospel According to Mark*, 215; cf. Guelich, *Mark 1–8:26*, 326–7.

143. See S. J. Nortje, 'John the Baptist and the Resurrection Traditions in the Gospels', *Neot* 23 (1989): 349–58; Nathanael Vette and Will Robinson, 'Was John the Baptist Raised from the Dead? The Origins of Mark 6:14-29', *BibAn* 9 (2019): 343–8.

144. Similarly Cummins, 'Integrated Scripture, Embedded Empire', 44–7.

145. See Matthew Thiessen, *Contesting Conversion: Genealogy, Circumcision, and Identity in Ancient Judaism and Christianity* (Oxford: Oxford University Press, 2011), 87–110.

3. Scripturalized Narrative in the Gospel of Mark

and Persia and for all the satraps and generals and district governors that were under him in the hundred [and] twenty-seven satrapies from India to Ethiopia' (3:1-2: πᾶσιν τοῖς μεγιστᾶσιν τῆς Μηδίας καὶ τῆς Περσίδος καὶ πᾶσιν τοῖς σατράπαις καὶ στρατηγοῖς καὶ τοπάρχαις τοῖς ὑπ' αὐτὸν ἀπὸ τῆς Ἰνδικῆς μέχρι τῆς Αἰθιοπίας ἐν ταῖς ἑκατὸν εἴκοσι ἑπτὰ σατραπείαις). This appears to be borrowed from the description of Ahasuerus in Est. 1:1-3, where the king 'gave a banquet' (1:3: עשׂה משׁתה; cf. LXX: δοχὴν ἐποίησεν) 'for all his officials and ministers' (לכל־שׂריו ועבדיו), along with the 'army of Persia and Media and the nobles and governors of the provinces' (חיל פרס ומדי הפרתמים ושׂרי המדינות; cf. LXX: καὶ τοῖς Περςῶν καὶ Μήδων ἐνδόξοις καὶ τοῖς ἄρχουσιν τῶν σατραπῶν) – which are enumerated in v. 1 as 'one hundred twenty-seven provinces from India to Ethiopia' (מהדו ועד־כושׁ שׁבע ועשׂרים ומאה מדינה). Following the banquet, Darius calls 'all the nobles of Persia and Media and the satraps and generals and governors and prefects' to hear the three bodyguards debate 'what one thing is strongest' (1 Esdr. 3:14-17; cf. 3:5).[146] The first argues wine is the strongest (3:17-24) and the second for the king (4:1-12), whereas the third, Zerubbabel the Jew, argues women are stronger than wine and the king (4:13-32), but truth is 'strongest of all' (4:33-41). As Zerubbabel emerges the undisputed victor of the symposium, Darius says to him, 'Ask what you wish, even beyond what is written, and we will give it to you' (4:42: αἴτησαι ὃ θέλεις πλείω τῶν γεγραμμένων, καὶ δώσομέν σοι). Darius' promise to Zerubbabel recalls Ahasuerus's promise to Esther, 'What is your wish, it shall be given you. And what is your request? Even to the half of my kingdom, it shall be fulfilled' (Est. 5:6; 7:2; cf. 5:3; 9:12).[147] In some respects the wording of 1 Esdr. 4:42 is even closer to Antipas' first question to the girl, 'Ask me for whatever you wish, and I will give it' (Mk 6:22: αἴτησόν με ὃ ἐὰν θέλῃς, καὶ δώσω σοι; also LXX Est. O 5:3; Est A 5:6). In any case, the author of 1 Esdras 3–4 appears to have found in Esther suitable material on which to model an episode in the royal court of the Median king Darius of Jewish legend – a royal court which understandably resembles that of the Persian king Ahasuerus (also of Jewish legend). On this point, the speech of Zerubbabel strikes a

---

146. Cf. the similar debate among three rulers before Ahasuerus in LXX Est. 1:15 (expanded in later literature).

147. The wording in 1 Esdr. 4:42 is in some respects closer to LXX Est. 5:3: τί θέλεις, Εσθηρ, καὶ τί σού ἐστιν τὸ ἀξίωμα; ἕως τοῦ ἡμίσους τῆς βασιλείας μου καὶ ἔσται σοι; Est. A 5:6: τί τὸ θέλημά σου; αἴτησαι ἕως ἡμίσους τῆς βασιλείας μου, καὶ ἔσται σοι ὅσα ἀξιοῖς.

156   *Writing with Scripture*

remarkably familiar tone: women are even stronger than kings, he argues, because they rule over them. In this, Darius is no exception, following the whims of Apame, his concubine (4:28-31). One wonders here if the author also had in mind another woman who ruled over a king: Queen Esther, the wife of Ahasuerus.

For the episode in Mk 6:21-28, it may simply have been the knowledge that John was executed in a palace by a mercurial ruler (Josephus, *Ant.* 18.119) that led to the scripturalization of the Baptist's death with material from Esther. The author's decision to use Esther in this way does not, however, appear to be important for the interpretation of the passage. Indeed, it is the only time Esther features in the Gospel.[148] Rather, the author of Mk 6:21-28 supplied some of the language from a Greek text of Esther as well as related traditions to the story of John's death. Whilst the scriptural source is significant for the interpretation of some scripturalized narratives – the influence of Daniel 3 on *LAB* 6 reveals an interpretation of Gen. 15:7; the use of Genesis 13–15 in 1QapGen 11 shows the Abrahamic promise originates with Noah; the Deuteronomic material in 1 Macc. 5:45-51 shows Judas' obedience to the law – in other cases the scriptural source contributes little to the meaning of the narrative. The pseudo-historical figure of Judith is fashioned in part out of the scriptural Jael (Judg. 4–5; and *vice versa* in *LAB* 31), but there is no sign the author intended or expected readers to pick up on it. The transferal of narrative details about Job to the figure of Abraham in the A recension of the *Testament of Abraham* appears to arise from little more than a comparison of the two figures. The use of Gideon and the rout of the Midianites with the three-hundred (Judg. 7) as the model for Kenaz's rout of the Amorites with the three-hundred (*LAB* 27) appears to serve no purpose other than as a means to tell a story. The use of Greek Esther in Mk 6:21-28 belongs to this last category. It could be the author had access to other details about the execution of John that brought Esther to mind. It might even be the execution of John originated in the promise of a ruler to a young girl. Whereas one can only speculate as to the historical sources for the episode in Mk 6:21-28, a literary source is readily available. The author invokes Esther as a way of telling the story of John's death, a story in which a young girl pleases a king who offers her 'even half of [his] kingdom', but she instead singles out one man for death.

---

148. *Pace* Roger D. Aus, 'The Release of Barabbas (Mark 15:6-15 par. John 18:39-40), and Judaic Traditions in the Book of Esther', in *Barabbas and Esther and Other Studies*, ed. Roger D. Aus (Atlanta, GA: Scholars Press, 1992), 1–27.

3. Scripturalized Narrative in the Gospel of Mark 157

The Jewish scriptures in the Passion Narrative

Whilst relatively little has been written about the use of scriptural elements in the foregoing episodes, the same cannot be said for the Markan Passion Narrative. There has been a steady stream of scholarship on the extensive use of scriptural language in the scenes of the last supper, Gethsemane, the trial and crucifixion ever since Martin Dibelius.[149] Dibelius proposed that the scriptures were a major source for the composition of the Passion Narrative.[150] Although he was not the first to broach the subject – Dibelius' conclusions were anticipated by Karl Weidel[151] – most scholarship on the Passion Narrative in the century since the publication of *Die Formgeschichte des Evangeliums* can be seen as a response to Dibelius. Form-critical questions concerning the integrity and genre of the supposed pre-Markan source for the Passion Narrative have thus dominated scholarship.[152] At the same time, Dibelius' comments on the formative role of scriptural elements in the Passion Narrative have influenced much of the subsequent debate. For the form critic, a good

149. Notable studies include Suhl, *Die Funktion der alttestamentlichen Zitate*, 26–66; Kee, 'The Function of Scriptural Quotations'; Steichele, *Der leidende Sohn Gottes*, 193–279; Moo, *The Old Testament in the Gospel Passion Narratives*; Raymond E. Brown, *The Death of the Messiah: A Commentary on the Passion Narratives in the Four Gospels*, 2 vols., ABRL (New York, NY: Doubleday, 1994), 2:1445–67; O'Brien, *The Use of Scripture in the Markan Passion Narrative*.

150. Dibelius, *Die Formgeschichte des Evangeliums*, 179–88, 205–6, 217–18; also in Dibelius, 'Das historische Problem der Leidengeschichte', in *Botschaft und Geschichte. Gesammelte Aufsätze. Band 1: Zur Evangelienforschung*, ed. Martin Dibelius (Tübingen: Mohr Siebeck, 1963), 248–57.

151. Weidel, 'Studien über den Einfluss' (1910): 83–109, 163–95; (1912): 167–86.

152. Following Dibelius, *Die Formgeschichte des Evangeliums*, 178–218; notably in Bultmann, *History of the Synoptic Tradition*, 275–84; Ludger Schenke, *Studien zur Passionsgeschichte des Markus. Tradition und Redaktion in Markus 14,1-42*, FZB 4 (Würzburg: Echter, 1971); Detlev Dormeyer, *Die Passion Jesu als Verhaltensmodell*, NTAbh NF 11 (Münster: Aschendorff, 1974); Pesch, *Das Markusevangelium*, 2:1–27; Étienne Trocmé, *The Passion as Liturgy: A Study in the Origin of the Passion Narrative in the Four Gospels* (London: SCM, 1983); John Dominic Crossan, *The Cross That Spoke: The Origins of the Passion Narrative* (San Francisco, CA: Harper & Row, 1988). Against Dibelius: Eta Linnemann, *Studien zur Passionsgeschichte*, FRLANT 102 (Göttingen: Vandenhoeck & Ruprecht, 1970), 54–68; the influential criticism of Pesch's views in Frans Neirynck, 'L'Évangile de Marc (II). À propos de R. Pesch, *Das Markusevangelium, 2. Teil*. Review of Pesch, R. *Das Markusevangelium. II Teil: Kommentar Zu Kap. 8,27-16,20*', *ETL* 55 (1979): 1–42; Johannes Schreiber, *Die Markuspassion*, 2nd ed., BZNW 68 (Berlin: W. de Gruyter, 1993).

158 *Writing with Scripture*

portion of the Passion Narrative can be traced to scriptural reflection and not to history – in other words, the influence flowed from scripture to history and not *vice versa*.[153] The darkness at noon occurs in Mk 15:33, not because any such event ever took place, but because the author supplied the image from Amos 8:9. For conservative exegetes, on the other hand, the influence flowed in the other direction, from history to scripture. Early Christians were led to certain scriptural passages by their uncanny resemblance to the historical recollections of the events surrounding Jesus' death.[154] This process may have even been initiated by Jesus himself, who utters the words of Ps. 22:1 (LXX 21:1), 'My God, my God, why have you forsaken me?' (Mk 15:34). Again, Crossan has memorably, and somewhat pejoratively, described these two polarities as 'prophecy historicized' and 'history remembered' – contrasting the nuance of the former with the naïveté of the latter.[155]

But as Mark Goodacre counters, this binary fails to capture the complexity of the narrative. Whilst few would doubt the darkness at noon of Mk 15:33 was created almost entirely on the basis of Amos 8:9, at other times scriptural language is merged with traditional material.[156] For example, the inclusion of named women at the crucifixion of Jesus appears to be traditional, but the detail that they looked on 'from a distance' (Mk 15:40: ἀπὸ μαχρόθεν; cf. 14:54) nonetheless reflects the language of LXX

153. Following Dibelius are Bultmann, *History of the Synoptic Tradition*, 262; Maurer, 'Knecht Gottes und Sohn Gottes im Passionsberichte'; Burton L. Mack, *A Myth of Innocence: Mark and Christian Origins* (Philadelphia, PA: Fortress, 1988), 249–312; Helmut Koester, *Ancient Christian Gospels: Their History and Development* (London: SCM, 1990), 216–40; Crossan, *Birth of Christianity*, 519–23; cf. the critical comments in Allison, *Constructing Jesus*, 387–92.

154. Gottfried Schille, 'Das Leiden des Herrn. Die evangelische Passionstradition und ihr "Sitz im Leben"', *ZTK* 52 (1955): 161–205, esp. 164; Lindars, *New Testament Apologetic*, 33–4; Moo, *The Old Testament in the Gospel Passion Narratives*, 380–1; cf. the more cautious comments in Brown, *Death of the Messiah*, 1:14–24.

155. Crossan, *The Birth of Christianity*, 520–21; also Crossan, *Who Killed Jesus? Exposing the Roots of Anti-Semitism in the Gospel Story of the Death of Jesus* (San Francisco, CA: HarperSanFrancisco, 1995), 1–2. Suhl made the same observation three decades earlier: 'Von hier aus ergaben sich für die Beurteilung der Passionsgeschichte zwei Standpunkte: Die einen meinen, in der Überlieferung noch sehr viel Historie entdecken zu können, die anderen halten mehr oder weniger alles für Konstruktion aus dem Weissagungsbeweis' (*Die Funktion der alttestamentlichen Zitate*, 26; also 44–5).

156. See Goodacre, 'Scripturalization in Mark's Crucifixion Narrative'; 'Prophecy Historicized or Tradition Scripturalized?'.

3. Scripturalized Narrative in the Gospel of Mark 159

Ps. 37:12 (MT 38:11): 'My friends and fellows approached opposite me and stood, and my next of kin stood *from a distance* (ἀπὸ μακρόθεν)'. It is in this vein that Goodacre proposes *scripturalization* as an alternative to 'prophecy historicized' and 'history remembered':

> It is not as if the women's witness has been created on the basis of Ps. 38.11, which does not refer solely to women, let alone to those particular named women. Rather, the traditional element is being retold in the light of the passage that they saw it fulfilling. In other words, in this verse we see the exact opposite of the process of 'prophecy historicized'. A verse taken to be historical has been expressed using the terminology of the scriptures. Tradition was scripturalized.[157]

Although Goodacre does not attempt to show scripturalization in other Second Temple works, his comments could easily apply to *scripturalized narratives* from the period. In the examples surveyed so far, only one appears to have been composed entirely out of scriptural elements, with no recourse to traditional or historical sources: Kenaz's Gideon-inspired defeat of the Amorites (*LAB* 27).[158] In the other examples, scripturalization takes place in relation to some pre-existing material. This includes the scripturalization of a *primary scriptural* narrative with *secondary scriptural* material (Gen. 13–15 in 1QapGen 11; cf. Gen. 9:1-7), scripturalized narratives composed on the basis of an exegetical tradition (Dan. 3 in *LAB* 6 and 38; cf. Gen. 15:7 and Judg. 10:5), scripturalization of an episode in the career of a historical person (Deut. 2:26-36 and 20:10-14 in 1 Macc. 5:45-51) and the scripturalization of a legend derived from the scriptural text (LXX Job 1–2 in *T. Ab.* A 1-15; cf. Gen. 18:1-15). Even the non-historical figure of Judith was not composed entirely out of Jael in Judges 4–5 (or Deborah or Miriam); rather, the scripturalization occurs within a much larger pseudo-historical narrative. In each of these examples, something existed prior to scripturalization. The scripturalized narrative of 1QapGen 11, for example, preserves much of Gen. 9:1-4, whilst incorporating material from Gen. 13:7, 15:1 and 26:24. In the two fiery furnace narratives (*LAB* 6; 38), the episodes have been spun out of a single word in the primary scripture (אור in Gen. 15:7; קמון in Judg. 10:5). The scripturalized account of Judas' siege of Ephron (1 Macc. 5:45-51), which is told in the language of Moses' defeat of Sihon and the laws of

---

157. Goodacre, 'Prophecy Historicized or Tradition Scripturalized?', 44–5.

158. The stories of Kenaz and the stones (*LAB* 25–26) and Zebul (*LAB* 29) can also be included here.

160   *Writing with Scripture*

ḥērem, may result from little more than a faint knowledge of a military altercation at an obscure village. But there is still something of history to the episode, or at least to the military campaign described in 1 Maccabees 3–5.

Turning to Mark, the scripturalized narratives surveyed thus far seem to have a similarly tenuous connection to historical memory, but nevertheless seem to have been triggered by some genuine aspect of Jesus' career – his reputation as a teacher with disciples (Mk 1:12-20) or as a miracle-worker (6:35-44; 8:1-9) – as well as the sordid details surrounding John's death (6:21-28). One might expect a similar interaction between pre-existing tradition and scriptural material in the Passion Narrative of Mark 14–15. The description of Jesus' trial and execution contains many elements that cannot be chalked up to scripturalization. The Jesus of the Passion Narrative is no Kenaz. Take away the scriptural material from Mark 14–15 and a coherent narrative still remains.[159] But the presence of an underlying narrative does not limit the potential for creative embellishment. The fantastic darkness at noon in Mk 15:33 is as extraneous to the brute historical events surrounding Jesus' death as the 83,500 who die in a fiery furnace are to the 'fire' of Gen. 15:7 (*LAB* 6). There was always room for wholesale invention. But scholars are able to tell when texts like the *Liber Antiquitatum Biblicarum* and the *Genesis Apocryphon* diverge from their underlying sources for one simple reason: the sources have survived – in this case, the Jewish scriptures. No comparable sources survive for broadly historical narratives like 1 Maccabees and the Gospel of Mark. This means Maccabean and Markan scholars can judge with some confidence when their texts depend on the Jewish scriptures for their content, but not when they depend on historical memory. Judas may well have destroyed 'every male by the edge of the sword' (1 Macc. 5:51) when he besieged Ephron, but the only sure thing is the language comes from Deut. 20:13. It could be those who crucified Jesus gambled for his clothes (Mk 15:24) – such mockery would surely fit the gruesome spectacle of crucifixion – but as it is, the historian only knows the language comes from LXX Ps. 21:19 (MT 22:18).

But what motivated Mark or their source to scripturalize the details of Jesus' death in this way? For 1 Maccabees, the answer is clear: it was the conviction that Judas and the Maccabean brothers behaved 'according to the law' (1 Macc. 3:56; 4:47, 53; 15:21: κατὰ τὸν νόμον) that led the author to compose a scripturalized narrative of Judas besieging like the lawgiver Moses (Deut. 2:26-36; Judg. 11:19-21) according to the laws of *ḥērem*

---

159. As Allison, *Constructing Jesus*, 387–433; *pace* Crossan, *The Birth of Christianity*, 521.

(Deut. 20:10-14).[160] Scholars have proposed similar interpretive frameworks for understanding the use of the Jewish scriptures in the Passion Narrative. To some, it presents Jesus as the Davidic messiah.[161] To others, it demonstrates that Jesus is the Isaianic 'suffering servant'.[162] For others, the scriptural elements are subsumed under Mark's eschatological framework.[163] All of these scholars tend to agree that the scriptures function in the Passion Narrative to demonstrate the fulfilment of prophecy – i.e. the *Weissagungs-* and *Schriftbeweis* of Weidel and Dibelius. But only

160. Likewise, it was the conviction that the Hasmonaeans were the heirs to the Phinehaic priesthood that led to the scripturalized episode of Mattathias at Modeïn (1 Macc. 2:23-26; cf. Num. 25:6-13).

161. See Juel, *Messianic Exegesis*, 91–117. More recently, Robert D. Rowe, *God's Kingdom and God's Son: The Background to Mark's Christology from Concepts of Kingship in the Psalms*, AGAJU 50 (Leiden: Brill, 2002), 295–306; Harold W. Attridge, 'Giving Voice to Jesus: Use of the Psalms in the New Testament', in *Psalms in Community: Jewish and Christian Textual, Liturgical, and Artistic Traditions*, ed. Attridge and Margot E. Fassler, SymS 25 (Atlanta, GA: SBL, 2003), 101–12; Rikki E. Watts (also Isaiah), 'The Psalms in Mark's Gospel', in *The Psalms in the New Testament*, ed. Steve Moyise and Maarten J. J. Menken (London: T&T Clark, 2004), 41–5; Jocelyn McWhirter, 'Messianic Exegesis in Mark's Passion Narrative', in van Oyen and Shepherd, eds., *The Trial and Death of Jesus*, 69–97; Stephen P. Ahearne-Kroll, *The Psalms of Lament in Mark's Passion: Jesus' Davidic Suffering*, SNTSMS 142 (Cambridge: Cambridge University Press, 2007); J. Samuel Subramanian, *The Synoptic Gospels and the Psalms as Prophecy*, LNTS 351 (London: T&T Clark, 2007), 64–9; Max Botner, *Jesus Christ as the Son of David in the Gospel of Mark*, SNTSMS 174 (Cambridge: Cambridge University Press, 2019), 174–88.

162. See Schweitzer (also eschatology), *The Mystery of the Kingdom of God: The Secret of Jesus' Messiahship and Passion*, trans. Walter Lowrie (New York, NY: Dodd, Mead & Co., 1914), 236–9; Jeremias, *TDNT* 5:709–17; Dodd, *According to the Scriptures*, 123–5; Maurer, 'Knecht Gottes und Sohn Gottes'; Lindars, *New Testament Apologetic*, 77–82, 89; Moo, *The Old Testament in the Gospel Passion Narratives*, 360; Marcus, *The Way of the Lord*, 186–96; Watts, *Isaiah's New Exodus*, 365; Otto Betz, 'Jesus and Isaiah 53', in *Jesus and the Suffering Servant: Isaiah 53 and Christian Origins*, ed. William H. Bellinger Jr. and William R. Farmer (Harrisburg, PA: Trinity Press International, 1998), 83–7; Darell L. Bock, 'The Function of Scripture in Mark 15.1-39', in Hatina, ed., *Biblical Interpretation in Early Christian Gospels: Volume 1*, 8–17; cf. Hooker, *Jesus and the Suffering Servant*, 86–92 and *passim*; Kee, 'The Functions of Scriptural Quotations', 182–3.

163. See Schweitzer, *The Mystery of the Kingdom of God*, 223–39. More recently, Dale C. Allison Jr., *The End of the Ages Has Come: An Early Interpretation of the Passion and Resurrection of Jesus* (Philadelphia, PA: Fortress, 1985), 26–39; to some extent Marcus, *The Way of the Lord*, 177–9; O'Brien, *The Use of Scripture in the Markan Passion Narrative*, 192–200; Hays, *Echoes of Scripture in the Gospels*, 87–91.

162 *Writing with Scripture*

two instances of scriptural language are explicitly tied to the fulfilment of prophecy (14:21, 49). Elsewhere the use of the Jewish scriptures resembles other texts from the Second Temple period, where the suffering of a righteous person is described using scriptural language, but not as the fulfilment of prophecy. This final section proposes that no one model is sufficient for understanding the use of the Jewish scriptures in the Markan Passion Narrative. As before, the focus will be on instances where unmarked scriptural language appears as part of the narrative, or where an episode or scene seems to be modelled extensively on scriptural elements. It will be my contention that the Passion Narrative utilizes scriptural elements in a manner similar to the scripturalized narratives surveyed thus far, often using the same language as other contemporaneous texts to depict the suffering of the righteous. One episode in particular appears to be modelled on a specific passage: the scene of Jesus' crucifixion (Mk 15:21-41). But first, we will examine the use of the scriptures in the narrative leading up to that episode.

The use of the Jewish scriptures in Mark 14:1–15:20

The first time scriptural language appears as part of the narrative is in Jesus' prediction of his betrayal. Jesus says to the disciples, 'Truly I tell you, one of you will betray me, one who is eating with me' (Mk 14:18: ἀμὴν λέγω ὑμῖν ὅτι εἷς ἐξ ὑμῶν παραδώσει με ὁ ἐσθίων μετ' ἐμοῦ).[164] After the disciples protest their innocence, Jesus again says, 'It is one of the twelve, one who is dipping [bread] into the bowl with me' (14:20: εἷς τῶν δώδεκα, ὁ ἐμβαπτόμενος μετ' ἐμοῦ εἰς τὸ τρύβλιον). This image appears to come from Ps. 41:9, 'Even my bosom friend in whom I trusted, who ate of my bread, has lifted the heel against me' (נֶם־אִישׁ שְׁלוֹמִי אֲשֶׁר־בָּטַחְתִּי בוֹ אוֹכֵל לַחְמִי הִגְדִּיל עָלַי עָקֵב). The agreement is closer with the LXX: 'he who would eat of my bread' (LXX Ps. 40:10: ὁ ἐσθίων ἄρτους μου).[165] As Marcus notes, the 'very awkwardness of the belated

---

164. Though the language of 'three days' (Mk 8:31; 9:31; 10:34) in the Gospel may allude to Hos. 6:2, the similarity of 'after two days' (μετὰ δύο ἡμέρας) in Mk 14:1 with LXX Hos. 6:2 (μετὰ δύο ἡμέρας) could be incidental. It is part of the chronological arrangement of Mk 14–16, which marks the first day of the Feast of Unleavened Bread (14:12), the night of Passover (14:16-17), the day of Passover (15:1, 25), the day of preparation for the Sabbath (15:42) and the first day of the week (16:2). In favour of the allusion is O'Brien, *The Use of Scripture in the Markan Passion Narrative*, 113–17.

165. Compare with the more literal translation of σ' and θ' Ps. 40:10: κατεμεγαλύνθη μου πτέρνα.

3. Scripturalized Narrative in the Gospel of Mark

phrase "the one eating with me" supports such an identification'.[166] O'Brien, on the other hand, finds the association with Ps. 41:9 (LXX 40:10) weak for the following reason: 'Simply adding ἄρτους (*bread*) to Mk 14.18 would have strengthened the verbal correspondence, in a very natural way'.[167] But after Jesus announces his betrayal in Mk 14:18-20, he does, in fact, share 'bread' (ἄρτος) with his betrayer, as in the psalm (Mk 14:22; implied in 14:20). It is for this reason Bultmann concludes that the pericope in Mk 14:17-21 'ist von der christlichen Legende das Motiv gewonnen' – growing out of Ps. 41:9.[168]

The scene is appended by Jesus' cryptic comment, 'For the Son of Man goes as it is written of him' (Mk 14:21: ὅτι ὁ μὲν υἱὸς τοῦ ἀνθρώπου ὑπάγει καθὼς γέγραπται περὶ αὐτοῦ). The Markan formula καθὼς/ὅτι γέγραπται often precedes a marked citation with a named (1:2; 7:6) or unnamed but otherwise clear source (11:17; 14:27), though in one instance it comes with no clear scriptural referent (9:12-13). So, does the formula in Mk 14:21 have Ps. 41:9 in mind? Matthew seems not to think so. Whilst Matthew includes the καθὼς γέγραπται περὶ αὐτοῦ of Mk 14:21 (par. Mt. 26:24), they remove the clearest reference to LXX Ps. 40:10 in the passage, so it simply reads, 'one of you will betray me' (Mt. 26:21: ὅτι εἷς ἐξ ὑμῶν παραδώσει με; cf. Mk 14:18: ὁ ἐσθίων μετ' ἐμοῦ).[169] For Matthew there is a different scriptural source behind Jesus' betrayal.[170] Judas hands over Jesus for 'thirty pieces of silver' (Mt. 26:15), an image borrowed from Zech. 11:13. The same passage also lies behind Judas' suicide in

---

166. Marcus, *The Way of the Lord*, 172; likewise Suhl, *Die Funktion der alttestamentlichen Zitate*, 51.

167. O'Brien, *The Use of Scripture in the Markan Passion Narrative*, 91, emphasis original.

168. Rudolph Bultmann, *Geschichte der synoptischen Tradition*, 4th ed., FRLANT 29 (Göttingen: Vandenhoeck & Ruprecht, 1961), 284. Frederick W. Danker, 'The Literary Unity of Mark 14:1-25', *JBL* 85 (1966): 467–72, goes further to suggest that Ps. 41 provides the structure for Mk 14:1-25 as a whole, connecting 'those who consider the poor' (Ps. 41:1) with the episode at Bethany (Mk 14:3-9). This argument is more appropriate for the Johannine parallel. Cf. Lohmeyer who thinks the reference to Ps. 41:10 is a later gloss (*Markus*, 301), or Suhl, who attributes it to the Markan redactor (*Die Funktion der alttestamentlichen Zitate*, 51–2).

169. At the same time, Mt. 26:23 adds a 'hand' (χείρ) to the dipping bowl whilst deleting the redundant 'one of the twelve' (also missing in some early mss. of Mk 14:20: A a ff²).

170. See Frédéric Manns, 'Un midrash chrétien: le récit de la mort de Judas', *RSR* 54 (1980): 197–203. Cf. the maximalist approach of Charlene McAfee Moss, *The Zechariah Tradition and the Gospel of Matthew*, BZNW 156 (Berlin: W. de Gruyter, 2009), 171–88, who finds multiple levels to Matthew's use of Zechariah.

164 *Writing with Scripture*

Mt. 27:3-10, though Matthew incorrectly names Jeremiah as the source: 'Then was fulfilled what had been spoken through the prophet Jeremiah' (Mt. 27:9: τότε ἐπληρώθη τὸ ῥηθὲν διὰ Ἰερεμίου τοῦ προφήτου). By contrast, Luke omits the καθὼς γέγραπται altogether, instead taking Mk 14:21 to imply predestination, 'For the Son of Man is going as it has been determined' (Lk. 22:22: ὅτι ὁ υἱὸς μὲν τοῦ ἀνθρώπου κατὰ τὸ ὡρισμένον πορεύεται).[171]

But John, either under the influence of Mark or a remarkably similar tradition, interprets the scene as the prophetic fulfilment of Ps. 41:9. Before Jesus announces one of his disciples will betray him, he says, 'But it is to fulfill the scripture, "The one who ate my bread has lifted his heel against me"' (Jn 13:18: ἀλλ' ἵνα ἡ γραφὴ πληρωθῇ· ὁ τρώγων μου τὸν ἄρτον ἐπῆρεν ἐπ' ἐμὲ τὴν πτέρναν αὐτοῦ). This quotation more closely resembles the MT of the psalm than the LXX: '[the one] who ate of my bread, has lifted the heel against me' (בו אוכל לחמי הגדיל עלי עקב). The following section then appears to expand on Mk 14:18-20: again Jesus announces he will be betrayed (Jn 13:21; cf. Mk 14:18), which perplexes the disciples (Jn 13:22; cf. Mk 14:19), leading Peter and the beloved disciple to enquire further in private (Jn 13:24-25). In response, Jesus says, 'It is the one to whom I give this *piece of bread* (ψωμίον) when I have dipped [it in the dish]'. Following this, Jesus gives the 'piece [of bread]' to Judas (Jn 13:26-27, 30). When Jesus grants him leave, Judas departs (13:27-30), leading some to wonder whether Judas, the treasurer, left to 'give something to the poor' (πτωχοῖς ἵνα τι δῷ). With this comment, John ties the scene to the anointing at Bethany earlier in the narrative (Jn 12:1-8; cf. Mk 14:1-9), where Judas is identified as the one who complains that the perfume could have been sold and the money given to the poor, adding, 'He said this not because he cared about the poor, but because he was a thief' (Jn 12:6: εἶπεν δὲ τοῦτο οὐχ ὅτι περὶ τῶν πτωχῶν ἔμελεν αὐτῷ, ἀλλ' ὅτι κλέπτης ἦν). Judas' feigned concern for the poor may too reflect Psalm 41, which begins, 'Happy are those who consider the poor' (Ps. 41:1).[172] This much, however, is clear: John has further scripturalized the details of Jesus' betrayal under the influence of Ps. 41:9, indicating that early readers saw in Mk 14:18-20, or a similar tradition, the fulfilment of the psalm.

171. It could be Luke understood Mark correctly, and the καθὼς γέγραπται of Mk 9:13 and 14:21 simply expresses the will of God rather than a scriptural referent. This may explain the rejoinder emphasizing human responsibility, 'but woe to that one by whom the Son of Man is betrayed!' (14:21b). At the same time, perhaps the scriptural source *and* divine predestination are in view.

172. Danker, 'The Literary Unity', 469–70, believes the use of Ps. 41 in the anointing originated with Mark.

3. Scripturalized Narrative in the Gospel of Mark 165

Perhaps the author of Mk 14:18-21, like John, saw Judas' betrayal as the fulfilment of Ps. 41:9 (LXX 40:10).[173] If so, it would be one of two passages in the Passion Narrative where the idea of prophetic-fulfilment is explicit – the other being the reference to Zech. 13:7 in Mk 14:49 (introduced in 14:27). In both of these examples, however, the formulae only relate to their immediate contexts: Judas' betrayal and the desertion of the disciples. They do not introduce a schema of prophetic-fulfilment for the Passion Narrative as a whole.[174] Elsewhere in the Gospel, there are isolated instances where certain events correspond to, or happen in fulfilment of, the Jewish scriptures.[175] But Mark lacks the explicit interpretive schema one finds in the editorial comments of Matthew (1:22; 2:17, 23; 4:14; 8:17; 12:17; 13:35; 21:4; 27:9) and John (12:16, 38; 15:25; 18:9; 19:24, 36).[176] For the most part, the concept of prophetic-fulfilment is undeveloped in Mark. Thus Suhl concludes it is more appropriate to speak of Mark composing 'in den "Farben" des Alten'.[177] But by preferring poetry over clarity, Suhl overlooks models more sensitive to the literary methods of the Second Temple period. Returning to Dimant's schema, here a better distinction can be made between the *expositional* use of scriptural material and its *compositional* use.

Instances where the scriptures are explicitly invoked to interpret the events in the narrative would fall under the first, *expositional* type. Here, the scriptures appear as something external to the narrative and aim to interpret it, providing a precedent for (LXX Isa. 29:13 in Mk 7:6-7), or giving meaning to (LXX Exod. 23:20 and LXX Isa. 40:3 in Mk 1:2-3),

---

173. A conclusion reached by scholars as dissimilar as Feigel (*Der Einfluß des Weissagungsbeweises*, 47) and Moo (*The Old Testament in the Gospel Passion Narratives*, 238).

174. *Pace* Donald Juel, *An Introduction to New Testament Literature*, with James S. Ackerman and Thayer S. Warshaw (Nashville, TN: Abingdon, 1978), 145; cf. also the influential comments on prophetic-fulfilment in Kee, 'The Function of Scriptural Quotations', 174, 177.

175. Mk 1:2-3; 7:6-7; 9:12-13; as noted *contra* Suhl, in Grässer, 'Review', 667–9.

176. As observed (sans John) by Suhl, *Die Funktion der alttestamentlichen Zitate*, 42–5; Anderson, 'The Old Testament in Mark's Gospel', 281, 305–6. For an enthusiastic interpretation of prophetic-fulfilment in Luke, see Darrell L. Bock, *The Proclamation from Prophecy and Pattern: Lucan Old Testament Christology*, LNTS 12 (Sheffield: Sheffield Academic, 1997).

177. Suhl, *Die Funktion der alttestamentlichen Zitate*, 47. See here the criticism of Herman Mueller, 'Review of Suhl, *Die Funktion*', *CBQ* 28 (1966): 95–7, 'one wonders at times if one can clearly penetrate the distinction' between prophetic-fulfilment and OT colours (97).

166   *Writing with Scripture*

the events described therein. In the Passion Narrative, the words of Jesus in 14:21 would fit this description, as would 14:49 (14:27). The use of LXX Ps. 40:10 (MT Ps. 41:9) to describe Jesus' betrayal is, by contrast, *compositional*. The details of the psalm have been merged with the narrative, so it does not appear as something external to the text, but as part of it.[178] This can also be compared to two other texts which contain references to Ps. 41:9. In *b. Sanh.* 7a, it reads, 'There was a man who went around saying, "The man on whom I relied raised his club against me". Said Samuel to R. Judah, "There is a pertinent verse of Scripture, 'Yes, mine own familiar friend, in whom I trusted and who ate my bread, has lifted up his heel against me'"'.' In this example, the scriptural material appears with an introductory formula (קרא כתיב) and seeks to interpret the aforesaid episode – in other words, it is an *expositional* use of Ps 41:9. Compare this with the *compositional* use of the same passage in 1QH 13:22-25 (esp. 23b-24a):

> But I have been the target of sl[ander for my rivals,] cause for quarrel and argument to my neighbours, for jealousy and anger to those who have joined my covenant, for challenge and grumbling to all my followers. *Ev[en those who e]at my bread have raised their heel against me* (ג]מ או[כלי עלי הגדילו עקב); they have mocked me with an unjust tongue all those who had joined my council; the men of my [congrega]tion are stubborn, and mutter round about.

In this instance, the language of Ps. 41:9 has been applied almost verbatim to the first-person speaker of the *Hodayot*.[179] But here it does not appear as something external to the text; rather, it becomes part of the hymnist's own experience, the narrative of suffering (*Leidensgeschichte*) that lies

---

178. In the corresponding account in Jn 13:18-30, Ps. 41:9 is used in both ways: the formal quotation in Jn 13:18 is *expositional*, whereas the incorporation of scriptural details into the narrative is *compositional*.

179. For the classic view that the hymnist of the *Hodayot* should be identified with the Teacher of Righteousness, see Jean Carmignac and Pierre Guilbert, *Les textes de Qumran: traduits et annotes*, 2 vols. (Paris: Letouzey et Ane, 1961), 1:132–3. For the alternative view that the first-person speaker of the *Hodayot* is constructed for performance in a congregational setting, see Carol A. Newsom, *The Self as Symbolic Space: Constructing Identity and Community at Qumran*, STDJ 52 (Leiden: Brill, 2004), 196–208. On the significance of the *Hodayot* for the study of the Jewish scriptures in the Markan Passion Narrative, see Yarbro Collins, 'The Appropriation of the Individual Psalms of Lament by Mark', in *The Scriptures in the Gospels*, ed. Christopher M. Tuckett, BETL 131 (Leuven: Leuven University Press, 1997), 223–41.

3. Scripturalized Narrative in the Gospel of Mark

behind the hymn. Indeed, this is one of many instances in the *Hodayot* where the hymnist incorporates unmarked language from the Psalms to describe their own experience.[180] This *compositional* use of Ps. 41:9 is of a piece with Mk 14:18-20. Like the hymnist of the *Hodayot*, Mark or their source has incorporated unmarked scriptural language into the story of suffering, thereby creating a scripturalized narrative of Jesus' betrayal. Whether the narrative of the betrayal was created entirely under the influence of Ps. 41:9 (in this case, LXX 40:10), or whether the author incorporated scriptural elements into a pre-existing narrative of Judas' treachery, the pericope in Mk 14:18-20 is the first clear instance of scripturalization in the Passion Narrative.

The Servant at the Supper: Mark 14:24 and Isaiah 53:12?

The scene then moves to the supper (Mk 14:22-25), with Jesus announcing what appears to be an echo of Exod. 24:8: 'This is my blood of the covenant' (Mk 14:24: τοῦτό ἐστιν τὸ αἷμα μου τῆς διαθήκης).[181] However, the clause that follows – 'which is poured out for many' (Mk 14:24: τὸ ἐκυννόμενον ὑπὲρ πολλῶν) – is unparalleled in Exodus 24 and related traditions. For some – often conservative – commentators, the clause is seen as part of Mark's presentation of Jesus as the 'suffering servant' of

---

180. Ps. 7:2 in 1QH 13:13-14; Ps. 12:6 in 1QH 13:16; Ps. 18:5 in 1QH 11:28-29; Ps. 22:15 in 1QH 13:31; Ps. 26:12 in 1QH 10:29-30; Ps. 31:10 in 1QH 13:34; Ps. 31:13 in 1QH 12:9; Ps. 42:6-7 in 1QH 16:31-32; Ps. 54:3 [86:14] in 1QH 10:21; Ps. 69:21-22 in 1QH 12:11-12; Ps. 88:3-4 in 1QH 16:29-30. On the form of the allusions, see John Elwolde, 'The Hodayot's Use of the Psalter: Text-Critical Contributions (Book 1)', in *Psalms and Prayers: Papers Read at the Thirteenth Joint Meeting of the Society of Old Testament Study and Het Oudtestamentisch Werkegezelschap in Nederland en België, Apeldoorn 21–24 August 2006*, ed. Bob Becking and Eric Peels, OS 55 (Leiden: Brill, 2007), 79–108; Elwode, 'The Hodayot's Use of the Psalter: Text-Critical Contributions (Book 2: Pss 42-72)', in *The Dead Sea Scrolls In Context: Integrating the Dead Sea Scrolls in the Study of Ancient Texts, Languages, and Cultures*, ed. Armin Lange, Emmanuel Tov and Matthias Weigold, VTSup 140 (Leiden: Brill, 2011), 1:79–99; Elwode, 'The Hodadyot's Use of the Psalter: Text-critical Contributions (Book 3: Pss 73-89)', *DSD* 17 (2010): 159–79.

181. LXX Exod. 24:8: ἰδοὺ τὸ αἷμα τῆς διαθήκης. Cf. Zech. 9:11. Compare with the words of institution in 1 Cor. 11:25: 'This cup is the new covenant in my blood' (τοῦτο τὸ ποτήριον ἡ καινὴ διαθήκη ἐστὶν ἐν τῷ ἐμῷ αἵματι). This raises the possibility the words of institution in Mk 14:24 owe to common tradition and not directly to Exod. 24. But as it is, the language of Mk 14:24 is closer to LXX Exod. 24:8 than it is to 1 Cor. 11:25.

Deutero-Isaiah.[182] Jesus is thus depicted as the sufferer of Isa. 53:12, who 'poured out himself to death…yet he bore the sin of many' (…הערה למות. והוא חמא־רבים נשא). The image of the 'suffering servant' is likewise thought to lie behind a number of other passages in the Passion Narrative (i.e. Mk 14:61, 65; 15:5, 19, 27, 43-46).[183] Language from the so-called Servant Songs does occasionally appear in other texts (Isa. 49:6 in *1 En.* 48:4; Isa. 52:7 in 11QMelch 2:15-16, 23; Isa. 50:4 in 1QH 15:13; 16:37; Isa. 52:1 in *Ps. Sol.* 11:7).[184] But is there any precedent for using Isa. 53:12 to describe the suffering of an individual?

One such example is found in the *Psalms of Solomon*: 'For a moment my soul was poured out to death; (I was) near the gates of Hades with the sinner' (*Ps. Sol.* 16:2: παρ' ὀλίγον ἐξεχύθη ἡ ψυχή μου εἰς θάνατον, σύνεγγυς πυλῶν ᾅδου μετὰ ἁμαρτωλοῦ). Like Mk 14:24, the first part resembles MT Isa. 53:12c (הערה למות נפשו), whereas the second part recalls the reckoning with the transgressors in the following clause. The influence of Isa. 53:12d is even more evident in *Ps. Sol.* 16:5: 'I will give thanks to you, O God, who came to my aid for (my) salvation, and who did not count me with the sinners for (my) destruction' (ἐξομολογήσομαί σοι, ὁ θεός, ὅτι ἀντελάβου μου εἰς σωτηρίαν, καὶ οὐκ ἐλογίσω με μετὰ τῶν ἁμαρτωλῶν εἰς ἀπώλειαν). Compare this with Isa. 53:12d: 'and [he] was numbered with the transgressors' (ואת־פשעים נמנה; cf. LXX: καὶ ἐν τοῖς ἀνόμοις ἐλογίσθη).

The image of a righteous one numbered with sinners in death also appears in the Passion Narrative. Jesus is crucified between 'two bandits, one on his right and one on his left' (Mk 15:27: δύο λῃστάς, ἕνα ἐκ δεξιῶν καὶ ἕνα ἐξ εὐωνύμων αὐτοῦ). An early copyist apparently saw Isa. 53:12 in the scene, adding under the influence of Lk. 22:37, 'And the scripture was fulfilled that says, "And he was counted among the lawless"' (Mk 15:28:

---

182. For conservative commentators, the use of Isa. 53:12 is evidence of a Markan theory of 'vicarious' atonement: Lindars, *New Testament Apologetic*, 78–9; R. T. France, *Jesus and the Old Testament: His Application of Old Testament Passages to Himself and His Mission* (Grand Rapids, MI: Baker, 1982), 122–3; Moo, *The Old Testament in the Gospel Passion Narratives*, 397; Craig A. Evans, *Mark 8:27–16:20*, WBC 34B (Nashville, TN: Thomas Nelson, 2001), 394. See the persuasive criticism in Hooker, *Jesus and the Servant*, 82; Joel B. Green, *The Death of Jesus*, WUNT 2/33 (Tübingen: Mohr Siebeck, 1988), 320–3.

183. See the survey of proposed allusions in Marcus, *The Way of the Lord*, 186–90.

184. See also 1QH 12:8 (also 12:23), 'They do not esteem me' (ולא יחשבוני), which may echo Isa. 53:3 'We esteemed him not' (ולא חשבנהו).

3. *Scripturalized Narrative in the Gospel of Mark* 169

καὶ ἐπληρώθη ἡ γραφὴ ἡ λέγουσα, καὶ μετὰ ἀνόμων ἐλογίσθη).[185] If the copyist was able to see Isa. 53:12 in the description of the two thieves, one might also ask whether the description of Jesus' burial by a member of the ruling class (Mk 15:43-46) owes to Isa. 53:9 – 'They made his grave with the wicked and his tomb with the rich' – or if the 'spitting' (ἐμπτύω) and 'striking' (κολαφίζω) Jesus endures (Mk 14:65; 15:19; cf. 10:34) owes to the 'spitting' (רק) and 'striking' (מכים) endured by the sufferer in Isa. 50:6. Given the absence of close verbal agreement with surviving texts of Isaiah, none of these allusions can be established with certainty. But this did not stop one of Mark's earliest – and closest – readers from finding Isaiah in these passages.

Whilst Mark describes Joseph of Arimathea as a 'respected member of the council, who was also himself waiting expectantly for the kingdom of God' (Mk 15:43), Matthew simply describes Joseph as a 'rich man' (Mt. 27:57: ἄνθρωπος πλούσιος) and a 'disciple of Jesus' (ἐμαθητεύθη τῷ Ἰησοῦ). These changes are brought on by two things. The first is the problem posed by Mark's assertion that Joseph was a 'member of the council' (βουλευτής), the same 'council' that had just sentenced Jesus to death (Mk 14:55: συνέδριον; 15:1: συμβούλιον). Whilst Luke absolves Joseph, 'who, though a member of the council, had not agreed to their plan and action' (Lk. 23:50-51), Matthew removes Joseph's involvement with the council altogether. The second appears to be an effort to strengthen the association with Isaiah 53 by describing Joseph as a 'rich man' (ἄνθρωπος πλούσιος) – as it reads in Isa. 53:9, 'They made his grave with the wicked and his tomb with the rich' (ויתן את־רשעים קברו ואת־עשיר במתיו).[186] A similar attempt to bring the passage more in line with Isaiah may be found in the description of Jesus' abuse. In Mk 14:65 (cf. 15:19), Jesus is spat upon, blindfolded and struck, whereas in Mt. 27:67 it reads, 'Then they spat in his face and struck him' (τότε ἐνέπτυσαν εἰς τὸ πρόσωπον αὐτοῦ καὶ ἐκολάφισαν αὐτόν). Compare this with Isa. 5:6: 'I gave my back to those who struck me… I did not hide my face from insult and spitting' (גוי נתתי למכים...פני לא הסתרתי מכלמות ורק). Here, Matthew may be conforming the wording of Mark to Isa. 50:6, so that, like the sufferer, Jesus' abusers spit in his face.[187] This has an unintended consequence, however, as by

---

185. The verse appears in mss. L Θ 0112 0250 $f^{1.13}$ 𝔐 lat syr[p.h].

186. LXX Isa. 53:9 likewise uses πλούσιος, though the meaning is antithetical to both the MT and Mt. 27:57-61.

187. The image also appears in some early mss. of Mk 14:65 (D it[(a), (d), f] syr[p] arm geo) presumably under the influence of Mt. 27:67.

170   *Writing with Scripture*

removing the 'blindfold' of Mk 14:65, the taunt of Jesus' abusers no longer makes sense: 'Prophecy to us, you Messiah! Who is it that struck you?' (Mt. 26:68).

Returning to the words of institution, here too there may be an effort to conform Mark closer to Isaiah. Matthew makes only slight alterations to Mk 14:24 – 'For this is my blood of the covenant, which is poured out for many' (Mt. 26:28: τοῦτο γάρ ἐστιν τὸ αἷμα μου τῆς διαθήκης τὸ πολλῶν ἐκχυννόμενον) – before adding, 'for the forgiveness of sins' (εἰς ἄφεσιν ἁμαρτιῶν).[188] Given the above efforts, it is possible Matthew added the prepositional phrase to intensify an allusion to Isa. 53:12, as the sufferer 'poured out himself to death' (הערה למות) and 'yet he bore the *sin* of many' (והוא חמא־רבים נשא).[189] Elsewhere, Matthew alters the wording of Mark in order to make the scriptural source more clear: for example, Mt. 17:11, changes the present ἀποκαθιστάνει of Mk 9:12 to the future ἀποκαταστήσει to better reflect LXX Mal. 3:23; and Mt. 27:46 replaces the εἰς τί of Mk 15:34 with ἱνατί to conform it closer to LXX Ps. 21:1. Matthew even adds narrative details to Mark's story in order to better reflect the scriptural source: in Mt. 21:2-8, Jesus rides into Jerusalem, not on a colt as in Mk 11:2-7, but on a colt *and* a donkey as in LXX Zech. 9:9. If Matthew was able to find – and exploit – allusions to Isaiah 50–53 in the Markan Passion Narrative, it would be tempting to see this as evidence that the allusions existed in the first place. But Matthew was equally capable of finding scriptural sources for Mark where none existed.[190] In the final analysis, one cannot easily dismiss the possibility that Mark or their source scripturalized details in Mark 14–15 on the basis of Isaiah 50–53, especially given the similar use of Isa. 53:12 in the *Psalms of Solomon* and the reception of the passages in Matthew. And yet, given the faint and fleeting nature of the parallels, one must cautiously conclude with Kee that, in the Markan Passion Narrative, 'There are no *sure* references to Isa 53'.[191]

---

188. Some early mss. of Mk 14:24 follow Matthew here (i.e. W a).

189. As Robert H. Gundry, *The Use of the Old Testament in St. Matthew's Gospel*, NovTSup 18 (Leiden: Brill, 1967), 57–9; Moo, *The Old Testament in the Gospel Passion Narratives*, 130–2. A reference to Jer. 31:34 here is unlikely; see Davies and Allison, *Matthew*, 3:474–5.

190. Matthew views Jesus' entrance into Capernaum as the fulfilment of Isa. 9:1-2 (Mt. 4:13-16), despite no sign of this in Mk 1:21; nor is there a scriptural basis for the location of Jesus in Nazareth (Mk 1:9), cf. the unknown source of the fulfilment formula in Mt. 2:23.

191. Kee, 'The Function of Scriptural Quotations', 183, emphasis mine.

3. Scripturalized Narrative in the Gospel of Mark   171

The Shepherd and the Sheep: Mark 14:27 and Zechariah 13:7

Following the supper, the scene shifts to the Mount of Olives, which begins with the only marked citation in the Passion Narrative. Jesus says to the disciples, 'You will all become deserters; for it is written, "I will strike the shepherd, and the sheep will be scattered"' (Mk 14:27: ὅτι πάντες σκανδαλισθήσεσθε, ὅτι γέγραπται· πατάξω τὸν ποιμένα, καὶ τὰ πρόβατα διασκορπισθήσονται).[192] The source here is Zech. 13:7, in a form close to LXX A: 'Strike the shepherd, and the sheep will be scattered' (πάταξον τὸν ποιμένα, καὶ διασκορπισθήσονται τὰ πρόβατα).[193] It is one of a series of prophecies Jesus makes during the course of the Passion Narrative (14:7-9, 13-15, 18, 25, 28, 30, 62). Some of these prophecies find fulfilment in the narrative itself: the burial (14:7-8; cf. 15:46-47); the preparations for Passover (14:13-15; cf. 14:16); the betrayal (14:18; cf. 14:41-45). Other details in the Passion Narrative fulfil earlier prophecies of Jesus: the testimony before the council (13:9; cf. 14:53-65; 15:1); the testimony before the governor (13:9; cf. 15:1-15); the betrayal (13:12; cf. 14:41-45); the darkening of the sun (13:24; cf. 15:33); and indeed, the Passion itself (8:31; 9:12, 31; 10:33-34, 40; cf. 14:43–15:39). Some prophecies in Mark 14–15 were understood to have already reached their fulfilment outside of the narrative (14:9, 28), or were to be fulfilled imminently (14:62; cf. 13:26).[194]

By contrast, Jesus' prophecy in Mk 14:27 is fulfilled almost immediately. This is announced in 14:49 with a fulfilment formula unusual for Mark: Jesus says, 'But let the scriptures be fulfilled' (ἀλλ' ἵνα πληρωθῶσιν αἱ γραφαί). This is the second of two instances in the Passion Narrative where the scriptures are interpreted in terms of prophetic-fulfilment – the other being 14:21. That Jesus has Zech. 13:7 in mind is indicated by

---

192. The location of the Mount of Olives may be significant. The narrative has already presented Judas in the language of Ps. 41:9 (Mk 14:18-20), a verse which was traditionally understood as referring to Ahithophel, who betrayed David (2 Sam. 15:12; *b. Sanh.* 106b). News of Ahithophel's betrayal reaches David as he is mourning on the Mount of Olives (2 Sam. 15:30-31).

193. LXX A is closer to the MT than the 'Old Greek' of LXX B; see the comments in Stendahl, *The School of St. Matthew*, 80–3. The same passage relates to the execution of R. Simeon ben Gamaliel II in *ARN* A 38, '[R. Ishmael b. Elisha said] Concerning you Scripture says, "Awake, O sword, against my shepherd and against the man who is near to me"'.

194. For Lohmeyer and Marxsen, the appearance in Galilee is in the future for the Markan audience: Ernst Lohmeyer, *Galiläa und Jerusalem*, FRLANT 34 (Göttingen: Vandenhoeck & Ruprecht, 1936), 11–13; Lohmeyer, *Markus*, 355–56; Marxsen, *Der Evangelist Markus*, 33–77.

172   *Writing with Scripture*

the following verse: 'All of them deserted him and fled' (Mk 14:50: καὶ ἀφέντες αὐτὸν ἔφυγον πάντες).[195] But Jesus confusingly uses the plural 'scriptures' (αἱ γραφαί).[196] Does this imply that the formula refers to scriptural material beyond Zech. 13:7?[197] It could conceivably refer back to the scriptural source for Jesus' betrayal 'as it is written of him' (Mk 14:21).[198] At the same time, it may be a reference to the scene that follows. In what may well be the strangest moment in the Gospel, Mark or their source inserts the following detail: 'A certain young man was following him, wearing nothing but a linen cloth. They caught hold of him, but he left the linen cloth and ran off naked' (Mk 14:51-52).

The all-too-brief cameo of this scantily clad character has understandably perplexed scholars. Some have followed the fantasy that Mark is identifying themselves to the reader as the naked young man.[199] Others have speculated that Mark is identifying an eyewitness source, which could explain the inclusion of other conspicuous characters in the Passion Narrative (15:21, 40, 47).[200] Perhaps the naked young man is to be contrasted with Jesus: Jesus does not flee, is stripped and then wrapped in a linen cloth (15:46: σινδών), whereas the young man flees, and is stripped of his linen cloth (14:51-52: σινδών).[201] Could the comparison even be a perverse interpretation of Mk 4:25: 'For to those who have, more will be given; and from those who have nothing, even what they have will be taken away' – in this case, linen cloths? Then again, it is equally possible

---

195. *Pace* Schenke, *Studien zur Passionsgeschichte*, 360.

196. Matthew instead interprets it generally, 'so that the scriptures *of the prophets* may be fulfilled' (Mt. 26:56; cf. some early mss. of Mk 14:49: N W).

197. In Mt. 21:42, αἱ γραφαί refers to only one passage (LXX Ps. 117:22-23).

198. A reference to Ps. 41:9 (LXX 40:10; as in Mk 14:21) would be appropriate given the betrayal occurs in 14:41-45. Cf. Pesch, *Das Markusevangelium*, 2:401, who thinks the referent is the various Psalms applied to the Passion Narrative; cf. Walter Schmithals (*Das Evangelium nach Markus: Kapitel 9,2-16*, OTK 2/2 [Gütersloh: Mohn, 1979], 646), and Marcus (*Mark: 8–16*, 994) who see Isa. 53:12 behind the formula. That Mk 14:49 is a general statement *à la* 1 Cor. 15:3, see Gnilka, *Das Evangelium nach Markus*, 2:271.

199. Theodor Zahn, *Einleitung in das Neue Testament*, 3rd ed., 2 vols. (Leipzig: Deichert, 1907), 2:250; Josef Schmid, *The Gospel According to Mark* (Staten Island, NY: Alba House, 1968), 273.

200. Lohmeyer, *Markus*, 323–4; Taylor, *The Gospel According to St. Mark*, 562; Barbara Saunderson, 'Gethsemane: The Missing Witness', *Biblica* 79 (1989): 224–33.

201. Albert Vanhoye, 'La fuite de jeuene homme nu (Mc 14,51-52)', *Bib* 52 (1971): 401–6; Harry Fleddermann, 'The Flight of a Naked Young Man (Mark 14:51-52)', *CBQ* 41 (1979): 412–18.

3. Scripturalized Narrative in the Gospel of Mark 173

the scene owes to scriptural language.[202] In Amos 2:16 it reads, 'And those who are stout of heart among the mighty shall flee away naked in that day' (ואמיץ לבו בגבורים ערום ינוס ביום־ההוא). Though the LXX reads, 'the naked shall pursue' (ὁ γυμνὸς διώξεται), Aquila, Symmachus and Theodotion offer the more literal 'shall flee naked' (γυμνὸς φεύξεται). In this regard, the γυμνὸς ἔφυγεν of Mk 14:52 is closer to the MT (α', σ' and θ') of Amos 2:16 than the LXX. If Mark or their source composed the detail on the basis of Amos 2:16, it would not be the only detail from Amos in the Passion Narrative (i.e. Amos 8:9 in Mk 15:33).[203]

The description of the naked young man may at the same time reflect another scriptural source. When Potiphar's wife attempts to seduce Joseph, who is elsewhere described as a 'young man' (LXX Gen. 41:12: νεανίσκος), by laying hold of his garments, he resists her advances, 'and leaving his garments behind in her hands he fled and went outside' (LXX Gen. 39:12: καὶ καταλιπὼν τὰ ἱμάτια αὐτοῦ ἐν ταῖς χερσὶν αὐτῆς ἔφυγεν καὶ ἐξῆλθεν ἔξω). As in Mk 14:51-52, a 'young man' (νεανίσκος) is caught and 'fled' (ἔφυγεν), 'leaving' (καταλιπὼν) his garment. One ancient text even has Joseph fleeing naked, possibly under the influence of Amos 2:16: 'When I saw, therefore, that in her madness she had seized my garment, I shook loose and left it and fled naked' (*T. Jos.* 8:3: ὡς οὖν εἶδον ὅτι μαινομένη βίᾳ κρατεῖ τὰ ἱμάτιά μου, γυμνὸς ἔφυγον).[204] This raises the possibility that Mark or their source composed the scene in 14:51-52 using the image of Joseph fleeing Potiphar's wife in Gen. 39:12, possibly to illustrate the flight of Amos 2:16.[205] The fleeting and incidental nature of the scene does resemble others in the Passion Narrative which clearly depend on a scriptural source (Mk 15:24, 33, 36).[206] The verbal similarities,

---

202. So Alfred Loisy, *L'Évangile selon Marc* (Paris: Nourry, 1912), 425; Eric Klostermann, *Das Markusevangelium*, 5th ed., HNT 3 (Tübingen: Mohr Siebeck, 1971), 153.

203. Note the interesting parallel with Jesus' interjection at Rev. 16:15: 'See, I am coming like a thief! Blessed is the one who stays awake and is clothed, not going about naked and exposed to shame.'

204. Note the similar use of κρατέω as in Mk 14:51.

205. Compare also with the description of the wicked in *2 En.* 10:5-6, who, 'to supply clothing, take away the last garment of the naked'.

206. Like the use of Amos 8:9, the use of Amos 2:16 would be eschatologically significant (cf. Allison, *The End of the Ages*, 26–30). The flight of the disciples echoes the words of Jesus in Mk 8:35-38. Given this pericope reflects a knowledge of the Passion (8:31, 34), it may be intended as an indictment of the disciples for deserting Jesus (14:50-52, 66-72). They were not those who endured till the end and were saved (13:13), but those who fled away naked on the day of the LORD (Amos 2:16).

174   *Writing with Scripture*

however, are slight. As it is, the only passage certainly behind the αἱ γραφαί formula in Mk 14:49 is the marked citation of Zech. 13:7 in Mk 14:27.[207]

Was the flight of the disciples composed on the basis of Zech. 13:7, however? The question deserves consideration. Mark appears to be the only source for the desertion. Matthew simply repeats Mk 14:50 (Mt. 26:56) whilst omitting the flight of the naked man, whereas Luke omits the desertion in its entirety, only noting that Peter followed at a distance (Lk. 22:54; cf. Mk 14:54). John appears to be rebutting the tradition of the desertion when they have Jesus explain the absence of the disciples: 'So if you are looking for me, let these men go', adding, 'This was to fulfill the word that he had spoken, "I did not lose a single one of those whom you gave me"' (Jn 18:8-9).[208] So, why would Mark or their source offer such a damning portrait of the men whom Jesus chose? Mark elsewhere presents the disciples in an unflattering light. They are shown to be haughty (Mk 8:32-33; 14:31), jealous (9:33-34, 38; 10:13, 37) and, above all, ignorant (4:40-41; 6:37, 51-52; 8:4, 16-21; 9:5-6, 28, 32; 10:24).[209] Jesus even calls their leader, Peter, 'Satan' (σατανᾶ). The Passion Narrative shows them to be more than imperfect disciples of Jesus: Judas betrays him, three fail to keep watch, Peter denies him and all desert him. Some apparently questioned the authority of those who claimed to be Jesus' disciples (2 Cor. 11:1, 5, 13; 12:11; Gal. 2:11-14) and it is conceivable Mark thought this way.[210] Thus, the desertion of the disciples in Mk 14:50-52 could have originated in a sectarian context, with the disciples' desertion invalidating their authority over Mark's community.[211]

It could, at the same time, be intended to explain a problem posed by the earliest kerygma. None of Jesus' followers were known to have been crucified with him. That the disciples deserted Jesus may have been inferred solely on the basis of this fact. When the hour came, not one

207. As Yarbro Collins, *Mark*, 687.

208. Cf. Jn 6:39; 17:12.

209. On the function of Mark's negative portrait of the disciples, see Elizabeth Struthers Malbon, 'Disciples/Crowds/Whoever: Markan Characters and Readers', *NovT* 28 (1986): 104–30.

210. So Theodore J. Weeden, 'The Heresy That Necessitated Mark's Gospel', *ZNW* 59 (1968): 145–58; Weeden, *Mark – Traditions in Conflict* (Philadelphia, PA: Fortress, 1971), 26–43; Werner Kelber, *Mark's Story of Jesus* (Philadelphia, PA: Fortress, 1979), 30–42, 88–96.

211. As Günter Klein notes, Mk 14:66-72 stands in some tension with the ἔφυγον πάντες of 14:50, but this too may contain an anti-Petrine element, 'Die Verleugnung des Petrus: Eine traditionsgeschichte Untersuchung', *ZTK* 58 (1961): 285–328.

3. Scripturalized Narrative in the Gospel of Mark

of Jesus' disciples was willing to 'drink the cup' he was about to drink. Why had they not 'taken up their crosses' and died with him, as Jesus demanded (Mk 8:34) and Peter promised (14:31)? Why had they not defended Jesus from those who persecuted him until the very end? The other Gospels address this last charge by having Jesus rebuke the disciple who molests the slave of the high priest (Mt. 26:51-54; Lk. 22:49-51; Jn 18:10-11; cf. Mk 14:47).[212] For Mark, however, the answer is simple albeit undeveloped: the disciples betrayed and deserted Jesus because of what is written in the scriptures. This does not absolve them of moral responsibility. As those who were unwilling to 'take up their cross' (Mk 8:34), who were 'ashamed' (8:38) of the Son of Man and did not endure 'till the end' (13:13), they should expect retribution, worst of all the betrayer (14:21). And yet, there is still an air of fatalism in Jesus' words, 'But let the scriptures be fulfilled'. It could not have been any other way. It may be that Mark or their source sought to explain the absence of the disciples at Jesus' crucifixion by invoking the scriptures. The cowardly and duplicitous disciples were, after all, simply playing their part in the divine plan.

Whether or not Mark authored this tradition in its entirety, the question remains as to whether the scriptures – in this case, Zech. 13:7 – influenced the narrative beyond the words of Jesus' prophecy. Did it lead to the creation of narrative details, as Ps. 41:9 led to Jesus' betrayer eating bread with him? The council and the guards 'strike' (Mk 14:65: κολαφίζω; 15:19: τύπτω) the shepherd (Jesus), though not in the same words as Zech. 13:7 (πατάσσω). The disciples scatter in the sense that they 'deserted him and fled' (Mk 14:50: καὶ ἀφέντες αὐτὸν ἔφυγον), though not in the words of Jesus' prophecy (διασκορπίζω). The crowd comes with clubs and 'swords' (μάχαιραι), though not in the same words as LXX Zech. 13:7, 'Awake, *O sword* (ῥομφαία), against my shepherd'. It would appear then the words of Zech. 13:7 serve to interpret the flight of the disciples, not to describe the act of desertion itself. The use of Zech. 13:7 in the Passion Narrative can be compared to the *expositional* use of the same passage in the *Damascus Document*, where it becomes a prophecy concerning the eschatological fate of the wicked: 'But (over) all those who despise the precepts and the ordinances, may be emptied over them the punishment of the wicked, when God visits the earth, when there comes the word which is written by the hand of the prophet Zechariah: "Wake up, sword, against my shepherd, and against the male who is my companion – oracle of God – strike the shepherd, and the flock may scatter, and I shall turn my hand against the little ones"' (CD B 19:5-9). Both texts use Zech. 13:7 to

---

212. There is no such rebuke in Mk 14:47.

176 *Writing with Scripture*

describe future events: in the *Damascus Document* it foretells what God will do to the wicked, whereas in Mk 14:27 it foretells what the disciples will do when the Son of Man is handed over.[213] For Mark, this future arrives swiftly in the night, as the disciples lie sleeping.[214] When it comes, the disciples do what is written of them, forsaking their master. Peter lingers for a little while longer (14:54, 66-72), but once the cock crows for a second time, Peter and the disciples vanish from the narrative, never to re-appear, leaving Jesus to face his dreadful fate alone.

Grief in the Garden: Mark 14:34 and Psalm 42:6

The desertion of the disciples forms an *inclusio* with the prophecy of Zech. 13:7 in Mk 14:27. Placed in between these two markers is the brief interlude in Gethsemane. As he has done before (5:37; 9:2), Jesus withdraws from the other disciples with Peter, James and John. There he confesses to them, 'My soul is deeply grieved, even to death; remain here, and keep awake' (14:34: περίλυπός ἐστιν ἡ ψυχή μου ἕως θανάτου· μείνατε ὧδε καὶ γρηγορεῖτε).[215] Jesus' command to 'keep awake' (γρηγορεῖτε), and the disciples failure to heed the command (14:37-42), ties the scene to the Olivet discourse (13:35, 37). This is one of many details in the Passion Narrative which mirrors the signs of the end of the age in Mark 13, signaling that for Mark the death of Jesus is a cosmic, eschatological event.[216] But still another text may lie behind the words of Jesus here. His words echo those of the Psalmist in Ps. 42:6 (LXX 41:7), 'My soul is cast down within me' (עלי נפשי תשתוחח).[217] Whilst the LXX renders the third person hitpolel תשתוחח as ἐταράχθη, the second person תשתוחח in the Psalmist's refrain appears as it does in Mk 14:34: 'Why are you deeply grieved, O my soul' (LXX Pss. 41:6, 12; 42:5: ἵνα τί περίλυπος εἶ, ψυχή). This leaves some confusion as to whether Jesus' words reflect the Hebrew or an unknown Greek variant of Ps. 42:6 (LXX 41:7), or if they reflect the repeated refrain of Psalms 42–43 (LXX 41–42).[218] This is further compli-cated by the fact no parallel exists in either psalm to Jesus' words, 'even

213. Cf. the application of Zech. 13:7 to the execution of R. Simeon ben Gamaliel II in *ARN* A 38.

214. Foreshadowed by Mk 13:35-37.

215. Translation mine.

216. For an overview of the parallels, see Allison, *The End of the Ages*, 36–8.

217. Cf. MT Ps. 6:3 (LXX 6:4).

218. The updated *Loci Citati vel Allegati* in NA[28] favours the latter. See also Marcus, *Mark: 8–16*, 974–5; Ahearne-Kroll, *The Psalms of Lament in Mark's Passion*, 66–9; O'Brien, *The Use of Scripture in the Markan Passion Narrative*, 125–8.

to death' (ἕως θανάτου). Some have followed Jerome in thinking Jesus' words owe instead to LXX Jon. 4:9, where Jonah mourns the loss of the pumpkin, 'I am exceedingly grieved, unto death' (σφόδρα λελύπημαι ἐγὼ ἕως θανάτου).[219] Another often overlooked parallel is found in the story of Samson, where Delilah taunts him until 'his soul was vexed to death' (Judg. 16:16: ותקצר נפשו למות).[220] But the fact Psalm 42 (LXX 41) was used to depict the suffering of individuals elsewhere in Second Temple literature makes it the most likely source for the words of Jesus in Mk 14:34.

The most striking parallel is found in the *Hodayot*: 'Breakers rush against me and my soul within me has weakened right to destruction' (1QH 16:32: ויתעופפו עלי משברים ונפשי עלי תשתוחה לכלה). The second clause reflects *mutatis mutandis* the Hebrew of Ps. 42:6, 'My soul is cast down within me' (עלי נפשי תשתוחח). The first clause may also reflect the pelagic imagery of Ps. 42:7: 'All your waves and your billows have gone over me' (כל־משבריך וגליך עלי עברו). Interestingly, the *Hodayot* adds the expression, '[right] to destruction' (לכלה), which, appearing as it does after the language of Ps. 42:6 (LXX 41:7), corresponds to the phrase in Mk 14:34, 'even to death' (ἕως θανάτου).[221] This, again, shows the *Hodayot* similarly using the Psalms to compose a narrative of suffering (*Leidengeschichte*) for the hymnist. Moreover, the *Hodayot* uses the language of Psalm 42 elsewhere: the words of the hymnist in 1QH 13:33-34 – 'I am eating the bread of weeping, my drink is tears without end' (ואוכלה בלחם אנחה ושקוי בדמעות אין כלה) – appear to build on the imagery of Ps. 42:3, 'My tears have been my food day and night' (היתה־לי דמעתי לחם יומם ולילה).

The language of Psalm 42 is likewise used in narrative descriptions of suffering.[222] Pseudo-Philo features a scripturalized narrative of Hannah's despair as told in 1 Samuel 1. Peninnah taunts Hannah using imagery from Isa. 56:3, 'What does it profit you that Elkanah your husband loves you, for you are a *dry tree*' (*LAB* 50:1: *lignum siccum*; cf. Isa. 56:3: עץ יבש).

---

219. *Jérôme, commentaire sur Jonah*, ed. Yves-Marie Duval, SC 323 (Paris: Cerf, 1985), 107–8; similarly Origen, *Comm. Matt.* 90. So also Gundry, *Mark*, 867; cf. Moo, *The Old Testament in the Gospel Passion Narratives*, 240–1.

220. My translation. The similarity is noted by Klostermann, *Das Markus-evangelium*, 168.

221. As noted in Gnilka, *Das Evangelium nach Markus*, 2:259.

222. There is also good reason to suspect Ps. 42:1 lies behind the description of Jacob in the fragmentary *History of Joseph*: 'to see [Ja]cob as a deer...the water' (*Hist. Jos. verso* C).

178   *Writing with Scripture*

To which she adds, 'And I know that my husband will love me, because he delights in the sight of my sons standing around him *like a plantation of olives trees*' (*tamquam plantation oliveti*) – reflecting Ps. 128:3: 'Your children will be *like olive shoots* (כשתלי זיתים)'. In her grief, Hannah begins praying to the LORD, only to stop, for fear that 'Penninah will then be even more eager to taunt me as she does daily when she says, "Where is your God in whom you trust?"' (*LAB* 50:5: *et erit ut plus me zelans improperet mihi Fenenna sicut quotidie dicit: Ubi est Deus tuus in quo confides?*). The image of one who 'taunts' (*impropero*) 'daily' (*quotidie*) saying 'Where is your God?' (*Ubi est Deus tuus*) comes directly from Ps. 42:3: 'While people say to me continually (*lit.* all-day), "Where is your God?" (באמר אלי כל־היום איה אלהיך).[223]

As the hymnist of 1QH 16:23 and Hannah in *LAB* 50:5 use Psalm 42 to describe their own suffering, the Markan Jesus uses the language of Ps. 42:6 to describe his own suffering to the disciples. Jesus then departs to pray alone (Mk 14:35), as he has done before (1:35; 6:46). He utters an anguished prayer (14:36, 40), which is paltry and pathetic when compared to the effusive prayers of the great Jewish heroines on the eve of their respective contests: Esther before Ahasuerus (LXX Est. 14) and Judith before Holofernes (Jdt. 9). Instead, Jesus pleads to be delivered from the fate he earlier said was inevitable (Mk 8:31; 9:12, 31; 10:33-34; 14:21). What accounts for the sudden reluctance on Jesus' part? Interestingly, Matthew and Luke preserve Mk 14:36 in some form (Mt. 26:39, 42; Lk. 22:42). Only John is uncomfortable with the Gethsemane prayer, so Jesus says, 'And what should I say – "Father, save me from this hour"? No, it is for this reason that I have come to this hour' (Jn 12:27; cf. 18:11). On the one hand, Mark or their source may have sought to capture the deep humanity of Jesus' suffering. As his hour of tribulation arrives, Jesus begs for deliverance, all the while entrusting his fate to God, a model for those who would 'endure to the end' (Mk 13:13). At the same time, it may be an attempt to distance Jesus from the lust for martyrdom that so characterized the First Jewish Revolt, after which Mark wrote.[224] For Mark, Jesus' death,

---

223. *LAB* 50:5 provides one of the rare agreements between *LAB* and the Vulgate: cf. Vg. Ps. 42:2: *Ubi est Deus tuus*. In the medieval *Midrash Tehillim*, Ps. 42:3 refers to Elkanah's words to Hannah in 1 Sam. 1:8.

224. The speech of Josephus against suicide (*War* 3.361-382) reflects a distaste for martyrdom following the conflict; contrasted with the speech of Eleazar (*War* 7.358-360). Later Rabbinic literature appears to condemn taking one's own life: *b. B. Kam.* 91b; *b. Avod. Zar.* 18a; *Gen. Rab.* 34:13; *Sem.* 2:1-5. The lust for martyrdom in early Christianity finds its purest expression in Ignatius of Antioch, esp. *Rom.* 1-8.

3. Scripturalized Narrative in the Gospel of Mark 179

though inescapable, was no suicide. He died, not by his own design, but according to God's will.[225] One imagines Mark would have gladly heard the Pauline hymn, 'He humbled himself and became obedient to the point of death – even death on a cross' (Phil. 2:8).[226]

As the scene departs from Gethsemane, the story nevertheless hurtles towards the inevitable – not just Jesus' impending death, but the end of all things. Like the elect in the Olivet discourse, Jesus is 'handed over' (παραδίδωμι) to 'councils' (συνέδρια) and 'governors' (ἡγεμόνες) where he is 'beaten' (δέρω; cf. κολαφίζω/τύπτω). The reader cannot help but see shades of the *eschaton* in Jesus' final hours. The Markan Jesus invites them to make this connection, as he tells the high priest, 'And you will see the Son of Man seated at the right hand of the Power, and coming with the clouds of heaven' (Mk 14:62). With these words, Jesus draws upon unmarked scriptural language from Ps. 110:1 and LXX Dan. 7:13, whilst at the same time recapitulating the final sign of the end of the age in Mk 13:26: 'Then they will see the Son of Man coming in the clouds with great power and glory'. This signals that the rejection of Jesus by the Temple elite will have eschatological consequences: the reader already knows 'not one stone' will be left of the Temple (13:2). The fate of the Temple and its leaders will be sealed at the moment of Jesus' death (15:38). Thus for Mark, the crucifixion of Jesus is as much about the events of 70 CE as those of *c.* 30 CE.[227] The crucifixion of Jesus establishes a direct line to the destruction of the Temple (14:58; 15:29), a nuance the otherwise sharp John was apparently unable to appreciate (Jn 2:21). It is part of Mark's design that sole responsibility for the death of Jesus lies with the defeated (Mk 14:55-65; 15:11-14) and not the victors of the Jewish war (15:2-15). In this way, the Passion Narrative functions as a theodicy. The wrongful execution of Jesus explains, if not rationalizes, the catastrophic losses suffered by the Judaeans, especially the Jerusalem elite, in 66–74 CE. The outcome of the war was seen as proof of the Jewish leaders' guilt,

---

225. Clement of Alexandria likewise distinguishes between seeking martyrdom and heeding the will of God: *Strom.* 4.77; 7.66; see Arthur J. Droge and James D. Tabor, *A Noble Death: Suicide and Martyrdom Among Christians and Jews in Antiquity* (San Francisco, CA: HarperSanFrancisco, 1992), 141–44.

226. On the self-abnegation of Jesus' death in Mark, see Helen K. Bond, 'A Fitting End? Self-Denial and a Slave's Death in Mark's *Life of Jesus*', *NTS* 65 (2019): 425–42.

227. As Paula Fredriksen, 'Jesus and the Temple, Mark and the War', in *SBL 1990 Seminar Papers*, ed. David J. Lull, SBLSP 29 (Atlanta, GA: Scholars Press, 1990), 293–310, esp. 304–7.

180   *Writing with Scripture*

as it was proof of the Roman leaders' innocence (15:6-15, 39). Mark's early readers could not have read the gross miscarriage of justice in Jesus' trial without recalling what befell the leaders of the Temple.[228] The scene tempts readers to draw a causal connection between the events of *c.* 30 CE and 70 CE – which one reader fatefully did, with tragic consequences.[229]

For the duration of the trial, along with Peter's denial and Pilate's sentencing, few narrative details have their origin in the scriptures. The pleonastic repetition of 'false testimony' (Mk 14:56-57: ἐψευδομαρτύρουν) might reflect the Mosaic prohibition against bearing false witness (LXX Exod. 20:17; LXX Deut. 5:16: ψευδομαρτυρήσεις) or the 'false witnesses' who rise up to accuse the Psalmist (Ps. 27:12: עדי־שקר).[230] A scriptural source may also lie behind the awkward detail that Jesus 'was silent and did not answer' (Mk 14:61: ἐσιώπα καὶ οὐκ ἀπεκρίνατο οὐδέν),[231] right before he answers the high priest (14:62) – a scene which recalls LXX Isa. 36:21: 'But they were silent, and no one answered him a word' (καὶ ἐσιώπησαν, καὶ οὐδεὶς ἀπεκρίθη αὐτῷ λόγον).[232] The scene where the high priest 'tore his clothes' (Mk 14:63: διαρρήξας τοὺς χιτῶνας αὐτοῦ) may also reflect the Levitical rule that the high priest 'shall not tear his vestments' (LXX Lev. 21:10: τὰ ἱμάτια οὐ διαρρήξει).[233] But in the final analysis, the

228. The request to release the 'rebel' (στασιαστής) Barabbas foreshadows the popular and institutional support for rebel leaders in the period leading up to the war. The involvement of the chief priests appears especially foreboding in light of the slaughter of the Temple elite by rebel factions (Josephus, *War* 4.197-333).

229. Mt. 27:24-25; see Amy-Jill Levine, *The Misunderstood Jew: The Church and the Scandal of the Jewish Jesus* (San Francisco, CA: HarperSanFrancisco, 2006), 99–102, 168.

230. Cf. the translations of α' (μάρτυρες ψεύδος) and σ' (ψευδομάρτυρες). For the influence of Ps. 27:12, see Gnilka, *Das Evangelium nach Markus*, 2:279–80; Josef Ernst, *Das Evangelium nach Markus*, RNT 2 (Regensburg: Pustet, 1981), 441; Yarbro Collins, *Mark*, 704. Cf. Suhl, *Die Funktion der alttestamentlichen Zitate*, 60; Gundry, *Mark*, 898. For the influence of Exod. 20:17, see O'Brien, *The Use of Scripture in the Markan Passion Narrative*, 133–5. For both, see Pesch, *Das Markusevangelium*, 2:432.

231. Cf. the silence in Mk 15:5.

232. The verbal agreement is slightly closer in D^ea: ουδεν απεκριθη. In favour of the allusion is O'Brien, 'Innocence and Guilt: Apologetic, Martyr Stories, and Allusion in the Markan Trial Narratives', in van Oyen and Shepherd, eds., *The Trial and Death of Jesus*, 219–21; O'Brien, *The Use of Scripture in the Markan Passion Narrative*, 135–8.

233. In favour of the allusion is Marcus, *Mark: 8–16*, 1008; as Davies and Allison note, Mt. 27:65 brings the Markan passage closer to LXX Lev. 21:10 (*Matthew*, 3:533).

3. Scripturalized Narrative in the Gospel of Mark 181

only sure sign of scriptural language in Mk 14:53–15:20 is the unmarked composite citation of Ps. 110:1 and LXX Dan. 7:13 in Jesus' words to the high priest, which signals that the spectre of the end of the age hangs over all that follows. From here on in, the most colourful images drawn from the Jewish scriptures will be reserved for the penultimate episode in the Gospel, the crucifixion of Jesus. The following focuses on the episode from the moment of Jesus' crucifixion to his last breath (Mk 15:21-41). As with the other scripturalized narratives surveyed earlier (Mk 1:12-20; 6:21-28, 35-44; 8:1-9), the episode is modelled primarily on one scriptural passage – though, as will become clear, this is not the only scriptural source for the narrative.

The Song of the Cross: Mark 15:21-41 and Psalm 22

The scene begins with Pilate reluctantly bowing to the will of the chief priests, first by releasing Barabbas (Mk 15:7-11) and then by handing over Jesus to be crucified (15:14-15). But Pilate has the last laugh over the Jewish leaders, putting words in their mouth – 'the man *you* call King of the Jews' (15:12: ὑμῖν τὸν βασιλέα τῶν Ἰουδαίων)[234] – an appellation repeated by the soldiers in their mockery (15:17-18) and in a moment of grim irony, affixed to the cross (15:26). The chief priests and the scribes play along with this farce, not knowing the joke is on them: 'Let the Messiah, the King of Israel, come down from the cross now, so that we may see and believe' (15:32). Throughout the sentencing, the mockery and the crucifixion, up until his final moment, Jesus remains silent. The narrative focuses instead on a series of abuses perpetrated against him, beginning with the flogging and mock coronation (15:15-23).[235] But from the moment of Jesus' crucifixion until his death, one scriptural source comes to the fore: the episode of Jesus on the cross is framed by its use of Psalm 22 (LXX 21).

---

234. Emphasis mine. This time, the irony was not lost on John (19:21-22).

235. The offer of expensive wine and the carrying of Jesus' cross may be a continuation of the royal mockery, see Evans, *Mark 8:27–16:20*, 501; Helen K. Bond, 'Paragon of Discipleship? Simon of Cyrene in the Markan Passion Narrative', in *Matthew and Mark Across Perspectives: Essays in Honour of Stephen C. Barton and William R. Telford*, ed. Kristian A. Bendoraitis and Nijay K. Gupta, LNTS 538 (London: T&T Clark, 2016), 18–35; cf. T. E. Schmidt, 'Mark 15.16-32: The Crucifixion Narrative and the Roman Triumphal Procession', *NTS* 41 (1995): 1–18 (11–12). That the entire Passion Narrative is styled after a Roman Triumph, see Adam Winn, *Reading Mark's Christology Under Caesar: Jesus the Messiah and Roman Imperial Ideology* (Downers Grove, IL; IVP Academic, 2018), 151–62.

182   *Writing with Scripture*

The words of the psalm are enacted by the soldiers (Mk 15:24), the crowds (15:29-32) and, finally, Jesus himself (15:34). This begins with the detail that Jesus' executioners 'divided his clothes among them, casting lots to decide what each should take' (15:24: διαμερίζονται τὰ ἱμάτια αὐτοῦ [ℵ: εαυτου], βάλλοντες κλῆρον ἐπ' αὐτὰ τίς τί ἄρῃ). There is little doubt Mark or their source composed this detail using LXX Ps. 21:19 (MT 22:18): 'They divided my clothes among themselves, and for my clothing they cast lots' (διεμερίσαντο τὰ ἱμάτιά μου ἑαυτοῖς καὶ ἐπὶ τὸν ἱματισμόν μου ἔβαλον κλῆρον). Whilst there may well be a historical basis for the scene – the victims of crucifixion were, by some accounts, stripped naked[236] – Mark's early readers were aware of its scriptural origin. Matthew and Luke omit the superfluous ἐπ' αὐτὰ τίς τί ἄρῃ, absent in the psalm, conforming the scene closer to the LXX.[237] John, who is using a source resembling Mk 15:24, expands the scene, making the scriptural source explicit (Jn 19:23-25). Much like the quotation of LXX Psalm 40 applied to the betrayal scene (Jn 13:18-30; cf. Mk 14:18-20), John introduces a verbatim quotation from LXX Ps. 21:19 with a fulfilment formula following the scene.[238]

Returning to Mark, language from the same psalm appears again in the very next scene. Having noted the time, the inscription and those crucified with Jesus, it reads, 'Those who passed by derided him, shaking their heads and saying, "save yourself, and come down from the cross!"' (Mk 15:29-30: καὶ οἱ παραπορευόμενοι ἐβλασφήμουν αὐτὸν κινοῦντες τὰς κεφαλὰς αὐτῶν καὶ λέγοντες … σῶσον σεαυτὸν καταβὰς ἀπὸ τοῦ στραυροῦ). This taunt is then echoed by the chief priests and the scribes: 'He saved others; he cannot save himself' (15:31: ἄλλους ἔσωσεν, ἑαυτὸν οὐ δύναται σῶσαι). The image of Jesus' hecklers 'shaking their heads' (κινοῦντες τὰς

---

236. Dionysius of Halicarnassus, *Ant. rom.* 7.29.2; Josephus, *Ant.* 19.270; Artemidorus Daldianus, *Onir.* 2.61.

237. Mt. 27:35: διεμερίσαντο τὰ ἱμάτια αὐτοῦ βάλλοντες κλῆρον; Lk. 23:24: διαμεριζόμενοι δὲ τὰ ἱμάτια αὐτοῦ ἔβαλον κλήρους.

238. The decision not to 'tear' (σχίζω) the 'seamless tunic' (χιτὼν ἄραφος) may also reflect the prohibition against tearing the clothes of the high priest (Lev. 21:10), contrasted with the high priest who tears his own clothes in Mk 14:63; see Helen K. Bond, 'Discarding the Seamless Robe: The High Priesthood of Jesus in John's Gospel', in *Israel's God and Rebecca's Children: Christology and Community in Early Judaism and Christianity: Essays in Honor of Larry W. Hurtado and Alan F. Segal*, ed. David B. Capes, April D. DeConick, Helen K. Bond and Troy A. Miller (Waco, TX: Baylor University Press, 2007), 183–94. Elsewhere, John presents Jesus as a priestly figure, see John Paul Heil, 'Jesus as the Unique High Priest in the Gospel of John', *CBQ* 57 (1995): 729–45.

κεφαλὰς) and saying 'save yourself' (σῶσον σεαυτὸν) reflects the language of LXX Ps. 21:8-9: 'All who saw me mocked at me; they talked with the lips; *they moved the head* (ἐκίνησαν κεφαλήν): "He hoped in the Lord; let him rescue him; *let him save him* (σωσάτω αὐτόν), because he wanted him"'. This time, only Matthew is aware of the scriptural source, putting more words of the psalm into the mouths of the hecklers: 'He trusts in God; let God deliver him, if he wants to' (Mt. 27:43: πέποιθεν ἐπὶ τὸν θεόν, ῥυσάσθω νῦν εἰ θέλει αὐτόν) – which loosely follows LXX Ps. 21:9 (ἤλπισεν ἐπὶ κύριον, ῥυσάσθω αὐτόν...ὅτι θέλει αὐτόν). The scene of mockery in Mk 15:29-32 also recalls the words of the wicked in the Wisdom of Solomon, who taunt the righteous one: 'He professes to have knowledge of God and calls himself a child of the Lord... Let us see if his words are true, and let us test what will happen at the end of his life; for if the righteous man is God's child, he will help him, and will deliver him from the hand of his adversaries... Let us condemn him to a shameful death, for, according to what he says, he will be protected' (Wis. 2:13, 17-18, 20).[239] The scene in Wisdom may itself rely on the language of Psalm 22.[240] There is no sign, however, the division of clothes (Ps. 22:18) or the mocking gestures (22:7-8) were used in other narrative descriptions in Jewish antiquity,[241] with the possible exception of the two mute men healed by R. Judah in *b. Ḥag..* 3a, who would 'shake their heads, and move their lips' (ומניידי ברישייהו ומרחשין שפוותייהו). The case is somewhat different regarding the final image from Psalm 22 in Mk 15:21-39.

After the sun is darkened, Jesus cries out with a loud voice, 'Eloi, Eloi lema sabachthani' (ελωι ελωι λεμα σαβαχθανι), his first and only words on the cross, which the text translates as 'My God, my God, why have you forsaken me?' (15:34: ὁ θεός μου ὁ θεός μου, εἰς τί ἐγκατέλιπές με;). The second part clearly reflects the opening line of the psalm in Greek – 'My God, my God, [attend to me;] why did you forsake me?' (LXX Ps. 21:2: ὁ θεὸς ὁ θεός μου, [πρόσχες μοι·] ἵνα τί ἐγκατέλιπές με;) – whereas the first part appears to be a transliteration of the psalm in Aramaic, resembling

239. Maurer, 'Knecht Gottes und Sohn Gottes im Passionsberichte', 26; Stendahl, *The School of St. Matthew*, 140–1; Frederick W. Danker, 'The Demonic Secret in Mark: A Reexamination of the Cry of Dereliction', *ZNW* 61 (1970): 48–69, esp. 57. Cf. Suhl, *Die Funktion der alttestamentlichen Zitate*, 59–60.

240. See Heike Omerzu, 'Die Rezeption von Psalm 22 im Judentum zur Zeit des Zweiten Tempels', in *Psalm 22 und die Passiongeschichten der Evangelien*, ed. Dieter Sänger, BthSt 88 (Neukirchen-Vluyn: Neukirchener, 2007), 33–76.

241. Though the psalm is applied to the division of Esther's clothes and the mocking of Haman's sons in the much later *Midr. Teh.* 22:7, 21, 27.

the later Targum: אלי אלי מטול מה שבקתני (*Tg. Ps.* 22:2).[242] The inclusion of the Aramaic may have been intended to create the misunderstanding of the following verse, the bystanders mistaking Jesus' cry to God (ελωι) as an invocation of Elijah ('Ηλίας). Matthew, apparently recognizing ελωι and 'Ηλίας did not sound alike, amends the transliteration to the more homophonous ηλι ηλι (Mt. 27:46).[243] The inclusion of Elijah again reflects the eschatological character of the crucifixion. Elijah was, of course, the figure most commonly associated with the end of the age (Mal. 4:5 [3:22]; Sir. 48:10). But the (non-)appearance of Elijah also ties the scene to the transfiguration earlier in the Gospel (Mk 9:2-8). The crucifixion is in some sense a reversal of the transfiguration: Jesus appears, not with the righteous, but the unrighteous; not in dazzling raiment, but naked; not in light, but darkness; not in the glory of the father, but forsaken by God – and this time Elijah is nowhere to be found. If George Boobyer is right, and the transfiguration represents the same scene as Mk 13:26-27, then this would be another instance of the Passion Narrative enacting the Olivet Discourse.[244]

The words of Ps. 22:1, appearing as they do on the lips of Jesus, continue the theme of suffering evoked by the other material from the psalm. Here is the Son of Man, alone on a cross, abandoned and bewildered. The scene is one of utter dejection and humiliation. There is no sign Mark or their source envisioned the vindication that the Psalmist experiences at the end of the psalm (22:21b-31).[245] If the author wished to express this, they could have inserted language from the *rettungteil* of the psalm at any point in the narrative.[246] Instead, the narrative draws exclusively from the *klageteil* of Psalm 22, like other texts from the period.[247]

---

242. So Gnilka, *Das Evangelium nach Markus*, 2:322; Marcus, *Mark: 8–16*, 1054–5.

243. Whilst also altering the Greek to better reflect the wording of the LXX (ἱνατί με ἐγκατέλιπες); see Davies and Allison, *Matthew*, 3:629. Luke may have omitted it for the very same reason; so Brown, *Death of the Messiah*, 2:1066–7 n. 95.

244. See George H. Boobyer, *St. Mark and the Transfiguration Story* (Edinburgh: T. & T. Clark, 1942), 29, 119.

245. *Pace* Watts, 'The Psalms in Mark's Gospel', 43–4; Holly Carey, *Jesus' Cry from the Cross: Towards a First-Century Understanding of the Intertextual Relationship between Psalm 22 and the Narrative of Mark's Gospel*, LNTS 398 (London: T&T Clark, 2009), 139–70; Rebekah Eklund, *Jesus Wept: The Significance of Jesus' Laments in the New Testament*, LNTS 515 (London: T&T Clark, 2016), 43–5; Hays, *Echoes of Scripture in the Gospels*, 84–6.

246. So Foster, 'Echoes without Resonance', 101.

247. Omerzu, 'Die Rezeption von Psalm 22', 58.

3. Scripturalized Narrative in the Gospel of Mark

The language of LXX Ps. 21:2 thus gives voice to Jesus' grief in the midst of tribulation. If there is any silver lining, it is in the impending judgment of Jesus' enemies (alluded to in Mk 15:38) – which was in the past for Mark's audience – and the imminence of the eschaton foreshadowed by the darkness at noon (15:33; cf. 13:24-25) – which was yet to come. This image of Jesus, anguished and powerless, appears to have been unacceptable to Luke, who replaces the passivity of Ps. 22:1 with the equanimity of Ps. 31:5: 'Father into your hands I commend my spirit' (Lk. 23:46: πάτερ, εἰς χεῖράς σου παρατίθεμαι τὸ πνεῦμά μου; cf. LXX Ps. 30:6: εἰς χεῖράς σου παραθήσομαι τὸ πνεῦμά μου).[248] But whilst Luke may have found it distasteful, Jesus' cry of dereliction (Mk 15:34; par. Mt. 27:46) is not the only instance where the opening line of Psalm 22 appears in the narrative description of a suffering individual.

Jesus and Esther: The Compositional Use of Psalm 22

The Talmudic tractate *Megillah* provides a midrashic commentary on the narrative of Esther by associating verses from the scroll with others in the Jewish scriptures, often with the formula 'as it is stated' (שנאמר). For example: 'What did Esther see that she invited Haman? R. Eliezer says: She set traps for him, *as is said* (שנאמר) "let their table be a trap for them"' (*b. Meg.* 15b) – thus citing Ps. 69:23. At the same time, the *Megillah* features the *compositional* use of scriptural elements, as in one scene where Esther is shown enacting the words of Psalm 22.[249] Like the Greek versions of Esther, the Gemara has Esther in the throes of despair before she approaches Ahasuerus (*b. Meg.* 15b; cf. Est. 5:1). According to R. Levi, 'When [Esther] reached the idol room, the divine presence left her. She said: "My God, my God, why have you abandoned me?"' (לבית הצלמים נסתלקה הימנה שכינה אמרה אלי אלי למה עזבתני).[250] Esther

---

248. Compare with Jn 19:30.

249. *B. Yom.* 29a likewise associates the psalm with Esther; cf. *Gen. Rab.* 46:7, where the psalm is associated with the *Aqedah*.

250. On the possibility Jewish exegesis of Ps. 22 was formulated in response to the use of the psalm by Christians, see Abraham Jacob Berkovitz, 'Jewish and Christian Exegetical Controversy in Late Antiquity: The Case of Psalm 22 and the Esther Narrative', in *Ancient Readers and their Scriptures: Engaging the Hebrew Bible in Early Judaism and Christianity*, ed. Garrick Allen and John Anthony Dunne, AGAJU 107 (Leiden: Brill, 2018), 222–39. See also the early Byzantine Jewish poem in Aramaic, which associates Jesus and Haman using language from the psalm, in Ophir Münz-Manor, 'Carnivalesque Ambivalence and the Christian Other in Aramaic Poems from Byzantine Palestine', in *Jews in Byzantium: Dialectics of Minority and*

186   *Writing with Scripture*

then speculates as to why God has forsaken her, asking if it was 'because I called [Haman] a dog' (על שקראתיו כלב) – in the words of Ps. 22:21. So instead she 'called him a lion' (וקראתו אריה) – in the words of Ps. 22:22. The later collection of the *Midrash Tehillim* builds on the scripturalized narrative of *b. Meg.* 15b, showing how each line of Psalm 22 applies to the *megillah*.[251] The words of the psalm become, almost in their entirety, the words of Esther, with the opening line (אלי אלי) featuring most prominently (*Midr. Teh.* 22:2, 6, 16, 17). Details from the psalm also become part of the narrative, as the people of the palace plot to divide Esther's clothes: 'And everyone said, "I shall take Esther's apparel", this one saying "Me, I shall take her ornaments"; and that one saying "Me, I shall take her earrings"; and another one saying "Me, I shall take her royal vesture", as is known from Esther's statement: They part my garments among them, and cast lots upon my vesture' (*Midr. Teh.* 22:7; also 22:27).[252]

Evidence that the opening line of the psalm was used in texts contemporaneous to the Gospel is more fragmentary. Although fragments of the psalm survive at Qumran (4Q88 Frg. 1-2; 5/6ḤevPs Frg. 1-2), the opening line is thought to be unattested.[253] The language of Ps. 22:1 could, however, lie behind the unknown psalm (Frg. 79) in the collection of 4Q381: 'my [G]od, do not forsake [me...]' ([...א]להי אל תעזוב[ני...]). A still more intriguing reference may be found in the *Apocryphon of Joseph* (4Q372), in the narrative corresponding to Gen. 37:12-36. When Joseph's brothers sell him to the gentiles, it reads, '[they] consumed his strength and broke *all his bones* (כל עצמיו)', so Joseph '*summoned the powerful God to save him* (וקרא אל אל גבור להושיעו) from their hands. And he said: "*My father and my God, do not abandon me* (אבי ואלהי אל תעזבני) in the hands of

---

Majority Cultures, ed. Guy G. Stroumsa et al. (Leiden: Brill, 2012), 831–45. That the psalm was used polemically in later Jewish conceptions of the Messiah, see Rivka Ulmer, 'Psalm 22 in Pesiqta Rabbati: The Suffering of the Jewish Messiah and Jesus', in *The Jewish Jesus: Revelation, Reflection, Reclamation*, ed. Zev Garber (West Lafayette, IN: Purdue University Press, 2011), 106–28.

251. To such an extent the psalm becomes a prophecy of Esther: 'As soon as David foresaw by the help of the Holy Spirit...blessed be He, David, thinking upon Esther, arranged this Psalm' (*Midr. Teh.* 22:7). See Lerner, 'The Works of Aggadic Midrash and the Esther Midrashim', 152, on difficulties with dating this midrash.

252. Note also the following: '"All they that see me laugh to scorn; they shoot out the lip, they shake the head" refers to Haman's sons who laughed Jews to scorn, shot out their lips at them, and shook their heads at them, saying, "On the morrow these will be slain, or hanged"' (*Midr. Teh.* 22.21).

253. The fragments contain Ps. 22:14-17 and 22:4-21, respectively.

gentiles"' (4Q372 1:15-16).[254] The emphatic address to God concerning 'abandonment' (עזב) could reflect the opening line of the psalm, whilst the detail that 'all his bones' (כל עצמיו) were broken evokes the words of Ps. 22:14: 'And all my bones are out of joint' (והתפרדו כל־עצמותי).[255]

That the rest of the psalm was used elsewhere in Qumran is much more certain. Three times the *Hodayot* adapts the language of Ps. 22:14: 'All [my bones] have fractured, my heart has melted like wax in front of the fire, my knees give way like water which flows down a slope' (1QH 12:33-34); 'The foundations of my building have crumbled, my bones have been disjointed, my entrails heave like a boat in the rage of the storm, my heart pulsates to destruction, a whirlwind swallows me' (1QH 15:4-5); 'My heart pours out like water, my flesh melts like wax, the vitality of my loins has turned into listlessness, my arm is broken at the elbow [with]out my being able to wave my hand' (1QH 16:32-33).[256] Language from the psalm occurs at 1QH 13:31 (cf. 4Q429 4:4), where the hymnist declares, 'My tongue sticks to {my} palate' (ולשוני לח{כי}ך תדבק) – which is close to MT Ps. 22:15b: ולשוני מדבק מלקוחי. The deliverance of the hymnist from the lions, who 'did not open their mouths against me' (1QH 13:10-11: ולא פצו עלי פיהם) appears to reflect the language of Ps. 22:13: 'they open wide their mouths at me, like a ravening and roaring lion' (פצו עלי פיהם אריה טלף ושאג). Indeed, the song of deliverance from the lions in 1QH 13:6-19 may build upon the imagery of Ps. 22:13-21 more broadly, though it also contains a clear allusion to Ps. 58:6: 'You closed the mouth of the lion cubs, whose teeth are like a sword, whose fangs are like a sharpened spear' (1QH 13:9-10; also 13:13-15). The lion imagery of Ps. 22:21 is found again in *Joseph and Aseneth*, a Greek text dating to the same era as the Gospel.[257] In one scene, Aseneth prays for deliverance from the Egyptian – 'From his mouth deliver me, lest he carry me off like a lion' (*Jos. Asen.* 12:11: ἐκ τοῦ στόματος αὐτοῦ ἐξελοῦ

---

254. The invocation of God as father closely resembles Sir. 51:10, 'I cried out, "Lord, you are my Father; do not forsake me in the days of trouble"'. The language of 4Q372 can also be compared to Pss. 27:9; 38:21; 71:9, 18.

255. The exhaustion of Joseph's 'strength' (כח) may also allude to the withering of 'strength' (כחי) in Ps. 22:15.

256. See Omerzu, 'Die Rezeption von Psalm 22', 58–67; Cavicchia Alessandro, *Le sorti e le vesti*, Tesi Gregoriana Serie Teologia 181 (Rome: Editrice Pontifica Università Gregoriana, 2010), 135–52; cf. Elwolde, 'The Hodayot's Use of the Psalter (Book 1)', 93.

257. John J. Collins favours a first-century CE date; see his 'Joseph and Aseneth: Jewish or Christian?', *JSP* 14 (2005): 97–112.

188   *Writing with Scripture*

με, μήποτε ἁρπάσῃ με ὡς λέων) – which reflects the language of LXX Ps. 21:14: ἤνοιξαν ἐπ' ἐμὲ τὸ στόμα αὐτῶν ὡς λέων ὁ ἁρπάζων. The language of the psalm resurfaces later in the prayer, where Aseneth declares, 'And my mouth has become dry as a drum, and my tongue as a horn, and my lips as a potsherd...and my entire strength has left (me)' (*Jos. Asen.* 13:9: καὶ τὸ στόμα μου γέγονε ξηρὸν ὡς τυμπανον καὶ ἡ γλῶσσά μου ὡς κέρας καὶ τὰ χείλη μου ὡς ὄστρακον...καὶ ἡ ἰσχύς μου πᾶσα ἐκέλοιπεν). This builds upon LXX Ps. 21:16: 'My strength was dried up like a potsherd, and my tongue stuck to my throat' (ἐξηράνθη ὡς ὄστρακον ἡ ἰσχύς μου, καὶ ἡ γλῶσσά μου κεκόλληται τῷ λάρρυγί μου).

In each of these examples, unmarked language from Psalm 22 – exclusively from the *klageteil* of the psalm (22:1-21a) – is used to describe the suffering of an individual. Only in the *Hodayot* does the sufferer speak from the standpoint of salvation, referring to the hymnist's past experience of suffering. In the other examples, the language is used to describe a righteous person in the midst of suffering. Multiple images from the psalm are applied to the individuals: for Esther (Ps. 22:1, 21-22 in *b. Meg.* 15b), the hymnist (Ps. 22:13-15 in 1QH *passim*) and Aseneth (LXX Ps. 21:14, 16 in *Jos. Asen.* 12:11; 13:9).[258] Not once does the whole psalm appear to be in view.[259] Nor does the purported Davidic authorship of the psalm play a role in its use. Rather, the psalm appears to have been selected simply because it relates to suffering.

Mark, on the other hand, shows some concern for Davidic authorship elsewhere. In one of the few marked citations in the Gospel, Jesus quotes LXX Ps. 109:1 (MT 110:1) with the formula, 'David himself, by the Holy Spirit, declared' (Mk 12:26: αὐτὸς Δαυὶδ εἶπεν ἐν τῷ πνεύματι τῷ ἁγίῳ). With this citation, the Markan Jesus appears to argue the messiah is really the 'son of God' (υἱὸς θεοῦ) and not the 'son of David' (υἱὸς Δαυιδ).[260] Other allusions to Davidic Psalms further contribute to the identification of Jesus as the 'son of God' (Ps. 2:7 in Mk 1:11; 9:7; Ps. 110:1 in Mk 14:62). This is also reflected in non-Davidic Psalms: when the crowds at the triumphal entry invoke the house of David using the words of the *hallel* (LXX Ps. 117:26 in Mk 11:9-10), the implication could be they have misunderstood Jesus' true identity. Only once outside of the Passion Narrative does Mark use language from the Psalms (Mk 12:10-11) – also

258. To this may be added Ps. 22:1, 14 in 4Q372 1:15-16.

259. Unlike the medieval *Midrash Tehillim*.

260. See Bousset, *Kyrios Christos*, 17; Werner Kelber, *The Kingdom in Mark: A New Place and a New Time* (Philadelphia, PA: Fortress, 1974), 80–1; more recently, Elizabeth Struthers Malbon, *Mark's Jesus: Characterization as Narrative Christology* (Waco, TX: Baylor University Press, 2009), 159–69.

3. Scripturalized Narrative in the Gospel of Mark 189

from the *hallel* (Ps. 118:22) – without referencing Jesus' identity: in the context of the parable of the wicked tenants it refers to the rejection of Jesus by the Temple elite. The Psalmic language of sonship does appear in the Passion Narrative in the direct speech of Jesus to the high priest (Mk 14:62). Though unmarked, the use of the psalm here resembles other *expositional* marked citations in the direct speech of characters (Mk 12:10-11, 36) or those resembling a citation (1:11; 9:7; 11:9). By contrast, the other examples in the Passion Narrative are of a *compositional* nature as they are unmarked and embedded into the narrative itself (LXX Ps. 40:10 in Mk 14:18-20; Ps. 42:6 in Mk 14:34; LXX Ps. 21 in Mk 15:24-34; LXX Ps. 68:22 in Mk 15:36; LXX Ps. 37:12 in Mk 15:40 [also 14:54]). There is no clear sign the *compositional* use of the Psalms in the Passion Narrative is intended to contribute to the identification of Jesus, either as the Davidic messiah,[261] or – Mark's preferred title – 'son of God'.[262] The declaration of the centurion, 'Truly this man was God's son' (Mk 15:39: ἀληθῶς οὗτος ὁ ἄνθρωπος υἱὸς θεοῦ ἦν), is not in response to the Psalmic imagery of the crucifixion, but the events of the foregoing narrative (15:37-38). This particular scene dramatizes the judgment envisioned earlier in the parable of the wicked tenants: 'He will come and destroy the tenants and give the vineyard to others' (12:9). In this case, the tearing of the Temple curtain preludes the coming judgment of the Temple elite whilst the confession of the centurion announces the coming of the age of the gentiles.[263]

In the final analysis, it is the description of suffering that led the author to scripturalize the details of Jesus' crucifixion with LXX Psalm 21 (MT 22).[264] The use of the psalm is of a piece with the Psalmic descriptions

261. *Pace* Frank J. Matera, *The Kingship of Jesus: Composition and Theology in Mark 15*, SBLDS 66 (Atlanta, GA: Scholars Press, 1982), 125–35; Juel, *Messianic Exegesis*, 93–117; Rowe, *God's Kingdom and God's Son*, 295–304; Watts, 'The Psalms in Mark's Gospel', 43–5; Ahearne-Kroll, *The Psalms of Lament in Mark's Passion*, 215–23; Botner, *Jesus Christ as the Son of David in the Gospel of Mark*, 182–8.

262. *Pace* Hays, *Echoes of Scripture in the Gospels*, 83–6.

263. As does the success of the gentile mission (Mk 7–8).

264. One other detail may have recommended the psalm to the author: in the Septuagint it reads, 'They *gouged* (ὤρυξαν) my hands and feet' (LXX Ps. 21:17c). A similar variant occurs in the Hebrew of 5/6ḤevPs 8-9: 'They *pierced* (כארו) my hands and feet' (cf. MT Ps. 22:17: 'like a lion' [כארי]). Whilst this variant could have been easily associated with the ordeal of crucifixion, there is no clear sign the earliest Christians made the association (cf. Zech. 12:10 in Jn 19:34, 37). On issues with the passage, see Kristin M. Swenson, 'Psalm 22:17: Circling around the Problem Again', *JBL* 123 (2004): 637–48.

190   *Writing with Scripture*

of Esther (*b. Meg.* 15b), the hymnist of the *Hodayot* (1QH *passim*) and Aseneth (*Jos. Asen.* 12:11; 13:9). Unmarked language from the psalm has been merged into the narrative description of a suffering righteous person. Much like the scripturalized narratives surveyed earlier in the work, Mark or their source repeatedly draws on one scriptural source during the episode – in this case LXX Psalm 21. But scripturalized narratives often incorporate material beyond their primary scriptural model: for instance, the episode of Abram in the fiery furnace, modelled on Daniel 3, uses the language of Gen. 37:22 to describe Joktan (*LAB* 6:6); the episode of the fiery furnace of Jair, also modelled on Daniel 3, attributes the words of Joshua (Josh. 1:7-8) and Elijah (1 Kgs 18:24) to different characters (*LAB* 38:2); Kenaz's victory over the Amorites, modelled on Judges 7, borrows phrases from 1 Sam. 10:6 and 2 Sam. 23:10 (*LAB* 27:10-11); and the siege of Ephron, modelled on Deut. 2:26-36 (par. Judg. 11:19-21), also uses language from Deut. 20:10-14 (1 Macc. 5:48-51). The episode of Jesus' crucifixion is no exception to this. Beyond the primary model of LXX Psalm 21, isolated details are also drawn from other scriptural sources.

Other Uses of the Jewish Scriptures in Mark 15:21-41

The first of these is the darkness at noon of Mk 15:33: '[and] when it was noon, darkness came over the whole land' (καὶ γενομένης ὥρας ἕκτης σκότος ἐγένετο ἐφ' ὅλην τὴν γῆν). At least since the time of Irenaeus (*Adv. Haer.* 4.33.12), commentators have recognized Amos 8:9 as the source for the image: 'And it will come to pass on that day, says the Lord, and the sun will go down at noon, and the light will become dark upon the earth in daytime' (LXX: καὶ ἔσται ἐν ἐκείνῃ τῇ ἡμέρᾳ, λέγει κύριος ὁ θεός, καὶ δύσεται ὁ ἥλιος μεσημβρίας, καὶ συσκοτάσει ἐπὶ τῆς γῆς ἐν ἡμέρᾳ τὸ φῶς).[265] The 'ninth hour' (ὥρας ἕκτης) establishes the time as midday (μεσημβρία), and whilst Mark has the noun σκότος instead of the verb σκοτάζω, the image of 'darkness...over [the] land' plainly recalls the scene of LXX Amos 8:9.[266] Of the early inheritors of Markan tradition, only the *Gospel of Peter* heightens the agreement with LXX Amos 8:9: '*And it was noon and darkness covered all Judaea* (ἦν δὲ μεημβρία, καὶ σκότος κατέσχε[ν] πᾶσαν τὴν Ἰουδαίαν). And they were troubled and distressed *lest the sun had already set* (μήποτε ὁ ἥλιος ἔδυ) since he was alive. It is written by

---

265. Cf. the translations of σ' and θ' Amos 8:9: καὶ συνεσκότασε τὴν γῆν.
266. The addition of ὅλος is characteristically Markan (1:28, 33, 39; 6:55).

3. Scripturalized Narrative in the Gospel of Mark   191

them, "The sun is not to set on one who has been put to death"' (*Gos. Pet.* 5:15).[267] The inclusion of μεσημβρία and ἥλιος conforms the scene closer to LXX Amos 8:9, whilst the Jews' concern is based on Deut. 21:23: '[the criminal's] corpse must not remain all night upon the tree; you shall bury him that same day'.[268] Whether the *Gospel of Peter* developed this image under the influence of Mark or – as is more likely – Matthew, the fact remains that LXX Amos 8:9 has clearly shaped the Markan narrative at this point.

But has the scene been created in its entirety out of Amos 8:9? Attempts to trace a possible historical origin for this scene invoke far-fetched meteorological phenomena (i.e. black sirocco) or appeal to long-discredited reconstructions of lost sources (i.e. Phlegon, Thallus).[269] Crossan's judgment on the matter is sound, if not a little simplistic: 'that no such *historical* three-hour-long midnight at noon accompanied the death of Jesus, but that learned Christians searching their Scriptures found this ancient description of future divine punishment, maybe facilitated by its mention of "an only son" in the second-to-last line, and so created that *fictional* story about darkness at noon'.[270] Whilst the fantastical nature of the scene can hardly be disputed, it is more than a pure fabrication on the basis of Amos 8:9. The darkness at noon should be compared to the second, and equally fantastical, sign of the crucifixion: the tearing of the Temple curtain (Mk 15:38). This alludes to the prophecy of the Temple's destruction in 13:2, the 'beginning of the birth pangs' (13:8: ἀρχὴ ὠδίνων) which will precede the end. The darkness likewise harkens back to the vision of the end, where it appears in the words of Joel 2:30-31: 'But

---

267. Text and translation taken from Paul Foster, *The Gospel of Peter: Introduction, Critical Edition and Commentary*, TENT 4 (Leiden: Brill, 2010), 308. The addition of ἐπὶ πᾶσαν in Mt. 27:45 may be an attempt to evoke the darkness of Exod. 10:22; see Dale C. Allison Jr., *Studies in Matthew: Interpretation Past and Present* (Grand Rapids, MI: Baker Academic, 2005), 82–3. It is not clear whether the eclipse of Lk. 23:45, 'while the sun's light failed' (τοῦ ἡλίου ἐκλιπόντος), is an attempt to make the scene closer to Amos 8:9, though the variant καὶ ἐσκοτίσθη ὁ ἥλιος (A C³ W Δ Θ Ψ; cf. D) makes the scene closer to Joel 2:30-31 (LXX 2:10).

268. Following Brown, *The Death of the Messiah*, 2:1037; Foster, *The Gospel of Peter*, 313.

269. See the survey in Allison, *Studies in Matthew*, 88–96, for examples in the last century, see 96–7 nn. 67–8.

270. Crossan, *Who Killed Jesus?*, 1–4 (4, emphasis original). Before him was Bultmann, *History of the Synoptic Tradition*, 282, who classified it as one of several 'pure novelistic motifs' in the Passion Narrative.

192   *Writing with Scripture*

in those days, after that suffering, the sun will be darkened' (Mk 13:24: ἀλλ᾽ ἐν ἐκείναις ταῖς ἡμέραις μετὰ τὴν θλῖψιν ἐκείνην ὁ ἥλιος σκοτισθήσε-ται).[271] The darkness at noon and the rending of the veil, along with the command to be awake (14:37-41; cf. 13:33-37), the betrayal (14:43-46; cf. 13:12), the testimony before council (14:53-65; cf. 13:9) and governor (15:1-5; cf. 13:9), present the crucifixion as a cosmic, eschatological event. For Mark and their readers, it signals the beginning of the end. Matthew is acutely aware of this, adding still more fantastical elements to the eschatological drama of the crucifixion: an earthquake (Mt. 27:51; cf. Mk 13:8) and a mass resurrection (Mt. 27:52-53; cf. Mk 13:27). Against this it may be argued that cosmic darkness was thought to accompany non-eschatological events, such as the deaths of great men, mythical (i.e. Romulus) and historical (i.e. Julius Caesar).[272] Cosmic darkness may also be found in Jewish literature accompanying the deaths of Adam (*LAE* 46:1; *T. Adam* 3:6) and Enoch (*2 En.* 67:1-2). Rabbinic literature associates the darkness of Amos 8:9 with the death of R. Pedat: 'When R. Pedat's soul came to rest, R. Isaac b. Eleazar commenced with these words: "This day is as hard for Israel as the day on which the sun set at noon, as it is written, 'And it shall come to pass in that day...that I will cause the sun to set at noon and darken the earth on a clear day'"' (*b. Moed. Kat.* 25b). But given the close relationship between the Olivet Discourse and the events of Mark 14–15, an eschatological context featuring the language of LXX Amos 8:9 seems most appropriate for the darkness at noon in Mk 15:33.

The use of eschatological imagery in the crucifixion continues with the invocation of Elijah following Jesus' cry of dereliction. Having misheard the Aramaic 'God' (ελωι) as 'Elijah' (Ἡλίας), the bystanders assume Jesus is calling Elijah, with one running to offer Jesus something to drink, saying, 'Wait, let us see whether Elijah will come to take him down' (Mk 15:36: ἄφετε ἴδωμεν εἰ ἔρχεται Ἡλίας καθελεῖν αὐτόν). Later literature speaks of Elijah's ability to intervene to save the righteous (*b. Avod. Zar.* 17b; 18b; *b. Taan.* 21a; *b. Sanh.* 109a; *PRE* 50:10). Whilst the bystanders appear to imagine a similar role for Elijah here, it might also reflect

---

271. Later exegetes also applied images from Joel 2 to the crucifixion, see Allison, *Studies in Matthew*, 87 n. 36.

272. Romulus: Cicero, *Rep.* 2.10; 6.21-22; Dionysius Halicarnassus, *Ant. rom.* 2.56; Livy, *Hist.* 1.16; Ovid, *Fast.* 485-498; Plutarch, *Rom.* 27; Florus, *Epit.* 1.1; Julius Caesar: Virgil, *Georg.* 1.466-467; Pliny, *Nat.* 2.30; Josephus, *Ant.* 14.309; Plutarch, *Caes.* 69; also Augustus: Dio Cassius, *Hist.* 56.29.3; see the other examples in Allison, *Studies in Matthew*, 95–6 n. 63.

3. *Scripturalized Narrative in the Gospel of Mark*   193

Mark's peculiar eschatology, set forth in the Olivet Discourse.[273] We have noted the language of the Olivet Discourse is re-purposed in the Passion Narrative. There is also an overlooked parallel in the Transfiguration (Mk 9:2-8). As Mk 13:26-27 speaks of the 'Son of Man' (υἱὸς τοῦ ἀνθρώπου) appearing with 'clouds' (νεφέλαι) with the 'angels' (ἄγγελοι), so the Transfiguration features the 'Son' (υἱὸς) appearing in a 'cloud' (νεφέλη) with 'Elijah with Moses' (Ἠλίας σὺν Μωϋσεῖ). In the preceding passage, Jesus speaks of the 'Son of Man' coming 'in the glory of his Father with the holy angels' (8:38: ἐν τῇ δόξῃ τοῦ πατρὸς αὐτοῦ μετὰ τῶν ἀγγέλων τῶν ἁγίων). It could be that the Transfiguration provides Jesus' inner-circle – and thereby readers – with a glimpse of the eschatological scene alluded to in Mk 8:38, 13:26-27 and 14:62. One may then wonder if the 'angels' (ἄγγελοι) of the *parousia* are not also Elijah and Moses.[274] Both prophets were expected to return in the last days,[275] and are sometimes referred to as 'angels' (ἄγγελος/מלאך).[276] It could even be the image of Jesus crucified

---

273. Cf. Öhler, *Elia im Neuen Testament*, 150–2, who thinks the purpose is to counter the popular expectation of Elijah (6:14-16; 8:28); Mark F. Whitters, 'Why Did the Bystanders Think Jesus Called Upon Elijah Before He Died (Mark 15:34-36)? The Markan Position', *HTR* 95 (2002): 119–24, who thinks the scene is included to show Jesus should not be identified with Elijah.

274. Cf. Christine E. Joynes, 'The Returned Elijah? John the Baptist's Angelic Identity in the Gospel of Mark', *SJT* 58 (2005): 455–67, who argues Elijah is identified as an angel in the person of John the Baptist.

275. Elijah: Mal. 4:5; Sir. 48:10; 4Q521 2:3?; 4Q588 1:2?; *Sib. Or.* 2:187-189, 194-202; *Apoc. El.* 4:7; 5:32; Justin, *Dial.* 8:4; 49:1; *m. Eduy.* 8:7; *m. Sot.* 9:15; *b. Erub.* 43a-b; Moses: *Liv. Pro.* 2:12-19; *Frg. Tg.* on Exod. 12:42; *Frg. Tg.* (P) on Deut. 33:21; *Sib. Or.* 5.256-257; *Mem. Mar.* 2:8; both: Mal. 4:4-6?; *LAB* 48:1?; Rev. 11:3-13; *4 Ezra* 6:26?; *Sib. Or.* 2.245-248; *Deut. Rab.* 3:17; *Sifre* to Deut. 342.

276. Elijah: Mal. 3:1; *b. Ber.* 4b; *Judg. Rab.* 16:1; *PRE* 29:18; Origen, *Comm. Jo.* 2.31; *Comm. Matt.* 10.20; Moses: Sir. 45:2?; *T. Mos.* 1:14; *Mem. Mar.* 2:12; 4:3, 6, 12; 5:3; 6:3. On the angelic identity of Elijah in Rabbinic literature, see Kristen H. Lindbeck, *Elijah and the Rabbis: Story and Theology* (New York, NY: Columbia University Press, 2010), 44–62. On the angelic identity of Moses in Jewish and Samaritan literature, see Jarl E. Fossum, *The Name of God and the Angel of the Lord: Samaritan and Jewish Concepts of Intermediation and the Origins of Gnosticism*, WUNT 36 (Tübingen: Mohr Siebeck, 1985), 130–5, 141; Ruth M. M. Tuschling, *Angels and Orthodoxy: A Study in Their Development in Syria and Palestine from the Qumran Texts to Ephrem the Syrian*, STAC 40 (Tübingen: Mohr Siebeck, 2007), 91–2. Cf. the possibility Moses was identified as an angel at Qumran is explored and rejected in Phoebe Makiello, 'Was Moses Considered to be an Angel by Those at Qumran?', in *Moses in Biblical and Extra-Biblical Traditions*, ed. Axel Graupner and Michael Wolter, BZAW 372 (Berlin: W. de Gruyter, 2007), 115–27.

194 *Writing with Scripture*

between two criminals is an anti-type of the Transfiguration/parousia, where Jesus appears with the angels Elijah and Moses.[277] At the very least, the invocation of Elijah, the figure most commonly associated with the end-time in contemporary thought, once more evokes the *eschaton* in Jesus' final moments.

But the detail that Jesus was offered 'sour wine' (ὄξους) 'to drink' (ἐπότιζεν) is a continuation of the Psalmic imagery found elsewhere in the crucifixion. It comes from LXX Ps. 68:22 (MT 69:21): 'And they gave gall as my food, and for my thirst they gave me vinegar to drink' (καὶ ἔδωκραν εἰς τὸ βρῶμά μου χολὴν καὶ εἰς τὴν δίψαν μου ἐπότισάν με ὄξος). This is the second time Jesus has been offered something to drink during the crucifixion. The first is in Mk 15:23: 'And they offered him wine mixed with myrrh; but he did not take it' (καὶ ἐδίδουν αὐτῷ ἐσμυρνισμένον οἶνον). Jesus' refusal to drink no doubt reflects 14:25: 'Truly I tell you, I will never again drink of the fruit of the vine until that day when I drink it new in the kingdom of God'. The offer of wine mixed with myrrh, which may have been a delicacy (cf. Pliny, *Hist. nat.* 14.15), could also be a continuation of the mockery of Mk 15:16-20 (cf. Lk. 23:36), or even a sedative to lessen the pain of execution (cf. *b. Avod. Zar.* 38b; *b. Sanh.* 43a).[278] By contrast, the offer of sour wine in Mk 15:36 is presumably meant to prolong Jesus' life so the bystanders can witness the coming of Elijah, apparently to no avail (15:37). Only Matthew follows Mark in having two offerings of wine. There, the first offering is also fashioned after LXX Ps. 68:22, as Jesus is given 'wine mixed with gall' (Mt. 27:34: οἶνον μετὰ χολῆς).[279] In Lk. 23:36, the offer of 'sour wine' (ὄξος) becomes part of the soldiers' mockery, whereas John conforms the scene even closer to LXX Ps. 68:22: 'He said (in order to fulfill the scripture), "I am thirsty". A jar full of sour wine was standing there. So they put a sponge full of the wine on a branch of hyssop and held it to his mouth' (Jn 19:28-29). The image of Ps. 69:21 is again found in the *Hodayot*, as the enemies of the hymnist are said to have 'denied the drink of knowledge to the thirsty, *but for their thirst they have given them vinegar to drink*' (1QH 12:11: ולצמאם ישקום חומץ). The verse also appears in *b. Ḥul.* 87a, where R. Yehuda HaNasi cites Ps. 69:21 in exasperation at the prospect of

---

277. Cf. Mk 10:40; explored in Vette, 'Who is Elijah in the Gospel of Mark?', 809–10.

278. Cf. LXX Prov. 31:6-7; see the relevant sources in Yarbro Collins, *Mark*, 740–4, 756–8.

279. Jesus becomes the speaker of Ps. 69:10 in Rom. 15:3. On this and other similarities between Paul and the Markan Passion Narrative, see Allison, *Constructing Jesus*, 407–11.

3. Scripturalized Narrative in the Gospel of Mark 195

having to dine with a heretic. In Mk 15:36, however, the language of the psalm is unmarked and embedded into the narrative. Once more, the offer of 'sour wine' (ὄξος) to Jesus appears to have been created on the basis of LXX Ps. 68:21.[280]

The final instance of Psalmic imagery, however, may reflect something of historical tradition. The detail that certain women were looking on 'from a distance' (Mk 15:40: ἀπὸ μακρόθεν) recalls LXX Ps. 37:12 (MT 38:11): 'My friends and my fellows approached opposite me and stood, and my next of kin *stood far off* (ἀπὸ μαρκόθεν ἔστησαν)'. The phrase can also be found in Mk 14:54, where Peter follows Jesus 'at a distance' (ἀπὸ μαρκόθεν) to the courtyard of the high priest. Whilst ἀπὸ μαρκόθεν appears elsewhere in the Gospel in different contexts (5:6; 8:3; 11:13), given the similar use of Psalmic imagery elsewhere in the Passion Narrative, the image of Jesus' companions standing 'far off' from his affliction (14:54; 15:40) likely owes to LXX Psalm 37. Luke, apparently aware of this, makes the scene closer to the psalm: 'But all his acquaintances, including the women who had followed him from Galilee, *stood at a distance* (εἰστήκεισαν...ἀπὸ μαρκόθεν)' (Lk. 23:49). Elsewhere, the wording of LXX Ps. 37:12 appears to lie behind Rev. 18:9-19, where the kings, merchants, shipmasters, seafarers and sailors 'stood far off' (18:17: ἀπὸ μαρκόθεν ἔστησαν) from the suffering of Babylon.[281]

Unlike the darkness at noon and the offer of sour wine, however, the detail in Mk 14:50 is unlikely to have been created entirely out of scriptural language. The conspicuous naming of the women – 'Mary Magdalene, and Mary the mother of James the young and of Joses, and Salome' – mentioned here for the first time, can hardly be chalked up to the influence of LXX Psalm 37. They may be compared to the individual who carries Jesus' cross, who the text names 'Simon of Cyrene, the father of Alexander and Rufus' (Mk 15:21) – a detail which presumably identified him to earliest readers.[282] Two of the women are said to witness the burial of Jesus (15:47) and all three are present in the closing scene at the empty tomb (16:1-8). Whilst the writers of Jewish antiquity were

---

280. The absence of scriptural language favours the priority of Mk 15:23 over 15:36, so Gundry, *Mark*, 956; cf. John Dominic Crossan, *Four Other Gospels: Shadows on the Contours of Canon* (Minneapolis, MN: Winston, 1985), 138–9.

281. Also Rev. 18:10, 15. An allusion to Ps. 38:11 is uncertain in 1QH 6:20-21: 'to the deg[ree...I lov]e him, and to the extent that you place him *far off* (וברחקך), I hate him'.

282. So Lane, *Mark*, 563; Gerd Theissen, *Lokalkolorit und Zeitgeschichte in den Evangelien. Ein Beitrag zur Theorie der synoptischen Tradition*, NTOA 8 (Göttingen: Vandenhoeck & Ruprecht, 1992), 188.

more than capable of fabricating names for the sake of narrative – the bizarre names of the seven in the furnace of Jair spring to mind (*LAB* 38:1: 'Defal, Abiesdrel, Getaliabl, Selumi, Assur, Ionadali, Memihel') – the relation of the women to other named figures, James the Younger and Joses, suggests the names belong to tradition. But why would Mark or their source introduce new characters at such a late point in the narrative? The naïve view that the named women owe to historical memory has some points in its favour.[283] At the same time, their inclusion may owe to the sensitive nature of Mk 15:42–16:8. The author appears to have been aware the tradition was not widely known.[284] The fact that in 16:8 the women fail to tell the disciples what they had just witnessed implies their testimony differed from that commonly associated with 'the twelve' (i.e. 1 Cor. 15:3-8). If Mark or their source was the first to offer a detailed description of the burial and empty tomb of Jesus, named witnesses might be expected (*à la* 1 Cor. 15:5-8). Whether the named women were early on associated with an empty tomb tradition, or whether their presence was inferred by some other factor,[285] Mk 16:8 implies they provided an alternative testimony for the Markan community equivalent to the testimony of 'the twelve' in other communities (16:7). An analogy to this may be found in the unique disciples of John's Gospel (Jn 1:35-51; 21:2), who represent the true belief of the Johannine community in the narrative, often in contrast to Peter – and by extension the communities he represented.[286] But whatever the origin of the names in Mk 15:40, the fleeting detail from LXX Ps. 37:12 (ἀπὸ μαρκόθεν) plays second fiddle to the role of pre-existing tradition, so that, in the words of Goodacre, 'Tradition was scripturalized'.[287]

283. See Allison, *Constructing Jesus*, 389–91.

284. Mk 16:8: 'And they said nothing to anyone'. So Michael D. Goulder, 'Jesus' Resurrection and Christian Origins: A Response to N. T. Wright', *JSHJ* 3 (2005): 187–95 (192); James D. Crossley, 'Against the Historical Plausibility of the Empty Tomb Story and the Bodily Resurrection of Jesus: A Response to N. T. Wright', *JSHJ* 3 (2005): 171–86 (176 [n. 22], 184–5); cf. D. C. Allison Jr., 'Explaining the Resurrection: Conflicting Convictions', *JSHJ* 3 (2005): 117–33 (127–30).

285. Perhaps their presence at the tomb was inferred solely from the detail that they were known to have accompanied Jesus in Jerusalem at the time of his death. Though some take the simplicity of Mk 15:42–16:8 as a sign of authenticity, the narrative anticipates several objections, so is not free of apologetics.

286. So Raymond E. Brown, *The Community of the Beloved Disciple* (London: Chapman, 1979), 81–8.

287. Goodacre, 'Prophecy Historicized or Tradition Scriptuarlized?', 45.

3. Scripturalized Narrative in the Gospel of Mark 197

Mk 15:21-41	Psalm 22 (Pss. 38; 69; Amos 8)
Jesus' executioners 'divided his clothes among them' by 'casting lots' (15:24).	The Psalmist's enemies 'divided [his] clothes among themselves' and 'for [his] clothing they cast lots' (LXX Ps. 21:19).
Those mocking Jesus were 'shaking their heads' and saying 'save yourself' (15:29-30).	Those mocking the Psalmist 'shake their heads' and say 'let him save him' (LXX Ps. 21:8-9).
'Darkness' covers the 'earth' at noon (15:33).	The sun goes down at noon and 'darkens' over the 'earth' (LXX Amos 8:9).
Jesus cries, 'My God, my God, why have you forsaken me?' (15:34).	The Psalmist cries, 'My God, my God, why have you forsaken me?' (LXX Ps. 21:1; cf. MT 22:1).
Jesus is given 'sour wine' to drink (15:36).	The Psalmist is given 'sour wine' to drink (LXX Ps. 68:22).
Jesus' female followers look on 'at a distance' (15:40; cf. Peter in 14:45).	The Psalmist's friends and kin stand 'at a distance' (LXX Ps. 37:12).

Summary

The episodes surveyed in this chapter have drawn on the Jewish scriptures in a variety of ways. In Jesus' forty-day sojourn in the wilderness and the call of the first disciples (Mk 1:12-20), the episode roughly follows the forty-day sojourn of Elijah in the wilderness and the call of Elisha (1 Kgs 19), seen in distinctive narrative details – the forty-day sojourn; the ministry of angels; the disciple[s] at work; taking leave of father and trade – and minor verbal agreement: 'in the wilderness'; 'forty days'. The two feedings of the multitude (Mk 6:35-44; 8:1-9) are modelled on the miracle of Elisha (2 Kgs 4:42-44), loosely following the structure of that episode and incorporating memorable details – the small amount of loaves; the command to feed the people; the doubting disciple[s]; the feeding of many people; some food left over – though featuring no verbal agreement. The execution of John the Baptist (Mk 6:21-28), on the other hand, features language borrowed directly from a Greek text of Esther, including the verbatim promise of 'up to half of my kingdom' (ἕως ἡμίσους τῆς βασιλείας μου). The episode itself is modelled on Esther's banquet (Est. 7:1-10) along with traditional material. The crucifixion of Jesus (Mk 15:21-41), however, differs from the previous examples, as it does not draw on a narrative text but on imagery from the Psalms, primarily Psalm 22 (LXX 21:1, 8-9, 19) – but also LXX Pss. 37:12, 68:22 and Amos 8:9.

198   *Writing with Scripture*

In this episode, verbatim phrases and details are taken from the scriptural source and woven seamlessly into the narrative description of Jesus' final moments.

A similar variety of compositional approaches can be seen in the other scripturalized narratives. Some feature extensive (Deut. 2:26-36; 20:10-14 and Judg. 11:19 in 1 Macc. 5:45-51; LXX Job 1–2 in *T. Ab.* 1–4; 15:14-15) or fragmentary (Judg. 7:6-22 in *LAB* 27; Gen. 13:17 and 15:1 in 1QapGen 11) verbal agreement with their scriptural models, whilst others feature little (Dan. 3 in *LAB* 6; Judg. 4–5 in Jdt. 10–13) to no (Dan. 3 in *LAB* 38) verbal similarities. For the most part, these episodes rely on narrative texts as their model – i.e. Genesis, Judges, Daniel – though they occasionally rely on non-narrative texts (i.e. Deut. 20:10-14 in 1 Macc. 5:45-51). Some episodes follow the structure of their scriptural model (Dan. 3 in *LAB* 6; 38; Judg. 7 in *LAB* 27; Deut. 2:26-36 in 1 Macc. 5:45-51; Judg. 4–5 in Jdt. 10–13), whereas others simply insert narrative details or phrases into a pre-existing story (Gen. 13:7; 15:1 and 26:24 in 1QapGen 11; LXX Job 1–2 in *T. Ab.* 1–4; 15:14-15).

Mark, like these works, sometimes used scriptural elements to compose new narrative. At times this was done with a *whole episode modelled on a scriptural story* (1 Kgs 19 in Mk 1:12-20; 2 Kgs 2:42-44 in Mk 6:35-44; 8:1-9; Est. 7:1-10 in Mk 6:21-28). At other times it was done by *inserting unmarked scriptural details into the body of a traditional narrative* (Est. 5:3 in Mk 6:23; *sic passim* Mk 14–15). In this way, Mark or their source was able to compose scripturalized narratives of Jesus calling his disciples from the wilderness like Elijah, multiplying bread for the multitude like Elisha and enduring great suffering like the Psalmist, with John even meeting his fate like the wicked Haman of Esther. What all this means for the interpretation of the Gospel and its relationship to historical memory will be discussed in the concluding remarks.

4

CONCLUSION

The claim that the scriptural character of early Christian narrative illustrates its non-historical character is one conservative exegetes have been anxious to dismiss and radical exegetes have been eager to embrace. For conservative exegetes, the scriptural language of the Gospel narratives always has its basis in 'fact'. Since the literature of Jewish antiquity was not involved in the 'fabrication of contemporary historical events' on the basis of the scriptures, neither were the Gospels.[1] When events were described in scriptural language, like the Passion Narrative, 'the influence proceeded from the history to the text rather than vice versa'.[2] It was precisely the 'correspondence of prophecy with the facts' that generated interpretation.[3] The early Christians came to tell Jesus' final moments using the language of Psalm 22 because of the 'astonishingly accurate details' concerning his death.[4] Simply by searching the scriptures, the early Christians found an 'unexpected *foreshadowing* of the later story' of Jesus.[5] The early narratives about Jesus thus gained their scriptural character almost by accident. Fictions fabricated on the basis of the scriptures they were not.

1. Moo, *The Old Testament in the Gospel Passion Narratives*, 381 (and 55); also R. T. France, 'Jewish Historiography, Midrash, and the Gospels', in France and Wenham, eds., *Studies in Midrash and Historiography*, 99–127, esp. 120.

2. Moo, *The Old Testament in the Gospel Passion Narratives*, 380; also C. H. Dodd, *History and the Gospel* (London: Nisbet, 1938), 61–3; Schille, 'Das Leiden des Herrn', 164; Lindars, *New Testament Apologetic*, 33–4; Craig A. Evans, 'The Passion of Jesus: History Remembered or Prophecy Historicized?', *BBR* 6 (1996): 159–65, esp. 160–1; Hays, *Echoes of Scripture in the Gospels*, 360.

3. Dodd, *The Apostolic Teaching and Its Developments*, 53; cited approvingly by Moo, *The Old Testament in the Gospel Passion Narratives*, 381.

4. Lindars, *New Testament Apologetic*, 34.

5. Hays, *Reading Backwards*, 94, emphasis original.

Radical exegetes, on the other hand, begin by assuming the non-historical character of the Gospels. On this basis, anything and everything can be seen to have a scriptural origin. At its most extreme: 'Virtually the entirety of the gospel narratives and much of the Acts are wholly the products of haggadic midrash upon previous scripture'.[6] The same has been said for Mark: 'Each pericope in the Gospel has been demonstrated to have possible midrashic sources which could explain its origin without recourse to memories of the church, whether oral or written, going back to historical events'.[7] Few have gone this far, but many have questioned the historical character of Mark 14–15 along similar lines: 'Take the scriptural references away, and the story of death has vanished'.[8]

There is more in common between these positions than either side would like to admit. Both are remarkably confident about the ability of scholarship to uncover the historical details behind the Gospels, in their presence or their absence. Both affirm that the scriptural character of the Gospels has its basis in either 'fact' or 'fabrication' – with conservative exegetes opting for the former, radical exegetes the latter. Whereas conservative exegetes compare the Gospels to historical works – i.e. 1–2 Maccabees; Josephus; Greco-Roman historiography and biography – and conclude that they must have their basis in history not scripture, radical exegetes compare the Gospels to exegetical works – i.e. 'midrash' – and conclude that they must have their basis in scripture not history. Given the choice between 'history remembered' and 'prophecy historicized', the exegete will inevitably choose whichever confirms their presuppositions.

But this is a false choice. The historicity or non-historicity of Gospel material should be a conclusion not a starting point. What applies to one pericope may not apply to another. Though few would doubt the miraculous darkness at noon has been created out of scripture, the scripturalized image of named women looking on 'from a distance' has a better claim to history.[9] The interplay between historical memory and scriptural language

---

6. Price, 'New Testament Narrative as Old Testament Midrash', 1:534–5.

7. Miller and Miller, *The Gospel of Mark as Midrash*, 385.

8. Werner Kelber, *The Oral and the Written Gospel* (Philadelphia, PA: Fortress, 1983), 196; also Helmut Koester, 'Apocryphal and Canonical Gospels', *HTR* 73 (1980): 105–30 (126–8); Mack, *A Myth of Innocence*, 257; Crossan, *Who Killed Jesus?*, 11; *The Birth of Christianity*, 521. This approach can be traced back to Maurer, 'Knecht Gottes und Sohn Gottes', 10.

9. So Goodacre, 'Scripturalization in Mark's Crucifixion Narrative', 40–1; 'Prophecy Historicized or Tradition Scripturalized?', 44–5; Allison, *Constructing Jesus*, 387–9.

4. *Conclusion*   201

may be even more convoluted. Whilst the detail that Jesus' executioners divided his clothes and cast lots for them has indeed been created out of Psalm 22, it may still reflect a kernel of historical truth.[10] This truth may be specific – that Jesus was stripped of his clothes before being crucified – or more general – that the spectacle of crucifixion was a deeply humiliating experience for the victim. Showing a particular detail or episode owes to the scriptures is not the same as showing it does not owe to historical memory, though in some cases that conclusion is inevitable.

We found that scripturalized narratives usually have their basis in some underlying tradition. This is seen most clearly in those episodes which relate to a scriptural figure or episode. At one end, scripturalized narratives can result from a close and profound exegetical engagement with their source: by narrating Gen. 9:1-7 in the language of Genesis 13 and 15, the *Genesis Apocryphon* ties the Abrahamic covenant to the Noachide covenant. At the other end, long and complicated narratives can be triggered by a single word – i.e. the two fiery furnaces of Pseudo-Philo – or simply reflect the similarity of one figure with another – i.e. Abraham with Job in the *Testament of Abraham*. Whilst it is possible for a figure to be pieced together entirely out of scriptural material for no perceptible reason – i.e. Pseudo-Philo's Kenaz and Zebul – this is the exception not the norm. In most cases, the compositional use of scriptural elements in scripturalized narratives has been triggered by some aspect of the source text or tradition.

But where these texts may be compared with their primary sources – the Jewish scriptures – the historiographical narratives of 1 Maccabees, Judith and the Gospel of Mark may not. The precise relation of these texts to historical memory is for the most part unrecoverable. Some provisional comments can nevertheless be made. On the one hand, scholars are relatively confident 1 Maccabees reflects the broad outlines of history, though its function as dynastic propaganda should not be minimized. On the other hand, scholars are equally confident the book of Judith, though presented as historiography, contains almost nothing of history. Where the Gospel of Mark sits in relation to these two works is not immediately clear, especially since the events narrated in the Gospel are often of a supernatural or thaumaturgic character, unlike 1 Maccabees and Judith.

Each of these historiographical works contains episodes that have been modelled on scriptural elements and include unmarked scriptural language embedded into the narrative. In 1 Maccabees, Judas' siege of Ephron is

---

10. A possibility even Dibelius concedes, *Die Formgeschichte*, 188.

modelled on Moses' siege of Amorite territories with other details drawn from the laws of *ḥērem*. It is unlikely the small military force amassed by Judas was capable of waging the scale of warfare described in 1 Macc. 5:45-51 or its corresponding account in 2 Macc. 12:27-28. However, it is plausible that Judas modelled himself on Moses or sought to enact the Deuteronomistic laws; indeed, the author of 1 Maccabees presents Judas as behaving 'according to the law' (κατὰ τὸν νόμον).[11] But that the episode as narrated in 1 Macc. 5:45-51 has been fashioned almost entirely out of scriptural material is certain.

In the book bearing her name, Judith's beheading of the enemy general Holofernes in a tent is modelled on Jael's slaying of the enemy general Sisera in a tent, so that in both accounts victory is won 'by the hand of a woman'.[12] Unlike 1 Maccabees, there is no sign the story of Judith is rooted in historical memory; though there is likewise no reason to suspect it was a self-styled work of fiction. The legendary tale of Judith has nevertheless been presented as historiographical narrative, a pseudo-historical episode that allegedly took place in the post-exilic period. Much of Judith cannot be traced to a scriptural source, but the murder of an enemy general in a tent 'by the hand of a woman' unmistakably comes from Judges 4–5, a fact which was recognized early on by the author of *LAB* 31.

In the Gospel of Mark, Jesus' forty-day sojourn in the wilderness and the call of the first disciples from their work is modelled on Elijah's forty-day sojourn in the wilderness and the call of Elisha from his work. It is possible Jesus patterned his own actions after Elijah, as John the Baptist may have done, and later Rabbis and Christian ascetics certainly did.[13] Jesus appears to have been associated with Elijah at an early stage (Mk 6:15; 8:28) and it is possible the episode originates from this identification.[14] But at the same time, the scripturalized episode could have been triggered by the knowledge of a single detail: the widely known fact that Jesus himself had disciples may have led Mark or their source to the most famous of teacher–disciple relationships: Elijah and Elisha.

---

11. 1 Macc. 3:56; 4:47, 53.

12. Jdt. 9:10; 13:15; 16:5; cf. Judg. 4:9.

13. That John modelled himself on Elijah has been argued most recently by Marcus, *John the Baptist in History and Theology*, 46–61. On the emulation of Elijah in Christian circles, see Frankfurter, *Elijah in Upper Egypt*, 65–74; in Rabbinic literature, see Geza Vermes, 'Ḥanina ben Dosa', *JJS* 23 (1972): 28–50; *JJS* 24 (1973): 51–64.

14. The possibility that Jesus emulated Elijah is explored in Robinson, 'Elijah, John and Jesus', 263–81.

4. *Conclusion* 203

Thus, as Elijah emerged from the wilderness to call Elisha, so did Jesus to his disciples.

The two feedings of the multitude are modelled on Elisha's feeding of the multitude at Gilgal. As the episode pertains to the miraculous, its origins are not easily sought in historical memory. Unlike Elijah, there is no sign Jesus was identified with Elisha at an early stage. The reputation of Jesus as a miracle-worker, however, is well attested (Mk 3:22; 6:14-16) and no scriptural figure is better associated with the miraculous than Elisha.[15] It may have been this association alone that led Mark to compose not one but two scripturalized narratives of Jesus multiplying bread like Elisha.

The episode narrating the banquet of 'king' Antipas, his promise to the pleasing young girl and the execution of John the Baptist is modelled on the banquet in the court of King Ahasuerus, his promise to the pleasing young girl Esther and the execution of Haman the Assyrian. The oath of Ahasuerus of 'even half of my kingdom' appears on the lips of Antipas and the tradition of Vashti's severed head being carried in on a platter now applies to John. The broad historical outlines of the episode are, however, confirmed by the independent account of Josephus (*Ant.* 18.116-119): John was indeed executed by Herod Antipas – though Josephus understands it as a political calculation by the tetrarch. By contrast, the sensational character of the Markan episode owes in large part to its use of Esther. But by using Esther, the author is not drawing an equivalence between Haman and John the Baptist. Rather, the Esther material is mostly incidental to the episode. Although there may be some significance in the depiction of the Herodian court as a Persian – and therefore gentile – banquet, the Esther material was probably selected simply for its ability to narrate a courtly scene, as it is likewise used in 1 Esdras.

The execution of Jesus, like that of John, has been fashioned partly out of scriptural language. The division of clothes and the casting of lots, the shaking heads of the hecklers and the cry of 'My God, my God, why have you forsaken me?' are modelled on the division of clothes and the casting of lots, the shaking heads of the hecklers and the cry of 'My God, my God, why have you forsaken me?' in Psalm 22. Other details in the episode are drawn from elsewhere in the scriptures: the darkness at noon comes from Amos 8, the offer of sour wine to drink comes from Psalm 69 and the image of companions looking on 'from a distance' comes from

---

15. Sir. 48:12-14; *Liv. Pro.* 22; *Mek.* 12:1. The similarities between Jesus and Elisha are explored in Brown, 'Jesus and Elisha'.

Psalm 38. Whilst some have seen the role of Psalm 22 as proof of Jesus' Davidic messiahship or a foreshadowing of his vindication, the psalm appears to be used here as it is elsewhere in Second Temple literature: as a way to describe the suffering of an individual. Whilst the cosmic upheaval of the Amos-inspired darkness at noon has its roots in the eschatological interpretation of the crucifixion by Mark's community, the other psalmic imagery in the narrative simply expands upon the image of suffering initiated by Psalm 22.

If the scriptural language is taken away from the crucifixion, however, the bulk of the narrative remains: the compelling of Simon of Cyrene to carry the cross, the location of Golgotha, the offer of wine mixed with myrrh, the crucifixion itself, the time of the crucifixion, the inscription, the crucifixion of two bandits – though this was later seen to have scriptural significance (Mk 15:28) – the mockery of the chief priests, scribes and bandits, the time of Jesus' death, the non-appearance of Elijah, Jesus' final breath, the tearing of the Temple curtain, the confession of the centurion and the presence of named women from Galilee. Not all of these details can be easily traced back to the historical memory of Jesus' death. The invocation of the Temple's destruction, the tearing of the curtain, the confession of the centurion and even the rejection of Jesus by the chief priests and scribes are perhaps best seen as an attempt to foreshadow the destruction of the Temple and its elite, as well as the victory of the Romans, in the unjust death of Jesus. The other details may well be genuine historical recollections preserved in the earliest kerygma or else speak in some way to the present situation of Mark's community, or both in the case of the named men and women.

The one indispensable presupposition of the narrative is the brute fact of the crucifixion itself. Jesus was crucified by the Roman authorities in Jerusalem. Everything else, including the scriptural language, is framed around this fact. The scriptural origin of some of the details in the crucifixion does not preclude the possibility of a historical origin, except perhaps for the fantastic darkness at noon. It does, however, put the case for non-historicity on more solid ground. The historian may never know whether Jesus' tormentors cast lots for his clothing. But they do know the detail, as it appears in Mk 15:24, was composed out of LXX Ps. 21:19. It could be that if everything incidental was peeled away from the crucifixion narrative, all that would be left is Mk 15:20, 'Then they led him out to crucify him'.

This study had two major findings: that Mark composed and incorporated scripturalized narratives at several crucial moments in their Gospel; and that Mark was not the only author to have done so. The process of

4. *Conclusion* 205

composing new episodes by following a scriptural model or inserting unmarked scriptural elements into a narrative has been observed across diverse works of the Second Temple period. These include works originally composed in Hebrew, Aramaic and Greek, concerning subjects scriptural and historical. Like these works, the Gospel of Mark features episodes that follow a scriptural model with unmarked scriptural language embedded into the narrative. It appears then that scripturalized narrative is a stylistic feature of the Gospel, and of Second Temple literature more generally. When it came to composing their account of Jesus' ministry leading up to his death, scripturalization was one of the tools Mark had at their disposal.[16]

There is more to be said about scripturalization in Jewish antiquity. No doubt there is more to be said about scripturalization in the Gospel of Mark: the echoes of Jonah (esp. Jon. 1:4-16) in the stilling of the storm (Mk 4:35-41), the images from Exodus 24 in the Transfiguration (Mk 9:2-8) and the parallels between Moses' reaction to Eldad and Medad (Num. 11:26-29) and Jesus' reaction to the exorcist (Mk 9:38-41) deserve further consideration. It is clear also Mark's greatest expositor, Matthew, made use of scripturalization, i.e. in the scriptural details embellishing the birth narrative (Mt. 1:18-2:23) and the scripturalized account of Judas' betrayal (26:14-16; 27:3-10). That scripturalization continued in the narratives of early Christian and Rabbinic literature has been observed throughout this study. The Gospel of Mark itself would eventually become the subject of scripturalization: the *Arabic Infancy Gospel* relates an episode where the virgin Mary cast a demon out of a naked woman who lived among the tombs and could not be restrained by chains (*Arab. Gos. Inf.* 14), a legend based on that of the Gerasene demoniac (Mk 5:1-20). This way of composing new literature by following a scriptural model can be traced back to the scripturalized narratives of Jewish antiquity, at least to the Second Temple period and probably earlier.[17] When the first-century CE author of the Passion Narrative set out to compose their account of Jesus'

---

16. This would equally apply to hypothetical pre-Markan sources. Whether or not Mark authored all these traditions, each bears the marks of scripturalization. Differences in the use of scripture are not sufficient to assign the episodes to different authors; Pseudo-Philo, for example, rarely uses scripture in the same way twice. As it is, the simplest explanation is that the scripturalization owes to the Markan author or redactor, but the possibility of scripturalized pre-Markan sources cannot be ruled out.

17. Some examples of 'inner-biblical typology' within the Jewish scriptures identified by Fishbane (*Biblical Interpretation in Ancient Israel*, 350–79) might be classified as scripturalized narrative.

death, they were able to make use of this literary convention. A century later, the Valentinian author of the *Gospel of Truth* could write that Jesus was not crucified naked, but clothed in a book.[18] Mark was no Valentinian, but the image is one they might have used: Jesus lived and died as one clothed in the scriptures.

---

18. *Gos. Truth* 20:24; see Anne Kreps, 'The Passion of the Book: The Gospel of Truth as Valentinian Scriptural Practice', *JECS* 24 (2016): 311–35.

Bibliography

Primary sources

Acta Sanctorum. 68 vols. Antwerp: Société des Bollandistes, 1643–1940.

Aland, Barbara, Kurt Aland, Johannes Karavidopoulos, Carlo M. Martini and Bruce M. Metzger. *Novum Testamentum Graece*. 28th rev. ed. Stuttgart: Deutsche Bibelgesellschaft, 2012.

Alexander, Philip S. *The Targum of Canticles*. ArBib 17A. London: T&T Clark, 2003.

The Ante-Nicene Fathers. Edited by Alexander Roberts and James Donaldson. 10 vols. Buffalo, NY: Christian Literature, 1885–96. Repr. Peabody, MA: Hendrickson, 1994.

The Babylonian Talmud. Edited by Isidore Epstein. 30 vols. London: Soncino, 1960–90.

Bell, David N. *The Life of Shenoute*. CS 73. Kalamazoo, MI: Cistercian, 1983.

Bellman, Simon, and Anathea Portier-Young. 'The Old Latin Book of Esther: An English Translation'. *JSP* 28 (2019): 267–89.

Berman, Samuel A. *Midrash Tanhuma-Yelammedenu: An English Translation of Genesis and Exodus from the Printed Version of Tanhuma-Yelammedenu with an Introduction, Notes, and Indexes*. Hoboken, NJ: Ktav, 1996.

Bidez, J., and L. Parmentier. *The Ecclesiastical History of Evagrius, with the Scholia*. London: Methuen, 1898.

Braude, William G. *The Midrash on Psalms*. YJS 13. New Haven, CT: Yale University Press, 1959.

Braude, William G., and Israel J. Kapstein. *Tanna Debe Eliyyahu: The Lore of the School of Elijah*. Philadelphia, PA: JPS, 1981.

Burkitt, Francis Crawford. *Evangelion da-Mepharreshe: The Curetonian Version of the Four Gospels, with the Readings of the Sinai Palimpsest and the Early Syriac Patristic Evidence*. 2 vols. Cambridge: Cambridge University Press, 1904.

Burton, Philip. *Sulpicius Severus' Vita Martini*. Oxford: Oxford University Press, 2017.

Charlesworth, James H. *The Old Testament Pseudepigrapha*. 2 vols. Garden City, NY: Doubleday, 1983–85.

Chilton, Bruce D. *The Isaiah Targum*. ArBib 11. Edinburgh: T. & T. Clark, 1987.

Clarke, W. K. Lowther. *The Lausiac History of Palladius*. London: SPCK, 1918.

Corpus Scriptorum Ecclesiasticorum Latinorum. Vienna: Geroldi, 1886–.

Danby, Herbert. *The Mishnah: Translated from the Hebrew with Introduction and Brief Explanatory Notes*. Oxford: Oxford University Press, 1933.

Eidelberg, Shlomo. *The Jews and the Crusaders: The Hebrew Chronicles of the First and Second Crusades*. Madison, WI: University of Wisconsin Press, 1977.

Elliott, J. K. *The Apocryphal New Testament: A Collection of Apocryphal Christian Literature in an English Translation based on M. R. James*. Oxford: Clarendon, 1993.

208   *Bibliography*

Field, Frederick. *Origenis Hexaplorum quae supersunt.* 2 vols. Oxford: Clarendon, 1867–75.

Friedlander, Gerald. *Pirke de Rabbi Eliezer.* London, 1916. Repr. New York, NY: Sepher-Hermon, 1981.

Gaster, Moses. *The Chronicles of Jerahmeel.* London, 1899. Repr. 2 vols. New York, NY: Ktav, 1971.

Gibson, Margaret Dunlop. *The Commentaries of Isho'dad of Merv: Bishop of Ḥadatha (c. 850 A.D.): In Syriac and English.* Cambridge: Cambridge University Press, 1911.

Ginzberg, Louis. *Legends of the Jews.* Translated by Henrietta Szold and Paul Radin. 7 vols. Philadelphia, PA: JPS, 1909–38.

Godden, Malcolm, and Susan Irvine. *The Old English Boethius: An Edition of the Old English Versions of Boethius's De Consolatione Philosophiae.* 2 vols. Oxford: Oxford University Press, 2009.

Grau, Angel Fábrega. *Passionario hispánico.* 2 vols. MHS. SL 6. Barcelona: Instituto P. Enrique Florez, 1953.

Greenfield, Jonas C., Michael E. Stone and Esther Eshel. *The Aramaic Levi Document: Edition, Translation, Commentary.* SVTP 19. Leiden: Brill, 2004.

Gregory of Tours. *Glory of the Martyrs.* Translated by Raymond Van Dam. TTH 4. Liverpool: Liverpool University Press, 1988.

Grossfeld, Bernard. *The First Targum to Esther: According to the MS Paris Hebrew Manuscript 110 of the Bibliothèque Nationale.* New York, NY: Sepher-Hermon, 1983.

Haelewyck, Jean-Claude. *Hester.* VL 7/3. Freiburg: Herder, 2003–2008.

Halkin, François. *Euphémie de Chalcédoine.* LB. SHG 41. Brussels: Société des Bollandistes, 1965.

Hanhart, Robert. *Esther.* SVTGAASGE 8/3. Göttingen: Vandenhoeck & Ruprecht, 1966.

Harrington, Daniel J., and A. J. Saldarini. *Targum Jonathan of the Former Prophets.* ArBib 10. Edinburgh: T. & T. Clark, 1987.

Iudith. SVTGAASGE 8/4. Göttingen: Vandenhoeck & Ruprecht, 1979.

Jerome. *Commentaire sur Jonah.* Edited by Yves-Marie Duval. SC 323. Paris: Cerf, 1985.

Jonge, Marinus de. *The Testament of the Twelve Patriarchs: A Critical Edition of the Greek Text.* Leiden: Brill, 1978.

Josephus. Edited and translated by H. St. J. Thackery, Ralph Marcus, Louis H. Feldman and Allen Wilkgren. 10 vols. LCL. Cambridge, MA: Harvard University Press, 1926–65.

Kiraz, G. A. *Comparative Edition of the Syriac Gospels, Aligning the Sinaiticus, Curetonianus, Peshîṭṭâ and Ḥarklean Versions.* 4 vols. NTTS 21. Leiden: Brill, 1996.

Lehrman, S. M. *Midrash Rabbah: Exodus.* London: Soncino Press, 1951.

Leloir, L. *Saint Éphrem: Commentaire de l'Évangile Concordant Texte Syriaque (Manuscrit Chester Beatty 709) Folios Additionnels.* CBM 8. Leuven: Peeters, 1990.

Macdonald, John. *Memar Marqah: The Teaching of Marqah.* BZAW 83. Berlin: Töpelmann, 1963.

Machiela, Daniel A. *The Dead Sea Genesis Apocryphon: A New Text and Translation with Introduction and Special Treatment of Columns 13–17.* STDJ 79. Leiden: Brill, 2009.

Maher, M. J. *Targum Pseudo-Jonathan: Genesis.* ArBib 1B. Edinburgh: T. & T. Clark, 1992.

Martínez, Florentino García, and Eibert J. C. Tigchelaar. *The Dead Sea Scrolls Study Edition.* 2 vols. Leiden: Brill, 1997–98. Rev. ed. 2000.

McNamara, Martin J. *Targum Neofiti 1: Genesis.* ArBib 1A. Edinburgh: T. & T. Clark, 1992.

Bibliography

Mekhilta de-Rabbi Ishmael. Edited by Ḥayyim S. Horovitz and Israel A. Rabin. Jerusalem: Wahrmann, 1970.

Metzger, Bruce M., and Roland E. Murphy. *The New Oxford Annotated Bible with Apocryphal/Deuterocanonical Books: New Revised Standard Version.* Oxford: Oxford University Press, 1991.

Midrash Bereshit Rabbah. Edited by Julius Theodor and Chanoch Albeck. 3 vols. 2nd ed. Jerusalem: Wahrmann, 1965.

Midrash Tanḥuma. Edited by Solomon Buber. 2 vols. New York, NY: Sefer, 1946.

Midrash Tanḥuma. Edited by H. Zundel. Repr. Jerusalem: Lewin-Epstein, 1965.

Midrash Tehillim. Edited by Solomon Buber. Vilna, 1891.

Murray, A. T. *Homer: The Iliad Books 1–12.* LCL 170. Cambridge, MA: Harvard University Press, 1924. Repr. 1998.

Neusner, Jacob. *Genesis Rabbah: The Judaic Commentary on Genesis: A New American Translation.* 3 vols. BJS 104–106. Atlanta, GA: Scholars Press, 1985.

Neusner, Jacob. *The Nicene and Post-Nicene Fathers.* Edited by Philip Schaff. Series 1. 14 vols. Buffalo, NY: Christian Literature, 1886–89. Repr. Peabody, MA: Hendrickson, 1994.

Neusner, Jacob. *Sifre to Deuteronomy: An Analytical Translation.* 2 vols. BJS 98, 101. Atlanta, GA: Scholars Press, 1987.

Neusner, Jacob. *The Talmud of the Land of Israel, a Preliminary Translation and Explanation.* 35 vols. Chicago: University of Chicago Press, 1982.

Neusner, Jacob. *The Tosefta.* 6 vols. New York, NY: Ktav, 1977–86.

Noah, Moredcai Manuel. *Sefer ha-Yashar or The Book of Jasher Referred to in Joshua and Second Samuel.* New York, NY: W. Reid Gould, 1840. Repr. Salt Lake City, UT: J. H. Parry & Co., 1887.

Patrologia cursus completus. Series Graeca. Edited by Jacques-Paul Migne. 166 vols. Paris: Migne, 1857–86.

Patrologia cursus completus. Series Latina. Edited by Jacques-Paul Migne. 221 vols. Paris: Migne, 1844–64.

Pesikta Rabbati. 2 vols. New Haven, CT: Yale University Press, 1968.

Philo. Translated by F. H. Colson, G. H. Whitaker and Ralph Marcus. 10 vols. LCL. Cambridge, MA: Harvard University Press, 1929–62.

Pietersma, Albert, and Benjamin G. Wright. *A New English Translation of the Septuagint.* Oxford: Oxford University Press, 2007.

Pirqe Rabbi 'Eli'ezer. Edited by David Luria. Warsaw: Bomberg, 1852.

'Preface to Judith'. Page 691 in *Biblia Sacra Iuxta Vulgatum Versionem.* Edited by Robert Weber. Stuttgart: Deutsche Bibelgesellschaft, 1969.

Rahlfs, Alfred, and Robert Hanhart. *Septuaginta.* 2nd ed. Stuttgart: Deutsche Bibelgesellschaft, 2006.

Rudolph, Wilhelm, and Karl Elliger. *Biblia Hebraica Stuttgartensia.* 5th ed. Stuttgart: Deutsche Bibelgesellschaft, 1997.

Russell, Normal. *Lives of the Desert Fathers.* CS 34. Kalamazoo, MI: Cistercian, 1980.

Schmidt, Francis. *Le Testament grec d'Abraham: Introduction, edition critique des deux recensions grecques, traduction.* TSAJ 11. Tübingen: Mohr Siebeck, 1986.

Seder 'Eliyahu Rabbah we-Seder 'Eliyahu Zuta. Edited by Meir Friedmann. Vienna: Achiasaf, 1902.

Stec, David M. *The Targum of Psalms.* ArBib 16. London: T&T Clark, 2004.

The Targum of Lamentations. ArBib 17B. Collegeville, MN: Liturgical, 2007.

The Targum Onqelos to the Torah: Genesis. ArBib 6. Edinburgh: T. & T. Clark, 1988.

210

The Targum Sheni to the Book of Esther: A Critical Edition Based on MS. Sassoon 282 with Critical Apparatus. New York, NY: Sepher-Hermon, 1994.

Torrey, Charles Cutler. *Lives of the Prophets: Greek Text and Translation.* SBLMS 1. Philadelphia, PA: Society of Biblical Literature and Exegesis, 1946.

The Two Targums of Esther. ArBib 18. Edinburgh: T. & T. Clark, 1991.

Ulrich, Eugene. *The Biblical Qumran Scrolls: Transcriptions and Textual Variants.* 3 vols. Leiden: Brill, 2013.

Vivian, Tim. *Histories of the Monks of Upper Egypt; and the Life of Onnophrius by Paphnutius.* CS 140. Kalamazoo, MI: Cistercian, 1993.

Voragine, Jacobus de. *Legenda aurea: vulgo historia lombardica dicta; ad optimuorum liborum fidem.* Edited by Theodor Graesse. 3rd ed. Breslau: Gulielmum Koebner, 1890.

Weber, Robert. *Biblia sacra iuxta vulgatam versionem.* 2 vols. Stuttgart: Deutsche Bibelgesellschaft, 1983.

Wilson, Katharina. *Hrotsvit of Gandersheim: A Florilegium of Her Works: Translated with Introduction, Interpretative Essay and Notes.* LMW. New York, NY: Brewer, 1998.

Secondary works

Abel, Félix-Marie, and Jean Starcky. *Les Livres des Maccabées.* Paris: Cerf, 1961.

Ahearne-Kroll, Stephen P. *The Psalms of Lament in Mark's Passion: Jesus' Davidic Suffering.* SNTSMS 142. Cambridge: Cambridge University Press, 2007.

Aland, Barbara, and Kurt Aland. *The Text of the New Testament: An Introduction to the Critical Editions and to the Theory and Practice of Modern Textual Criticism.* Translated by Erroll F. Rhodes. Grand Rapids, MI: Eerdmans, 1987.

Alessandro, Cavicchia. *Le sorti e le vesti.* TGST 181. Rome: Editrice Pontifica Università Gregoriana, 2010.

Alexander, Philip S. 'Midrash and the Gospels'. Pages 1–18 in *Synoptic Studies: The Ampleforth Conferences of 1982 and 1983.* Edited by Christopher M. Tuckett. JSNTSup 7. Sheffield: JSOT Press, 1984.

Alexander, Philip S. 'Notes on the "Imago Mundi" of the Book of Jubilees'. *JJS* 38 (1982): 197–213.

Alexander, Philip S. 'Rabbinic Judaism and the New Testament'. *ZNW* 74 (1983): 237–46.

Allen, David M. 'Introduction: The Study of the Use of the Old Testament in the New'. *JSNT* 38 (2015): 3–16.

Allison Jr., Dale C. 'Behind the Temptations of Jesus: Q 4:1-13 and Mark 1:12-13'. Pages 195–213 in *Authenticating the Activities of Jesus.* Edited by Bruce D. Chilton and Craig A. Evans. Leiden: Brill, 2002.

Allison Jr., Dale C. *Constructing Jesus: Memory, Imagination, and History.* Grand Rapids, MI: Baker Academic, 2010.

Allison Jr., Dale C. 'Elijah Must Come First'. *JBL* 103 (1984): 256–8.

Allison Jr., Dale C. *The End of the Ages Has Come: An Early Interpretation of the Passion and Resurrection of Jesus.* Philadelphia, PA: Fortress, 1985.

Allison Jr., Dale C. 'Explaining the Resurrection: Conflicting Convictions'. *JSHJ* 3 (2005): 117–33.

Allison Jr., Dale C. *The Intertextual Jesus: Scripture in Q.* Harrisburg, PA: Trinity Press International, 2000.

Allison Jr., Dale C. 'Job in the Testament of Abraham'. *JSP* 12 (2001): 131–47.

Bibliography

Allison Jr., Dale C. *The New Moses: A Matthean Typology* (Minneapolis, MN: Fortress, 1993).

Allison Jr., Dale C. 'Psalm 23 (22) in Early Christianity: A Suggestion'. *IBS* 5 (1983): 132–7.

Allison Jr., Dale C. *Studies in Matthew: Interpretation Past and Present.* Grand Rapids, MI: Baker Academic, 2005.

Allison Jr., Dale C. *Testament of Abraham.* CEJL. Berlin: W. de Gruyter, 2003.

Anderson, Hugh. *The Gospel of Mark.* NCB. London: Oliphants, 1976.

Anderson, Hugh. 'The Old Testament in Mark's Gospel'. Pages 280–306 in *The Use of the Old Testament in the New and Other Essays: Studies in Honor of William Franklin Stinespring.* Edited by J. M. Efird. Durham, NC: Duke University Press, 1972.

Attridge, Harold W. 'Giving Voice to Jesus: Use of the Psalms in the New Testament'. Pages 101–12 in *Psalms in Community: Jewish and Christian Textual, Liturgical, and Artistic Traditions.* Edited by Harold W. Attridge and Margot E. Fassler. SymS 25. Atlanta, GA: SBL, 2003.

Aune, David. *Prophecy in Early Christianity and the Ancient Mediterranean World.* Grand Rapids, MI: Eerdmans, 1983.

Aus, Roger D. *Feeding the Five Thousand: Studies in the Judaic Background of Mark 6:30-44 par. and John 6:1-15.* Studies in Judaism. Lanham, MD: University Press of America, 2010.

Aus, Roger D. 'Jesus' Calling the First Four Disciples in Mark 1:16-20 and Judaic Traditions on Elijah's Calling Elisha as his Disciple in 1 Kgs 19:19-21'. Pages 89–135 in *Stilling the Storm: Studies in Early Palestinian Judaic Traditions.* Edited by Roger D. Aus. Binghamton, NY: Global Publications, 2000.

Aus, Roger D. 'The Release of Barabbas (Mark 15:6-15 par. John 18:39-40), and Judaic Traditions in the Book of Esther'. Pages 1–27 in *Barabbas and Esther and Other Studies.* Edited by Roger D. Aus. Atlanta, GA: Scholars Press, 1992.

Aus, Roger D. *Water into Wine and the Beheading of John the Baptist.* BJS 150. Atlanta, GA: Scholars Press, 1988.

Babota, Vasile. *The Institution of the Hasmonean High Priesthood.* JSJSup 165. Leiden: Brill, 2014.

Bakhos, Carol. 'Method(ological) Matters in the Study of Midrash'. Pages 161–88 in *Current Trends in the Study of Midrash.* Edited by Bakhos. JSJSup 106. Leiden: Brill, 2006.

Barthélemy, Dominique. *Critique textuelle de l'Ancien Testament I.* OBO 50/1. Fribourg: Éditions Universitaires – Göttingen: Vandenhoeck & Ruprecht, 1982.

Bartlett, John R. *The First and Second Books of the Maccabees.* Cambridge: Cambridge University Press, 1973.

Batsch, Christophe. *La guerre et les rites de guerre dans le judaïsme du deuxième Temple.* JSJSup 93. Leiden: Brill, 2005.

Bauckham, Richard. 'The Liber Antiquitatum Biblicarum of Pseudo-Philo and the Gospels as "Midrash"'. Pages 33 76 in *Gospel Perspectives: Studies in Midrash and Historiography: Volume III.* Edited by R. T. France and David Wenham. Sheffield: JSOT, 1983.

Beavis, Mary Ann. *Mark.* Paideia. Grand Rapids, MI: Baker Academic, 2011.

Beetham, Christopher. *Echoes of Scripture in the Letter of Paul to the Colossians.* BibInt 96. Leiden: Brill, 2008.

Berkovitz, Abraham Jacob. 'Jewish and Christian Exegetical Controversy in Late Antiquity: The Case of Psalm 22 and the Esther Narrative'. Pages 222–39 in *Ancient Readers and their Scriptures: Engaging the Hebrew Bible in Early Judaism and Christianity*. Edited by Garrick Allen and John Anthony Dunne. AGAJU 107. Leiden: Brill, 2018.

Bernstein, Moshe J. 'The Genesis Apocryphon: Compositional and Interpretive Perspectives'. Pages 157–79 in *A Companion to Biblical Interpretation in Early Judaism*. Edited by Matthias Henze. Grand Rapids, MI: Eerdmans, 2012.

Bernstein, Moshe J. '"Rewritten Bible": A Generic Category Which Has Outlived Its Usefulness?' *Textus* 22 (2005): 169–96.

Berthelot, Katell. 'The Biblical Conquest and the Hasmonean Wars According to 1 and 2 Maccabees'. Pages 45–60 in *The Books of the Maccabees: History, Theology, Ideology: Papers of the Second International Conference on the Deuterocanonical Books, Pápa, Hungary, 9–11 June, 2005*. Edited by Géza G. Xeravits and Jósef Zsengellér. JSJ 118. Leiden: Brill, 2007.

Berthelot, Katell. 'Casting Lots and Distributing Territories: The Hellenistic Background of the Book of Jubilees and the Genesis Apocryphon'. Pages 148–66 in *Sibyls, Scriptures, and Scrolls: John Collins at Seventy*. Edited by Joel Baden, Hindy Najman and Eibert J. C. Tigchelaar. JSJSup 175. Leiden: Brill, 2017.

Best, Ernest. *The Temptation and the Passion: The Markan Soteriology*. 2nd ed. SNTSMS 2. Cambridge: Cambridge University Press, 1990.

Betz, Otto. 'Jesus and Isaiah 53'. Pages 83–7 in *Jesus and the Suffering Servant: Isaiah 53 and Christian Origins*. Edited by William H. Bellinger Jr. and William R. Farmer. Harrisburg, PA: Trinity Press International, 1998.

Bickerman, Elias. *The God of the Maccabees: Studies on the Meaning and Origin of the Maccabean Revolt*. Translated by Hoerst R. Moehring. SJLA 32. Leiden: Brill, 1979.

Bickerman, Elias. 'Notes on the Greek Book of Esther'. *PAAJR* 20 (1950): 101–33.

Blair, H. J. 'Putting One's Hand to the Plough: Luke ix.62 in the Light of 1 Kings xix.19-21'. *ExpTim* 79 (1967–68): 342–3.

Bloch, Renée. 'Écriture et traditions dans le judaïsme – Aperçus sur l'origine du Midrash'. *CS* 8 (1954): 9–34.

Bloch, Renée. 'Note méthodologique pour l'étude de la littérature rabbinique'. *RScR* 43 (1955): 194–227.

Bock, Darell L. 'The Function of Scripture in Mark 15.1-39'. Pages 8–17 in *Biblical Interpretation in Early Christian Gospels: Volume 1: The Gospel of Mark*. Edited by Thomas R. Hatina. SSEJC 16. London: T&T Clark, 2006.

Bock, Darell L. *The Proclamation from Prophecy and Pattern: Lucan Old Testament Christology*. LNTS 12. Sheffield : Sheffield Academic, 1997.

Bond, Helen K. 'Discarding the Seamless Robe: The High Priesthood of Jesus in John's Gospel'. Pages 183–94 in *Israel's God and Rebecca's Children: Christology and Community in Early Judaism and Christianity: Essays in Honor of Larry W. Hurtado and Alan F. Segal*. Edited by David B. Capes, April D. DeConick, Helen K. Bond and Troy A. Miller. Waco, TX: Baylor University Press, 2007.

Bond, Helen K. 'A Fitting End? Self-Denial and a Slave's Death in Mark's *Life of Jesus*'. *NTS* 65 (2019): 425–42.

Bond, Helen K. 'Paragon of Discipleship? Simon of Cyrene in the Markan Passion Narrative'. Pages 18–35 in *Matthew and Mark Across Perspectives: Essays in Honour of Stephen C. Barton and William R. Telford*. Edited by Kristian A. Bendoraitis and Nijay K. Gupta. LNTS 538. London: T&T Clark, 2016.

Bibliography

Boobyer, George H. *St. Mark and the Transfiguration Story*. Edinburgh: T. & T. Clark, 1942.

Borchardt, Francis. *The Torah in 1 Maccabees: A Literary Critical Approach to the Text*. DCLS 19. Berlin: W. de Gruyter, 2014.

Boring, M. Eugene. *Mark A Commentary*. NTL. Louisville, KY: Westminster John Knox, 2006.

Botner, Max. *Jesus Christ as the Son of David in the Gospel of Mark*. SNTSMS 174. Cambridge: Cambridge University Press, 2019.

Bousset, Wilhelm. *Kyrios Christos: Geschichte des Christusglaubens von den Anfängen des Christentums bis Irenaeus*. Göttingen: Vandenhoeck & Ruprecht, 1913. Rev. ed. 1921.

Bowman, John. *The Gospel of Mark: The New Christian Jewish Passover Haggadah*. SPB 8. Leiden: Brill, 1965.

Box, George H. *The Testament of Abraham: Translated from the Greek Text with Introduction and Notes*. London: SPCK, 1927.

Brandt, Wilhelm. *Die Evangelische Geschichte und der Ursprung des Christentums auf Grund einer Kritik der Berichte über das Leiden und die Auferstehung Jesu*. Leipzig: Reisland, 1893.

Brine, Kevin R., Elena Ciletti and Henrike Lähnemann, eds. *The Sword of Judith: Judith Studies Across the Disciplines*. Cambridge: OpenBook Publishers, 2010.

Brockelmann, Carl. *Lexicon Syriacum*. 2nd ed. Halle: Max Niemeyer, 1928.

Brodie, Thomas L. *The Crucial Bridge: the Elijah–Elisha Narrative as an Interpretive Synthesis of Genesis–Kings and a Literary Model for the Gospels*. Collegeville, MN: Liturgical, 2000.

Brown, Raymond E. *The Community of the Beloved Disciple*. London: Chapman, 1979.

Brown, Raymond E. *The Death of the Messiah: A Commentary on the Passion Narratives in the Four Gospels*. 2 vols. ABRL. New York, NY: Doubleday, 1994.

Brown, Raymond E. 'Jesus and Elisha'. *Perspective* 12 (1971): 85–104.

Bruns, J. Edgar. 'Judith or Jael?' *CBQ* 16 (1954): 12–14.

Buchanan, George W. 'The Use of Rabbinic Literature for New Testament Research'. *BTB* 7 (1977): 110–22.

Bultmann, Rudolf. *Geschichte der synoptischen Tradition*. 4th ed. FRLANT 29. Göttingen: Vandenhoeck & Ruprecht, 1961.

Bultmann, Rudolf. *The History of the Synoptic Tradition*. Translated by John Marsh. 2nd ed. Oxford: Blackwell, 1968.

Burge, Stephen R. *Angels in Islam: Jalāl al-Dīn al-Suyūṭī's al-Ḥabā'ik fī akhbār al-malā'ik*. CCME. London: Routledge, 2012.

Buschmann, Gerd. *Das Martyrium des Polykarp: Ubersetzt Und Erklart*. Kommentar zu den Apostolischen Vätern 6. Göttingen: Vandenhoeck & Ruprecht, 1998.

Caneday, Ardel B. 'Mark's Provocative Use of Scripture in Narration: "He Was with the Wild Animals and Angels Ministered to Him"'. *BBR* 9 (1999): 19–36.

Caponigro, Mark Stephen. 'Judith, Holding the Tale of Herodotus'. Pages 47 59 in *'No One Spoke Ill of Her': Essays on Judith*. Edited by James C. VanderKam. SBLEJL 2. Atlanta, GA: Scholars Press, 1992.

Carey, Holly. *Jesus' Cry from the Cross: Towards a First-Century Understanding of the Intertextual Relationship between Psalm 22 and the Narrative of Mark's Gospel*. LNTS 398. London: T&T Clark, 2009.

Carmignac, Jean, and Pierre Guilbert. *Les textes de Qumran: traduits et annotes*. 2 vols. Paris: Letouzey et Ane, 1961.

Carrington, Philip. *According to Mark: A Running Commentary on the Oldest Gospel.* Cambridge: Cambridge University Press, 1960.

Carrington, Philip. *The Primitive Christian Calendar: A Study in the Making of the Marcan Gospel.* Cambridge: Cambridge University Press, 1952.

Chilton, Bruce D. *A Galilean Rabbi and His Bible.* London: SPCK, 1984.

Cohn, Leopold. 'An Apocryphal Work Ascribed to Philo of Alexandria'. *JQR* 10 (1898): 311–13.

Collins, John J. 'Joseph and Aseneth: Jewish or Christian?' *JSP* 14 (2005): 97–112.

Collins, Adela Yarbro. 'The Appropriation of the Individual Psalms of Lament by Mark'. Pages 223–41 in *The Scriptures in the Gospels.* Edited by Christopher M. Tuckett. BETL 131. Leuven: Leuven University Press, 1997.

Collins, Adela Yarbro. *Mark: A Commentary.* Hermeneia 55. Minneapolis, MN: Fortress, 2007.

Conway, Colleen M. *Sex and Slaughter in the Tent of Jael: A Cultural History of a Biblical Story.* Oxford: Oxford University Press, 2016.

Cook, Edward M. '"In the Plain of the Wall" (Dan 3:1)'. *JBL* 108 (1989): 115–16.

Cranfield, C. E. B. *The Gospel According to St. Mark.* CGTC. Cambridge: Cambridge University Press, 1959.

Craven, Toni. *Artistry and Faith in the Book of Judith.* SBLDS 70. Chico, CA: Scholars Press, 1983.

Crawford, Sidnie White. 'Esther and Judith: Contrasts in Character'. Pages 61–76 in *The Book of Esther in Modern Research.* Edited by Crawford and Leonard J. Greenspoon. London: A. & C. Black, 2003.

Crawford, Sidnie White. 'Esther not Judith: Why One Made It and the Other Didn't'. *Bible Review* 18 (2002): 22–31.

Crawford, Sidnie White. 'In the Steps of Jael and Deborah: Judith as Heroine'. Pages 5–16 in *'No One Spoke Ill of Her': Essays on Judith.* Edited by James C. VanderKam. SBLEJL 2. Atlanta, GA: Scholars Press, 1992.

Crawford, Sidnie White. *Rewriting Scripture in Second Temple Times.* Studies in the Dead Sea Scrolls and Related Literature. Grand Rapids, MI: Eerdmans, 2008.

Crossan, John Dominic. *The Birth of Christianity: Discovering What Happened in the Years Immediately After the Execution of Jesus.* Edinburgh: T. & T. Clark, 1998.

Crossan, John Dominic. *The Cross That Spoke: The Origins of the Passion Narrative.* San Francisco, CA: Harper & Row, 1988.

Crossan, John Dominic. *Four Other Gospels: Shadows on the Contours of Canon.* Minneapolis, MN: Winston, 1985.

Crossan, John Dominic. *Who Killed Jesus? Exposing the Roots of Anti-Semitism in the Gospel Story of the Death of Jesus.* San Francisco, CA: HarperSanFrancisco, 1995.

Crossley, James G. 'Against the Historical Plausibility of the Empty Tomb Story and the Bodily Resurrection of Jesus: A Response to N.T. Wright'. *JSHJ* 3 (2005): 171–86.

Crossley, James G. 'History from the Margins: The Death of John the Baptist'. Pages 147–61 in *Writing History, Constructing Religion.* Edited by James G. Crossley and Christian Karner. Aldershot: Ashgate, 2005.

Crossley, James G. *Jesus and the Chaos of History: Redirecting the Life of the Historical Jesus.* Oxford: Oxford University Press, 2015.

Cummins, S. Anthony. 'Integrated Scripture, Embedded Empire: The Ironic Interplay of "King" Herod, John and Jesus in Mark 6.1-44'. Pages 31–48 in *Biblical Interpretation in Early Christian Gospels, Volume 1: The Gospel of Mark.* Edited by Thomas R. Hatina. SSEJC 16. London: T&T Clark, 2006.

Daise, Michael A. *Feasts in John: Jewish Festivals and Jesus' 'Hour' in the Fourth Gospel.* WUNT 2/229. Tübingen: Mohr Siebeck, 2007.

Dancy, John C. *A Commentary on 1 Maccabees.* Oxford: Blackwell, 1954.

Danker, Frederick W. 'The Demonic Secret in Mark: A Reexamination of the Cry of Dereliction'. *ZNW* 61 (1970): 48–69.

Danker, Frederick W. 'The Literary Unity of Mark 14:1-25'. *JBL* 85 (1966): 467–72.

Daube, David. 'Judith'. Pages 849–70 in *The Collected Works of David Daube.* Vol. 3, *Biblical Law and Literature.* Edited by Calum M. Carmichael. Berkeley, CA: Robbins Collection, 1992.

Davies, W. D., and D. C. Allison, Jr. *The Gospel According to Saint Matthew.* 3 vols. ICC. Edinburgh/London: T&T Clark, 1988–97.

Day, Linda. *Three Faces of a Queen: Characterization in the Books of Esther.* JSOTSup 186. Sheffield: Sheffield Academic, 1995.

Delcor, Mathias. *Le Testament d'Abraham: Introduction, traduction du texte grec et commentaire de la recension grecque longue, suivi de la traduction des Testaments d'Abraham, d'Isaac et de Jacob d'après les versions orientales.* SVTP 2. Leiden: Brill, 1973.

Derrett, J. Duncan M. *The Making of Mark: The Scriptural Bases of the Earliest Gospel.* Shipston-on-Stour: P. Drinkwater, 1985.

Dibelius, Martin. *Die Formgeschichte des Evangeliums.* Tübingen: Mohr Siebeck, 1919. 6th ed. 1966.

Dibelius, Martin. 'Das historische Problem der Leidengeschichte'. Pages 248–57 in *Botschaft und Geschichte. Gesammelte Aufsätze. Band 1: Zur Evangelienforschung.* Edited by Martin Dibelius, Heinz Kraft and Günther Bornkamm. Tübingen: Mohr Siebeck, 1963.

Dijk-Hemmes, Fokkelein van. 'Gezegende onder de vrouwen: een moeder in Israël en een maagd in de kerk'. Pages 123–47 in *'t Is kwaad gerucht, als zij neit binnen blijft: Vrouwen in oude culturen.* Edited by Fokkelein van Dijk-Hemmes. TM. Utrecht: HES, 1986.

Dimant, Devorah. 'Use and Interpretation of Mikra in the Apocrypha and Pseud-epigrapha'. Pages 379–419 in *Mikra: Text, Translation, Reading and Interpretation of the Hebrew Bible in Ancient Judaism and Early Christianity.* Edited by Martin J. Mulder. Philadelphia, PA: Fortress, 1988.

Dodd, C. H. *According to the Scriptures: The Sub-Structure of New Testament Theology.* London: Nisbet & Co., 1952.

Dodd, C. H. *The Apostolic Preaching and its Development.* London: Hodder & Stoughton, 1936.

Dodd, C. H. *History and the Gospel.* London: Nisbet, 1938.

Donahue, John R., and Daniel J. Harrington. *The Gospel of Mark.* SP 2. Collegeville, MN: Liturgical Press, 2002.

Dormeyer, Detlev. *Die Passion Jesu als Verhaltensmodell.* NTAbh NF 11. Münster: Aschendorff, 1974.

Droge, Arthur J., and James D. Tabor. *A Noble Death: Suicide and Martyrdom Among Christians and Jews in Antiquity.* San Francisco, CA: HarperSanFrancisco, 1992.

Drury, John. 'Midrash and Gospel'. *Theology* 77 (1974): 291–6.

Dubarle, André-Marie. *Judith: Formes et sens des diverses traditions.* 2 vols. AnBib 24. Rome: Institut Biblique Pontifical, 1966.

Edwards, James R. *The Gospel According to Mark.* Pillar New Testament Commentary. Grand Rapids, MI: Eerdmans, 2002.

Einbinder, Susan L. *Beautiful Death: Jewish Poetry and Martyrdom in Medieval France*. Jews, Christians, and Muslims from the Ancient to the Modern World 8. Princeton, NJ: Princeton University Press, 2002.

Einbinder, Susan L. 'The Jewish Martyrs of Blois'. Pages 537–60 in Medieval Hagiography: An Anthology. Edited by Thomas Head. London: Routledge, 2000.

Eissfeldt, Otto. *The Old Testament: An Introduction*. Translated by P. R. Ackroyd. New York, NY: Harper & Row, 1965.

Eklund, Rebekah. *Jesus Wept: The Significance of Jesus' Laments in the New Testament*. LNTS 515. London: T&T Clark, 2016.

Elwolde, John. 'The Hodayot's Use of the Psalter: Text-Critical Contributions (Book 1)'. Pages 79–108 in *Psalms and Prayers: Papers Read at the Thirteenth Joint Meeting of the Society of Old Testament Study and Het Oudtestamentisch Werkegezelschap in Nederland en België, Apeldoorn 21–24 August 2006*. Edited by Bob Becking and Eric Peels. OS 55. Leiden: Brill, 2007.

Elwolde, John. 'The Hodayot's Use of the Psalter: Text-Critical Contributions (Book 2: Pss 42–72)'. Pages 79–99 in vol. 1 of *The Dead Sea Scrolls in Context: Integrating the Dead Sea Scrolls in the Study of Ancient Texts, Languages, and Cultures*. Edited by Armin Lange, Emmanuel Tov and Matthias Weigold. 2 vols. VTSup 140. Leiden: Brill, 2011.

Elwolde, John. 'The Hodadyot's Use of the Psalter: Text-critical Contributions (Book 3: Pss 73–89)'. *DSD* 17 (2010): 159–79.

Emadi, Samuel. 'Intertextuality in New Testament Scholarship: Significance, Criteria, and the Art of Intertextual Reading'. *CBR* 14 (2015): 8–23.

Ernst, Josef. *Das Evangelium nach Markus*. RNT 2. Regensburg: Pustet, 1981.

Eshel, Esther. 'The Dream Visions in the Noah Story of the Genesis Apocryphon and Related Texts'. Pages 41–61 in *Northern Lights on the Dead Sea Scrolls: Proceedings of the Nordic Qumran Network 2003–2006*. Edited by Anders Klostergaard Petersen et al. STDJ 80. Leiden: Brill, 2009.

Eshel, Esther. 'The Imago Mundi of the Genesis Apocryphon'. Pages 111–31 in *Heavenly Tablets: Interpretation, Identity and Tradition in Ancient Judaism*. Edited by Lynn LiDonnici and Andrea Lieber. JSJSup 119. Leiden: Brill, 2007.

Esler, Philip. '"By the Hand of a Woman": Culture, Story and Theology in the Book of Judith'. Pages 64–101 in *Social Scientific Models for Interpreting the Bible: Essays by the Context Group in Honor of Bruce J. Malina*. Edited by Bruce J. Malina and John J. Pilch. BibInt 53. Leiden: Brill, 2001.

Ettelson, H. W. 'The Integrity of 1 Maccabees'. *TCAAS* 27 (1925): 249–384.

Evans, Craig A. 'The Baptism of John in a Typological Context'. Pages 45–71 in *Dimensions of Baptism: Biblical and Theological Studies*. Edited by Stanley E. Porter and Anthony R. Cross. JSNTSup 234. London: Sheffield Academic, 2002.

Evans, Craig A. 'Josephus on John the Baptist and Other Jewish Prophets of Deliverance'. Pages 55–63 in *The Historical Jesus in Context*. Edited by Amy-Jill Levine, D. C. Allison and John Dominic Crossan. Princeton, NJ: Princeton University Press, 2006.

Evans, Craig A. *Mark 8:27–16:20*. WBC 34B. Nashville, TN: Thomas Nelson, 2001.

Evans, Craig A. 'The Passion of Jesus: History Remembered or Prophecy Historicized?' *BBR* 6 (1996): 159–65.

Faierstein, Morris M. 'Why do the Scribes Say that Elijah Must Come First?' *JBL* 100 (1981): 75–86.

Falk, Daniel K. *The Parabiblical Texts: Strategies for Extending the Scriptures among the Dead Sea Scrolls*. LSTS 63. London: T&T Clark, 2007.

Farrer, Austin. *A Study in Mark*. London: A. & C. Black, 1951.

Feigels, Friedrich K. *Der Einfluß des Weissagungsbeweises und anderer Motive auf die Leidensgeschichte*. Tübingen: Mohr, 1910.

Feldman, Ariel. *The Dead Sea Scrolls Rewriting Samuel and Kings: Texts and Commentary*. BZAW 469. Berlin: W. de Gruyter, 2015.

Feldman, Louis H. 'Hellenizations in Josephus' Version of Esther'. *TAPA* 101 (1970): 143–70.

Feldman, Louis H. 'Prolegomenon'. Pages ix–clxix in M. R. James, *The Biblical Antiquities of Philo*. TED 1. London: SPCK, 1917. Repr. New York, NY: Ktav, 1971.

Feuillet, André. 'L'episode de la tentation d'après l'Evangile selon Saint Marc (1,12-13)'. *EstBíb* 19 (1960): 49–73.

Fishbane, Michael A. *Biblical Interpretation in Ancient Israel*. Oxford: Clarendon, 1985.

Fishbane, Michael A. 'Use, Authority and Interpretation of Mikra at Qumran'. Pages 339–77 in *Mikra: Text, Translation, Reading and Interpretation of the Hebrew Bible in Ancient Judaism and Early Christianity*. Edited by Martin J. Mulder. Philadelphia, PA: Fortress, 1988.

Fisk, Bruce N. *Do You Not Remember? Scripture, Story and Exegesis in the Rewritten Bible of Pseudo-Philo*. JSPSup 37. Sheffield: Sheffield Academic, 2001.

Fitzmyer, J. A. '"4Q Testimonia" and the New Testament'. Pages 59–89 in *Essays on the Semitic Background of the New Testament*. Edited by J. A. Fitzmyer. SBS 5. Missoula, MT: Scholars Press, 1974.

Fitzmyer, J. A. *The Genesis Apocryphon of Qumran Cave 1 (1Q20): A Commentary*. 3rd ed. BibOr 18B. Rome: Editrice Pontificio Istituto Biblico, 2004.

Fitzmyer, J. A. 'More About Elijah Coming First'. *JBL* 104 (1985): 295–6.

Fleddermann, Harry. 'The Flight of a Naked Young Man (Mark 14:51-52)'. *CBQ* 41 (1979): 412–18.

Focant, Camille. *The Gospel According to Mark: A Commentary*. Translated by L. R. Keylock. Eugene, OR: Pickwick, 2012.

Focke, Friedrich. 'Synkrisis'. *Hermes* (1923): 327–68.

Fossum, Jarl E. *The Name of God and the Angel of the Lord: Samaritan and Jewish Concepts of Intermediation and the Origins of Gnosticism*. WUNT 36. Tübingen: Mohr Siebeck, 1985.

Foster, Paul. 'Echoes without Resonance: Critiquing Certain Aspects of Recent Scholarly Trends in the Study of the Jewish Scriptures in the New Testament'. *JSNT* 38 (2015): 96–111.

Foster, Paul. *The Gospel of Peter: Introduction, Critical Edition and Commentary*. TENT 4. Leiden: Brill, 2010.

France, R. T. *Jesus and the Old Testament: His Application of Old Testament Passages to Himself and His Mission*. Grand Rapids, MI: Baker, 1982.

France, R. T. 'Jewish Historiography, Midrash, and the Gospels'. Pages 99–127 in *Studies in Midrash and Historiography*.

Frankfurter, David T. M. *Elijah in Upper Egypt: The Apocalypse of Elijah and Early Egyptian Christianity*. Minneapolis, MN: Fortress, 1993.

Fredriksen, Paula. 'Jesus and the Temple, Mark and the War'. Pages 293–310 in *SBL 1990 Seminar Papers*. Edited by David J. Lull. SBLSP 29. Atlanta, GA: Scholars Press, 1990.

Frye, Northrop. *Fearful Symmetry: A Study of William Blake*. Princeton, NJ: Princeton University Press, 1947.

Frye, Northrop. *The Great Code: The Bible and Literature*. New York, NY: Harcourt Brace Jovanovich, 1982.

Frye, Northrop. *The Stubborn Structure: Essays on Criticism and Society*. Ithaca, NY: Cornell University Press, 1970.

Gera, Deborah Levine. 'The Jewish Textual Traditions'. Pages 23–40 in Kevin R. Brine, Elena Ciletti and Henrike Lähnemann, eds. *The Sword of Judith: Judith Studies Across the Disciplines*. Cambridge: OpenBook Publishers, 2010.

Gera, Deborah Levine. *Judith*. CEJL. Berlin: W. de Gruyter, 2013.

Gerhardsson, Birger. *The Testing of God's Son (Matt. 4:1-11 & Par): An Analysis of an Early Christian Midrash*. Lund: Gleerup, 1966.

Gibson, Jeffrey B. *The Temptations of Jesus in Early Christianity*. London: T&T Clark, 2004.

Glickler-Chazon, Esther. 'Moses' Struggle for his Soul: A Prototype for the Testament of Abraham, the Greek Apocalypse of Ezra, and the Apocalpse of Sedrach'. *The Second Century: A Journal of Early Christian Studies* 5 (1985/86): 151–64.

Gnilka, Joachim. *Das Evangelium nach Markus*. 2 vols. EKK 2. Zurich: Benziger, 1978.

Goldstein, Jonathan A. *I Maccabees: A New Translation with Introduction and Commentary*. AB 41. Garden City, NY: Doubleday, 1976.

Goodacre, Mark. 'Prophecy Historicized or Tradition Scripturalized? Reflections on the Origins of the Passion Narrative'. Pages 37–51 in *The New Testament and the Church: Essays in Honour of John Muddiman*. Edited by John Barton and Peter Groves. LNTS 532. London: T&T Clark, 2016.

Goodacre, Mark. 'Scripturalization in Mark's Crucifixion Narrative'. Pages 33–47 in *The Trial and Death of Jesus: Essays on the Passion Narrative in Mark*. Edited by Geert van Oyen and Thomas Shepherd. Leuven: Peeters, 2006.

Goulder, Michael D. *The Evangelist's Calendar: A Lectionary Explanation of the Development of Scripture*. London: SPCK, 1978.

Goulder, Michael D. 'Jesus' Resurrection and Christian Origins: A Response to N.T. Wright'. *JSHJ* 3 (2005): 187–95.

Goulder, Michael D. *Midrash and Lection in Matthew*. London: SPCK, 1974.

Grässer, Erich. 'Review of A. Suhl, *Die Funktion der alttestamentlichen Zitate und Anspielungen im Markusevangelium*'. *TLZ* 91 (1966): 667–9.

Green, Joel B. *The Death of Jesus*. WUNT 2/33. Tübingen: Mohr Siebeck, 1988.

Guelich, Robert A. *Mark 1–8:26*. WBC 34A. Dallas, TX: Word, 1989.

Gundry, Robert H. *Mark: A Commentary on His Apology for the Cross, Chapters 1–8*. Grand Rapids, MI: Eerdmans, 2000.

Gundry, Robert H. *The Use of the Old Testament in St. Matthew's Gospel*. NovTSup 18. Leiden: Brill, 1967.

Haag, Ernst. *Studien zum Buche Judith: Seine theologische Bedeutung und literarische Eigenart*. TThSt 16. Trier: Paulinus, 1963.

Habermann, Abraham. *Sefer Gezerot Ashkenaz ve-Zarefat*. Jerusalem: Tarshish, 1945.

Haenchen, Ernst. *Der Weg Jesu*. Berlin: Töpelmann, 1966.

Hanhart, Robert. *Text und Textgeschichte des Buches Judith*. MSU 14. Göttingen: Vandenhoeck & Ruprecht, 1979.

Harrington, Daniel J. 'The Biblical Text of Pseudo-Philo's "Liber Antiquitatum Biblicarum"'. *CBQ* 33 (1971): 1–17.

Harrington, Daniel J. *The Hebrew Fragments of Pseudo-Philo's Liber Antiquitatum Biblicarum Preserved in the Chronicles of Jerahmeel*. TAT 3. Pseudepigrapha Series 3. Missoula, MT: SBL, 1974.

Harrington, Daniel J. 'Pseudo-Philo'. Pages 304–77 in vol. 2 of *OTP*.

Harrington, Daniel J. 'The Original Language of Pseudo-Philo's "Liber Antiquitatum Biblicarum"'. *HTR* 63 (1970): 503–14.

Harrington, Daniel J. *Text and Biblical Text in Pseudo-Philo's Liber Antiquitatum Biblicarum*. Cambridge, MA: Harvard University Press, 1969.

Harris, J. Rendel. *Testimonies*. 2 vols. Cambridge: Cambridge University Press, 1916–20.

Harris, Sarah. *The Davidic Shepherd King in the Lukan Narrative*. LNTS 558. London: Bloomsbury, 2016.

Harvey, John E. *Retelling the Torah: The Deuteronomistic Historian's Use of Tetrateuchal Narratives*. JSOTSup 403. London: T&T Clark, 2004.

Hatina, Thomas R. 'Embedded Scripture Texts and the Plurality of Meaning: The Announcement of the "Voice from Heaven" in Mark 1.11 as a Case Study'. Pages 81–99 in *Biblical Interpretation in Early Christian Gospels, Volume 1: The Gospel of Mark*. Edited by Thomas R. Hatina. SSEJC 16. London: T&T Clark, 2006.

Hatina, Thomas R. *In Search of a Context: The Function of Scripture in Mark's Narrative*. JSNTSup 232. Sheffield: Sheffield Academic, 2002.

Haupt, Paul. 'Purim'. *Beiträge zur Assyriologie* 6 (1906): 1–53.

Hauser, Alan J. 'Two Songs of Victory: A Comparison of Exodus 15 and Judges 5'. Pages 265–84 in *Directions in Biblical Hebrew Poetry*. Edited by Elaine R. Follis. JSOTSup 40. Sheffield: JSOT, 1987.

Hays, Richard B. *Echoes of Scripture in the Gospels*. Waco, TX: Baylor University Press, 2016.

Hays, Richard B. *Echoes of Scripture in the Letters of Paul*. New Haven, CT: Yale University Press, 1989.

Hays, Richard B. *Reading Backwards: Figural Christology and the Fourfold Gospel Witness*. Waco, TX: Baylor University Press, 2014.

Hayward, Robert. 'Phinehas – the Same is Elijah: The Origins of a Tradition'. *JJS* 29 (1978): 22–34.

Heil, John Paul. 'Jesus as the Unique High Priest in the Gospel of John'. *CBQ* 57 (1995): 729–45.

Heising, Alkuin. *Die Botschaft der Brotvermehrung*. SBS 15. Stuttgart: Kohlhammer, 1966.

Heising, Alkuin. 'Exegese und Theologie der Alt- und Neutestamentlichen Speisewunder'. *ZKT* 86 (1964): 80–96.

Henten, Jan Willem van. 'Daniel 3 and 6 in Early Christian Literature'. Pages 149–69 in volume 1 of *The Book of Daniel: Composition and Reception*. Edited by John J. Collins and Peter W. Flint. 2 vols. VTSup 83. Leiden: Brill, 2001.

Henten, Jan Willem van. 'Judith as Alternative Leader: A Rereading of Judith 7–13'. Pages 224–52 in *A Feminist Companion to Esther, Judith and Susanna*. Edited by Athalya Brenner. London: T&T Clark, 1995.

Henten, Jan Willem van. 'Zum Einfluß jüdischer Martyrien auf die Literatur des frühen Christentums. II: Die Apostolischen Väter'. *ANRW* II.27 (1993): 700–723.

Hieke, Thomas. 'The Role of "Scripture" in the Last Words of Mattathias'. Pages 61–74 in *The Books of the Maccabees*.

Hill, Andrew E. *Malachi: A New Translation with Introduction and Commentary*. AB 25D. New York, NY: Doubleday, 1998.

Himmelfarb, Martha. '"He Was Renowned to the Ends of the Earth" (1 Maccabees 3:9)'. Pages 77–97 in *Jewish Literatures and Cultures: Context and Intertext*. Edited by Anita Norich and Yaron Z. Eliav. BJS 349. Providence, RI; Brown Judaic Studies, 2008.

Hodgson Jr., R. 'The Testimony Hypothesis'. *JBL* 98 (1979): 361–78.

Hoehner, Harold W. *Herod Antipas: A Contemporary of Jesus Christ*. Grand Rapids, MI: Zondervan, 1980.

Hoffeditz, David M., and Gary E. Yates. 'Femme Fatale Redux: Intertextual Connection to the Elijah/Jezebel Narratives in Mark 6:14-29'. *BBR* 15 (2005): 199–221.

Hollander, John. *The Figure of Echo: A Mode of Allusion in Milton and After*. Berkeley, CA: University of California Press, 1981.

Hooker, Morna D. *The Gospel According to St Mark*. London: A. & C. Black, 1991.

Hooker, Morna D. *Jesus and the Servant: The Influence of the Servant Concept of Deutero-Isaiah in the New Testament*. London: SPCK, 1959.

Hooker, Morna D. 'Mark'. Pages 220–30 in *It is Written: Scripture Citing Scripture: Essays in Honour of Barnabas Lindars, SSF*. Edited by D. A. Carson and H. G. M. Williamson. Cambridge: Cambridge University Press, 1988.

Horsley, Richard A. 'Prophetic Envoys for the Renewal of Israel: Q 9:57–10:16'. Pages 228–59 in *Whoever Hears You Hears Me: Prophets, Performance, and Tradition in Q*. Edited by Richard A. Horsley and Jonathan A. Draper. Harrisburg, PA: Trinity Press International, 1999.

Huizenga, Leroy A. 'The Old Testament in the New, Intertextuality and Allegory'. *JSNT* 38 (2015): 17–35.

Hurtado, Larry W. *Mark*. NIBC. Peabody, MA: Hendrickson, 1989.

Hutton, Jeremy M. 'Topography, Biblical Traditions, and Reflections on John's Baptism of Jesus'. Pages 149–77 in *Jesus Research: New Methodologies and Perceptions: The Second Princeton-Prague Symposium on Jesus Research Research, Princeton 2007*. Edited by James H. Charlesworth and Brian Rhea. Grand Rapids, MI: Eerdmans, 2014.

Iersel, Bas M. F. van. *Mark: A Reader-Response Commentary*. Translated by W. H. Bisscheroux. JSNTSup 164. Sheffield: Sheffield Academic, 1998.

Ilan, Tan, and Vared Noam, eds. *Josephus and the Rabbis*. 2 vols. Jerusalem: Yad Ben-Zvi, 2017.

Iverson, Kelly R. *Gentiles in the Gospel of Mark: 'Even the Dogs Under the Table Eat the Children's Crumbs'*. LNTS 339. London: T&T Clark, 2007.

Jacobson, Howard. *A Commentary on Pseudo-Philo's Liber Antiquitatum Biblicarum: With Latin Text & English Translation*. 2 vols. AGAJU 31. Leiden: Brill, 1996.

James, M. R. *The Biblical Antiquities of Philo*. TED 1. London: SPCK, 1917. Repr. New York, NY: Ktav, 1971.

James, M. R. *The Testament of Abraham: The Greek Text Now First Edited with an Introduction and Notes*. TS 2/2. Cambridge: Cambridge University Press, 1892.

Janes, Regina. 'Why the Daughter of Herodias Must Dance (Mark 6.14-29)'. *JSNT* 28 (2006): 443–67.

Jeremias, Joachim. 'παῖς θεοῦ'. *TDNT* 5:700–709.

Jobes, Karen H. *The Alpha-Text of Esther: Its Character and Relationship to the Masoretic Text*. SBLDS 153. Atlanta, GA: Scholars Press, 1996.

Joynes, Christine E. 'The Returned Elijah? John the Baptist's Angelic Identity in the Gospel of Mark'. *SJT* 58 (2005): 455–67.

Juel, Donald. *An Introduction to New Testament Literature*. Nashville, TN: Abingdon, 1978.

Juel, Donald. *Messianic Exegesis: Christological Interpretation of the Old Testament in Early Christianity*. Philadelphia, PA: Fortress, 1988.

Juel, Donald. 'Review of Joel Marcus, *The Way of the Lord*'. *JBL* 114 (1995): 147–50.

Kaminski, Carol M. *From Noah to Israel: Realization of the Primaeval Blessing After the Flood.* JSOTSup 413. London: T&T Clark, 2004.

Kasher, Aryeh. *Jews and Hellenistic Cities in Eretz-Israel: Relations of the Jews in Eretz-Israel with the Hellenistic Cities During the Second Temple Period (332 BCE–70 CE).* TSAJ 21. Tübingen: Mohr Siebeck, 1990.

Katz, Paul. 'Jesus als Vorläufer des Christus: Mögliche Hinweise in den Evangelien auf Elia als den "Typos" Jesu'. *TZ* 52 (1996): 225–35.

Katz, Paul. 'Wie einer der Propheten? Das biblische Markusevangelium als Darbietung eines "Vorevangeliums"'. *TZ* 58 (2002): 46–60.

Kazmierski, Carl R. *Jesus, the Son of God: A Study of the Markan Tradition and its Redaction by the Evangelist.* Wurzburg: Echter, 1979.

Kee, Howard Clark. *Community of the New Age: Studies in Mark's Gospel.* London: SCM, 1977.

Kee, Howard Clark. 'The Function of Scriptural Quotations and Allusions in Mark 11–16'. Pages 165–88 in *Festschrift für Werner Georg Kümmel.* Edited by Erich Grässer and E. Earle Ellis. Göttingen: Vandenhoeck & Ruprecht, 1975.

Keesmaat, Sylvia C. *Paul and His Story: (Re)Interpreting the Exodus Tradition.* JSNTSup 181. Sheffield: Sheffield Academic, 1999.

Kelber, Werner. *The Kingdom in Mark: A New Place and a New Time.* Philadelphia, PA: Fortress, 1974.

Kelber, Werner. *Mark's Story of Jesus.* Philadelphia, PA: Fortress, 1979.

Kelber, Werner. *The Oral and the Written Gospel.* Philadelphia, PA: Fortress, 1983.

Kelhoffer, James A. *The Diet of John the Baptist: 'Locusts and Wild Honey' in Synoptic and Patristic Interpretation.* WUNT 176. Tübingen: Mohr Siebeck, 2005.

Klein, Günter. 'Die Verleugnung des Petrus: Eine traditionsgeschichte Untersuchung'. *ZTK* 58 (1961): 285–328.

Klostermann, Eric. *Das Markusevangelium.* 5th ed. HNT 3. Tübingen: Mohr Siebeck, 1971.

Knauf, Ernst Axel. 'Joshua Maccabeus: Another Reading of 1 Maccabees 5'. Pages 203–12 in *'Even God Cannot Change the Past': Reflections on Seventeen Years of the European Seminar in Historical Methodology.* Edited by Lester L. Grabbe. LHBOTS 663. London: T&T Clark, 2018.

Koester, Helmut. *Ancient Christian Gospels: Their History and Development.* London: SCM, 1990.

Koester, Helmut. 'Apocryphal and Canonical Gospels'. *HTR* 73 (1980): 105–30.

Koller, Aaron. *Esther in Ancient Jewish Thought.* Cambridge: Cambridge University Press, 2014.

Kozlowski, Jan M. 'And He Saw His Pillow Being Consumed by Fire (*Martyrium Polycarpi* 5,2): A Proposal of Interpretation'. *ETL* 85 (2009): 147–58.

Kreps, Anne. 'The Passion of the Book: The Gospel of Truth as Valentinian Scriptural Practice'. *JECS* 24 (2016): 311–35.

Kugel, James. *A Walk Through Jubilees: Studies in the Book of Jubilees and the World of its Creation.* JSJSup 156. Leiden: Brill, 2012.

Kushelevsky, Rella. *Moses and the Angel of Death.* STML 4. New York, NY: Peter Lang, 1995.

Labahn, Michael. *Offenbarung in Zeichen und Wort.* WUNT 2/17. Tübingen: Mohr Siebeck, 2000.

Lacocque, André. *The Feminine Unconventional: Four Subversive Figures in Israel's Tradition.* Minneapolis, MN: Fortress, 1990.

222 *Bibliography*

Lane, William. *The Gospel According to Mark.* NICNT 2. Grand Rapids, MI: Eerdmans, 1974.

Lang, Judith. 'The Lord Who Crushes Wars: Studies on Judith 9:7, Judith 16:2, and Exodus 15:3'. Pages 179–87 in *A Pious Seductress: Studies in the Book of Judith.* Edited by Géza G. Xeravits. DCLS 14. Göttingen: Vandenhoeck & Ruprecht, 2012.

Lange, Armin, and Matthias Weigold. *Biblical Quotations and Allusions in Second Temple Jewish Literature.* JAJSup 5. Göttingen: Vandenhoeck & Ruprecht, 2011.

LaVerdiere, Eugene. *The Beginning of the Gospel: Introducing the Gospel According to Mark, Volume 1.* Collegeville, MN: Liturgical, 1999.

Lerner Myron B. 'The Works of Aggadic Midrash and the Esther Midrashim'. Pages 133–229 in *The Literature of the Sages: Second Part.* Edited by Shmuel Safrai, Zeev Safrai, Peter J. Tomson and Joshua Schwartz. CRINT 2.3. Assen: Royal Van Gorcum, 2006.

Levine, Amy-Jill. *The Misunderstood Jew: The Church and the Scandal of the Jewish Jesus.* San Francisco, CA: HarperSanFrancisco, 2006.

Li, Tarsee. *The Verbal System of the Aramaic of Daniel: An Explanation in the Context of Grammaticalization.* SAIS 8. Leiden: Brill, 2009.

Liebengood, Kelly D. *The Eschatology of 1 Peter: Considering the Influence of Zechariah 9–14.* SNTSMS 157. Cambridge: Cambridge University Press, 2014.

Lightfoot, Robert H. *History and Interpretation in the Gospels.* London: Hodder & Stoughton, 1935.

Lim, Timothy H. *The Formation of the Jewish Canon.* New Haven, CT: Yale University Press, 2013.

Lim, Timothy H. 'Origins and Emergence of Midrash in Relation to the Hebrew Bible'. Pages 595–612 in vol. 2 of *Encyclopedia of Midrash: Biblical Interpretation in Formative Judaism.* Edited by Jacob Neusner. 2 vols. Leiden: Brill, 2005.

Lindars, Barnabas. *New Testament Apologetic: The Doctrinal Significance of Old Testament Quotations.* London: SCM, 1961.

Lindbeck, Kristen H. *Elijah and the Rabbis: Story and Theology.* New York, NY: Columbia University Press, 2010.

Linnemann, Eta. *Studien zur Passionsgeschichte.* FRLANT 102. Göttingen: Vandenhoeck & Ruprecht, 1970.

Loader, William. *The Pseudepigrapha on Sexuality: Attitudes towards Sexuality in Apocalypses, Testaments, Legends, Wisdom, and Related Literature.* Grand Rapids, MI: Eerdmans, 2011.

Loewenstamm, Samuel E. 'The Death of Moses'. Pages 185–217 in *Studies in the Testament of Abraham.* Edited by George W. E. Nickelsburg. SBLSCS 6. Missoula, MT: Scholars Press, 1976.

Loewenstamm, Samuel E. 'The Testament of Abraham and the Texts Concerning Moses' Death'. Pages 219–25 in *Studies in the Testament of Abraham.* Edited by George W. E. Nickelsburg. SBLSCS 6. Missoula, MT: Scholars Press, 1976.

Lohmeyer, Ernst. *Das Evangelium des Markus.* Göttingen: Vandenhoeck & Ruprecht, 1953.

Lohmeyer, Ernst. *Galiläa und Jerusalem.* FRLANT 34. Göttingen: Vandenhoeck & Ruprecht, 1936.

Loisy, Alfred. *L'Évangile selon Marc.* Paris: Nourry, 1912.

Loos, Hendrick van der. *The Miracles of Jesus.* Leiden: Brill, 1965.

Lowin, Shari L. *The Making of a Forefather: Abraham in Islamic and Jewish Exegetical Narratives.* IHC 65. Leiden: Brill, 2006.

MacDonald, Dennis R. *The Homeric Epics and the Gospel of Mark*. New Haven, CT: Yale University Press, 2000.

Machiela, Daniel A. '"Each to His Own Inheritance": Geography as an Evaluative Tool in the Genesis Apocryphon'. *DSD* 15 (2008): 50–66.

Mahnke, Hermann. *Die Versuchungsgeschichte im Rahmen der synoptischen Evangelien. Ein Beitrag zur frühen Christologie*. BBET 9. Frankfurt: Lang, 1978.

Mack, Burton L. *A Myth of Innocence: Mark and Christian Origins*. Philadelphia, PA: Fortress, 1988.

Majoros-Danowski, Johannes. *Elija im Markusevangelium. Ein Buch im Kontext des Judentums*. BWANT 180. Stuttgart: Kohlhammer, 2008.

Makiello, Phoebe. 'Was Moses Considered to be an Angel by Those at Qumran?' Pages 115–27 in *Moses in Biblical and Extra-Biblical Traditions*. Edited by Axel Graupner and Michael Wolter. BZAW 372. Berlin: W. de Gruyter, 2007.

Malbon, Elizabeth Struthers. 'Disciples/Crowds/Whoever: Markan Characters and Readers'. *NovT* 28 (1986): 104–30.

Malbon, Elizabeth Struthers. *Mark's Jesus: Characterization as Narrative Christology*. Waco, TX: Baylor University Press, 2009.

Mann, Jacob. *The Bible as Read and Preached in the Old Synagogue*. 2 vols. Cincinnati, OH: JPS, 1940.

Manns, Frédéric. 'Un midrash chrétien: le récit de la mort de Judas'. *RSR* 54 (1980): 197–203.

Marcus, Joel. *John the Baptist in History and Theology*. SPNT. Columbia, SC: University of South Carolina, 2018.

Marcus, Joel. *Mark: 8–16: A New Translation with Introduction and Commentary*. AB 27A. New York, NY: Doubleday, 2009.

Marcus, Joel. *The Way of the Lord: Christological Exegesis of the Old Testament in the Gospel of Mark*. Edinburgh: T. & T. Clark, 1992.

Marxsen, Willi. *Der Evangelist Markus: Studien zur Redaktionsgeschichte des Evangeliums*. FRLANT 49. Göttingen: Vandenhoeck & Ruprecht, 1959.

Matera, Frank J. *The Kingship of Jesus: Composition and Theology in Mark 15*. SBLDS 66. Atlanta, GA: Scholars Press, 1982.

Matera, Frank J. 'The Prologue as the Interpretative Key to Mark's Gospel'. *JSNT* 34 (1988): 3–20.

Maurer, Christian. 'Knecht Gottes und Sohn Gottes im Passionsberichte des Markusevangeliums'. *ZTK* 50 (1953): 1–38.

Mauser, Ulrich W. *Christ in the Wilderness: The Wilderness Theme in the Second Gospel and its Basis in the Biblical Tradition*. SBT 39. Eugene, OR: Wipf & Stock, 1963.

McNamara, Martin. *Targum and Testament Revisited: Aramaic Paraphrases of the Hebrew Bible: A Light on the New Testament*. 2nd ed. Grand Rapids, MI: Eerdmans, 2010.

McWhirter, Joceyln. 'Messianic Exegesis in Mark's Passion Narrative'. Pages 69–97 in *The Trial and Death of Jesus: Essays on the Passion Narrative in Mark*. Edited by Geert van Oyen and Thomas Shepherd. Leuven: Peeters, 2006.

Meier, J. P. 'The Circle of the Twelve: Did it Exist During Jesus' Public Ministry?' *JBL* 116 (1997): 635–72.

Meier, J. P. *A Marginal Jew: Rethinking the Historical Jesus, Vol. 2: Mentor, Message, and Miracles*. New York, NY: Doubleday, 1994.

Mell, Ulrich. 'Jesu Taufe durch Johannes (Markus 1,9-15) – zur narrative Christologie vom neuen Adam'. *BZ* 40 (1996): 161–78.

Meye, Robert P. *Jesus and the Twelve: Discipleship and Revelation in Mark's Gospel.* Grand Rapids, MI: Eerdmans, 1968.

Meyer, Rudolf. 'προφήτης C'. *TDNT* 6:812–28.

Millard, Allan. 'Judith, Tobit Ahiqar and History'. Pages 195–203 in *New Heaven and New Earth: Prophecy and the Millenium. Essays in Honour of Anthony Gelston.* Edited by Peter J. Harland and Robert Hayward. VTSup 77. Leiden: Brill, 1999.

Miller, Dale, and Patricia Miller. *The Gospel of Mark as Midrash on Earlier Jewish and New Testament Literature.* SBEC 21. Lewiston, NY: Edwin Mellen, 1990.

Moo, Douglas J. *The Old Testament in the Gospel Passion Narratives.* Sheffield: Almond, 1983.

Moore, Carey A. *Judith: A New Translation with Introduction and Commentary.* AB 40. Garden City, NY: Doubleday, 1985.

Moore, Carey A. 'Why Wasn't the Book of Judith Included in the Hebrew Bible?' Pages 61–71 in *No One Spoke Ill of Her.*

Moore, George F. *Judaism in the First Centuries of the Christian Era: The Age of the Tannaim.* 3 vols. Cambridge, MA: Harvard University Press, 1927.

Moss, Charlene McAfee. *The Zechariah Tradition and the Gospel of Matthew.* BZNW 156. Berlin: W. de Gruyter, 2009.

Motyer, Stephen. 'The Rending of the Veil: A Markan Pentecost?' *NTS* 33 (1987): 155–7.

Moyise, Steve. 'Is Mark's Opening Quotation the Key to his Use of Scripture?' *IBS* 20 (1998): 146–58.

Mroczek, Eva. *The Literary Imagination in Jewish Antiquity.* Oxford: Oxford University Press, 2016.

Mueller, Herman. 'Review of Suhl, *Die Funktion*'. *CBQ* 28 (1966): 95–7.

Mueller, James R. 'The *Apocalypse of Abraham* and the Destruction of the Second Jewish Temple'. Pages 341–9 in *The Society of Biblical Literature 1982 Seminar Papers.* Edited by Kent Harold Richards. SBLSP 21. Chico, CA: Scholars Press, 1982.

Munk, Eliyahu. *Torah Commentary of Rabbi Bachya Ben Asher,* 7 vols. Jerusalem: Urim, 1998.

Munoa, Phillip B. *Four Powers in Heaven: The Interpretation of Daniel 7 in the Testament of Abraham.* JSPSup 28; Sheffield: Sheffield Academic, 1998.

Münz-Manor, Ophir. 'Carnivalesque Ambivalence and the Christian Other in Aramaic Poems from Byzantine Palestine'. Pages 831–45 in *Jews in Byzantium: Dialectics of Minority and Majority Cultures.* Edited by Guy G. Stroumsa et al. Leiden: Brill, 2012.

Murphy, Frederick J. *Pseudo-Philo: Rewriting the Bible.* Oxford: Oxford University Press, 1993.

Murphy, Frederick J. 'Retelling the Bible: Idolatry in Pseudo-Philo'. *JBL* 107 (1988): 275–87.

Neirynck, Frans. 'L'Évangile de Marc (II). À propos de R. Pesch, *Das Markusevangelium, 2. Teil.* Review of Pesch, R. *Das Markusevangelium. II Teil: Kommentar Zu Kap. 8,27–16,20'. ETL* 55 (1979): 1–42.

Neuhaus, Günter. *Studien zu den poetischen Stücken im ersten Makkabäerbuch.* Würzburg: Echter, 1974.

Newman, Judith H. *Before the Bible: The Liturgical Body and the Formation of Scriptures in Early Judaism.* Oxford: Oxford University Press, 2018.

Newman, Judith H. *Praying by the Book: The Scripturalization of Prayer in Second Temple Judaism.* EJL 14. Atlanta, GA: Scholars Press, 1999.

Newsom, Carol A. *The Self as Symbolic Space: Constructing Identity and Community at Qumran.* STDJ 52. Leiden: Brill, 2004.

Nickelsburg, George W. E. *Jewish Literature Between the Bible and the Mishnah*. Minneapolis, MN: Fortress, 2011.

Nickelsburg, George W. E. 'Patriarchs Who Worry About Their Wives: A Haggadic Tendency in the Genesis Apocryphon'. Pages 177–99 in vol. 2 of *George W. E. Nickelsburg in Perspective: An Ongoing Dialogue of Learning*. Edited by Jacob Neusner and Alan J. Avery-Peck. 2 vols. JSJSup 82. Leiden: Brill, 2003.

Nickelsburg, George W. E. 'Structure and Message in the Testament of Abraham'. Pages 85–93 in *Studies on the Testament of Abraham*. Edited by George W. E. Nickelsburg. SACS 6. Missoula, MT: Scholars Press, 1976.

Nineham, Dennis E. *Saint Mark*. PGC. Harmondsworth: Penguin, 1963.

Nortje, S. J. 'John the Baptist and the Resurrection Traditions in the Gospels'. *Neot* 23 (1989): 349–58.

O'Brien, Kelli S. 'Innocence and Guilt: Apologetic, Martyr Stories, and Allusion in the Markan Trial Narratives'. Pages 205–28 in *The Trial and Death of Jesus: Essays on the Passion Narrative in Mark*. Edited by Geert van Oyen and Thomas Shepherd. Leuven: Peeters, 2006.

O'Brien, Kelli S. *The Use of Scripture in the Markan Passion Narrative*. LNTS 384. London: T&T Clark, 2010.

Öhler, Marcus. *Elia im Neuen Testament: Untersuchungen zur Bedeutung des alttestamentlichen Propheten im frühen Christentum*. BZNW 88. Berlin: W. de Gruyter, 1997.

Omerzu, Heike. 'Geschichte durch Geschichten. Zur Bedeutung jüdischer Traditionen für die Jesusdarstellung des Markusevangeliums'. *EC* 2 (2011): 77–99.

Omerzu, Heike. 'Die Rezeption von Psalm 22 im Judentum zur Zeit des Zweiten Tempels'. Pages 33–76 in *Psalm 22 und die Passiongeschichten der Evangelien*. Edited by Dieter Sänger. BthSt 88. Neukirchen-Vluyn: Neukirchener, 2007.

Otzen, Benedict. *Tobit and Judith*. Guides to Apocrypha and Pseudepigrapha. London: Sheffield Academic, 2002.

Owen, Paul. 'Jesus as God's Chief Agent in Mark's Christology'. Pages 40–58 in *Mark, Manuscripts, and Monotheism: Essays in Honor of Larry W. Hurtado*. Edited by Dieter Roth and Chris Keith. LNTS 528. London: Bloomsbury, 2016.

Parker, Neil R. *The Marcan Portrayal of the "Jewish" Unbeliever: A Function of the Marcan References to Jewish Scripture*. SBL 79. New York, NY: Lang, 2008.

Paton, Lewis Bayles. *A Critical and Exegetical Commentary on the Book of Esther*. ICC 19. Edinburgh: T. & T. Clark, 1908.

Pearson, Lionel. 'The Pseudo-History of Messenia and Its Authors'. *Historia: Zeitschrift für Alte Geschichte* (1962): 397–426.

Pellegrini, Silvia. *Elija – Wegbereiter des Gottesohnes: Eine textsemiotische Untersuchung im Markusevangelium*. HBS 26. Freiburg: Peterson, 2000.

Perkins, Larry. '"The Lord is a Warrior" – "The Lord Who Shatters Wars": Exodus 15:3 and Judith 9:7; 16:2'. *BIOSCS* 40 (2007): 121–38.

Perrot, Charles, Pierre-Maurice Bogaert and Daniel J. Harrington. *Pseudo-Philon: Les Antiquités Bibliques*. 2 vols. SC 230. Paris. Cerf, 1976.

Pervo, Richard I. 'Panta Kiona: The Feeding Stories in the Light of Economic Data and Social Practice'. Pages 163–94 in *Religious Propaganda and Missionary Competition in the New Testament World*. Edited by Lukas Bormann. Leiden: Brill, 1994.

Pesch, Rudolf. 'Anfang des Evangeliums Jesu Christi. Eine Studie zum Prolog des Markusevangeliums (Mark 1,1-15)'. Pages 108–44 in *Die Zeit Jesu: Festschrift für Heinrich Schlier*. Edited by Günther Bornkamm and Karl Rahner. Freiburg: Herder, 1970.

Pesch, Rudolf. 'Berufung und Sendung, Nachfolge und Mission: Eine Studie zu Mk 1,16-20'. *ZKT* 91 (1969): 1–31.

Pesch, Rudolf. *Das Markusevangelium*. 2 vols. HTKNT. Freiburg: Herder, 1976–77.

Petersen, David L. *Late Israelite Prophecy: Studies in Deutero-prophetic Literature and in Chronicles*. SBLMS 23. Atlanta, GA: Scholars Press, 1977.

Pokorny, Petr. 'The Temptation Stories and Their Intention'. *NTS* 20 (1974): 115–27.

Porton, Gary G. 'Defining Midrash'. Pages 55–92 in vol. 1 of *The Study of Ancient Judaism*. Edited by Neusner. New York, NY: Ktav, 1981.

Price, Robert M. 'New Testament Narrative as Old Testament Midrash'. Pages 534–74 in vol. 1 of *Encyclopedia of Midrash*.

Pyeon, Yohan. *You Have Not Spoken What Is Right About Me: Intertextuality and the Book of Job*. SBL 45. New York, NY: Lang, 2003.

Rajak, Tessa. 'Hasmonean Kingship and Tradition'. Pages 39–60 in *The Jewish Dialogue with Greece and Rome: Studies in Cultural and Social Interaction*. Edited by Tessa Rajak. AGAJU 48. Leiden: Brill, 2001.

Rakel, Claudia. '"I Will Sing a New Song to my God": Some Remarks on the Intertextuality of Judith 16.1-17'. Pages 27–47 in *Judges: A Feminist Companion to the Bible*. Edited by Athalya Brenner. Sheffield: Sheffield Academic, 1999.

Rakel, Claudia. *Judit – über Schönheit, Macht und Widerstand im Krieg: Eine feministisch-intertextuelle Lektüre*. BZAW 334. Berlin: W. de Gruyter, 2003.

Rappaport, Uriel. 'A Note on the Use of the Bible in 1 Maccabees'. Pages 175–79 in *Biblical Perspectives: Early Use and Interpretation of the Bible in Light of the Dead Sea Scrolls: Proceedings of the First International Symposium of the Orion Center for the Study of the Dead Sea Scrolls and Associated Literature, 12–14 May, 1996*. Edited by Michael E. Stone and Esther G. Chazon. STDJ 28. Leiden: Brill, 1998.

Reeves, John C. *Jewish Lore in Manichaean Cosmogony: Studies in the Book of Giants Traditions*. HUCM 14. Cincinnati, OH: Hebrew Union College, 1992.

Reiss, Jacob. 'Das Targum Scheni zu dem Buche Esther'. *MGWJ* 25 (1876): 398–406.

Reinmuth, Eckhart. *Pseudo-Philo und Lukas: Studien zum Liber Antiquitatum Biblicarum und seiner Bedeutung für die Interpretation des lukanischen Doppelwerks*. WUNT 2/74. Tübingen: Mohr Siebeck, 1994.

Reiterer, Friedrich V. 'Die Vergangenheit als Basis für die Zukunft Mattathias' Lehre für seine Söhne aus der Geschichte in 1 Makk 2:52-60'. Pages 75–100 in *The Books of the Maccabees*.

Robinson, J. A. T. 'Elijah, John and Jesus: An Essay in Detection'. *NTS* 4 (1958): 263–81.

Robinson, Marilynne. 'The Book of Books: What Literature Owes the Bible'. *The New York Times*. 22 December 2011, 22.

Roth, Wolfgang. *Hebrew Gospel: Cracking the Code of Mark*. Oak Park, IL: Meyer-Stone Books, 1988.

Rowe, Robert D. *God's Kingdom and God's Son: The Background to Mark's Christology from Concepts of Kingship in the Psalms*. AGAJU 50. Leiden: Brill, 2002.

Ruiten, Jacques T. A. G. M. van. *Abraham in the Book of Jubilees: The Rewriting of Genesis 11:26–25:10 in the Book of Jubilees 11:14–23:8*. JSJSup 161. Brill: Leiden, 2012.

Sanders, E. P. 'Testament of Abraham'. Pages 871–904 in vol. 1 of *OTP*.

Saunderson, Barbara. 'Gethsemane: The Missing Witness'. *Biblica* 79 (1989): 224–33.

Schedl, Claus. 'Nabochodonosor, Arpakšad und Darius'. *ZDMG* 115 (1965): 242–54.

Scheil, Jean-Vincent. 'Cylindres et Légendes Inédits (avec trois planches)'. *RA* 13 (1961): 5–25.

Schenke, Ludger. *Studien zur Passionsgeschichte des Markus. Tradition und Redaktion in Markus 14,1-42*. FZB 4. Würzburg: Echter, 1971.

Schille, Gottfried. 'Das Leiden des Herrn. Die evangelische Passionstradition und ihr "Sitz im Leben"'. *ZTK* 52 (1955): 161–205.

Schmid, Josef. *The Gospel According to Mark*. Staten Island, NY: Alba House, 1968.

Schmidt, Francis. 'Naissance d'une geographe juive'. Pages 13–30 in *Moïse géographe: Recherches sur les representations juives et chrétiennes de l'éspace*. Edited by Alain Desreumaux and Schmidt. Paris: Vrin, 1988.

Schmidt, T. E. 'Mark 15.16-32: The Crucifixion Narrative and the Roman Triumphal Procession'. *NTS* 41 (1995): 1–18.

Schmithals, Walter. *Das Evangelium nach Markus: Kapitel 9,2-16*. OTK 2/2. Gütersloh: Mohn, 1979.

Schnackenburg, Rudolf. 'Der Sinn der Versuchung Jesu bei den Synoptikern'. *TQ* 132 (1952): 297–326.

Schneck, Richard. *Isaiah in the Gospel of Mark, I-VIII*. BIBALDS 1. Vallejo, CA: BIBAL, 1994.

Scholz, Anton. *Das Buch Judith – eine Prophetie*. Würzberg: Leo Woerl, 1885.

Schreiber, Johannes. *Die Markuspassion*. 2nd ed. BZNW 68. Berlin: W. de Gruyter, 1993.

Schulz, Anselm. *Nachfolgen und Nachahmen*. StANT 6. Munich: Kösel, 1962.

Schulz, Siegfried. 'Markus und das Alte Testament'. *ZTK* 58 (1961): 184–97.

Schunck, Klaus-Dietrich. *1. Makkabäerbuch*. JSHRZ 1/4. Gütersloh: Mohn, 1980.

Schwartz, Daniel R. *2 Maccabees*. CEJL. Berlin: W. de Gruyter, 2008.

Schwartz, Seth. 'Israel and the Nations Roundabout: 1 Maccabees and the Hasmonean Expansion'. *JJS* 42 (1991): 16–38.

Schweitzer, Albert. *The Mystery of the Kingdom of God: The Secret of Jesus' Messiahship and Passion*. Translated by Walter Lowrie. New York, NY: Dodd, Mead & Co., 1914.

Schweizer, Eduard. *Das Evangelium nach Markus*. NTD 1. Göttingen: Vandenhoeck & Ruprecht, 1967.

Scott, James M. *Geography in Early Judaism and Christianity: The Book of Jubilees*. SNTS 113. Cambridge: Cambridge University Press, 2002.

Seethaler, Angelika. 'Die Brotvermehrung – Ein Kirchenspiegel?' *BZ* 34 (1990): 108–12.

Segal, Michael. *The Book of Jubilees: Rewritten Bible, Redaction, Ideology and Theology*. JSJSup 117. Leiden: Brill, 2007.

Sherman, Philip Michael. *Babel's Tower Translated: Genesis 11 and Ancient Jewish Interpretation*. BibInt 117. Leiden: Brill, 2013.

Siker, Jeffrey S. '"First to the Gentiles": A Literary Analysis of Luke 4:16-30'. *JBL* 111 (1992): 73–90.

Silva, David A. de. 'Judith the Heroine? Lies, Seduction, and Murder in Cultural Perspective'. *BTB* 36 (2006): 55–61.

Smith, Jessie Payne. *A Compendious Syriac Dictionary*. Oxford: Oxford University Press, 1902. Repr. ALR. Eugene, OR: Wipf & Stock, 1999.

Snodgrass, Klyne R. 'Streams of Tradition Emerging from Isaiah 40:1-5 and their Adaption in the New Testament'. *JSNT* 8 (1980): 24–45.

Standhartinger, Angela. '"And All Ate and Were Filled" (Mark 6.42 par.): The Feeding Narratives in the Context of Hellenistic-Roman Banquet Culture'. Pages 62–82 in *Decisive Meals: Dining Politics in Biblical Literature*. Edited by Nathan MacDonald, Luzia Sutter Rehman and Kathy Ehrensperger. LNTS 449. London: T&T Clark, 2012.

Stegner, William Richard. *Narrative Theology in Early Christianity*. Louisville, KY: Westminster John Knox, 1989.

228 *Bibliography*

Steichele, Hans-Jörg. *Der leidende Sohn Gottes: Eine Untersuchung einiger alttestamentlicher Motive in der Christologie des Markusevangeliums.* BU 14. Regensburg: Pustet, 1980.

Stein, Robert H. *Mark.* BECNT. Grand Rapids, MI: Baker Academic, 2008.

Stemberger, Günter. *Midrasch: Vom Umgang der Rabbinen mit der Bibel. Einführung – Texte – Erläuterungen.* Munich: Beck, 2002.

Stendahl, Krister. *The School of St. Matthew and Its Use of the Old Testament.* Philadelphia, PA: Fortress, 1968.

Stone, Michael E. 'Review of Munoa, *Four Powers in Heaven*'. *JQR* 90 (1999): 235–7.

Stott, Katherine M. 'Ezra's "Lost Manuscripts": Narrative Context and Rhetorical Function'. Pages 96–106 in *The One Who Reads May Run: Essays in Honour of Edgar W. Conrad.* Edited by Roland Boer, Michael Carden and Julie Kelso. LHBOTS 553. London: T&T Clark, 2012.

Strauss, David Friedrich. *Das Leben Jesu: kritisch bearbeitet.* 2 vols. Tübingen: Osiander, 1835. 3rd ed. 1839. 4th ed. 1840.

Subramanian, J. Samuel. *The Synoptic Gospels and the Psalms as Prophecy.* LNTS 351. London: T&T Clark, 2007.

Suhl, Alfred. *Die Funktion der alttestamentlichen Zitate und Anspielungen im Markusevangelium.* Gütersloh: Mohn, 1965.

Swenson, Kristin M. 'Psalm 22:17: Circling around the Problem Again'. *JBL* 123 (2004): 637–48.

Swete, H. B. *The Gospel According to St Mark.* London: Macmillan, 1905.

Sydow, Carl W. von. 'Geography and Folk-Tale Oicotypes'. Pages 44–55 in *C. W. von Sydow, Selected Papers on Folklore.* Edited by L. Bødker; Copenhagen: Rosenkilde & Bagger, 1948.

Taylor, Joan E. *The Immerser: John the Baptist within Second Temple Judaism.* Grand Rapids, MI: Eerdmans, 1997.

Taylor, Vincent. *The Gospel According to St. Mark.* 2nd ed. London: Macmillan, 1966.

Teugels, Lieve. 'Midrash in the Bible or Midrash on the Bible? Critical Remarks about the Uncritical Use of a Term'. Pages 43–63 in *Bibel und Midrasch: zur Bedeutung der rabbinischen Exegese für die Bibelwissenschaft.* Edited by G. Bodendorfer and M. Millard. FAT 22. Tübingen: Mohr Siebeck, 1998.

Theissen, Gerd. *Lokalkolorit und Zeitgeschichte in den Evangelien. Ein Beitrag zur Geschichte der synoptischen Tradition.* NTOA 8. Göttingen: Vandenhoeck & Ruprecht, 1992.

Thiessen, Matthew. *Contesting Conversion: Genealogy, Circumcision, and Identity in Ancient Judaism and Christianity.* Oxford: Oxford University Press, 2011.

Tilly, Michael. *Johannes der Taüfer und die Biographie der Propheten: Die synoptische Taüferüberlieferung und das jüdische Prophetenbild zur Zeit des Täufers.* BWANT 137. Stuttgart: Kohlhammer, 1994.

Tolbert, Mary Ann. *Sowing the Gospel: Mark's World in Literary-Historical Perspective.* Minneapolis, MN: Fortress, 1996.

Torrey, Charles Cutler. *Documents of the Primitive Church.* New York, NY: Harper & Brothers, 1941.

Torrey, Charles Cutler. *Lives of the Prophets: Greek Text and Translation.* SBLMS 1. Philadelphia, PA: Society of Biblical Literature and Exegesis, 1946.

Trocmé, Étienne. *The Passion as Liturgy: A Study in the Origin of the Passion Narrative in the Four Gospels.* London: SCM, 1983.

Turner, Nigel. *The Testament of Abraham: A Study of the Original Language, Place of Origin, Authorship, and Relevance*. London: University of London, 1953.

Tuschling, Ruth M. M. *Angels and Orthodoxy: A Study in Their Development in Syria and Palestine from the Qumran Texts to Ephrem the Syrian*. STAC 40. Tübingen: Mohr Siebeck, 2007.

Ulansey, David. 'The Heavenly Veil Torn: Mark's Cosmic *Inclusio*'. *JBL* 110 (1991): 123–5.

Ulmer, Rivka. 'Psalm 22 in Pesiqta Rabbati: The Suffering of the Jewish Messiah and Jesus'. Pages 106–28 in *The Jewish Jesus: Revelation, Reflection, Reclamation*. Edited by Zev Garber. West Lafayette, IN: Purdue University Press, 2011.

Upson-Saia, Kristi. 'Hairiness and Holiness in the Early Christian Desert'. Pages 155–72 in *Dressing Judeans and Christians in Antiquity*. Edited by Upson-Saia, Carly Daniel-Hughes and Alicia J. Batten. London: Routledge, 2014.

VanderKam, James C. *Jubilees 1–21*. Hermeneia. Minneapolis, MN: Fortress, 2018.

Vanhoye, Albert. 'La fuite de jeune homme nu (Mc 14,51-52)'. *Bib* 52 (1971): 401–6.

Vermes, Geza. '2. The Genesis Apocryphon from Qumran'. Pages 318–325 in vol. 3 of *The History of the Jewish People in the Age of Jesus Christ* by Emil Schürer. Rev. Geza Vermes, Fergus Millar and Martin Goodman. Edinburgh: T. & T. Clark, 1986.

Vermes, Geza. 'Ḥanina ben Dosa'. *JJS* 23 (1972): 28–50. *JJS* 24 (1973): 51–64.

Vermes, Geza. *Scripture and Tradition in Judaism: Haggadic Studies*. SPB. Leiden: Brill, 1961.

Vette, Nathanael. 'Who is Elijah in the Gospel of Mark?' Pages 799–810 in *Reading the Gospel of Mark in the Twenty-First Century*. Edited by Van Oyen. BETL 301. Leuven: Peeters, 2019.

Vette, Nathanael. 'Kenaz: A Figure Created out of the Scriptures?' *JSP* 29 (2020): 245–59.

Vette, Nathanael. 'The Many Fiery Furnaces of Daniel 3: The Evolution of a Literary Model'. *Biblical Interpretation* (forthcoming).

Vette, Nathanael, and Will Robinson. 'Was John the Baptist Raised from the Dead? The Origins of Mark 6:14-29'. *BibAn* 9 (2019): 335–54.

Vorster, Willem S. 'The Function of the Use of the Old Testament in Mark'. *NeoT* 14 (1980): 62–72.

Vorster, Willem S. 'The Production of the Gospel of Mark: Essay on Intertextuality'. *HTS* 49 (1993): 385–96.

Wacholder, Ben Z. 'How Long did Abram Stay in Egypt?' *HUCA* 35 (1964): 43–56.

Wadsworth, Michael. *The* Liber Antiquitatum Biblicarum *of Pseudo-Philo: Doctrine and Scriptural Exegesis in a Jewish Midrash of the First Century A.D.* 2 vols. Oxford: Oxford University, 1975.

Wadsworth, Michael. 'Making and Interpreting Scripture'. Pages 7–22 in *Ways of Reading the Bible*. Edited by Michael Wadsworth. Sussex: Harvester, 1981.

Walt, Charl Pretorius Van der. 'The Prayer of Esther (LXX) and Judith Against Their Social Backgrounds: Evidence of a Possible Common "Grundlage"?' *JSem* 17 (2008): 194–206.

Watts, Rikki E. *Isaiah's New Exodus*. WUNT 2/88. Tübingen: Mohr Siebeck, 1997.

Watts, Rikki E. 'The Psalms in Mark's Gospel'. Pages 25–45 in *The Psalms in the New Testament*. Edited by Moyise and Maarten J. J. Menken. London: T&T Clark, 2004.

Weeden, Theodore J. 'The Heresy That Necessitated Mark's Gospel'. *ZNW* 59 (1968): 145–58.

Weeden, Theodore J. *Mark – Traditions in Conflict*. Philadelphia, PA: Fortress, 1971.

Weidel, Karl. 'Studien über den Einfluss des Weissagungsbeweises auf die evangelische Geschichte'. *TSK* 83 (1910): 83–109, 163–95; *TSK* 85 (1912): 167–286.

Weinberg, Joanna. 'Job versus Abraham: The Quest for the Perfect God-Fearer in Rabbinic Tradition'. Pages 281–96 in *The Book of Job*. Edited by W. A. M. Beuken. BETL 114. Leuven: Peeters, 1994.

Weiss, Johannes. *Die Drei* Älteren *Evangelien*. 2nd ed. Die Schriften des NT 1. Göttingen, 1907.

Whitters, Mark F. 'Why Did the Bystanders Think Jesus Called Upon Elijah Before He Died (Mark 15:34-36)? The Markan Position'. *HTR* 95 (2002): 119–24.

Wills, Lawrence M. *Judith*. Hermeneia. Minneapolis, MN: Fortress, 2019.

Wink, Walter. *John the Baptist in the Gospel Tradition*. SNTSMS 7. Cambridge: Cambridge University Press, 1968.

Winn, Adam. *Mark and the Elijah–Elisha Narrative: Considering the Practice of Greco-Roman Imitation in the Search for Markan Source Material*. Eugene, OR: Wipf & Stock, 2010.

Winn, Adam. *Reading Mark's Christology Under Caesar: Jesus the Messiah and Roman Imperial Ideology*. Downers Grove, IL; IVP Academic, 2018.

Witherington III, Ben. *The Gospel of Mark: A Socio-Rhetorical Commentary*. Grand Rapids, MI: Eerdmans, 2001.

Zahn, Theodor. *Einleitung in das Neue Testament.* 3rd ed. Leipzig: Deichert, 1907.

Zakovitch, Yair. 'The Exodus from Ur of the Chaldeans: A Chapter in Literary Archaeology'. Pages 429–39 in *Ki Baruch Hu: Ancient Near Eastern, Biblical and Judaic Studies in Honor of Baruch Levine*. Edited by Robert Chazan, William Hallo and Lawrence Schiffman. Warsaw, IN: Eisenbrauns, 1999.

Zeitlin, Solomon. *The First Book of Maccabees*. With English translation of the text by Sidney Tedesche. New York, NY: Harper, 1950.

Zeitlin, Solomon. 'Introduction: The Books of Esther and Judith: A Parallel'. Page 1–37 in *The Book of Judith: Greek Text with an English Translation, Commentary and Critical Notes*. Edited by Enslin. JAL 7. Leiden: Brill, 1972.

Zelyck, Lorne R. 'Elisha Typology in Jesus' Miracle on the Jordan River (Papyrus Egerton 2,2v.6-14)'. *NTS* 62 (2015): 1–8.

Zeron, Alexander. 'Erwägungen zu Pseudo-Philos Quellen und Zeit'. *JSJ* 11 (1980): 38–52.

Zimmerman, Frank. 'Aids for the Recovery of the Hebrew Original of Judith'. *JBL* 57 (1938): 67–74.

INDEX OF REFERENCES

HEBREW BIBLE/ OLD TESTAMENT

Genesis

1.1-27	88
1.2	122
1.6-9	62
1.9	35
1.28-30	69, 74
1.28	69, 72
1.29	70, 72
2–3	131
2.11	56, 58
4.1-16	35
4.22	34
5–15	64
5.4-32	34
6.14	36
7.4	132
7.12	132
7.17	132
7.21-23	35
8.6	132
8.15-21	65
8.15-20	66
8.22	75
9.1-7	67, 70, 74, 159, 201
9.1-4	159
9.1	69, 72
9.2	88
9.3-4	70
9.3	72
9.4	72
9.7	72
9.13-15	35
9.18-27	65
9.21-27	66
10–11	40, 47
10	43
10.2-31	73
10.6-8	56
10.8-10	43
10.10	45
10.23	33
10.25-29	43
10.25	43
10.26-29	42
11	40, 45, 47
11.1-9	36, 40, 47–8
11.1-6	45
11.1	47
11.2-4	42
11.2	45
11.3	39, 42
11.4	47
11.9	44
11.16-19	43
11.17	128
11.18-29	42
11.28	39–40
11.31	47
12.7	73
12.10-20	69
12.11-13	65
12.11	68
12.18-19	66
13–15	108, 159
13	69, 201
13.7	159
13.14-17	66, 70, 74
13.15	73
13.17	70, 198
13.18	101
14.1	45
14.9	45
14.13	101
14.15	68
14.22-23	66
15	69, 201
15.1-6	74
15.1	70–1, 74, 159
15.3	35
15.6	77
15.7	38–9, 42, 44, 47, 51, 63, 109, 152, 156, 159–60
15.11	130
15.14	88
15.18-21	73
16.3	66
16.24	159
18–25	101
18.1-15	159
18.1	101
18.7	35
18.8	140
18.11-15	68
19.25	36, 98
19.28	44
20	69
20.4	69
20.7	69
22.1-19	77, 88
22.1	128
22.2-3	101
22.2	123–5
22.9	101

Index of References

Genesis (cont.)

22.11-12	101
22.12	123
22.16	101, 123
22.17	35, 101
24.31	113
25.7-11	100
25.30	96, 98
26	69
26.24	70–1, 74, 198
27.2	4
27.11	118
28.5	88
29.1–32.1	88
30.37-39	35, 98
32.24-27	35
34	95
37.12-36	186
37.18-28	3
37.19	118
37.22	46, 190
39.7-12	77
39.12	173
41.8	69
41.12	173
41.39-45	77
42.8	63
46.17	33
49.4	140
49.23	118
49.33	36, 63–4, 98

Exodus

2.3	36
3.8	35
5–14	86
7.11	69
7.28	44
9.8	44
9.10	44
9.11	69
10.22	191
12.37	144
14	35

14.12	89–90
14.21-22	120
14.22	35
14.27-28	35
15.1-20	89
15.1	89
15.3	87, 89
15.20-21	90
15.20	89
15.21	89
16	143
16.4-36	143
16.4-35	143
16.4	128
16.8	143
16.12	143
16.16	141
16.18	145
16.32	143
17.3	89
17.6	46, 129
17.7	128
18.21	79, 143–4
18.25	79, 143–4
19.18	44
20.2	48
20.13-14	34
20.13	34
20.15	34
20.17	180
20.20	128, 130, 140
23.20	15, 19, 112–14, 116, 125
23.20 LXX	4
23.21-22	112
24	167, 205
24.8	167
24.14	118
24.18	132
25	36
25.30	79
26.33	79
28.17-20	56
33.1-23 LXX	19

34.2	76
34.6	19
34.22	3
34.24	79
34.28	130, 132
40.4-5	79

Leviticus

2.4	44
2.13	67
2.14	145
4.18	67
4.19	67
7.9	44
7.26	67, 72
8.25	140
10.2	41
11.13-19	130
11.35	44
14.36	113
14.40	79
19.23-25	67
20.10	3
20.11	67
20.25	76
21.3-4	118
21.10	180
23.9-14	145
23.34-44	4
23.34	4
23.38	3
23.40-42	4
24.12	55–6, 63
26.26	44

Numbers

5.29	118
11	143
11.6-9	143
11.9	143
11.26-29	205
11.31-35	143
12.10	113
13–14	35
13.30	77
14.6-10	77

14.19	140	2.26-34	81	28.57	93
14.24	77	2.26-30	82	29.18	55
14.30	77	2.26	108	30.9	140
15–16	35	2.27-28	108	32.26	75, 79, 84
15.24-25	67	2.27	80–1, 83	33.2	34
15.24	67	2.28	81, 83	33.7	58, 61
15.34	55–6, 63	2.30-31	82	33.8	128
16	46	2.30	81, 83	33.12	123
16.31-35	46–7	2.31-33	81	34.1-6	103
16.32	101	2.32	81		
20.14-21	80	2.33	82	*Joshua*	
20.17	81	2.34	81	1.7-8	49, 190
20.19	81	2.35	82	2.10	87, 90
21.21-24	80–1	2.36	82	6.7	140
21.22	80	3.5	79, 84	6.21	82
21.23	81	3.14	48	6.25	90
21.24	81–2	3.23-29	103	7	36, 54–6
21.27	113	4.20	44	7.16-26	141
22–24	35	5.16	180	7.16-18	55
23.19	88	5.32	49	7.19-21	55
25.6-13	78, 161	6.13	129	7.21-22	56
25.6	78	6.16	128–9	7.25	62
25.7	78	7.18	78	7.26	56
25.10	78	8.3	129, 143	8.24	82
25.11-13	77–8	9.9	130, 132	10.13	38
27.1-33	36	9.18	130	13.30	48
27.1-11	62	9.22	128	14.8	35
27.17	143–4	13.1-4	37	15.7	54
27.21	55	14.22-23	4	15.17	54, 61
29.12-40	4	18.15-19	78	15.19	61–2
32.12	54, 77	19.8	79	23.6	55–6
32.41	48	20.5-8	79, 82	23.14	63
33.22	67	20.10-14	82–4, 109,	24.15	56, 62
36.1-12	37, 62		159, 161,	24.25	77
			190, 198	24.33	55
Deuteronomy		20.10-11	82		
1.15	79, 143	20.10	83	*Judges*	
1.33	114	20.12	82–3	1.1-10	55
2.13	83	20.13	83, 108,	1.1-2	55
2.20	68		160	1.1	55–6
2.24	82	20.14	82–3	1.2	62
2.26-37	80	21.23	191	1.13	54, 61
2.26-36	80, 83–4,	25.5-10	3	1.15	61–2
	108–9,	26.26-36	190	1.18	62
	159–60,	27.6	79	3.9-10	61
	198	28.14	55–6	3.9	54, 61

Index of References

Judges (cont.)

3.10	58–61
3.11	54
3.15-30	62
3.24	93
4–5	93–4, 96, 98, 156, 159, 198, 202
4	94
4.1-16	93
4.3	46
4.9	93–4, 97, 109, 202
4.13	46
4.17-22	108
4.17	93
4.18-19	93
4.18	94–5, 97
4.19	94, 96–8
4.21-22	95
4.21	93, 96–7
4.22	93, 97
4.23-24	93
5	90, 93–4
5.24	93–4, 97
5.25	94, 97
5.26	95, 97
5.27	93, 97
6.10	56–7, 62
6.14	113
6.16	61
6.34	58–9
6.36-40	57
7	36, 57, 156, 190, 198
7.2	58
7.6-22	198
7.6-9	59
7.7-11	58
7.7	60
7.8-9	57
7.8	63
7.9-14	57
7.9	60
7.10-11	59

7.11	58, 60–1
7.13-14	59
7.14-15	58, 60
7.14	57, 59, 63, 108
7.15	59
7.16-18	57, 59
7.22	58, 60, 63
9.28-41	62
9.54	96
10.3-5	48, 51
10.5	50, 52, 109, 159
10.6	51
11.19-21	80–4, 108–9, 160, 190
11.19	80–1, 83, 108, 198
11.20	81, 83
11.21	81–2
11.29	58
14.6	58
14.19	58
15	55
15.14	58
16.16	177
16.27	46

Ruth

1.16	90
2.14	140
3.7	93

1 Samuel

1	177
1.8	178
2.36	140
5.12	76
7.5-6	78
7.6	78
9–10	144
10.6	57–8, 60, 63, 190
13.17	113
14.23	76
14.36-46	55

17	55
24.4	93
30.16	55

2 Samuel

1.25	80
1.27	80
2.7	76
6	36
7.1-17	77
11.8	93
15.12	171
15.30-31	171
23.9-10	63
23.10	58, 60–1, 190

1 Kings

4.13	48
8	36
8.51	44
11.41	76
13.8	149
14.19	76
17	9, 24–5, 37
17.1	131
17.2-7	130–2
17.2	131
17.3-4	46
17.3	131–2
17.4-6	127, 131
17.4	129, 131
17.6	119, 130
17.7-16	26
17.17-24	9, 24
18–21	147
18.3-8	147
18.4	143
18.13	143
18.24	49, 51, 190
19	125–6, 128, 130, 133, 137, 139, 197, 198

19.1-9	46
19.1-8	129
19.2	133
19.3	130
19.4-21	24, 26, 28
19.4-18	130
19.4-8	127, 129–32, 138, 147
19.4	126–7, 130
19.5-7	126–7
19.6-8	129
19.6	119, 129
19.7	127
19.8	126–7, 129, 132–3
19.9-14	133
19.10	77, 130
19.11-18	126
19.13	117
19.14	77, 130
19.15-18	133
19.15-16	133
19.19-21	134–6, 138
19.19	117, 126–7, 135–6
19.20-21	127, 136, 147
19.20	126–7, 135–6
19.21	126, 135

2 Kings

1.8	116–19, 125, 129, 131, 147
1.8 LXX	5
1.10	102
2	37
2.1-12	26
2.7	120
2.8-12	120, 125
2.8	117, 120
2.9-15	121
2.9	120
2.11-14	137
2.11	120, 147
2.12	120, 137
2.13-14	117, 120
2.14	120
2.15	120
2.24	101
2.42-44	198
3.11	137
4.1	143
4.8	140
4.12	139
4.18-37	9, 24, 121
4.25	139
4.38-41	139
4.38	139, 145–6
4.40	140
4.41	139
4.42-44	24, 26, 28, 121, 138–42, 144–7, 197
4.42	139, 140, 144
4.43-44	140
4.43	139–41, 144, 146
4.44	139–41
5	9
5.1-19	26
5.9-14	121, 125
5.10	121
5.14	121
6.19	134
10.26-27	52
13	9, 24–5
13.20-21	121
13.21	9
17.17	76
19.19	88
23.5	75
23.11	75

1 Chronicles

2.22-23	48
2.51	35
4.10	61
4.13	54
4.15	35
7.20-27	35
15–16	36
29.17	128

2 Chronicles

20.29	58
28.15	140
36.7-18	77

Nehemiah

9.1	89
9.5-37	28
9.15	143
9.25	143

Esther

1.1-3	155
1.1	155
1.3	155
1.15	155
2.9	150
3.1-11	149
3.14-15	92
3.15	92
4.1-4	89
5.1	185
5.3	4, 148, 150, 152, 155, 198
5.5-8	91
5.6	4, 148, 150, 152, 155
6.14–7.1	91
6.24-25	150
6.27-28	150
7.1-10	149–50, 197–8
7.2	4, 148, 150, 152, 155

Esther (cont.)

7.3-6	152
7.3-4	149
7.5-6	150
7.9-10	150, 152
7.9	149, 152
8.15	68
9.12	148, 155
10.2	38
14–15	92
14	178
14.1–15.5	92
14.1-2	91
14.3-19	91
14.17	91
15.1-6	91
15.9	91
A 2.9	149, 152
A 5.3	150, 152
A 5.5	149, 152
A 5.6	150, 152, 155
A 7.1-12	149
A 7.12	152
A 7.2	150, 152
A 7.7	152
A 7.9	152
O 5.3	155

Job

1–2	103, 104, 106–8, 159, 198
1.1	103–5
1.6-12	104
1.8	103–5, 109
1.10	104
1.12	104, 105
1.14	104, 105
1.16-18	104, 105
1.20-22	104, 105
2.1-2	104, 105
2.3	104, 105, 109
2.6	104, 105
2.10	104, 105

4.2-6	105
4.7	105
4.12	106
12.10	107
19.3	105
23.10	128
28.23	107

Psalms

2	123
2.7	123–5, 188
7.2	167
12.6	167
14.10	162
17.3	128
18.5	167
18.9	35, 122, 125
19.5	101
21	181, 189–90
21.1	158, 170, 197
21.2	183, 185
21.8-9	183, 197
21.9	183
21.10	44
21.14	188
21.16	188
21.17	189
21.19	160, 182, 197, 204
21.19 LXX	5
22	181, 183–5, 188–9, 197, 199, 201, 203–4
22.1-21	188
22.1	158, 184–6, 188, 197
22.4-21	186
22.7-8	183
22.13-21	187
22.13-15	188

22.13	187
22.14-17	186
22.14	187–8
22.15	167, 187
22.17	189
22.18	160, 182–3
22.21-31	184
22.21-22	188
22.21	186–7
22.22	186
26.2	128
26.8	36
26.12	167
27.9	187
27.12	180
30.6	185
31.5	185
31.10	167
31.13	167
35.13	89
37	195
37.12	159, 189, 195–7
38	197, 204
38.11	159, 195
38.21	187
40	182
40.10	162–3, 165–7, 172, 189
41–42	176
41	163–4, 177
41.1	163–4
41.6	176
41.7	176–7
41.9	162–7, 171–2
41.12	176
42–43	176
42	177–8
42.1	177
42.2	178
42.3	177–8
42.5	176
42.6-7	167

42.6	176–8, 189	118.1	76	14.4	75
42.7	177	118.22	189	15.7	140
51.10	4	118.29	76	21.4	121
54.3	167	126.2	123	23.20	165
58.6	187	127.2	123	29.13	165
59.7	123	128.3	178	33.16	129
60.4	123	139.23	128	36.21	180
68.21	195	144.5	122, 125	40	143
68.22	189, 194, 197			40.1-5	113
		Proverbs		40.3	15, 19, 112–14, 116, 119, 125, 165
69	197	17.3	44, 128		
69.10-11	89	23.18	88		
69.10	194	27.21	44		
69.21-22	167	29.22	118	40.3 LXX	4
69.21	28, 194	31	68	40.3-5	113
69.23	185	31.6-7	194	40.4	114
71.9	187	31.10-31	68	40.15	125
71.18	187	31.29	68	41.8-9	123
77.24	143–4			42	124
77.29	143	*Ecclesiastes*		42.1-4	124
78.2-3	75	1.3	140	42.1	114, 123–5
78.18	128	2.11	140		
78.25	63	2.13	140	43.10	123
78.41	128	3.9	140	45.21-22	125
79.2-3	75	3.18	128	45.21	125
79.10	113	5.8	140	48.10	44
81.7	128	5.15	140	49.6	168
85.	125	6.8	140	50–53	170
86.14	167	7.11-12	140	50.4	168
88.3-4	167	10.10-11	140	50.6	169
89.44	75			51.1	125
92.13	68	*Song of Songs*		52.1	168
92.14	68	2.14	68	52.7	168
95.8-9	128	4.1	68	53	10, 24, 169–70
104.40	143	4.5	68		
106.9	36	5.15	68	53.3	168
106.14	128	6.5	68	53.7	63
107.7	123	7.1	68	53.9	169
108.6	123	7.3	68	53.12	167–70, 172
109.1	188	7.4	68		
110.1	179, 181, 188	7.7-8	68	56.3	177
				57.14	113
		Isaiah		58.5	89
114.4	125	1.31	44	62.10	113
116.15	125	4.3	140	64.1	122
117.22-23	172	7.20	93	65.20	4
117.26	188	9.1-2	170	66.24	88

Jeremiah		3.23	43	*Nahum*	
1.6	63	3.25-27	44	2.9	113
11.4	44	3.25	41–2, 49,		
11.20	128		52–3	*Habakkuk*	
12.3	128	3.26	44, 52	1.13	3
52.17-23	77	3.27-28	42		
		3.27	46, 53	*Haggai*	
Lamentations		3.46-50	49	1.9	113
2.21	77	3.47-48	47		
5.10	44	3.47	43	*Zechariah*	
		3.48	43–4, 52	3.15	113
Ezekiel		6	46	8.4	80
6.6	75	6.17-24	76, 77	8.12	80
16.25	93	7.13	179, 181	9.9	170
22.18-22	44	9.3	89	9.11	167
25.15	55	11.31	76	11.13	163
27.18	68	12.10	130	12.10	189
34	143			13.7	165, 171–
		Hosea			72, 174–6
Daniel		2.11	75		
1.2	45	6.2	162	*Malachi*	
2.22	48	7.4-7	44	2.13	113
2.37-38	88			3.1	4, 15, 19,
3	36–7,	*Joel*			111–14,
	39–40, 42,	1.13-14	89		116, 125,
	44–53,	2	192		193
	108, 135,	2.10	191	3.5	113
	152, 156,	2.30-31	191	3.19	44
	159, 190,			3.22-24	115
	198	*Amos*		3.22	111, 114,
3.1-30	76–7	2.16	173		184
3.1-18	133	8	197	3.23	116, 170
3.1-7	45, 51	8.9	28, 158,	4.4-6	115, 193
3.1	42, 45		173, 190–	4.5	37, 111,
3.3	46		2, 197		114, 116,
3.6	44				122, 184,
3.7	42	*Obadiah*			193
3.12	42, 43, 51	17–21	76	4.6	114
3.15	43, 45				
3.16-18	43, 47	*Jonah*		*1 Esdras*	
3.17-18	45	3.6-9	89	3–4	155
3.19-27	133	3.7-8	89	3.1-2	155
3.19-21	51	3.8	88–9	3.1	154
3.19	41, 43, 47			3.5	155
3.22	42–4, 46,	*Micah*		3.14-17	155
	49, 52,	1.4	88	3.17-24	155
	108, 141	4.4	80	4.1-12	155

Index of References

4.13-32	155	10–13	93, 108, 198	13.19	88
4.28-31	156			14.6	97
4.33-41	155	10.1-5	91	14.7	94, 97
4.42	155	10.2	95	14.10	90
		10.3-4	96	14.14-18	95
Tobit		10.4	93, 96	15.12-13	89–90
2.6	76	10.5	95	16.2-17	89–90, 93
		10.10	95	16.3	87, 89
Judith		10.17	95	16.5	94, 97, 109, 202
1.1	85–6, 88	10.20	94		
1.2	88	11.1	91	16.9	95
1.7	86	11.7	88	16.14	88
1.11	86	11.19	143	16.15	88
1.13	86	11.22-23	96	16.17	88
2.1	86	11.23	90	16.31	85
2.4	86	12.1-2	92		
3.2	88	12.5	94, 97	*Wisdom of Solomon*	
4.1	86	12.7	95, 121	2.2	44
4.3	86	12.8	95	2.13	183
4.7	95	12.10–13.10	93	2.17-18	183
4.9-12	89	12.10–13.1	95	2.20	183
4.9	88	12.10-16	94	3.7	44
4.11	88	12.10-15	95	11.18	44
4.12	88–9, 92	12.10	95	11.19	44
5.5-21	88	12.11-16	93	16.20	144
5.13	87, 90	12.12	96–7		
5.16	94	12.13–13.2	95	*Ecclesiasticus*	
5.19	86	12.13	97	2.1	128
7.16	89–90	12.15	93, 95–6	34.25	121
8.1-2	93	12.16	96–7	44.20	128
8.7	96	12.17–13.2	94	45.2	193
8.10	95	12.17-19	95	48.1-8	132
8.16	88	12.19	95	48.2-5	117
8.26	88	12.20	96–7	48.10-11	122
8.33	95	13	37	48.10	116, 184, 193
9–10	91–2	13.2	96–7		
9	178	13.3	95	48.12-14	203
9.1	91	13.4-5	95	51.10	187
9.2-14	28, 89, 95	13.6-10	94	51.12	76
9.2-5	95	13.6-7	97		
9.2	88	13.7-9	64	*Baruch*	
9.7	87, 89	13.7	95–7	4.16	123
9.10	94, 97, 109, 202	13.8	95–7		
		13.9	95–7	*1 Maccabees*	
9.14	88	13.15	94–5, 97, 109, 202	1.15	76
10–16	93, 96			1.39	76
		13.16	95	1.41-64	84

240 Index of References

1 Maccabees (cont.)

1.48	76
1.54	76
2	77
2.7-13	77
2.9	77
2.21	84
2.23-26	78, 161
2.23	78
2.25	78
2.26-27	84
2.26	78
2.42	84
2.50	84
2.51-60	77
2.52	128
2.54	78
2.58	117
2.59-60	76
2.64	84
2.67-68	84
3–5	160
3–4	79
3.5-6	84
3.8	78
3.46-56	84
3.46	78
3.48	84
3.55-56	84
3.55	79, 143
3.56	79, 82, 84, 109, 160, 202
3.58	76
4.8-9	78
4.24	76
4.25	76
4.42-59	84
4.42-53	84
4.46	78
4.47	84, 109, 160, 202
4.49-51	79
4.53	84, 109, 160, 202
5	83–4
5.6	76
5.28	82
5.31	76
5.35	82
5.45-51	80, 81, 83–4, 98, 108, 156, 159, 198, 202
5.45-48	81
5.45	80
5.46	80–1, 83, 108
5.47	83
5.48-51	190
5.48	79–83, 108
5.49-51	81
5.49-50	81-83
5.49	82
5.50	80, 82–3
5.51	80, 82–3, 108, 160
5.66	76
5.68	76, 84
7.17	75
9.21	80
9.22	76
9.50	79, 84
12.53	75, 79, 84
13.3	84
14.4-15	80
14.4	84
14.6	79
14.8	80
14.9	80
14.12	80
14.29	84
14.41	78
15.21	84, 160
16.23	76
16.24	78

2 Maccabees

2.4-8	56
7	49
12	84
12.27-28	83, 202

NEW TESTAMENT

Matthew

1.18–2.23	205
1.22	165
2.17	165
2.23	165, 170
3.3	114
3.4	116, 118
3.17	124
4.1-11	128
4.2	128, 132
4.4	129
4.7	128
4.10	129
4.13-16	170
4.14	165
6.25-31	145
7.3-5	152
8.17	165
8.18-22	136
8.21	136
8.22	136
11.13-14	122
11.14	115
12.17	165
12.18-21	124
12.18	124
13.35	165
14.1-12	154
14.1	153
14.6-11	151
14.21	144
15.38	144
16.8	145
17.5	124
17.10-13	122
17.11	170
17.13	115
21.2-8	170
21.4	165
21.42	172
26.14-16	205
26.15	163
26.21	163
26.23	163
26.24	163

26.28	170		131, 146,	1.35	178
26.39	178		147	1.39	190
26.42	178	1.7-8	116, 121,	1.40-45	9, 26
26.51-54	175		134	1.40-42	121
26.56	172, 174	1.7	121	1.44	4, 116
26.68	170	1.9-11	11, 15,	2.1-12	9
27.3-10	164, 205		124, 133	2.14	135
27.9	164–5	1.9-10	120	2.15-16	137
27.24-25	180	1.9	120, 132,	2.23	137
27.34	194		170	2.25-26	4, 116
27.35	182	1.10-11	120	3.7	137
27.43	183	1.10	120, 122	3.22	203
27.45	191	1.11	4, 116,	4.11-12	18
27.46	170, 184–5		120, 122–	4.12	4, 117
			5, 188,	4.25	172
27.51	192		189	4.35-41	205
27.52-53	192	1.12-20	24, 26, 28,	4.40-41	174
27.57-61	169		110, 125–	5.1-20	205
27.57	169		7, 133,	5.6	195
27.65	180		138–9,	5.21-43	9, 24–5
27.67	169		160, 181,	5.35-43	121
			197–8	5.37	176
Mark		1.12-13	127, 128,	5.41-42	149
1–12	23		130–32,	6.4-16	121
1–8	16		134, 146,	6.8	139
1.1-8	11		147	6.14-16	154, 203
1.1	134	1.12	125, 132	6.14	153
1.2-33	122, 125	1.13	125–7,	6.15	146, 202
1.2-20	110		131–3	6.17-29	115, 147–
1.2-11	110, 122	1.14-39	135		8, 152–4
1.2-3	4, 15–16,	1.14-15	18, 125,	6.17	153
	18–19, 21,		133	6.19	115
	111, 114–	1.14	133	6.21-28	110, 148–
	16, 121,	1.15	133		52, 154,
	124–5,	1.16-20	134–6,		156, 160,
	165		141, 146–		181, 197,
1.2	13, 111–	7			198
	15, 163	1.16	127, 136	6.21-22	150
1.3	112–3, 119	1.17	125, 127,	6.21	150, 152,
1.4-11	120–1,		134, 136		153
	124–5	1.18	126, 127	6.22	148, 151–
1.4-6	132	1.19	127, 134		3, 155
1.4	116, 119	1.20	126–7,	6.23	4, 21, 30,
1.5	120		134		148–50,
1.6	4, 111,	1.21	170		152
	115–18,	1.28	190	6.24-25	152
	120, 125,	1.33	190	6.25-27	153

Index of References

Mark (cont.)		7.6	13, 140, 163	9.2	176
6.25	115, 151			9.4-5	146
6.26	152	7.10	4, 116	9.4	115
6.27-28	151	7.24-30	24, 26	9.5-6	174
6.27	133, 151–3	7.25-29	9	9.5	137
		7.28	137	9.7	4, 117, 124, 188–9
6.28	152	7.31	141		
6.30-44	26, 144	8.1-10	26		
6.30-34	138	8.1-9	24, 28, 110, 121, 138–40, 142, 144, 146, 160, 181, 197, 198	9.9-13	11, 122
6.31-32	143			9.9-10	122
6.32	141			9.11-13	15, 115, 122, 146
6.34	138			9.11	122
6.35-44	24, 28, 110, 121, 138–40, 142, 144, 146, 147, 160, 181, 197, 198			9.12-13	116, 163, 165
		8.1-3	142	9.12	116, 170–1, 178
		8.1-2	140		
		8.1	138	9.13	111, 115, 117, 125, 140, 146–7, 164
		8.2	138		
6.35-37	142	8.3	138, 195		
6.35-36	138, 140	8.4	138–40, 142–3, 174		
6.35	142–3			9.17-29	9
6.37	138–40, 174			9.28	174
		8.5	138–40	9.31-32	26
6.38-43	144	8.6-7	139, 141	9.31	162, 171, 178
6.38	138–42, 146	8.6	140		
		8.7	141–2, 144	9.32	174
6.39-40	138			9.33-34	174
6.40	143	8.8-9	139	9.38-41	205
6.41	139–42, 146	8.8	138–43, 145–6	9.38	174
				9.42	137
6.42	138–9, 141, 143, 147	8.9	141	9.48	4, 117
		8.10	142	10.4	4, 116
		8.16-21	174	10.6-8	4, 116
		8.17-21	142	10.13-16	137
6.43	138–9, 141–2, 145–6	8.28	121, 146, 202	10.13	174
				10.19	4, 116
		8.31-32	26	10.24	174
6.44	138–9, 141	8.31	162, 171, 173, 178	10.33-34	26, 171, 178
6.45	141				
6.46	178	8.32-33	174	10.34	162, 169
6.48	19	8.34	173, 175	10.37	174
6.51-52	174	8.35-38	173	10.40	171, 194
6.55	190	8.38	193	10.51	137
7.6-7	4, 18, 116, 165	9.2-8	11, 15, 146, 184, 193, 205	11.2-7	170
				11.9-10	188

Index of References

11.9	4, 18, 117, 189	14.3-9	163	14.49	13, 116, 162, 165–6, 171–2, 174
11.13	195	14.7-9	171		
11.17	4, 116, 163	14.7-8	171		
		14.9	171		
11.21	137	14.12	140, 162	14.50-52	173–4
12.6	124	14.13-15	171	14.50	172, 174–5, 195
12.9	189	14.16-17	162		
12.10-11	4, 15, 116, 188–9	14.16	171	14.51-52	172–3
		14.17-21	163	14.51	173
12.26	4, 116, 188	14.18-21	165	14.52	173
		14.18-20	163–4, 167, 171, 182, 189	14.53–15.20	181
12.29-33	4, 116			14.53-65	171, 192
12.35-37	15	14.18	162–4, 171	14.54	158, 174, 176, 189, 195
12.36	4, 116, 189	14.19	164	14.55-65	179
12.39	149	14.20	163	14.55	169
13	176	14.21	13, 116, 162–4, 166, 171–2, 175, 178	14.56-57	180
13.2	5, 179, 191			14.58	179
				14.61	168, 180
13.8	191			14.62	4, 117, 171, 179–80, 188–9, 193
13.9	171, 192				
13.12	171, 192	14.22-25	167		
13.13	173, 175, 178	14.22	163		
		14.24	167–8, 170	14.63	180
13.14	4, 116			14.65	168–70, 175
13.24-27	18	14.25	171, 194		
13.24-25	4, 117, 185	14.27	4, 116, 163, 165–6, 171, 174, 176	14.66-72	26, 173–4, 176
13.24	171, 192			15.1-15	171
13.26-27	184, 193			15.1-5	192
13.26	171, 179	14.28	171	15.1	162, 169, 171
13.27	192	14.30	171		
13.33-37	192	14.31	174–5	15.2-15	179
13.35-37	176	14.34	176–7, 189	15.5	168, 180
13.35	176			15.6-15	180
13.37	176	14.35	178	15.7-11	181
14–16	162	14.36	178	15.11-14	179
14–15	7, 15, 110, 160, 170–1, 192, 198, 200	14.37-42	176	15.12	181
		14.37-41	192	15.14-15	181
		14.40	178	15.15-23	181
		14.41-45	171–2	15.16-20	194
		14.43–15.39	171	15.17-18	181
14.1–15.20	162	14.43-46	192	15.19	168–9, 175
14.1-9	164	14.45	137, 197		
14.1	162	14.47	175	15.20-41	11
				15.20	204

Index of References

Mark (cont.)

Reference	Pages
15.21-41	110, 162, 181, 190, 197
15.21-39	183
15.21	172, 195
15.23	194, 195
15.24-34	189
15.24	5, 160, 173, 182, 197, 204
15.25	162
15.26	181
15.27	168
15.28	168, 204
15.29-32	182, 183
15.29-30	182, 197
15.29	179
15.31	182
15.32	181
15.33	28, 158, 160, 171, 173, 185, 190, 192, 197
15.34	4, 117, 158, 170, 182–3, 185, 197
15.35-36	146
15.35	115
15.36	28, 173, 189, 192, 194–5, 197
15.37-38	189
15.38	122, 179, 185, 191
15.39	180, 189
15.40	158, 172, 189, 195–7
15.42–16.8	196
15.42	162
15.43-46	168–9
15.43	169
15.46-47	171
15.47	172, 195
15.64	172
16.1-8	195
16.2	162
16.4-8	121
16.4-6	154
16.7	196
16.8	196

Luke

Reference	Pages
3.4	114
4.1-13	128
4.2	132
4.25-26	117
4.27	142
7.27	114
7.36	145
9.14	143
9.47-62	136
9.59	136
9.60	136
9.61	136
9.62	136
19.8	149
22.22	164
22.37	168
22.42	178
22.49-51	175
22.54	174
23.24	182
23.36	194
23.45	191
23.46	185
23.49	195
23.50-51	169

John

Reference	Pages
1.4-16	205
1.35-51	196
2.21	179
4.9	177
6.1-15	144
6.9	144
6.13	144
6.31	144
6.32	144
6.39	174
6.49	144
12.1-8	164
12.6	164
12.16	165
12.27	178
12.38	165
13.18-30	166, 182
13.18	164, 166
13.21	164
13.22	164
13.24-25	164
13.26-27	164
13.27-30	164
13.30	164
15.25	165
17.12	174
18.8-9	174
18.9	165
18.10-11	175
18.11	178
19.21-22	181
19.23-25	182
19.24	165
19.28-29	194
19.30	185
19.34	189
19.36	165
19.37	189
21.2	142, 196

Acts

Reference	Pages
6.3	142
13.33	123
19.14	142

Romans

Reference	Pages
15.3	194

1 Corinthians

Reference	Pages
11.1	174
11.5	174
11.13	174
11.2.11	174
11.25	167
15.3-8	196
15.3-4	12, 14
15.3	172

Index of References

15.5-8	196	89.52	147	1.4	129
15.5	137	91.4	123	2.1	129

Galatians
2.11-14	174	*2 Baruch*		*Joseph and Aseneth*	
13.17	108	77.18-26	131	12.11	187–8,
		77.24	131		190
				13.9	188, 190

Philippians
2.8	179	*2 Enoch*		*Jubilees*	
		10.5-6	173	1.21	4
		67.1-2	192	2.33	67
1 Thessalonians				3.14	67
2.4	128	*3 Enoch*		4.15	65
		10.4-5	114	4.21	65
Hebrews				4.28	65
1.5	123	*3 Maccabees*		5.2	65
3.8-9	128	2.2-20	28	5.20	65
9.3	24			6.1-3	66
11.31	90	*4 Baruch*		6.2	65, 67
		3.10	56	6.3	67
James				6.5-9	67
2.25	90	*4 Ezra*		6.5-6	69
		6.26	193	6.5	69
1 Peter		7.28	123	6.6-7	70
1.7	23	7.109	117	6.14	67
		14.23	129	6.17	3
Revelation		14.36	129	7.2	67
11.3-13	193	14.44-45	129	7.6-7	66
12.16	102			8.10–9.13	73–4
18.9-19	195	*Apocalypse of Abraham*		8.12-21	73
18.10	195	5.1-14	39	9.2-6	73
18.15	195			9.11	34
18.17	195	*Apocalypse of Elijah*		12.14	39
21.14	137	4.7	193	13.8	65
		5.32	193	13.10-16	66
PSEUDEPIGRAPHA				13.11	65–6
1 Enoch		*Aramaic Levi Document*		13.12	65, 67
1.2	66	2.5	114	13.13-15	66
1.3	66			13.19-21	66
2–5	67	*Greek Apocalypse*		13.25	67
2	65	*of Ezra*		13.28-29	66
5.27	65	6.3–7.14	102	16.20-31	4
6–11	69	7.6	117	17.15-16	106
10.1	66	7.7	101	17.16-18	128
106-107	65			17.17-8.13	106
106.1	66	*History of the*		19.27	123
12.2	66	*Rechabites*		20.3-4	3
48.4	168	1.1	129		

Index of References

Jubilees (cont.)

21.1	4
23.28	4
23.32	67
32.3-10	4
32.10	67
33.1-9	67
33.16	67
36.20	67
39.6-7	3
49.17	67

Liber Antiquitatum Biblicarum

1.2-22	34
2.9	34
3.3	36, 98
3.10	34
4.6-7	56
4.9	33
5.1	46–7
6	36, 39, 41, 46, 49, 51, 63, 98, 108, 133, 135, 152, 156, 159–60, 198
6.1	45, 47
6.3-5	48
6.4	40, 45, 47
6.5	45
6.6-15	46, 133
6.6	46, 190
6.7-12	129
6.14	46–7
6.16-18	44, 108, 133
6.16	48
6.17	44, 47, 102, 141
6.18	44–5
7	48, 63
7.3	125
8.13	33
9.12	36
9.14	90
10.5	35
11.5	34
11.10-11	34
11.15	36
12.1	63
12.4	125
14–19	34, 35
14.1-4	35
15	35
15.1	35
15.3	35
15.5-6	35
15.6	125
16	35
16.2-3	35
16.18	47
17	35
17.3	35, 98
18	35
18.4-6	35
18.5	100
18.13	34
19	35
19.5	35, 63
20.6	61
21.7-10	36
22.3	48
23.4	125
23.5	47
23.6	100
23.10	125
24.5	36, 63–4, 98
25–28	36, 54
25–26	54, 56, 159
25	58
25.1	54, 56–7, 62
25.2	55, 58
25.3	55–7, 62–3
25.4	55–6, 63, 141
25.5	55
25.6	63
25.7	55
25.8-14	55
25.8	57
25.9-12	57
25.9	56, 63
25.10	56
25.11	56, 59
26.1	56, 102
26.2	56
26.3	63
26.5	58, 63
26.8	63
26.10-11	56
26.11	63
26.12-15	56
27	39, 54, 57, 59, 108, 156, 159, 198
27.1	55, 57, 62
27.2	57
27.3-4	57, 58
27.4	63
27.5-6	63
27.5	59
27.6	57, 59
27.7	57, 59, 61, 63
27.8	59
27.9	57, 59, 108
27.10-11	63, 190
27.10	49, 57–8, 60, 63
27.11-12	58
27.11	58, 60
27.15-16	58
27.15	56, 63
27.16	58, 61
28–29	61
28.6-9	61
29	36, 54, 62, 159
29.1-2	61
30.3	46
30.5	34, 63

31	37, 93, 95–6, 108, 156, 202	10.6	137	4.7-8	104
		10.9	54	4.10-11	104–5
		21.4-15	117, 132	4.10	99
31.1	97	21.13	131	5.10	99
31.3	96–7	22	203	5.14	99
31.4-6	96			6.1–7.11	100
31.4	98	*Psalms of Solomon*		6.2-6	100
31.5-7	96	11.7	168	6.4	101
31.6	97	16.2	168	7.12	104–5
31.7	64, 96–7	16.5	168	8.1-12	102
31.9	96–7	16.14	128	8.1-3	99
32.1	47			8.4–9.1	102
33.2	63	*Questions of Ezra*		8.7	125
34	37, 62	A 39	132	8.9	102
35–36	61	A 40	117	9.4	101
35.7	38			9.5	101
36.2	59	*Sibylline Oracles*		10–14	102
38	37, 39, 48, 51, 108, 135, 159, 198	2.187-189	193	10.1–14.14	100
		2.194-202	193	10.10	101
		2.245-248	193	10.11	102
		5.256-257	193	10.12	102
38.1	49, 51, 196	8.377	125	14.1-15	100
				15.11-15	102
38.2	49, 51, 190	*Syriac Sirach*		15.14-15	99, 104–5, 108, 198
		4.10	118		
38.3	49, 51–2			15.15	104–7
38.4	48–9, 52, 141	*Testament of Abraham*		16–20	102
		1–15	104, 159	16.1-6	102
40.4	125	1–4	108, 198	16.6-15	100
43.4	38	1.1	104	16.7	101
43.8	46	1.2	101	16.16	102
45.6	34	1.4-7	100, 104	17.11	102
48.1	37, 127, 130–2, 152, 193	1.5	101, 104	19.2-4	102
		1.6-7	104–5	20.4-5	102
		1.6	123	20.8-15	101
49.1	62	2–7	105	20.8-9	102, 107
50.1	177	2.1–5.14	100	20.11	101
50.5	178	2.1	101, 104	20.12	102
53.2	123	4–15	103	20.14	102
56.6	63	4.1	101	A 3.9-10	99
56.7	38	4.5-6	104–5		
62.8	34	4.5	99, 104–5	*Testament of Adam*	
63.5	38	4.6-11	102	3.6	192
		4.6	99, 103–5, 107, 109		
Lives of the Prophets				*Testament of Joseph*	
2.12-19	193	4.7–5.1	102	8.3	173
9.2	137	4.7-10	105		

Testament of Levi
10.3   24
18.6-7   123

Testament of Moses
1.14   193
9.4   128

Testament of Zebulun
3.4-5   3

QUMRAN
1Q28a
2.11-12   123

1QapGen
2.1–5.27   72
2.1   66
2.3-18   66
2.3-5   65
2.14   66
2.16   66
2.20-21   65
2.20   66
3.3   65
6.1-6   73
6.14-16   73
6.23   73
6.26   65
8.10–9.13   73
10.12-13   65
10.13–11.1 65
10.13   65, 67
10.14   67
10.15-16   67
10.15   67
10.17   67
11   69, 71, 73,
            108, 156,
            159, 198
11.1-10   71
11.6   70
11.11-19   69
11.11-17   74
11.11   70–1, 108
11.15   70–2, 74
11.16-17   67, 69, 72

11.16   69, 72
11.17   67, 70, 72
12–15   73
12.12   34
12.13–15.21 65, 66
12.13-16   67
14.9   68
16–17   73
16.16-25   73
17.7-14   73
19–20   69
19.7-8   65
19.9-10   65
19.9   67
19.14-21   65
19.14-15   68
19.17-21   66
19.23   65
19.25   66
19.29   66
20.2-8   68
20.2   68
20.3   68
20.4   68
20.6   68
20.7   68
20.16-19   66
20.17   69
20.18-19   69
20.20   69
20.22-23   66
20.23   69, 118
20.25   118
20.31   68
21–22   71
21.10-12   71
21.12   73
21.13-20   66
21.14   71
21.18-29   68
21.23   45
22.10   68
22.24-26   66
22.27-29   66
22.27   71
22.30-31   70
22.30   72, 74

22.31   71
22.34   74

1QH
6.20-21   195
10.21   167
10.29-30   167
11.28-29   167
12.8   168
12.9   167
12.11-12   167
12.11   194
12.23   168
12.33-34   187
13.6-19   187
13.9-10   187
13.10-11   187
13.13-15   187
13.13-14   167
13.16   167
13.22-25   166
13.23b-24a 166
13.31   167, 187
13.33-34   177
13.34   167
15.4-5   187
15.13   168
16.29-30   167
16.31-32   167
16.32-33   187
16.32   177
16.37   168

1QM
4.1-4   143

1QpHab
5.8-10   3

1QS
1.29–2.1   143
8.13-15   114

1QSa
1.29–2.1   143

Index of References

249

4Q12		*11QT*		*Targ. Psalms*		
1.4	71	54.12	128	2.7	123	
				22.2	184	
4Q88		*11QTa*				
Frg 1-2	186	42.15	143	*Targ. Neof. Gen.*		
				10.10	45	
4Q372		*CD*		11.2	45	
1.15-16	187–8	13.1-2	143	11.31	40	
		A 11.17-18	3	14.1	45	
4Q381		B 19.5-9	175	14.9	45	
Frg 79	186			15.7	40	
		TARGUMS		26.24	71–2	
4Q429		*Frag. Targ. Deut.*				
4.4	187	33.21	193	*Targ. Onq. Gen.*		
				14.1	45	
4Q481a		*Frag. Targ. Exod.*		6.14	36	
3.4	137	12.42	193			
				Targ. Onq. Exod.		
4Q521		*Frag. Targ. Gen.*		21.3	118	
2.3	193	1.10	151			
		1.19	151–2	*Targ. Ps.-J. Deut.*		
4Q588		1.21	151–2	1.33	114	
1.2	193	5.14	40	34.3	137	
		11.27-28	40			
4QCatena				*Targ. Ps.-J. Gen.*		
2.10	128	*Targ. 2 Chronicles*		11.28	40	
		28.3	40	13.17	70	
4QMa				15.1	70	
Frags 1-3.10	143	*Targ. 2 Kings*		15.7	40	
		1.8	118	20.3	118	
4QPsJoshua[a]		2.12	137			
Frag 3 2.6-7	143	4.43	140	MISHNAH		
				Abot		
4QTanh		*Targ. Canticles*		5.3	105	
1.6-9	114	2.12	122			
		7.9	68	*Eduyyot*		
4QpsJub[a]				8.7	193	
2.1-2	106	*Targ. Esth. II*				
		2.8	150	*Soṭah*		
5/6HevPs		5.3	151	9.15	122, 193	
Frg. 1-2	186					
8–9	189	*Targ. Isaiah*		*Ta'anit*		
		41.8-9	123	4.6	132	
11QMelch		42.1	123			
2.15-16	168	43.10	123			
2.23	168					

TALMUDS

b. Abodah Zarah
17b	192
18a	178
18b	192
22a	142
36b	142
38b	194
39b	145
53b	39

b. Arakin
16b	152

b. Baba Batra
100a	70
121b	48
15b	70, 105–6, 152
16a	70, 106

b. Baba Qamma
91b	178
93a	114

b. Berakot
3a	122
4b	193
39b	145

b. Erubin
43a-b	122, 193
53a	40, 41
81a	145

b. Ḥagigah
3a	183
15a	122
25a	120

b. Ḥullin
87a	194
89a	39

b. Horayot
10b	93–4

b. Ketubbot
105b	145
106a	137
77b	122

b. Megillah
11b	150
15b	185–6, 188, 190

b. Menaḥot
66b	139
99b	132

b. Mo'ed Qaṭan
25b	192
28a	145

b. Nazir
23b	93, 95

b. Pesaḥim
118a	40–1, 47, 50
118b	47, 52

b. Šabbat
89a	132
118a	70, 122

b. Sanhedrin
12a	139
38b	114
43a	194
89b	105
92b	46
93a	41
105b	137
106b	171
107b	137
109a	46, 102, 192
111a	70

b. Seder
61a	114

b. Soṭah
11b-12a	54
13a	137
47a	137
48b	145
49a	137

b. Sukkah
52a	123

b. Ta'anit
21a	192
25a	145
8a	132

b. Temurah
16a	54

b. Yebamot
23a	142
103a	93, 95

b. Yoma
4b	132
6.5	145
21b	50
29a	185
39a	145
76a	132

y. Berakot
14b	106

y. Sanhedrin
10.2	137

y. Soṭah
20c	106

TOSEFTA

t. Berakot
4.11	145

t. Šabbat
6.1–7.18	56

Index of References

t. Sanhedrin
2.9	145

t. Soṭah
4.8	137
12.5	137

t. Yoma
1.6	136

OTHER RABBINIC LITERATURE

ARN
A 7	105–6
A 33	40
A 38	171, 176

Canticles Rabbah
1.56	40–1
2.16	41
4.7	55, 61
4.11	137

Chronicles of Jerahmeel
34.12	41
34.13	41, 47
57	54
57.34	50
58.10	50

Deuteronomy Rabbah
3.17	193
4.11	111, 114
11.3	106
11.5	102
11.8	102
11.10	102, 107
11.19	114

Esther Rabbah
4.9-11	151
4.9	151–2
4.11	151–2

Exodus Rabbah
3.4	114

18.5	41, 46–7, 50, 52
23.4	40
32.9	114

Genesis Rabbah
4.2	62
30.7	68
34.9	40–1
34.13	178
38.6	39
38.13	40–1
41.1	68
44.13	40–1, 47
46.7	185
49.9	106
56.11	105

Judges Rabbah
16.1	37, 193

Lamentations Rabbah
4.25	137

Leviticus Rabbah
23.10	95

Mekhilta de-Rabbi Ishmael
12.1	203
13.19	137

Midrash Tanḥuma

B *Bo*
9.1	144

B *Noach*
5.6	36

B *Terumah*
11	62

B *Tetz*
12.2	41, 47

B *Toldot*
4.1	40–1, 47

B *Tsav*
1.1	142

Mish
17.7-8	114

Vayyiqra
8.2	105
10.1-2	114

Midrash Tehillim
2.9	123
22.2	186
22.6	186
22.7	183, 186
22.16	186
22.17	186
22.21	183, 186
22.27	183, 186
26.2	106
28.2	47
42.5	114
117.3	50
118.9	40

Pirkei Avot
5.1-6	105

PRE
24	39
26 188	40
29.18	114, 193
31.13	117
33.2	137
33.8	137
46.1-6	132
49.12	150–1
50.6	149
50.10	192

Pesiqta Rabbah
33.4	40

Seder Eliyahu Rabbah
17	137
27	40
32	135

Seder Eliyahu Zuta
2   145
173   141

Seder 'Olam Rabbah
19   137

Sefer haYashar
12.24-25   42
12.25   53
12.26   42
12.27-32   42
12.29-31   42

Semahot
2.1-5   178

Sifre Deuteronomy
2.2   132
305.5   102, 107
339.1   102
342   193
357.1-27   102

Sifre Numbers
89.1   145

Rashi
Numbers
32.12   54

PHILO
Legum allegoriae
3.48   132

Quaestiones in Genesin
2.33   132
2.56   69

De vita Mosis
2.14   132

JOSEPHUS
Antiquities
3.7   132
8.7   136

1.10.1   68
1.118-119   45
1.3.5   132
11.232-234 92
12.187-189 151
14.309   192
18.109-110 153
18.116-119 153, 203
18.119   156
18.136   153
19.270   182
20.263   152
5.182-184   54
5.220   145
5.254   48
5.3.3   58
8.13.2   131
8.13.4-9.2.2 117
8.13.7   135, 137
9.2.1   117
9.2.2   137
9.3.1   137

Apion
1.50   152
2.25   132

Life
11   117

War
3.361-382   178
4.197-333   180
4.460-464   146
5.427   145
7.358-360   178

OTHER CHRISTIAN
WRITINGS
1 Clement
23   90

Acts of John
93   145

Ambrose
Epistles
15.8-9   120, 137
63.28   130

Apostolic Constitutions
8.7.5   101

Athanasius
Vita Antonii
7.37   129

Clement of Alexandria
The Instructor
2.11   119

Miscellanies
3.7.1   132

Stromateis
4.77   179
7.66   179

Ephrem
*Commentary on the
Diatessaron*
1.17   118

Eusebius
Historia ecclesiastica
6.25.2   75

Theophania
3.55   132

Gospel of Peter
5.15   191

Hrotsvit of Gandersheim
Sapientia
144-145   53

Ignatius
To the Romans
1–8   178

Index of References

253

Irenaeus
Adversus haereses
3.22.2   132
4.33.12   190

Jerome
Epistolae
58.5   129

Prologus galeatus
28.593-604   75

*Quaestionum
hebraicarum liber
in Genesim*
43   40

Vita Paul
10   130

John Cassian
Conferences
18.6   129

John Chrysostom
Homilies
14.3   134

Martyrdom of Polycarp
15–16   52

Justin
Dialogue with Trypho
2.21   145
3.37   146
8.4   193
49.1   122, 193

Life of Shenoute
10   130

Origen
*Commentarii in
evangelium Joannis*
2.31   193
10.1   132

*Commentarium in
evangelium Matthaei*
10.20   193

Palladius
Historia Lausiaca
51   146

Paphnutius
Historia
10b   136

Paulinus of Nola
Epistulae
29.1   119

Pseudo-Chrysostom
Precatio in Obsessos
64.1065   101

Sulipicius Severus
Life of Martin
10   119

*Syriac Acts of Paul
and Thecla*
7–8   52

Tertullian
De resurrectione carnis
61   132

Vita S. Marco Atheniensi
4–5   129
8   129
13   129

CLASSICAL SOURCES
Aristophenes
Birds
69 70   131

Artemidorus Daldianus
Oneirocritica
2.61   182

Cicero
De republica
2.10   192
6.21-22   192

Dio Cassius
Historia
56.29.3   192

Diodorus Siculus
Bibliotheca Historica
16.47.3   86
17.5.3   86
31.19.2   86

Dionysius of
Halicarnassus
Antiquitates romanae
2.56   192
7.29.2   182

Florus
*Epitome of Roman
History*
1.1   192

*History of the Monks
of Upper Egypt*
8.46   146

Homer
Iliad
9.616   149

Odyssey
11.75   26

Livy
History of Rome
1.16   192

Ovid
Fasti
485-498   192

Index of References

Pliny
Natural History
2.30   192
14.15 194

Plutarch
Caesar
69   192

Romulus
27   192

Strabo
Geographica
16.1-3 88

Virgil
Aeneid
6.156-325 26

Georgica
1.466-467 192

Xenophon
Anabasis
3.4.10 88

QURAN
21.51-71 41
29.16-27 41
37.83-99 41

OTHER SOURCES
Arabic Gospel of the Infancy
14   205

Gospel of Truth
20.24 206

Memar Marqah
2.8   193
2.12 193
4.3   193
4.6   193
4.12 193
5.3   193
6.3   193

Index of Authors

Abel, F.-M. 75
Ahearne-Kroll, S. P. 161, 176, 189
Aland, B. 119
Aland, K. 119
Alessandro, C. 187
Alexander, P. S. 24, 37, 73
Allen, D. M. 17
Allison Jr., D. C. 9, 30–1, 99–107, 114, 122, 126, 129–30, 134, 136–7, 139, 142–4, 158, 160–1, 170, 173, 176, 180, 184, 191–2, 194, 196, 200
Anderson, H. 14, 148, 165
Attridge, H. W. 161
Aune, D. 78
Aus, R. D. 134–6, 139–45, 148, 150–2

Babota, V. 78
Bakhos, C. 24
Barthélemy, D. 119, 120
Bartlett, J. R. 75
Batsch, C. 82
Bauckham, R. 35–8, 40, 46, 50, 55, 61–2, 64, 98
Beavis, M. A. 126
Beetham, C. 17
Berkovitz, A. J. 185
Bernstein, M. J. 3, 65, 69
Best, E. 128, 131
Berthelot, K. 73, 77, 79, 82
Betz, O. 161
Bickerman, E. 78, 93
Blair, H. J. 136
Bloch, R. 37
Bock, D. L. 161, 165
Bogaert, P.-M. 33, 36–7, 49
Bond, H. K. 179, 181–2
Boobyer, G. H. 184
Boring, M. E. 141
Botner, M. 161, 189
Bousset, W. 123, 188

Bowman, J. 22–3
Brandt, W. 13
Brine, K. R. 85
Brockelmann, C. 118
Brodie, T. L. 25, 147
Brown, R. E. 146, 157–8, 184, 191, 196, 203
Bruns, J. E. 94
Buchanan, G. W. 151
Bultmann, R. 154, 157–8, 163, 191
Burge, S. R. 103
Burkitt, F. C. 118
Buschmann, G. 53

Caneday, A. B. 128
Caponigro, M. S. 99
Carey, H. 184
Carmignac, J. 166
Carrington, P. 22
Chilton, B. D. 124
Ciletti, E. 85
Cohn, L. 33, 37–8, 50
Collins, J. J. 187
Collins, A. Y. 122, 139, 148, 166, 174, 180, 194
Conway, C. M. 95
Cook, E. M. 45
Cranfield, C. E. B. 127, 148
Craven, T. 87
Crawford, S. W. 85, 92, 94–5, 118
Crossan, J. D. 27, 29, 157–8, 160, 191, 195, 200
Crossley, J. G. 148, 196
Cummins, S. A. 153–4

Daise, M. A. 145
Dancy, J. C. 75
Danker, F. W. 163–4, 183
Daube, D. 92
Davies, W. D. 114, 139, 170, 180, 184

Index of Authors

Day, L. 91
Delcor, M. 106
Derrett, J. D. M. 23
Dibelius, M. 7, 10, 12, 14, 157–8, 161, 201
Dijk-Hemmes, F. van 94
Dimant, D. 2, 4, 21, 27, 30, 80, 116, 165
Dodd, C. H. 5, 8–16, 18, 20–1, 161, 199
Donahue, J. R. 139, 148
Dormeyer, D. 147
Droge, A. J. 179
Drury, J. 23
Dubarle, A.-M. 86–90, 93, 95

Edwards, J. R. 135
Eissfeldt, O. 111
Eklund, R. 184
Elwolde, J. 167, 187
Emadi, S. 29
Ernst, J. 180
Eshel, E. 68, 73
Esler, P. 95
Ettelson, H. W. 74
Evans, C. A. 117, 121, 153, 168, 181, 199

Faierstein, M. M. 121
Falk, D. K. 65, 68–9, 71
Farrer, A. 8–9
Feigels, F. K. 6
Feldman, A. 137
Feldman, L. H. 33–4, 37, 54, 56, 92, 98
Feuillet, A. 127
Fishbane, M. A. 3, 28, 205
Fisk, B. N. 34–5, 37, 47, 64
Fitzmyer, J. A. 8, 64, 113, 122
Fleddermann, H. 172
Focant, C. 122, 131, 134, 139, 149
Focke, F. 106
Fossum, J. E. 193
Foster, P. 18, 184, 191
France, R. T. 168, 199
Frankfurter, D. T. M. 130, 202
Fredriksen, P. 179
Frye, N. 1

Gera, D. L. 85–91, 98–9
Gerhardsson, B. 128
Gibson, J. B. 127
Glickler-Chazon, E. 102
Gnilka, J. 111, 124, 134, 148, 172, 177, 180, 184

Goldberg, A. 37
Goldstein, J. A. 75, 77–8, 83
Goodacre, M. 27–9, 158–9, 196, 200
Goulder, M. D. 22–4, 37, 196
Grässer, E. 13, 165
Green, J. B. 168
Guelich, R. A. 111, 124, 142, 148
Guilbert, P. 166
Gundry, R. H. 117, 134–5, 142, 170, 177, 180, 195

Haag, E. 86, 88
Haenchen, E. 132
Hanhart, R. 87, 149
Harrington, D. J. 32–4, 36–7, 44, 48–50, 139, 148
Harris, J. R. 8–9
Harris, S. 17
Harvey, J. E. 81
Hatina, T. R. 13, 18–19, 124, 134
Haupt, P. 90
Hauser, A. J. 90
Hays, R. B. 17–21, 30, 111, 148, 161, 184, 189, 199
Hayward, R. 37
Heil, J. P. 182
Heising, A. 139, 144
Henten, J. W. van 52, 95
Hieke, T. 77
Hill, A. E. 111
Himmelfarb, M. 76
Hodgson Jr., R. 8
Hoehner, H. W. 148, 153
Hoffeditz, D. M. 147
Hollander, J. 19
Hooker, M. D. 16, 124, 128, 148, 161, 168
Horsley, R. A. 136
Huizenga, L. A. 17–18
Hurtado, L. W. 148
Hutton, J. M. 120

Iersel, B. M. F. van 25, 126
Ilan, T. 152
Iverson, K. R. 142

Jacobson, H. 33–6, 46–8, 54, 61
James, M. R. 33–4, 49, 100
Janes, R. 147
Jeremias, J. 123, 161
Jill-Levine, A. 180

Index of Authors

Jobes, K. H. 149
Joynes, C. E. 193
Juel, D. 14–15, 18, 161, 165, 189

Kaminski, C. M. 70, 72
Kasher, A. 84
Katz, P. 115, 126
Kazmierski, C. R. 123
Kee, H. C. 13, 157, 161, 165, 170, 174, 176
Keesmaat, S. C. 17
Kelber, W. 174, 188, 200
Kelhoffer, J. A. 119
Klein, G. 174
Klostermann, E. 173, 177
Knauf, E. A. 77
Koester, H. 158, 200
Koller, A. 91
Kozlowski, J. M. 53
Kreps, A. 206
Kugel, J. 66
Kushelevsky, R. 102

Labahn, M. 139
Lacocque, A. 90
Lähnemann, H. 85
Lane, W. 131, 154, 195
Lang, J. 87, 89
Lange, A. 32, 33
LaVerdiere, E. 148
Lerner M. B. 150, 186
Li, T. 46
Liebengood, K. D. 17
Lightfoot, R. H. 127
Lim, T. H. 2, 38
Lindars, B. 10–12, 20–1, 158, 161, 168, 199
Lindbeck, K. H. 193
Linnemann, E. 157
Loader, W. 95
Loewenstamm, S. E. 102–3
Lohmeyer, E. 111, 149, 163, 171–2
Loos, H. van der 147
Lowin, S. L. 41

MacDonald, D. R. 25
Machiela, D. A. 64, 68, 73
Mack, B. L. 158, 200
Majoros-Danowski, J. 126
Makiello, P. 193
Malbon, E. S. 174, 188

Mahnke, H. 132
Mann, J. 114
Manns, Frédéric 163
Marcus, J. 13, 15–16, 18, 114, 120–1, 126, 131, 134, 139, 143, 148, 153, 161–3, 168, 176, 180, 184, 202
Marxsen, W. 12, 171
Matera, F. J. 15, 114, 189
Maurer, C. 7, 158, 161, 183, 200
Mauser, U. W. 10, 11
McNamara, M. 71
McWhirter, J. 161
Meier, J. P. 117, 137
Mell, U. 131
Meye, R. P. 137
Meyer, R. 78
Millard, A. 86
Miller, D. 23–4, 200
Miller, P. 23–4, 200
Moo, D. J. 11, 18, 21, 157–8, 161, 165, 168, 170, 177, 199
Moore, C. A. 85–7, 89, 91, 98
Moore, G. F. 5
Moss, C. M. 163
Motyer, S. 123
Moyise, S. 114
Mroczek, E. 2, 51
Mueller, H. 165
Mueller, J. R. 129
Munoa, P. B. 99
Münz-Manor, O. 185
Murphy, F. J. 37, 46–7, 64

Neirynck, F. 157
Neuhaus, G. 75
Newman, J. H. 2, 27–8, 39, 89
Newsom, C. A. 166
Nickelsburg, G. W. E. 66, 69, 100
Nineham, D. E. 124
Noam, E. 152
Nortje, S. J. 154

O'Brien, K. S. 17, 157, 161–3, 176, 180
Öhler, M. 111, 132, 134–6, 193
Omerzu, H. 25, 126, 183–4, 187
Otzen, B. 86–7, 90, 99
Owen, P. 143

Parker, N. R. 148–9
Paton, L. B. 92
Pearson, L. 98

Pellegrini, S. 115
Perkins, L. 89
Perrot, C. 33, 36–7, 49
Pervo, R. I. 145
Pesch, R. 111, 121, 124, 131, 134–5, 139, 141, 148, 154, 157, 172, 180
Petersen, D. L. 112
Pokorny, P. 131
Porton, G. G. 37
Price, R. M. 24, 200
Pyeon, Y. 17

Rajak, T. 77
Rakel, C. 89
Rappaport, U. 76
Reeves, J. C. 68
Reiss, J. 150
Reiterer, F. V. 77
Robinson, J. A. T. 121, 154, 202
Robinson, M. 1
Robinson, W. 154
Roth, W. 24–6, 120, 141, 147
Rowe, R. D. 161, 189
Ruiten, J. T. A. G. M. van 106

Sanders, E. P. 99–100
Saunderson, B. 172
Schedl, C. 86
Scheil, J.-V. 45
Schenke, L. 157, 172
Schille, G. 158, 199
Schmid, J. 172
Schmidt, F. 73, 100
Schmidt, T. E. 181
Schmithals, W. 172
Schnackenburg, R. 127
Schneck, R. 16, 18
Scholz, A. 88
Schreiber, J. 157
Schulz, A. 134
Schulz, S. 13
Schunck, K.-D. 75
Schwartz, D. R. 83
Schwartz, S. 84
Schweitzer, A. 161
Schweizer, E. 134, 148
Scott, J. M. 73
Seethaler, A. 146
Sherman, P. M. 45, 47
Siker, J. S. 142

Silva, D. A. de 85
Smith, J. P. 118
Snodgrass, K. R. 113
Standhartinger, A. 147
Starcky, J. 75
Stegner, W. R. 143
Steichele, H.-J. 11, 13, 124, 157
Stein, R. H. 141
Stendahl, K. 8, 114, 171, 183
Stone, M. E. 99
Stott, K. M. 98
Strauss, D. F. 5–6, 8–9, 115, 134, 139, 141
Subramanian, J. S. 161
Suhl, A. 5, 7, 12–15, 18, 21, 148, 157–8, 163, 165, 180, 183
Swenson, K. M. 189
Swete, H. B. 148
Sydow, C. W. von 119

Tabor, J. D. 179
Taylor, J. E. 117, 153
Taylor, V. 148, 172
Teugels, L. 37–8
Theissen, G. 195
Thiessen, M. 154
Tilly, M. 153
Tolbert, M. A. 115
Torrey, C. C. 54, 118
Trocmé, É. 148, 157
Turner, N. 100
Tuschling, R. M. M. 193

Ulansey, D. 123
Ulmer, R. 186
Upson-Saia, K. 130

VanderKam, J. C. 66
Vanhoye, A. 172
Vermes, G. 37, 39, 65, 202
Vette, N. 53, 56, 61–2, 115, 154, 194
Vorster, W. S. 13–15, 21

Wacholder, B. Z. 66
Wadsworth, M. 37, 49
Walt, C. P. Van der 91
Watts, R. E. 13, 16–19, 114, 148, 161, 184, 189
Weeden, T. J. 174
Weidel, K. 6–7, 9–10, 157, 161

Weigold, M. 32–3
Weinberg, J. 106
Weiss, J. 6
Whitters, M. F. 193
Wills, L. M. 86–91
Wink, W. 111
Winn, A. 25–6, 126, 133–4, 139, 147, 181
Witherington III, B. 142–3

Yates, G. E. 147

Zahn, T. 172
Zakovitch, Y. 45
Zeitlin, S. 37, 75, 85, 87, 91–2
Zelyck, L. R. 146
Zeron, A. 33
Zimmerman, F. 87

Printed in the USA
CPSIA information can be obtained
at www.ICGtesting.com
LVHW020738041223
765477LV00003B/125